THE NEW AUSTRALIAN *Dream*

*Rethinking our homes and cities
to solve the housing crisis*

SERGIO FAMIANO

First published in Australia by Aurora House
www.aurorahouse.com.au

This edition published 2022
Copyright © Sergio Famiano 2022

Cover design: Donika Mishineva | www.artofdonika.com
Typesetting and e-book design: Amit Dey

The right of Sergio Famiano to be identified as Author of the Work has been asserted in accordance with the Copyright, Designs and Patents Act 1988.

ISBN number: 978-1-922697-80-6 (Paperback)

All rights reserved. No part of this publication may be reproduced, stored in a retrieval system, or transmitted, in any form or by any means without the prior written permission of the publisher, nor be otherwise circulated in any form of binding or cover other than that in which it is published and without a similar condition being imposed on the subsequent purchaser.

 A catalogue record for this book is available from the National Library of Australia

Distributed by: Ingram Content: www.ingramcontent.com
Australia: phone +613 9765 4800 |
email lsiaustralia@ingramcontent.com
Milton Keynes UK: phone +44 (0)845 121 4567 |
email enquiries@ingramcontent.com
La Vergne, TN USA: phone +1 800 509 4156 |
email inquiry@lightningsource.com

For the next generation who face a housing affordability crisis
and for those in the old generation who care and are brave enough
to do something about it...

ACKNOWLEDGEMENTS

In writing a book on housing affordability, I would first like to acknowledge the next generation, Generation Z (born after 1997), who will be the first generation in Australia since the Second World War to be confronted with the prospect of not being able to afford a house. This is a major concern, as housing is regarded as a human right, and everybody should have the ability and opportunity to own their own place. Like climate change, housing affordability is a major issue for Australia and should be considered, equally along with health, urban planning, transport, international security and human rights, to form part of the core policy initiatives that drive government action at the federal, state and local levels. Over the course of the past thirty years, there has been little that can be spoken of in terms of tangible attempts by the government or industry in maintaining housing affordability in Australia. My task is to bring attention to this issue, in the hope that policymakers and politicians alike are listening.

In writing this book, it would be remiss of me not to thank the many researchers, policy advocates and organisations who have researched and contributed significantly to the subject of housing affordability. I have drawn upon a wide area of research that touches on the housing industry to assist in framing the debate around the housing affordability crisis and to develop ideas I hope will form solutions to the housing crisis in Australia. The people I refer to include prominent academics such as Peter Hall, who has spent a life documenting urban and city form and its historical transition through the ages. Graeme Davies, for his pivotal work on how the rise of the automobile has influenced urban policy and urban form and created the suburban housing model that is tied to the Australian Dream.

The collective works of Peter Newman, Jeff Kenworthy, Leo Kosonen, Paul Cozens, Chris Butler, Tony Hall, David Yergin, David Hedgecock, Jago Dodson and Neil Sipe deserve a mention for being instrumental in examining sustainable cities, urban form, oil vulnerability and car dependency. This research has been illuminating and instrumental in understanding the current form of the Australian Dream and its symbiotic relationship with suburbia. The research has also contributed towards our understanding of the growing economic and ecological shadows that suburbia and the Australian Dream are casting over the Australian landscape. I have had the pleasure of meeting some of these researchers and authors and can say with certainty that they are influential in their areas of expertise and are passionate and dedicated. I have nothing but respect for them.

There are a number of government agencies I would like to thank for their insight into and dedication towards making a difference in the housing debate in Australia. They recognise the problems with housing affordability and are trying within their spheres of influence to make an impact. This includes organisations such as Development WA and Development Victoria. Both organisations and their New South Wales and Queensland counterparts have been instrumental in the delivery of transit-oriented development and housing diversity and, through demonstration, are attempting to shape the real estate market by promoting more sustainable and affordable housing. I have had the pleasure of working for the East Perth Redevelopment Authority and Landcorp in Western Australia for twelve years (both renamed Development WA) and can say with experience and certainty that organisations like Development WA are moving the goalposts on housing diversity and affordability and contributing towards the solution.

I would also like to acknowledge the work of urbanist Brett Woodgush from Urban Insight, who has been a confidant and support for this book in providing insight into urban problems and possible solutions. I am very grateful for his contributions and assistance in preparing some of the illustrations in this book. I would also like to acknowledge my close friends Steven Kovacs, Robert Whittingham, Shane Best and Greg Bowering, who are urban enthusiasts and avid readers of economics and history. Over many social outings, we have discussed housing affordability and other associated issues with our urban environment. The sum of our discussions has provided varied perspectives on housing affordability and has contributed towards the solutions identified in this book.

Jan Gehl, the prominent architect and humanistic urbanist, deserves a mention, not only for his historical work in making cities more human, but also because his method has always inspired me and has driven my approach to bringing 'human-centred' urban design and planning to the Australian context. Jan's approach is a blueprint for the rest of the world and is a method that urban planners and urban designers in Australia need to respect and follow.

Finally, I would like to thank my wife and children. My wife, Maria, has been supportive of the many nights and weekends I have devoted to researching and writing this book. She understands the importance of the subject matter and the need to get the message out so something can be done to address the housing affordability crisis in Australia. My children, Lucas and Claudia, who, at the time of writing this book, are seventeen and fourteen years old, respectively, deserve a mention. They represent the next generation who will struggle to realise the dream of home ownership in Australia unless something is done about it. I aspire to help my children and the many others like them, who will no doubt aspire to own their own home but have a much bigger hill to climb than previous generations. Their task deserves our attention and assistance to ensure Australia can continue to be an egalitarian nation where everyone gets a 'fair go'.

PREFACE

Home ownership is a human right, and it's a travesty that young Australians can no longer afford a home of their own...

The dream of home ownership has mesmerised Australians for more than a century. Its manifestation, whether it be the home or what goes in it, often resonates in the media and has earnt a special place in popular culture through sitcoms such as *Kingswood Country* and the more contemporary *Neighbours*. Since the 1950s, the pursuit of home ownership has been the driving force behind lifestyle changes and is a symbol of the growing prosperity in Australia.

Often described as a 'national obsession', the single-minded pursuit of owning a 'piece of Australia' spawned a legacy of big houses on big blocks and includes our love affair with the automobile. The automobile and the house have combined to create the notion of the 'good life' in suburban surroundings. But the unparalleled improvements to the standard of living that Australians have come to enjoy over the past seventy or so years, and the consequential explosion in the 'consumer-suburban culture', is beginning to show cracks, and questions have begun to emerge. Questions like: *Is the current form of the Australian Dream, namely the big house in a suburban setting, doing us harm? Is the suburban home a sustainable form of development, and does it have a future? Is the current form of the Australian Dream affordable?*

Despite the unparalleled growth in prosperity, lifestyle and comfort, Australians are faced with a housing affordability crisis. House prices are now beyond the reach of most young Australians, and, if you live in Sydney, the median house price will set you back a cool $1.5 million. How can this be, and are we still the lucky country? Instead of being easy going, Australians are now working themselves to death to pay for their mortgages and are steadily presenting as a nation of sick people. This is evidenced by growing issues with obesity and mental health. This begs the question of whether Australians are genetically predisposed to obesity and mental health problems, or if our environments, chosen forms of lifestyle and the housing affordability crisis plays a role in this growing malaise.

This book will preview the growing shadows that are forming behind our obsession with big homes and home ownership, as well as its symbiotic relationship with suburbia. The Australian obsession with home ownership and the corresponding 'consumption-suburban culture' are also examined as factors contributing towards an ever-growing public health and environmental concern. This book will also examine the growing issues with housing affordability and how, as a nation, we can combat this issue through changes in the way our cities are designed and the way houses are built, thereby reimagining the Australian Dream for future generations.

I would like to be clear that, in going on this journey with you, we will examine the inherent contradictions of our lifestyles. In other words, we will try to understand that, despite having a lifestyle envied by most of the world, Australians are actually emerging as one of the unhealthiest nations, encapsulating the notion that 'bigger' doesn't always mean 'better'.

I will also endeavour to examine some of the causes of our contemporary problems with housing affordability and its 'killing' of the Australian Dream of home ownership. The solutions I present in this book may be viewed as controversial and challenging, but, if future generations have any hope of accomplishing the Australian Dream, we must make changes *now*.

TABLE OF CONTENTS

I. Preface	ix
II. Introduction	01
The Changing Dream	04
From Dream to Obsession	07
The Growing Shadows	11
1. Creating Paradise	**13**
From Constraint to Freedom	13
The Mechanisation of Society	15
Housing and Population	18
A New Model for Growth	21
The Core Characteristics of Suburbia	24
From Suburbia to Sprawl	31
2. Shifting Sands: A Society in Transition	**37**
The Consequences of Suburbia	37
Public Life Versus Private	40
The Link Between Consumption and Private Life	41
The Breaking Up of Society	43
The House and Land Package	46
A Loss of Place and Time	48
3. Keeping Up with the Joneses and the Housing Affordability Crisis	**51**
House Sizes	52
Generating Wealth	55

Standard of Living: 1970s and 1980s to Today	62
Deregulation of the Banking Industry and Negative Gearing	64
Spending Wealth: The Housing Trap	65
Debt	68
Overworked Australians	72
Summarising the Crisis	75
4. The Growing Shadows	**77**
Physical Activity	77
Obesity	81
Mental Health	85
Piecing It Together	87
The Urban Footprint	92
No Homes among the Gum Trees	97
Traffic and Gridlock	101
Pollution	104
The Environmental Impacts of Residential Development	107
The Financial Cost of Urban Sprawl	113
Vulnerability: Car Dependency and Peak Oil	120
5. The Changing Foundations of the Australian Dream	**129**
As Safe as Bricks and Mortar	129
Demographic Time Bomb	139
Planning Theory and the Changing Market	145
Time to Reflect	147
6. Macro-Planning the New Australian Dream	**149**
Macro-Planning Our Cities	151
Dealing with Our Suburbs	155
Transport	162
Mid-Tier Transit	166
Public Transport Implementation	168
Implementing Light Rail	172
New Technology: Trackless Trams	175
Creating Places of Interest: Transit-Oriented Development	180

The Future of Transit-Oriented Development	195
New Growth Areas	199
A New Vision for Our Growth Areas	199
Creating People-Centred Town Centres	202
Summing It All Up	219
Planning in Motion	219
Creating People-Centred Residential Precincts	222
Building Alternative Transport into Suburbs	226
The Planning System and the Role of Government	230
The Role of Government Developers	238
Summary	258
7. Micro-Planning the Australian Dream	**261**
What Does the Australian Dream Look Like?	261
The Original 1980s Duplex	266
The 1980s Cul-de-sac	267
The 1990s and the Emergence of New Urbanist Housing	268
The 1990s Wasn't All Rosy: The Emergence of Group Housing	269
Housing Since the 2000s: A Mixture of Success and Failure	274
New Growth Areas	274
The Question of Affordability	277
Demonstration Housing: The Influence of the Government	280
The Future of the Australian Dream	287
New House Design for the Australian Dream in New Growth and Infill Areas	289
A Carrot or Stick Approach?	295
Reducing the Running Costs of a Home: The Role of Sustainability	301
Parting Words on the Australian Dream	305
About the Author	**311**

II
INTRODUCTION

The Australian Dream: "the desire to own a comfortable
and spacious home"

—The Oxford English Dictionary

The Great Australian Dream can be summarised succinctly as the common belief that home ownership leads to a better life.[1] The term also often goes hand in hand with the notion that home ownership is a symbol of success and security. While it can mean many things to many different people, one thing is for certain: it represents what almost all Australians aspire to achieve, including our migrant population who arrive at our shores mesmerised by how good we have it as a nation.

Growing up as a kid in the suburbs of north-western Perth as a son to Italian immigrants, home ownership was drummed into me at an early age, as my parents – who were first generation migrants – saw home ownership as the quintessential pinnacle of having 'made it'. Some of my earliest memories as a young adult include conversations with my mother and father over home ownership. My parents regarded it as one of the most important decisions I would ever make in my life.

When we talk about home ownership, we often refer to the single-storey home on a block of land in suburban surroundings, but this is not the only representation of home ownership. As we will see later in this book, the Australian Dream can equally apply to other built forms, such as apartments, as we start to see a grass-root shift in the perception of the Australian Dream.

---

[1] *'Sprawl Consumes All'*. Adelaide.com.au, 29 October 2004.

Although the Australian Dream has taken on a form that is well known to today's Aussies, it is not a recent phenomenon or fad, and, in fact, it has been one of the primary aspirations driving consumer decisions for decades. "Having a home among the gum trees" in a land that was plentiful is an idea that often resonates throughout the early literature of Australian heritage. Because Australia is so vast, early colonies established homesteads that took on the character of standalone homes in urban settings and larger farm homes in the emerging outback. Early evidence points to the vast open spaces of early colonial Australia as the factor that helped to inspire the notion of home ownership for Australian families, and the first ideal of a standalone house on a large block.[2]

It has also been argued that, when the British first arrived in Australia, they very quickly displaced the Indigenous population and pressed on with establishing colonies in Australia on a first-in-first-served basis. The British, under Arthur Phillip, believed land was free, so they took more or less what they wanted, which established a pattern of control and possession in Australia.[3] Freed convicts, officers of the law, soldiers and settlers were all given land as an incentive to support the colony.[4]

With the majority of migrants in the colonial days coming from the British Isles, their prior experience of home ownership was vastly different from the possibilities that Australia offered. The majority of British migrants who came to Australia in the early days of settlement were either convicts, military or people who'd previously lived in cramped quarters. Once in Australia, the combined appreciation for vast open spaces and the untouched landscape brought the hope of a new way of living and the possibility of home ownership for the first time.

While early homes in Australia were simple single-room cottages, the abundance of space and gradual prosperity saw houses expand from a single room to three to four rooms. Adaptation to the climate meant that most houses of the era had a veranda and high ceilings. As the Australian colonies expanded, so did the choice of housing, with many adopting the Old Colonial Georgian style and Old Colonial Regency style housing.[5] For convicts and immigrants, home ownership had previously been out of reach, but the creation of colonies in Australia and the people's adaptation to the Australian landscape made home ownership an attainable dream.

By the time of Governor Ralph Darling's arrival in 1825, a more organised approach to land ownership had taken hold, with the creation of the freehold land system. This system marketed home ownership as an attainable commodity for settlers arriving in Australia.[6] From the 1830s and 1840s onwards, property ownership was a bona fide proposition and was sought after by settlers as an essential step in life. In contrast,

---

[2] *'Suburbs and Suburbanisation'* E-Melbourne the City past and present, www.emelbourne.net.au, University of Melbourne, June 2008.
[3] Hughes, R, *'The Fatal Shore'*, Vintage Books, London, 2003.
[4] Hughes, R, *'The Fatal Shore'*, Vintage Books, London, 2003.
[5] Troy, P, *'A History of European Housing in Australia'*, Cambridge University Press, 2000.
[6] Hughes, R, *'The Fatal Shore'*, Vintage Books, London, 2003.

land tenure laws and critical ownership of large areas of land by the State and interests of the church precluded many people in Britain from ever owning a home. This was supported by the class system, which was driven largely by the social constructs of society at the time and made more acute by the Industrial Revolution, which created the earliest form of capitalism.

In Australia, it was very different. Land was immediately acquired by the Crown and was given to settlers through the freehold land system. By the 1850s, Australia started to see the subdivision of vast landholdings in Sydney and Melbourne; this created small towns and residential areas and allowed home ownership within the colonies on a large scale.[7]

A similar story unfolded in other parts of Australia. In South Australia, owning property was a pathway to attaining a vote in political proceedings. This created the notion that home ownership was a core part of being an Australian. Home ownership quickly became more widespread, and, by the 1880s, it was estimated that more than 40% of Australians owned a home – something that was rare to find in other countries, where only the wealthy owned land.[8] This was a time when capitalism was taking hold during the Industrial Revolution. This led to so much exploitation and division in society that it gave rise to the notions of socialism and communism.

As Australia approached the twentieth century, we started to see the Australian populace using their land to grow food to support themselves. This was very different from other countries, where housing and farmland were separate, with farmland placed outside of the town centres. By contrast, Australians grew food on their own land. This gave rise to the idea of putting a small house on a large quarter-acre block and using the rest of the land to grow food.

Figure 0.1: Difficult conditions in Industrial Britain[9]

---

[7] Hughes, R, *'The Fatal Shore'*, Vintage Books, London, 2003.

[8] Troy, P, *'A History of European Housing in Australia'*, Cambridge University Press, 2000.

[9] Rhodes, R, 'Energy: A Human History', Simon & Schuster, 2018.

Figure 0.2: Vast open spaces in colonial Australia[10]

The influx of immigrants into Australia, many from agrarian backgrounds, further reinforced the home and agricultural lifestyle. Looking back at the early 1900s, most Australian households had agricultural gardens; this included my own family, who purchased a quarter-acre block in Perth's northern suburbs in the 1950s.[11] They had a modest house and a large backyard, where they grew a wide range of vegetables and fruits, including avocados, lemons and leeks. What this gave rise to was the notion of the house in the suburban setting in Australia.

The Changing Dream

The advent of the automobile and the establishment of planning movements, such as Ebenezer Howard's garden city movement, in the early nineteenth century helped to transform the Australian Dream to the common notion of a single-storey detached home on a suburban quarter-acre block.[12] The garden city movement, which promoted planned and self-contained communities surrounded by 'greenbelts', was the first movement of its kind to advocate for the separation of land use, such as for homes, industry and agriculture. With its origins in the late 1890s, the movement was a reaction to the Industrial Revolution, which created poor living standards in Britain,

---

[10] 'Sydney circa 1800', State Library of NSW, 2022.
[11] Jupp, J, *'From White Australia to Woomera'*, Cambridge Press, April 2007.
[12] Hall, P, *'Cities of Tomorrow: An intellectual history of urban planning and design since 1880'*, John Wiley & Sons, 4th Edition, 2014.

with homes being cramped, beset with poor sanitation and burdened with a myriad of public health issues.[13]

This new movement was a complete revolution in city planning, reverting away from the ad hoc approach associated with industrial expansion in Britain and moving towards the creation of new estates based on clear land-use separation. For residential development, this was a move from cramped apartments and workman-like cottages to single-residential dwellings on a block with semi-detached or detached housing with a nearby park setting. The early incarnation of this new form of town planning can be seen in Britain today in the historic towns of Welwyn and Letchworth.

Figure 0.3: Welwyn Garden City[14]

This movement, which really took hold in the late 1890s and early 1900s, reinforced the hopes and desires of the early Australian migrants, who were coming to Australia seeking a better life. They aspired to escape from the squalid conditions of city life, which many people experienced in major cities such as Liverpool, Manchester and London. This was aptly articulated by British historian Peter Hall in his book *Cities of Tomorrow* in the chapter "City of Dreadful Night", which described the awful conditions faced by Britons in the 1880s, who lived as workers through the Industrial Revolution.[15]

With the garden city movement taking hold in Britain and the strong colonial and migrant ties between Britain and Australia, Australia began to introduce land-use segregation through subdivision and the creation of single-lot,

---

[13] Hall, P, *'Cities of Tomorrow: An intellectual history of urban planning and design since 1880'*, John Wiley & Sons, 4th Edition, 2014.

[14] 'Welwyn Garden City', The International Garden's City Institute, 2018.

[15] Hall, P, *'Cities of Tomorrow: An intellectual history of urban planning and design since 1880'*, John Wiley & Sons, 4th Edition, 2014.

single-use urban environments.[16] In the early to mid-1900s, new residential housing estates began to emerge in most fringe areas of Australian cities, comprising mostly single-residence homes on large blocks. In residential areas closer to the centres of Australian cities, such as Northbridge in Perth and North Melbourne in Melbourne, these suburbs included built forms such as workman's cottages resembling those in Britain, but they gradually expanded to include housing on standalone blocks.

While the notion of a single block and house started to take hold in Australia, spurred on by changing public health standards and radical city planning movements, the expansion of the city was constrained by the prevailing modes of transport at the time, which were limited to the tram, cycling and walking.[17] Only the social elite could afford an automobile, and it wasn't until later on in the middle of the twentieth century that the automobile would have a significant impact on city design in Australia.

Figure 0.4: Early automobile suburbs[18]

Although it is arguable that the Australian Dream has been part of Australian society since the beginning of colonial Australia, there can be little argument that the modern form of the Australian Dream truly came of age after the Second World War.

Following the Second World War, policymakers were faced with a serious dilemma of dealing with thousands of returning servicemen and women who needed jobs and houses. Policymakers also needed to find a way to reward these men and women for their years of service and sacrifice in a longer-than-expected war. What was dreamt up was unique in history and included the automobile as a particular catalyst for urban form and transportation. Through a combination of cheap credit,

---

[16] Goodhall, B, *'The Dictionary of Human Geography'*, Penguin, 1987.
[17] Hall, P, *'Cities of Tomorrow: An Intellectual History of Urban Planning and Design since 1800'*, John Wiley & Sons, 4th Edition, 2014.
[18] Praefcke, A, *'A Pictorial History of Suburbia'*, McMansion Hell, December 2016.

plentiful suburban land and the creation of new state government housing authorities charged with the responsibility to deliver government housing, the Australian Dream was re-packaged en masse to include an automobile, a piece of land and a two-to-three-bedroom home in a quiet suburban setting.[19] This was the payoff for years of sacrifice and the hiatus from living a normal life that war caused in the lives of people at the time. This scheme's success could be seen through an increase in the number of Australians who owned a home: only 50% of Australians owned their own home in the first half of the century, and that percentage jumped to 72% in the twenty years after the Second World War.[20] For many, the home ownership dream suddenly became a reality.

From Dream to Obsession

Somewhere along the line, the reality of home ownership got on steroids. It wasn't just enough for Australians to own a home, it had to be the biggest and best that money could buy. Australians now have the biggest homes in the world, even surpassing the United States, which have held the title since records commenced in the 1950s. Between 1950, when repackaging the Australian Dream started, and 2021, the average size of a home grew from a modest 100sqm to 238sqm – a whopping 240% increase in floor space. This extraordinary feat has been matched by few countries in the world, with the United States (232sqm in 2021), Canada (192sqm in 2021) and New Zealand (209sqm in 2021) being notable examples.[21]

Large single-storey and two-storey detached homes have become the norm in Australian suburbs, with many houses featuring three to four bedrooms, three bathrooms and a two-car garage. This obsession with housing is a cultural phenomenon spurred on by a real estate industry that knows no boundaries when it comes to selling the Australian Dream. Real estate agents will tell you that you need a two-car garage and a minimum of three bedrooms if you want good resale value, but this couldn't be further from the truth, with houses being grossly mismatched to household sizes.

---

[19] Praefcke, A, 'A Pictorial History of Suburbia', McMansion Hell, December 2016, Allen & Unwin, 2004.
[20] 'Home ownership in Australia, data and trends', Research Paper No.21, 2008-09, www.aph.gov.au.
[21] 'What countries have the largest homes', Quora, www.quora.com, 2021.

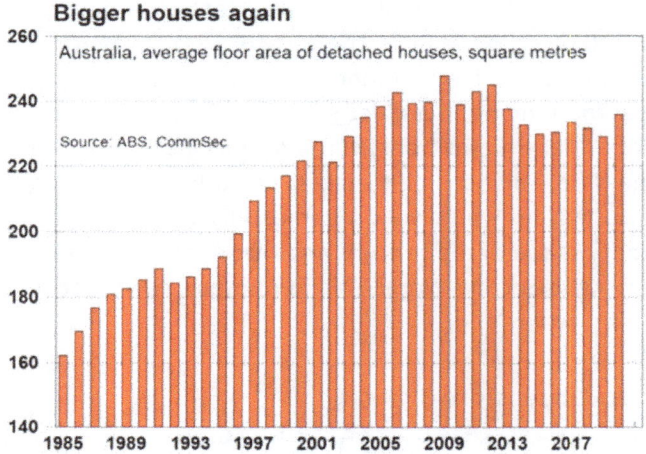

Figure 0.5: Average house sizes in Australia[22]

At the same time as housing sizes have been increasing, the average number of people living in each household has been steadily declining. This 'house flight' is illustrated below. In 1911, the average household size was approximately 4.5 people, with most households comprising a typical nuclear family: two parents and three children.[23] By 2011, this had changed dramatically, with the typical household falling to an average of 2.6 people.

The latest figures from the Australian Bureau of Statistics indicate that occupancy has dropped to an all-time low of 2.55 people per household.[24] Overlap this trend with growing house sizes, and we get an almost perfect inverse relationship which defies logic. This trend has been tracking virtually uninterrupted now for seventy years.

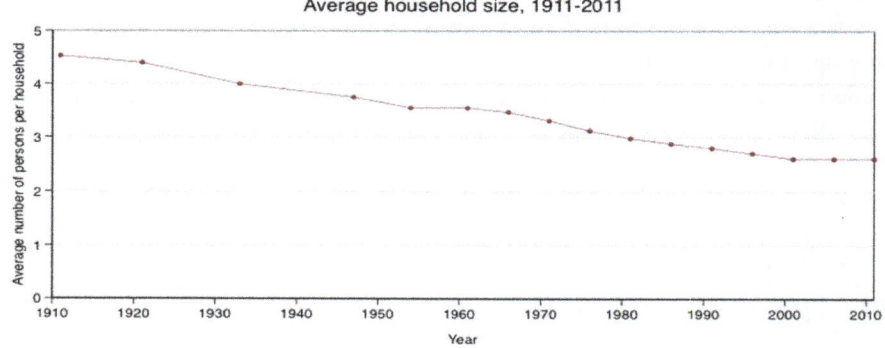

Figure 0.6: Average household size in Australia[25]

---

[22] 'Average House Sizes in Australia', Economic Insight, Commsec, December 2020.
[23] 'Population and Households', Australian Institute of Housing Studies, aif.gov.au, 2017.
[24] 'Population and Households', Australian Institute of Housing Studies, aif.gov.au, 2017.
[25] 'Population and Households', Australian Institute of Housing Studies, aif.gov.au, 2017.

Figure 0.7: Average house sizes and people per household[26]

---

[26] Images of Suburban housing', courtesy of WA State Library and archives Sergio Famiano and 'Various images of suburban families', Getty Images (various).

This isn't the only relationship that appears divergent. The sizes of our cities have grown enormously to accommodate our fascination with big houses, and this has seen a massive growth in low-density suburbia, which has transformed our urban and rural landscape from compact cities to a sprawling urban paradise. Perth, which has a population of just under 2.2 million people, spans over 6,418 square kilometres, starting from Alkimos in the north, to Mandurah in the south. London, by comparison, is 8,383 square kilometres in area, with seven times the population. Growth on steroids has meant that we can no longer walk to places; instead, we are now dependent on the automobile for getting around our cities, further entrenching the suburban malaise. This presents dilemmas for our city planners and policymakers, who have to grapple with the challenges that come with a rapidly growing city.

But this isn't the only issue causing policymakers to worry: debt is now reaching nightmarish proportions. With bigger houses come bigger mortgages, and Australians are now so in debt, total mortgages in Australia reached a staggering milestone of 1 trillion dollars in 2017 and are now approaching 1.2 trillion dollars.[27] Spiralling debt is becoming more difficult to service, even at historically low interest rates. It is no surprise now that one of the fastest growing professions in Australia is debt counselling, as more and more Australians find themselves unable to pay their mortgages.

This growing trend has led to the term 'mortgage stress' being coined, which refers to the portion of disposable income devoted to servicing a mortgage; once this portion reaches a third of disposable income, the household is under financial stress. Put simply: if mortgage servicing exceeds a third of a household's income, there is less money available for other essential items, such as education, food and bills. During the 1990s, this term didn't exist, but, by the 2000s, the term 'mortgage stress' had become commonplace in the vernacular, and it is a notion often referred to by the Reserve Bank Board when it meets monthly to determine monetary policy. This notion has become so important now that it is the primary cause of concern for decision makers when determining interest-rate movement.

And these concerns are justified.

Australian debt is now reaching even more nightmarish proportions, having soared to 203% of household income in 2021 from 70% in the early 1990s.[28] Such a massive explosion in debt is deeply concerning, especially when you consider that wages have been stagnant. With stagnant wages, more and more Australians are in debt and are increasingly having less income to purchase basic necessities. The situation is so bad that the Reserve Bank Governor is frequently quoted saying that interest

---

[27] 'With 1 trillion in Mortgages, the RBA might be getting worried', The Sydney Morning Herald, www.smh.com.au 2017.
[28] 'Household debt as a percentage of disposable income', OECD data, 2021.

rates on mortgages would only have to increase slightly from historic lows to cause widespread mortgage stress, leaving policymakers with few options for managing the economy.

This is true for the current state of the Australian economy. Despite having endured nearly thirty years without entering into a recession (changed now due to COVID-19), a feat that is unmatched by any Organisation for Economic Co-operation and Development (OECD) country in the developed world, Australia is now faced with an economic climate of stagnant wage growth, low economic growth and the prospect of near zero interest rates for the first time in its history.

Policymakers are faced with the dilemma that, despite low interest rates, wage growth remains stagnant and economic growth is barely treading water. Could it be that Australians are mortgaged out? With high mortgage levels and stagnant wage growth, there is very little room for Australians to move when it comes to spending. This alarming trend is compounded by the potential for falling house prices, which will add to mortgage stress and, in many instances, will result in negative equity in homes. Throw the potential for rising interest rates in the mix (we are starting to see this in 2022), and all of a sudden you have a perfect storm that will add to mortgage stress and falling house prices.

The Growing Shadows

The housing explosion and its tango with suburbia is taking its toll on other areas of Australian life. Emerging are the growing shadows in public health and environmental issues, which are reaching critical points in our history. Mental health decline, obesity, environmental degradation and loss of habitat are all synonymous with the rapid growth in the Australian Dream and suburbia. Ironic as it sounds, suburbia was created as a by-product of public health initiatives, which saw the growth in land-use segregation in our cities. Over seventy years of living this lifestyle has seen the Australian Dream and suburbia transform our landscape, some would say, for the worst and take on the mantle of public enemy number one.

1
CREATING PARADISE

From Constraint to Freedom

Aside from creating devastation, war also puts people's lives on hold and fuels dreams of a better life. For Australian servicemen and women, the Second World War deferred hopes and frustrated desires and aspirations. If you count the Great Depression as being a similar period in history, then, for over fifteen years, normal life was suspended with many Australians feeling as though they were in a long and drawn-out funk. Just as soon as the war ended, all the pent-up frustrations and desires experienced during the Great Depression, and especially the war years, were released. A new era of unprecedented confidence commenced, fuelled by the most enduring of human emotions: hopes and dreams.

The 1940s and 1950s were a time of unprecedented hope in Australian society. While Australian and American troops were still fighting their way through the Pacific, politicians, city planners, industrialists and the media at home began conjuring up a dream of a brighter and happier future. On the home front, politicians talked about better times, the media promoted the family unit, newspapers held competitions to design the post war 'dream home', and car designers began drawing plans for 'dream cars' that could be marketed and sold en masse to the general population. The people in power knew what people wanted, they just needed to package it up and deliver it to give a vision to all the hopes and desires of a tired and weary population.[29]

---

[29] Davidson, G, *'Car Wars: How the Car won our hearts and conquered our cities'*, Allen & Unwin, 2004.

Figure 1.1: Creating the image of the Australian Dream[30]

---

[30] Images from *'American Dream or Nightmare: Analysing Post Suburbia in America'*, Liam's look at history, 2016.

Winning the war required the drastic curtailment of people's freedoms, including their freedom of movement. Soldiers and civilians alike were subject to all sorts of controls and restrictions during the Depression and World War Two. During the war years, petrol was rationed, and car owners were limited to 3,200 kilometres of travel a year, with many car owners locking their vehicles away in the garage until the war was over or until better times resumed.[31] Rationing forced many motorists to catch the tram, cycle or walk. This constraint was preceded by years of economic depression, which resulted in other restrictions, such as those on housing, clothing and the purchase of everyday consumer items, as all aspects of life were constrained due to prolonged poor economic conditions.

As the war dragged on, war-weary Australians began to dream of a better life, and their dreams were shaped by the preceding decade of depression and war as they looked towards radical changes after years of long, drawn-out hardship. The war, which had relieved unemployment for a period of time, provided some respite to the troubles of the Depression era, but the threat of another Great Depression was ever present in the post-war period. This fear would shape the post-war world in many ways, not least of all through the promotion of consumption as a way to stimulate demand through creating supply.

Politicians were keen not to see a return to economic hardship after the Second World War, and it could be argued that the war was the final push that took most economies out of the Great Depression. The focus, therefore, fell on how society could continue economic development without the stimulus of a war and the mobilisation that comes with it. Population growth and consumerism would emerge as the panacea and would form the basis of economic policy to generate enduring economic growth.

The Mechanisation of Society

The Second World War also opened up the idea of all possibilities associated with a mechanised society. The Allied victory was won by rapid movement driven by engines, whether it be ships, aeroplanes, tanks or trucks; mechanisation and rapid movement was the key to success against the Axis nations. When the war ended, society was not immune to the new reality of a mechanised society, and a new industrial society based on mass movement began to take hold in places such as Europe and America. No sooner had America won the war in Europe and the Pacific than supreme Allied commander General Dwight D "Ike" Eisenhower, who later became US president in 1950, put to plan his dream of a motorised society. He did this by enacting America's Regional Highway Program, which sought to connect cities in America through a series of interconnected interstate highways. This was done at the expense of trams

---

[31] MeKernan, M, 'All in – Australia during World War Two', Melbourne, Thomas Nelson, Australia, 1983.

and trains, which, in many cities, were ripped up to make way for new highways.[32] It was said that Ike was inspired by the hundreds of kilometres of German Autobahns used to move German military and domestic vehicles. When the US army in turn conquered Western Germany, it was done via the speed with which American armoured tanks and troop carriers could move through Germany using these new highways. Eisenhower saw the model for the future and brought it to the United States. It wasn't long before this model was exported to Australia.

Figure 1.2: Autobahns in Hitler's 'modern' Germany[33]

Figure 1.3: Autobahns powering the allied victory in World War Two[34]

Just as quickly as highways began to spread across the United States linking cities with towns – thanks to the *Federal-Aid Highway Act of 1956* – Australia began

---

[32] Kunstler, J, 'The Geography of Nowhere', Touchstone and Simon & Schuster, New York, 1994.
[33] 'A concise history of Germany's autobahn's', Motor Trend, 2020.
[34] *'Thousands of Germans march down autobahn, near Gleeson'*, Everett Collection, 1974.

drawing plans for similar schemes.[35] Winning a world war and becoming a new superpower brought with it admirers, and the world looked towards the United States for inspiration and leadership. So, when the United States began its highway construction, Australia followed suit, sending its best and brightest town planners and civil engineers to the United States to see the new way of city planning.

Figure 1.4: Interstate highways in the US[36]

As Australia turned its attention towards the United States, it shunned its long-held tradition of town planning links with the United Kingdom and Europe. Small-scale neighbourhood planning fostered by the garden city movement gave way to mass-transit planning – a decisive shift that saw transport planning take centre stage in city planning. This led to numerous programs being established in Australia that sought to rapidly expand highways in Australian cities, allowing free movement of the automobile over other forms of transport.

In Perth, for example, this led to the enactment of the Metropolitan Region Scheme in the mid-1950s, which saw mass reserves of land being set aside for highway construction. This was quickly followed by the creation of the Mitchel Freeway and the Narrows Interchange in the 1960s, with the expansion of this road network still continuing today.[37] This was preceded by the establishment of the *Main Roads Act 1930* and the establishment of the State Government Department Main Roads WA, which is responsible for administering all arterial roads in Western Australia. Such is the power and influence granted to Main Roads WA, that the road network in West-

---

[35] Weingroff, R, *"Federal-Aid Highway Act of 1956, Creating the Interstate System"*. Public Roads. Federal Highway Administration. 60 (1). 1996.

[36] *'Interstate Highway Map'*, Wikimedia Commons, 2011.

[37] Hedgecock, D, and Yiftachel, O, *'Urban and Regional Planning in Western Australia'* Paradigm Press, 1992.

ern Australia has exploded in size over the last seventy years and now constitutes over 17,800 kilometres of roads.[38]

In Sydney and Melbourne, the stories were similar. In Sydney, the Department for Main Roads was established in 1932 and was initially responsible for road construction, upgrades and rerouting. This authority, which was later reconstituted and named the Roads and Traffic Authority in 1989, would oversee the construction of over 17,000 kilometres of road and 4,700 bridges.[39] In Melbourne, the Road Boards changed to the Road Safety and Traffic Authority in 1982, which later became the Road Corporation, or VicRoads, in 1989.[40] Following a similar trajectory to Sydney and Perth, Melbourne created over 23,000 kilometres of freeway and arterial road in what has become an interconnecting web of roads and towns across the eastern seaboard.[41] This mass expansion, which occurred over a relatively short period of history, opened up a number of possibilities, including housing growth along a low-density, suburban-based model.

The mass expanse of road construction in Australia went hand in hand with home building. A new form of housing took shape that saw suburban blocks serviced by easy access to arterial roads and highways, which allowed for quick transportation via the automobile to any part of town. This was in stark contrast to the pre-1945 period, which saw housing curtailed by economic depression and war, and transport technology largely limited to railways and trams.

Housing and Population

During the Great Depression and Second World War, housing remained in short supply, and it was only a matter of time before the government would need to address this issue. In war-torn Europe, the shortage in housing was brought about by years of devastation, with city after city succumbing to massive aerial bombardment. When the war ended, it sparked one of the biggest urban renewal and housing projects ever witnessed, affecting most major European cities. In Australia, the story was very different, with the housing shortage being caused by house building coming to a stop during the war, as resources had to be devoted to the war effort. The demand for houses was also curtailed by the Great Depression.

In the immediate post-war period, this housing shortage was compounded by an unprecedented influx in population from Britain and Southern Europe, predominantly refugees fleeing their war-torn countries in search of a better life. The latter became an enduring trend that dominated the post-war period.

---

[38] Edmonds, L, *'The vital link: A History of Main Roads 1926 to 1996'*, University of Western Australia Press, 1996.
[39] Clark, C, *'A History of Australia Vol 1'*, Melbourne University Press, Melbourne 1962.
[40] Lay, M. 'Melbourne miles: the story of Melbourne's roads', Australian Scholarly Publishing, Melbourne, 2003.
[41] Lay, M. 'Melbourne miles: the story of Melbourne's roads', Australian Scholarly Publishing, Melbourne, 2003.

After the Second World War, Australia threw its doors open to immigration. Having believed that Australia narrowly avoided Japanese invasion, Australia embarked upon an ambitious program of immigration to meet labour shortages and protect Australia from external threat. Prime Minister Ben Chifley declared "a powerful enemy looked hungrily toward Australia. In tomorrow's gun flash that threat could come again. We must populate Australia as rapidly as we can before someone else decides to populate it for us."[42]

This was a major break in policy for Australia. While supporting immigration wasn't new, the Australian Government entering into an agreement with the new International Refugee Organisation in July 1947 to settle displaced people from camps in Europe was a big change.[43] From the onset, it was intended that the bulk of these immigrants should mainly be from the United Kingdom, so that Australian society could maintain its 'British character'. This policy quickly shifted to include people from continental European countries, such as Greece, Italy, Germany and Yugoslavia.

Even as early as 1942, policymakers in Australia foreshadowed a massive housing shortage that would result from a combination of years of neglect and the policy of extended immigration that was expected to take hold in the post-war period. Together with the growing expectation that the 'slum housing' created during the Depression years would be removed, it was estimated that the immediate housing shortage in Australia would amount to at least 112,000 homes by 1945, while a further 46,000 houses would be declared unfit for human habitation.[44] To meet this demand, the Federal Government had to take immediate action and devised the establishment of the Commonwealth Housing Commission to make the issue a national priority, with separate State Housing Commissions also established to demolish the slums and deliver the new housing in their respective state jurisdictions.

The housing boom fuelled by returning servicemen and women and expanding immigration, which commenced in 1945, was supported by government schemes to promote home ownership through low-cost mortgage programs. Home loans were offered to servicemen at sustained low rates and deferred payment of land. This was done to incentivise housing and also to reward returning servicemen and women for their years of sacrifice and service.[45]

The housing boom that took hold in the post-war years was facilitated by a shift in town planning, which saw the establishment of the quarter-acre block as the new formula for suburban development. The new subdivision of land into quarter-acre

---

[42] Day, D, *'Chifley'*, Harper Collins, Sydney, 2001.

[43] National Archives of Australia, *'Land of Opportunity: Australia's Post War Construction'*, www.guides.naa.gov.au/land-of-opportunity/chapter14/.

[44] National Archives of Australia, *'Land of Opportunity: Australia's Post War Construction'*, www.guides.naa.gov.au/land-of-opportunity/chapter14/.

[45] Duffy-Jones, R, *'A Historical Geography of Housing Crisis in Australia'*, Australian Geographer, 49:1, 5-23, 2018.

blocks was supported by new housing taking the form of two-to-three-bedroom semi-detached and detached homes. Supported by the growing popularisation of the automobile, suburban developments like Joondanna in Western Australia and Waverly in Melbourne became the new template for post-war development, resulting in the vast expansion of Australian cities over a short period of time.

The Australian housing boom brought with it an unprecedented level of prosperity, as the mass construction of housing and the expansion of infrastructure projects to support the boom took hold. The immediate post-war period witnessed the rapid expansion in mining in Australia, the growth in manufacturing in Australia and, importantly, the establishment of significant infrastructure projects, such as the Snowy River Hydro Dam Project in New South Wales, which brought thousands of jobs and migrants to the country in search of a better life and home ownership.[46] For most migrants, who also suffered during the Great Depression and Second World War, home ownership prior to coming to Australia had only been a distant dream.

Fuelled by the promise of jobs, the establishment of cheap credit, deferred payment for land, state-sponsored housing and the growing accessibility and popularisation of the automobile, the elements collectively conspired to create the possibility of the Australian Dream of home ownership. The coming-together of these factors over a short period of time resulted in unprecedented population growth, with the population in Australia nearly doubling from 7.5 million to 13 million people between 1945 to 1975.[47] The Australian Dream was on its way.

Figures 1.5 and 1.6: Expansion of infrastructure and industry in the post-war period[48] [49]

---

[46] 'The Snowy Mountains Scheme', Culture and Recreation Portal, Department of the Environment, Water, Heritage and the Arts, Australia, 2008.
[47] Australian Bureau of Statistics, 'Population Growth: Australia's Population Growth', www.abs.gov.au.
[48] 'Two generations of Snowy Mountain Engineering – 70 years of impact', SMEC, 2020.
[49] Cheetham, C, 'Australian Cars – All in the Past', DM-Drive.com, 2017.

A New Model for Growth

When faced with how Australia would house its new and rapidly growing population, policymakers had to consider two fundamentally opposing models of growth. The first was based on the traditional neighbourhood design supported by a walkable and diverse transit urban form. The second was the new automobile-centric suburbia, or automobile urban form. The two models, for all intents and purposes, are completely different.

The traditional neighbourhood model was a fundamental form of historic European settlement and constituted a compressed urban form characterised by mixed land use, such as combining housing and retail, with a pedestrian-friendly urban morphology that supported a population of diversity in socio-economic background and age. This type of development was based on the pre-automobile urban form characterised by narrow street forms and compact housing, with housing consisting of a mixture of apartments and semi-detached and detached homes around a clear town centre square or main street. The town centre or main street, which formed the community hub of the neighbourhood, usually included shops, a post office, a church and a public meeting space. Life was generally lived on the streets, with the home being the place you slept. The streets and town centre were where people met, socialised and participated in community activities.

Characteristic of walkable neighbourhoods, these places were originally limited to a walking distance of eight-hundred metres to four kilometres. This distance expanded in the late 1800s, when the train and tram were established, linking neighbourhoods and towns. Despite these transport innovations, the town centre core and main street maintained a compact urban form, with housing located within walking distance of transport, shops and civic land uses. Because this urban form evolved prior to the popularisation of the automobile, the streets were generally narrow, built originally for the horse and cart and later adapted for the tram, and then the automobile.

The traditional walkable neighbourhood and the urban form that resulted could best be described through the notion of the Marchetti constant. This was developed by Italian Cesare Marchetti together with the work done by Australia's own Peter Newman on urban fabrics. Combined, their work helped to explain how cities had evolved over time. The Marchetti constant is a theory that articulates that there is a universal travel-time budget equivalent to one hour per person, per day, that influences travel patterns. This theory suggests people would be willing to travel a distance equivalent to one hour in time per day. Using this theory, Peter Newman described the various urban forms that resulted as transport technology evolved through history.[50]

---

[50] Newman, P, Kosonen, L, Kenworthy, J, *'Theory of urban fabrics: planning the walking, transit/public transport and automobile/motor car cities for reduced car dependency*, TPR, 87(4), 2016.

In the pre-heavy-transport era, walking and the horse and cart were the dominant forms of transport, and this limited the expansion of cities and towns based on the Marchetti constant. Accordingly, early towns and cities, up until the 1850s, were limited to a radius no greater than three to four kilometres – in most cases – since walking from the town's centre to the outskirts would take approximately one hour.[51] Because of the limitations associated with walking and the use of the horse and cart, historic towns in Europe are compact and dense in population, with everything being designed to be within walking distance of your home. This walkable 'urban fabric' stood for thousands of years until technology in transport progressed.[52]

When technology did progress during the Industrial Revolution period, it was initially in the form of the train and then the tram. This enabled cities to expand, since people could now travel greater distances in a one-hour period. Cities and towns began to grow along linear train and tram lines, like tentacles from the centre, beyond the original walkable catchment. Occurring during the 1850s to the 1920s, this saw the radius of the 'transit urban form' expand to up to twenty kilometres from the centre of the city.[53] Elements of the walkable neighbourhood or walkable urban form remained, with the establishment of walkable neighbourhoods now centring around train stops, which branched out from the town's centre. Dense nodes of development were created around train stations, which, in turn, created secondary commercial and civic spaces outside of the cities' centres.

Examples of the walkable and transit urban form can be found throughout most historic European towns and cities but also in the inner and middle locations of Australian cities – notably the traditional city centre cores of Melbourne, Sydney and Perth. Neighbourhoods such as Highgate in Perth's Central North are typical of development that expanded outwards from the city centre along linear transport corridors, which was facilitated through transport technological advancement such as trams. In these locations, residential housing is typically a mixture of apartments, detached terrace housing and semidetached homes close to the 'main street'. The main street includes a variety of places, including churches, cinemas, shops, medical centres, a post office, cafés, restaurants and offices.

The transit neighbourhood, such as Highgate, was facilitated through the establishment of a tram service, such as the one that ran from Barrack Street, in Perth's Central Business District (CBD), to Mt Lawley, via Beaufort Street. This form of development, which pre-dates the popularisation of the automobile, stood for a

---

[51] Newman, P, Kosonen, L, Kenworthy, J, 'Theory of urban fabrics: planning the walking, transit/public transport and automobile/motor car cities for reduced car dependency, TPR, 87(4), 2016.
[52] Newman, P, Kosonen, L, Kenworthy, J, 'Theory of urban fabrics: planning the walking, transit/public transport and automobile/motor car cities for reduced car dependency, TPR, 87(4), 2016.
[53] Newman, P, Kosonen, L, Kenworthy, J, 'Theory of urban fabrics: planning the walking, transit/public transport and automobile/motor car cities for reduced car dependency, TPR, 87(4), 2016.

large period of time and proved to be a sustainable form of growth, allowing people to live close to work and community areas and be less reliant on private transport for commuting. These areas today stand as some of the most popular places to live and work due to their vitality and ability to attract and accommodate a variety of amenities within walking distance of diverse housing types. They bring convenience and community together as cornerstones of this way of living. Around the world, these places are some of the most popular and most visited.

When you think of great cities, such as Paris, Rome and Florence, you think of the walkable centres that include public squares, tight streets and four-to-five-storey buildings that give a human scale to what are densely populated areas. These places are established along transport corridors serviced by rail and public transport.

Figure 1.7: Tram servicing Mt Lawley (inner suburbs of Perth) circa 1940s[54]

The urban form adopted for Australia, however, was vastly different from the traditional neighbourhood model. In keeping with the progressive change gripping the country after the Second World War, new urban development took the form of the mass privatised transit-orientated suburb. Using the Marchetti constant, the introduction of the automobile meant that cities could rapidly expand, since people could travel long distances in an automobile over a one-hour time period.[55] This meant cities could expand outward from the limits of the train line and the city's centre, taking on a whole new urban form through suburbia.

---

[54] 'Tram in Mt Lawley', courtesy of Maria Marsala, 1954.
[55] Newman, P, Kosonen, L, Kenworthy, J, 'Theory of urban fabrics: planning the walking, transit/public transport and automobile/motor car cities for reduced car dependency, TPR, 87(4), 2016.

Peter Newman identified this third urban fabric as the 'automobile urban fabric', which enables cities to expand not only in a linear pattern along former transit routes occupied by trains and trams (in many cities trains and trams were removed to make way for highways), but also between the railway transit corridors due to the accessibility of the automobile.[56] In other words, the original tentacles coming from the city centre, which were facilitated by linear train and tram routes, could now be widened, due to the growing availability of the automobile. Cities could now expand beyond the hinterland of a twenty-kilometre radius under the transit urban form to eighty kilometres under the automobile urban form.[57]

The suburban model, which really took hold after the Second World War, ignored past planning and design. It was a new form of transit-based planning, which prioritised the automobile as the dominant form of transport, rather than having people-centred places at the core of its design. The suburban model was made possible by technological advances that made the automobile popular. This new model was supported by planners, engineers and architects, who used this technological advancement to reshape planning by doing away with the traditional neighbourhood – a move that fitted the general mood for change following the Second World War.

Unlike the traditional neighbourhood town centre or main street design, which is human in scale and evolved over time, suburbia is a cookie cutter form of development: predictable and based on road planning. It also has another fundamental characteristic. Rather than the traditional neighbourhood model, which is community focused and outwardly oriented from a social perspective, the suburban model is inward looking and is individually focused.

The Core Characteristics of Suburbia

So, what is Australian suburbia? In the modern sense, suburbia has a number of core characteristics that set it apart from other forms of human settlement, which I will describe in turn.

Housing

Firstly, suburbia is all about housing, which is created through a series of subdivisions and is formed on the notion that each dwelling stands alone on a separate block of land, in most cases. This differs considerably from the traditional walkable

---

[56] Newman, P, Kosonen, L, Kenworthy, J, *'Theory of urban fabrics: planning the walking, transit/public transport and automobile/motor car cities for reduced car dependency*, TPR, 87(4), 2016.
[57] Newman, P, Kosonen, L, Kenworthy, J, *'Theory of urban fabrics: planning the walking, transit/public transport and automobile/motor car cities for reduced car dependency*, TPR, 87(4), 2016.

neighbourhood, which is compact and has a mixture of housing types placed next to other land uses. Importantly, suburbia includes housing that is largely homogenous, often resulting in suburbs containing only one type of urban form: a single or two-storey detached house on a large block. This form of development is homogenous compared to traditional neighbourhoods, which are defined as places where housing and a mixture of other land uses, such as shops, post office and the community type, come together. Contrary to the traditional neighbourhood, the homogenous suburb resembles a gated community, separating housing from other types of built form, such as shops and marketplaces. The homogenous suburb stands alone, separated from everything else, making it essential to have an automobile to travel.

The housing in suburbia, as a living arrangement itself, is sprawled, taking up large tracts of land compared to traditional neighbourhoods, which include compact and diverse housing typologies. However, in the early stages of mass suburbia, housing was modest, mainly comprising two-bedroom homes with a sleep-out between 80sqm and 120sqm in area. The house has since evolved, and now we have houses in excess of 400sqm in area.[58] Households in suburbia used to mainly consist of a typical nuclear family: a husband and wife and at least three children. As population composition changed, and Australia became more affluent as a society, households changed, with three and four-bedroom houses becoming the norm and household numbers dropping. Despite this change, which occurred over 1945 to 2000 and beyond, housing in suburbia is arranged in relatively the same way, with its form only changing in terms of street arrangement.

In the early stages of the suburban incarnation, the basis of the street form was an arrangement of grid-like streets interlocking in a series of right-angled, four-way intersections. This changed in form during the 1970s and 1980s to include the cul-de-sac suburb, which includes a series of short and mid-sized roads that lead to a dead-end. Most of these streets link to one or more distributor roads, which then feed to larger main roads that move traffic from suburb to suburb. These roads then lead to highways, which move traffic from suburbs to regions.

Nowadays, suburbia resembles a hybrid of grid and semi-circular roads, which are a bi-product of the New Urbanist movement that gripped America in the 1990s and then Australia shortly afterwards.[59] This new urban form, which we will discuss later, still maintains the suburban structure as a fundamental character, but has, at least, reverted back to the establishment of a grid-style layout and has introduced a greater mix of housing typology to bring diversity and increased

---

[58] *'How the post-war small home movement helped deliver the great Australian dream'*, www.abc.net.au.
[59] Cozens, P, *'New Urbanism, Crime and the Suburbs: A Review of the Evidence'*, Urban Policy and Research, 26(4), 429-444, 2008.

density.[60] New Urbanism is essentially a hybrid of the extreme suburbia developed in the 1950s, which was characterised by homogenous housing and land use, and the traditional neighbourhood, which includes a variety of land uses and housing types.

Despite there being some changes in the way land uses are included or excluded, these urban areas largely resemble residential suburbs with other land uses reserved for locations between residential suburbs. I can say, however, that New Urbanism is an improvement and a step in the right direction to creating a more pleasant and walkable urban form in Australia.

Shopping Centres

The shopping centre is another common characteristic of suburbia, and in Australia it took the form of 'big box' retail havens – places that are primarily for shopping. These places come in various shapes and sizes, from the small corner local shops to the large regional retail shopping centre, which are largely reliant on people driving there by car. Large shopping centres, such as Karrinyup Shopping Centre in Perth's north-western suburbs, are distinctly different from the main-street-style shopping centres located in the traditional neighbourhood, in that the shopping centres lack the combination of housing and offices that makes main street dynamic. Instead, the big box haven normally takes the form of a single-storey or, in some cases, a two-storey building surrounded by a sea of carparking between the building and the roadway.

Because these shopping centres are surrounded by low-density detached homes on large blocks, the commercial hinterland they serve is considerable. This causes people to come far and wide to undertake their shopping, which means these shopping complexes require lots of carparking to cater for the high volume of people coming via car. With big box shopping centres surrounded by carparks and high-volume vehicle movement, these places are typically congested and unfriendly, making alternative transport, such as walking and cycling, an impossible, and even scary, task.

Suburban shopping centres have one other overarching characteristic: they are places of mass consumption.[61] The box centre typically includes a large variety of shops, ranging from hairdressers to medical centres. They typically include large supermarkets and big department stores, such as Myer and David Jones. Among these places is a variety of food stores, cafés and restaurants, all designed to keep you in the centre. All functions are internalised through a system of malls, hence the term 'big box centre'.

---

[60] Cozens, P, *'New Urbanism, Crime and the Suburbs: A Review of the Evidence'*, Urban Policy and Research, 26(4), 429-444, 2008.

[61] Kunstler, J, *'The Geography of Nowhere'*, Touchstone and Simon & Schuster, New York, 1994.

Figure 1.8: Indooroopilly Shopping Centre[62]

Shopping centres, as opposed to town centres, are often difficult places to navigate, they're noisy and filled with a variety of visual distractions. Because you are housed within a large, air-conditioned box, the environment often feels artificial and can be challenging to the senses. The drive for the creation of shopping centres has come from the big retail department stores, which are often the anchor tenants to these centres, working to attract people in and then trapping them with the consumption-driven mall. While suburban malls have their incarnations throughout the world, they are a typically American invention that was imported to Australia during the 1960s as suburbanisation and mass automobile transit took hold. They still persist today.

Offices and Civic Places

Other land uses in suburbia include the office park and civic institutions. Office parks are places that are similar to big box shopping centres, in that they exist as freestanding buildings surrounded by carparks. Generally, these places include corporate businesses, showrooms, and trade and service centres that are pulled from other locations within a city and agglomerated into one homogeneous location. Examples include Herdsman Office Park in Perth's central west and Sydney's Business Park in western Sydney.

---

[62] Ellen, S, *'Indooroopilly Shopping town 1, circa 1970'*, flickr, 2019.

Figure 1.9: Sydney's Business Park West[63]

Civic institutions, or public buildings, are buildings such as town halls, churches and other places where people gather for cultural events and engagement. These were once found in the centres of traditional neighbourhoods, adjacent to a public square, but, in the suburban model, are now segregated and supported by a sea of carparking. These buildings are often inwardly focused, since the carparking that surrounds these places creates a poor connection with other nearby land uses. In the instance of community buildings, these land uses can be hidden away through a combination of carparking and landscaping.

In traditional neighbourhoods, these buildings usually serve as the town square's centrepiece and often come in the form of period architecture that separates it from other buildings, creating a landmark for the area. But, in suburbia, these buildings take an altered form, being large and infrequent and often lacking any celebrated architectural form.

Education Facilities

Education facilities – an important part of the community – in the traditional neighbourhood are integrated with other civic, shopping and religious-type uses at the centre of the neighbourhood. In suburbia, though, they take a different form. Smaller primary and secondary schools are often located away from each other and established as islands in the middle of residential suburbs. This allows, in some places, walking and cycling to and from the school, but, given that schools are similarly

---

[63] 'Sydney Business Park West', https://www.sydneybusinesspark.com.au/portfolio/location/.

surrounded by large single-storey houses on large blocks, the school catchment is often beyond the normal walking distance for most children. Accordingly, most parents need to drive their children to and from school. In some instances, schools can be well serviced by public transport via buses, and this offers some relief to the mass automobile transit that typically occurs around most schools.

In terms of cultural land uses, in the suburban model these facilities are often surrounded by a combination of playgrounds and car-parking, which results in the built form being oriented inwardly from the street. The outcomes are the same for regional universities. Universities in Australia, such as Murdoch University in Perth's southwest, are established as an island segregated away from other forms of development and surrounded by roads and carparking. Because of their isolationist designs and locations, often the only way to get to and from universities is by car. They are also monotonous places.

In Europe, by contrast, universities are integrated into the fabric of the town centre, allowing students to engage and mingle with people from other aspects of society and conduct other errands in addition to attending university, such as catching up with friends, going shopping or attending a part-time job. In the case of Australian universities, they are largely segregated from other land uses, creating a homogenous campus-style feel, where students attend classes, study and then are forced to leave if they wish to engage in other activities.

Industrial Parks

A common feature of modern land-use-segregation-based planning, which is quintessential to the suburban model, is the establishment of the industrial park. Up until the early 1900s, industrial parks were created in close proximity to housing quarters to enable ease of mobility between home and work.[64]

As the noxious base of industry began to take its toll on nearby residents, and importantly the workers themselves, modernist planning through zoning controls began to segregate industrial zones from other forms of land use, thereby reducing the health and environmental impacts that industrial complexes have on their surroundings. This resulted in a movement of industrial centres away from residential areas, in particular, and the specific zoning of industrial space near key service corridors, such as ports and major transport connects such as highways. As the years progressed, environmental legislation began to mature and dictate changes in industrial development itself, whereby industrial-type land uses changed dramatically, and their polluting nature was reduced significantly. This was a particular trend from the 1970s

---

[64] Horn, J, Rosenband, L, Smith, M, *'Reconceptualising the Industrial Revolution'*, Cambridge MA, London: MIT Press, 2010.

onwards as the environmental movement grew; this, in turn, impacted planning and environmental legislation and practices.

Despite environmental changes influencing industry, the nuisance factor associated with industrial-type land uses, such as smell and noise, still prevails and has resulted in modernist planning maintaining the approach of segregating this type of land use from other uses. Industrial parks, such as Osborne Park in Perth and Alliance Industrial Park in Melbourne, are typical examples of industrial areas. Similar to office parks, these areas are serviced by vast highways and main distributor roads, given these places are often high-volume vehicle areas, especially with large service vehicles and trucks. Characteristically, these places represent small island buildings surrounded by carparks, with buildings bearing very little relationship to their surroundings. With their functionality centred around the automobile and movement, these places are often uninviting and have little sense of aesthetics and streetscape.

Figure 1.10: Alliance Industrial Park, Melbourne[65]

Highways

The final element of suburbia, and perhaps its most enduring, is the advent of the roadway or highway. This component consists of miles of bitumen that are essential to connect all the other segregated land-use elements discussed above. Since each element that constitutes greater suburbia is single serving, and since daily life involves a wide variety of actions and activities, the residents of Australian suburbia spend an inordinate amount of time moving from one element

---

[65] 'Alliance Industrial Park', https://www.sydneybusinesspark.com.au/.

of suburbia to the next, usually on a highway or one of its many incarnations. Since most of this movement takes place via the private automobile, even a low populated area tends to generate a large concentration of traffic compared to traditional urban forms.

Expansive roadways are a necessary component of suburbia. Since suburbia consists of dispersed land uses, people must drive longer distances to gain access to services. When this is done en masse, walkability is largely non-existent, and people are dependent upon cars to move from place to place.

The highway is now a quintessential component of our car-dominated city, usually segregating areas like a giant wedge. They are polarising, difficult to look at and are often frustrating to experience, especially in peak hour when traffic becomes heavy, and you're stuck on a highway bumper to bumper for an hour or more.

Collectively, the Australian suburban model was a radical shift in urban planning. Movement shifted from predominately cycling, walking and catching the train or tram to driving a car or catching a bus. People began to live further away from all other forms of land use, and, instead of spending a large amount of time walking within a traditional neighbourhood, people began spending an inordinate amount of time travelling by car from place to place. This was fuelled by a rapid expansion in road infrastructure and the creation of freeways, which allowed vehicles to travel vast distances in relatively short periods of time. A by-product of this shift was that social experiences moved from taking place predominately in the public realm to the private home. Unbeknown to us at the time, society was undergoing a transformation never before experienced in human history.

From Suburbia to Sprawl

The size and scale of the urban transformation, which took place immediately after the Second World War, cannot be underestimated. Immigration combined with an increase in babies being born resulted in a massive population expansion. The near doubling of the Australian population in only a twenty-year timeframe led to suburban development becoming the dominant development form, which would reshape the Australian landscape forever.[66]

Population transformation became the impetus for change, but creating suburbia and turning it into what has now become known as 'urban sprawl' followed a series of historical events combined with legislative changes that transformed town planning profoundly. In Australia, town planning, up until the 1940s, was largely influenced by the British model. This influence initially focused on the town centre and the neighbourhood development form from the colonial days up until the early 1900s. This was then influenced by movements such as the garden city by Ebenezer

---

[66] Price, C, *'Post War Immigration: 1947-1998'*, Journal of Australian Population Association, 15 (2), 115-129, 1998.

Howard, which began to popularise the notion of the suburban block supported by parkland. The latter began to influence popular thinking, which would later be transformed into legislation and practice.

In Western Australia, for example, the genesis of the current planning framework was initiated in 1928 through the establishment of the *Town Planning and Development Act 1928*.[67] This act, which came about following the need for the orderly and proper planning of cities, gave powers through the Town Planning Board to enable local authorities to prepare district planning schemes. This allowed local authorities to assess and refer subdivision applications to the relevant co-ordinating authorities for approval, subject to conditions and rights of appeal.[68] This replaced the ad hoc approach to town planning that had occurred in Australian cities prior and came about at a time when technology was changing. This created a departure from the Industrial Revolution in the 1800s, which created squalor due to housing being located next to unfiltered noxious industries (remember, there were no environmental authorities in the 1800s).

For Western Australia, the *Town Planning and Development Act* was seen as a 'watershed' moment, being the first statutory framework that led to integrated community planning and development. This change gave birth to the modern subdivision design and development process, which dominated the post-war period.

In 1930, shortly after the establishment of the *Town Planning and Development Act*, the Report of the Metropolitan Town Planning Commission provided the next important step in regard to future metropolitan and regional planning and development.[69] The worldwide economic depression and world war effectively restricted any progressive development for another fifteen to twenty years. As a result, the 1930 report of the Metropolitan Town Planning Commission and its recommendations remained in hiatus until 1952, when the Brand Liberal Government appointed Professor Gordan Stephenson and Alistair Hepburn to report on the need for a Metropolitan Region Scheme for Perth and Fremantle.[70] As part of this investigation, Gordan Stephenson travelled to the United States and was influenced greatly by the mechanisation of the planning framework taking place there, with highways replacing train- and tramways as the preferred form of mass transit. Equally impressive was the resulting suburban model that Stephenson bore witness to in suburban developments, such as places like Levittown in Pennsylvania, which demonstrated how the automobile and private housing could work.

---

[67] Hedgecock, D, and Yiftachel, O, *'Urban and Regional Planning in Western Australia'*, Paradigm Press, 1992.
[68] Hedgecock, D, and Yiftachel, O, *'Urban and Regional Planning in Western Australia'*, Paradigm Press, 1992.
[69] Hedgecock, D, and Yiftachel, O, *'Urban and Regional Planning in Western Australia'*, Paradigm Press, 1992.
[70] Hedgecock, D, and Yiftachel, O, *'Urban and Regional Planning in Western Australia'*, Paradigm Press, 1992.

A modernist by tradition, Stephenson spent part of his career working for the Swiss-born Architect Charles Le Corbusier in Paris and developed a style of planning that centred around La Corbusier's Radiant City theory. The Radiant City radically departed from traditional neighbourhood planning; instead, the focus shifted to large-scale and dispersed planning that included high-rise buildings in wide open spaces supported by a transport network centred around the automobile and away from neighbourhood planning that was human in scale. This shaped Stephenson's philosophy, and his trip to the United States helped create the suburbanised version of this ideology.

When Professor Stephenson returned from the United States and published his report, he argued that there was a need for a Metropolitan Region Scheme to guide future development. This was an overarching plan that would guide land use and development in the metropolitan area in the broad sense and set the blueprint for the modern transport network.[71] The report was adopted by Parliament in 1955. In 1959, the *Metropolitan Region Scheme Act* provided for the statutory formation of a Metropolitan Regional Planning Authority with the power to prepare a Metropolitan Region Scheme. This was prepared and adopted in 1963.[72] This scheme was instrumental in developing the blueprint for the growth of Perth over the next sixty years, with mass-transit corridors reserved for highways, setting up the future development of suburbia along an intricate web of highways and distributor roads-type model. Although there were differences between state governments during the period, Australia's most populous States – Victoria, New South Wales and Queensland – followed similar planning stories.

With the town planning framework in place, the suburban model had the demand impetus and framework for the rapid expansion of suburbia. But these weren't the only factors pivotal in homogenising the urban form; other factors were also in play. The popularisation of the automobile came on the back of cheap energy, with oil being the principal catalyst for a successful motor industry.[73] During the Second World War and the post-war period, massive discoveries of oil were found and harnessed in the Middle East, which would seemingly guarantee that the model of mass transit based on the private automobile would have a long-lasting and successful future. Countries like Saudi Arabia, Iraq and Iran joined the United States and Soviet Union in being massive world suppliers of cheap oil, making the suburban experiment a very possible and viable living arrangement.[74]

---

[71] Hedgecock, D, and Yiftachel, O, '*Urban and Regional Planning in Western Australia*', Paradigm Press, 1992.
[72] Hedgecock, D, and Yiftachel, O, '*Urban and Regional Planning in Western Australia*', Paradigm Press, 1992.
[73] Yergin, D, '*The Prize: The Epic Quest for Oil, Money, and Power*', Simon and Schuster, 1990.
[74] Yergin, D, '*The Prize: The Epic Quest for Oil, Money, and Power*', Simon and Schuster, 1990.

Figure 1.11: Cheap oil fuelled the suburban model[75]

Another influencing factor was the advent of the Cold War, which had its origins in the rise of socialist Russia following the Bolshevik revolution of 1917. This revolution resulted in the overturning of over four-hundred years of Tsarist rule, which was replaced by a radical new socialist ideal. The rivalry between the USA and the USSR, which had been present since the beginning, became a serious proposition in the post-war period. The Second World War saw the decline of the United Kingdom as a superpower and the rise of the United States and the Soviet Union as the two new superpowers. Both nations had completely opposing ideologies, with the Soviet Union emphasising state control and servitude to the greater good, versus the democratic freedoms and free-market economy of the United States, which, while nationalistic, emphasised the importance of the individual.[76]

Both countries wanted to prove their ideologies were superior, and this battle played out in many forms – not the least of which were through the lifestyles that each ideology brought with it.[77] In the United States and its satellite countries, such as Australia, the doctrine was about freedom, consumption and a better life. This drive resulted in economic policy bias towards the promotion of mass consumption to feed the ambitions and desires of a tired and war-weary population. One of the manifestations of this doctrine was the creation of an economy that would enable the masses to have access to all forms of consumable items that inventors could conjure up. This included housing, cars, boats, holidays and all forms of freedoms that money could buy. The biggest consumable asset became the home and the ornaments that came within it. Everything from vacuum cleaners, TVs, lawn mowers, toasters and the like were invented to enable consumption and convenience to be a part of the American and Western way of life.[78]

---

[75] "Image of Oil Derricks", California', Getty Images, 2015.
[76] Gaddis, J, *'The Cold War: A New History'*, Penguin Books, 2006.
[77] Gaddis, J, *'The Cold War: A New History'*, Penguin Books, 2006.
[78] Yergin, D. *'The Prize: The Epic Quest for Oil, Money, and Power'*, Simon and Schuster, 1990.

Figure 1.12: Communism gave rise to an opposing ideology to capitalism ensuring reforms to please the population in Western societies[79]

In fact, I credit the Cold War and communism for why we have a 'middle class' in Australia. By providing favourable economic circumstances and giving people an opportunity to purchase and own their own home and the freedom of a car, it kept the 'revolutionary instincts' at bay. If you look at all countries that became communist during the post-World War Two period, there were a variety of factors that contributed towards it: corrupt governments; exploitive economic circumstances; a disparity between the wealthy and poor; and a lack of stability, food and housing.[80] If an economic system cannot provide the basics for the majority of the population – a good job, food, clothing and a roof over your head – then the economic system and government are in trouble. Look at countries like Vietnam, Laos, Cambodia, Cuba and so on. The battle of lifestyle envy was underway, and the field of battle was the suburban home and carport.

---

[79] Breslauer, G, 'The Rise and Demise of World Communism', Oxford Scholarship, 2021.
[80] Gaddis, J, *'The Cold War: A New History'*, Penguin Books, 2006.

2

SHIFTING SANDS: A SOCIETY IN TRANSITION

The Consequences of Suburbia

The suburban model, which took hold in the post-Second World War period, was an entirely different living arrangement from what people had become used to. The suburban allure was based around the concept that people would be using their car to travel to and from home. So, how does this concept look and feel? For starters, walkability does not come into the equation. In the past, cities were planned based on how far people could walk and were characterised by having places of work, shopping and community buildings within this walking distance. Remember the Marchetti constant? This was typically a radius of one to two kilometres.[81] With the advent of the automobile as the dominant mode of transport in the twentieth century, this radius shifted dramatically, as the automobile allowed people to travel greater distances. Planning for automobile-based suburbs, therefore, shifted from people planning to automobile planning; in other words: how do we fit the car in first then think of people later? This notion is a subtle one, but it has fundamental consequences to the organising of the geography of Australia's man-made landscape.

The suburban experiment goes hand in hand with the growth in popularity of and perceived freedoms associated with the automobile.[82] Planning for new towns and suburbs suddenly had a focus on how best to accommodate the automobile as the primary form of transportation, placing walking and cycling as secondary considerations. What this did was alter living arrangements in Australia dramatically. Land uses

---

[81] Newman, P, Kosonen, L, Kenworthy, J, *'Theory of urban fabrics: planning the walking, transit/public transport and automobile/motor car cities for reduced car dependency*, TPR, 87(4), 2016.

[82] Kunstler, J. *'The Geography of Nowhere'*, Touchstone and Simon & Schuster, New York, 1994.

became more dispersed, with separate enclaves created for office parks, residential, commercial and shops, all serviced by a hierarchy of roads. These roads started with highways, which dissected the city, through to lower-order roads – commonly referred to as district and local distributor roads – which filtered traffic from highways through to the suburban network.[83] The vernacular for city planning changed, with highway, district, neighbourhood and local road networks suddenly replacing references to walkability and people accessible areas.

With land uses segregated by roads, a distance was put between places, altering the landscape completely. While, from a bird's-eye view, housing appeared to be in close proximity to shopping centres, the two land uses were considerably more distant. Due to excessive noise caused by vehicles travelling between land uses (and the reliance on vehicles for moving about suburbia), residential areas are often constructed with estate walls around them, creating a physical segregation from road and land use. The resulting impact of this design is that pedestrians are discouraged from walking from residential locations to shops, resulting in people driving to go between places. This cycle perpetuates segregation, as more cars on the road results in more sound walls between communities. The spinoff of this phenomenon is that shops require ample car parking around them, further creating a barrier between land uses.

Other comparisons are perhaps just as dramatic. Previously, shops were located along main streets in most Australia cities and towns, where residential, commercial, retail and civic type uses typically shared the same street block, enabling walking to be a viable, and even pleasurable, experience. This, however, changed dramatically with the automobile suburb, as land uses were separated from other land uses, with access provided via the highway and district distributor road. This was made worse by the fact that many vehicles contain only one or two individuals, resulting in a higher need for carparking. Once you fit in all the parking and the road network, the elements that make the pedestrian and cycle movement viable have been sacrificed for the car. A new pattern of behaviour emerged, where people – now termed appropriately as 'consumers' – moved between single-serving places.[84] No longer were people lingering around, wandering from shop to shop, or shop to civic use (library), then to a friend's house. Instead, shopping centres were becoming single-serving places, and the enclosed environment of the typical mall made lingering a painful, noisy and, overall, a less than satisfying experience.

Perhaps one of the most enduring cultural changes in the shift towards the automobile suburb is the notion of convenience. In earlier urban forms, the viability of having a mixture of land uses in close proximity was achieved because people

---

[83] Kunstler, J, *'The Geography of Nowhere'*, Touchstone and Simon & Schuster, New York, 1994.
[84] Kunstler, J, *'The Geography of Nowhere'*, Touchstone and Simon & Schuster, New York, 1994.

were living closer to these locations. What this meant was that, in traditional neighbourhoods such as Mount Lawley in Perth's inner circle of suburbs, corner stores flourished, because they were accessible via walking within a smaller commercial hinterland. Automobile suburbs, on the other hand, prioritise automotive travel and have created homogenous living arrangements, such as large homes on large blocks.

This means corner stores are often no longer within walking distance and, therefore, no longer get the foot traffic they require to remain viable. As a bit of a 'canary in the coal mine', the corner store is perhaps the yardstick for understanding if a suburb has become too automobile dependent. Now, corner stores are a thing of the past, and, for residents in new suburbs, convenience shopping generally requires a car trip to the local or district shopping centre to get something as basic as the morning paper or a litre of milk.

In terms of transport, the low-density housing and segregation of land uses which comes with automobile-planned suburbs means the automobile becomes the most viable form of transport. In Australia's early history, cities had trams to support the walking and cycling that residents did to move between places, and the choice of transport mode was based on distance to travel.[85] This variety meant that people had options at their disposal, should one form of transport become untenable.

A fundamental element of the automobile suburb is that most other forms of transportation no longer become viable for the majority of people.[86] This means people become automobile dependent. Perhaps this isn't a problem if you are thirty years old with a job and without a family, but what happens to others who have families, or are too young or old to own a car? Movement all of a sudden becomes highly constrained, and, in modern suburbia, this has created large numbers of immobile people, which can lead to reduced socialisation and participation in society.[87] I know from my own experience that I dread the idea of growing old in Australia. The day I lose my ability to drive a car will be the day most of my social engagements come to an end. So much for the freedom of the automobile.

One of the other enduring elements of suburbia is that it is largely all the same. The standardisation of suburbia, combined with population expansion and favourable economic circumstances, has resulted in its mass expansion. This has brought with it the same types of housing and the same local shops, which all contain the same brand liquor stores, fast-food outlets and supermarkets. Every suburb looks the same, making wayfinding difficult.

---

[85] Newman, P and Kenworthy, J, *'Sustainability and Cities: Overcoming Automobile Dependence*, Island Press, United States, 1999.

[86] Newman, P and Kenworthy, J, *'Sustainability and Cities: Overcoming Automobile Dependence*, Island Press, United States, 1999.

[87] Newman, P and Kenworthy, J, *'Sustainability and Cities: Overcoming Automobile Dependence*, Island Press, United States, 1999.

I remember once driving through Craigie, Heathridge and Beldon in Perth's northern suburbs at night and getting lost. There were no distinguishing landmarks, no uniquely designed shopping centres, and the road networks and housing were all the same. At the time, I was young, and my faculties were in order, but, for an elderly person negotiating the suburbs at night, this has the potential to become a very frightening experience. The fact suburbia now looks largely the same has an impact on how we perceive and enjoy that environment, and this has had a discernible knock-on effect on people's mental health – something we will discuss later in this book.

Public Life Versus Private

Since the early inception of the suburban model, the house on a large block was always the jewel in the crown. Set against the backdrop of a city's fringe, the suburban home was always designed to be the place where city lifestyle met the rural areas, with suburbia promising large blocks and large houses near public open space, rivers and forests to create the pseudo-urban and rural lifestyle that was supposed to conjure up the best of both the urban and rural worlds.[88] It was supposed to be the offering that would bring people together and create better communities and a place for everyone. But this is not what has transpired, and the design of suburbs has had a profound impact on the way we interact and socialise as a people.

What occurred after the post-Second World War period was a decided shift away from public living to private, as the focus shifted to the individual rather than the community. This shift, you could argue, was intended by the government and people in positions of power as an offering to people that suffered during the Great Depression and through the war.[89] The home became a reward for a generation of sacrifice, and this would have a lasting impact on our urban geography and the way society functions. The fixation on the home combined with an expanded distance to travel, made possible by freeways, meant that the culture in the new suburban society changed dramatically, with individualism becoming the focus over community.

Throughout most of history, people have always lived in compact living arrangements facilitated by a closely located mix of land use; this, combined with the limits of long-distance transportation options, restrained the distances people could travel. The closeness of all daily activities to the home, combined with the modesty of homes, led to daily life largely occurring outside of the home. People were forced to engage with the community, as most activities took place outside of the home and with short distances to travel. This meant people could accommodate greater variety in their daily lives.

With few people owning telephones until the post-war period, where it became affordable and popular, people socialised in the public realm, often walking to markets,

---

[88] Clapson, M, *'The suburban aspiration in England since 1919'*, Contemporary British History, 14, 151-174, 2000.
[89] Davison, G, *'Car Wars: How the Car won our hearts and conquered our cities'*, Allen & Unwin, 2004.

shops, cafés and restaurants to meet with friends and family. Children walked to school and parents walked, cycled or took the tram to work – all of which occurred within walking distance of their place of residence. Occasionally, there would be a train ride if you were looking to travel further to a nearby town, but the majority of visits occurred through walking, cycling or tram rides. Because of the modesty associated with living prior to 1950, the house played, in most people's lives, a secondary role. It was a place where you ate dinner and slept, while entertaining and meeting people largely took place elsewhere in the town square, the main street or on the streets, in parks and civic places. This represented a much more harmonious and community-oriented living arrangement, which brought people together and kept people close.[90]

This lifestyle, however, changed radically in the post-war period, with suburbia and the advent of the 'automobile urban fabric' allowing people to live kilometres away from shops, places of employment and friends.[91] Travel, which had previously been limited to walking or taking a horse and cart over eight-hundred metres to four kilometres, all of a sudden became a major part of the day, with most consumers having to commute long distances to work or the shops, in what can only be described as single-serving visitation. The dispersed city, which resulted in the suburban experiment, caused land uses to spread out across the city, with housing separated from shops, schools, offices and civic places. This resulted in travel over long distances, which made people time poor.

Gone were the days where you could stroll down the public square or main street to watch a movie, buy groceries, visit friends and go to the town hall all in one visitation. With the suburban city, every visit was a bespoke exercise: a trip to the shops, then jump in the car to go to a friend's house, and then jump in the car to go home. Transport all of a sudden became a major part of our pastimes. As cities in the post-war era rapidly expanded, this was accentuated as suburbs were located further away from places of work and entertainment and civic places, meaning there was less time to spend walking and attending to daily activities. The car suddenly became a second home, and the house became the main area of entertainment for family and friends, not out of design, but through necessity.

The Link Between Consumption and Private Life

From its inception, suburbia, and the house, have been associated with consumption.[92] This, perhaps, is best explained by understanding what people living in suburbia

---

[90] Davison, G, *'Car Wars: How the Car won our hearts and conquered our cities'*, Allen & Unwin, 2004.
[91] Newman, P, Kosonen, L, Kenworthy, J, *'Theory of urban fabrics: planning the walking, transit/public transport and automobile/motor car cities for reduced car dependency*, TPR, 87(4), 2016.
[92] Dauvergne, P, *'The Shadows of Consumption: Consequences for the Global Environment'*, The MIT Press, 2010.

experience. If you spend a disproportionate amount of time travelling in isolation by car to single-serving destinations, not only do you find yourself time-poor, but your social interactions are greatly reduced, since most people are doing the same thing as you. Unlike the traditional neighbourhood, where the chances of meeting someone you knew or someone new were greatly enhanced, suburbia becomes the vehicle for consumption. The way this happens is twofold.

Firstly, people are lonelier in suburbia, as a greater distance to travel and the dispersion of land uses mean the people you know are farther away and more difficult to reach. This means fewer opportunities to engage and interact, with every instance requiring careful planning, since the distance required to travel between places is greater. Often, this leads to feelings of loneliness and isolation. When you are lonely, you find ways of filling the void; this can often turn people towards consumption – buying things, whether you need them or not, to please yourself.

The second aspect of the suburban model is that the entire construct is designed to be single serving and, therefore, is not conducive to encouraging people to stay, linger, meet people and socialise. Instead, you go to the shops to do your shopping then leave immediately to pick the kids up from school or to arrive home to make dinner, for example. The monotony that comes with this form of living can drive people to spend their way out of feelings of boredom and depression. People are gregarious creatures and constructing an environment that forces people apart is counterintuitive and dangerous, as we will discuss later on.

On a wider scale, you can see that the mass marketing of consumables was linked with the growing number of housing estates. In the post-Second World War period, this occurred for the first time in people's homes as the television and radio began to be more widespread. In the post-war period, companies of all sorts sprung up out of nowhere selling what appeared to be an endless supply of new consumer products designed to be used around the home. This included washing machines, refrigerators, barbeques, dining and lounge room furniture, lamps, toasters, kettles, vacuum cleaners... the list goes on. This didn't happen to the same extent before, with people in the pre-war period having to read the paper or take a trip to the local corner store or shop to be confronted with consumable items. Now with mobile phones, computers, TVs and so on, consumption is virtually all around and inescapable.

While Australians had lived strong public and civic lives, they began to internalise and live privatised lives.[93] This showed itself in many metrics of measurement: levels of volunteering, club associations and people participating in civic duties, for example. All of these activities began to decline in the post-war period, as more and more people chose to associate themselves within the private realm of their homes, rather than the civic and public realms where engagement with people of all walks of life

---

[93] Davison, G, 'Car Wars: How the Car won our hearts and conquered our cities', Allen & Unwin, 2004.

was greatly enhanced. All this was facilitated by the suburban model and entrenched by the consumer culture, which works hand in hand with this living arrangement. Club and civic participation rates have been in decline since the 1950s as a result; this decline is a worrying sign for society. Since people are naturally gregarious, human interaction is very important to health and wellbeing, and if this is in decline in society, then that can only lead to rising issues associated with isolation and disconnection from society.

The Breaking Up of Society

It is perhaps the nature of the suburban model, through its mass production, that has had the most poignant influence in the transition from public life to private life. It has resulted in Australians becoming more closed off, and this includes from other socio-economic groups.

As the suburban housing model rolled out, so did the standardisation of its construction. Similar to the model T-Ford, which created the world's first mass-produced car, suburbia in America – through places like Levittown in Pennsylvania – created the first mass-produced living arrangements.[94] Characterised with a semi-lineal road system, block sizes were made to be the same size and configuration in order to accommodate standard and configured homes.[95] The homogenous nature of the suburban rollout that was occurring in the United States in the post-war period found its way to Australia, with many estates being established with four to eight slightly different designs. These designs were rolled out block after block, like mass-produced vehicles on a production line. Many suburbs in Australia resembled a mass-produced form, with the style and design changing based on the socio-economic makeup of an area.

This reality, which was convenient to the creators of suburbia, created the world's first homogenous communities, with housing estates, such as Yokine and Innaloo in Perth, being developed for one group of people in society. In the period immediately following the Second World War, this was housing for returning war veterans, but, as migration began to fold into society and with it different socio-economic groups, suburbs changed to meet the new community based on their level of wealth.

Perhaps the strongest and most concerning artefact of the suburban model is its segregation of community.[96] Suburbs are created as homogenous centres where housing is similar, and this includes housing price. This form of organisation has created a new form of segregation within society – one dictated by income. There have always

---

[94] Rothstein, R, *'The Color of Law: A forgotten History of How Our Government Segregated America'*, Liveright, 2017.
[95] Rothstein, R, *'The Color of Law: A forgotten History of How Our Government Segregated America'*, Liveright, 2017.
[96] Butler, C, *'Reading the production of suburbia in post war Australia'*, University of Wollongong Australia, Legal Spaces Vol 9, 2005.

been suburbs that are better off than others and places separated by socio-economic differences, such as rich and poor, but never before in history has a form of development through subdivision created such division en masse. The segregation of housing through market conditions is a relatively new phenomenon driven by developers, creating exclusivity to a suburb by marketing it to a particular segment of society.

Similar to the housing estates created for returning war veterans in the late 1940s and early 1950s, estate developers began adopting this standardised model en masse to market their new suburbs via market segmentation and income.[97] What resulted was the creation of suburbs that housed only one group of society – i.e., middle-income earners with families, since the housing provided for each block within the suburb was developed by builders and developers who used one to eight variations of the same home design. Of course, it is horses for courses, and nowadays suburbs have been adjusted according to income levels, with suburb housing prices varying greatly. The point being is that the suburban model has created a new distinction within society, where people of different income levels are separated from each other.

It doesn't take much of an imagination to predict the society that evolves from such a construct. There is plenty of evidence throughout Australian cities where suburbs, like gated communities, create separation from society, with people living within a specific suburb associating primarily with people of their same socio-economic group. You may think "so what?" but the congregation of socio-economic clumps into one homogenous setting creates insulation from society, such that it is possible that, from a young age through to adolescence, children are exposed only to one group of people in society, resulting in a lack of awareness or empathy for other groups in society. You might think this is farfetched, but think about where you lived and grew up. If you grew up in a middle-income-earning household and lived somewhere such as Carine in Perth's northern suburbs, how often did you rub shoulders with the poorer people who lived in Balga (a less affluent suburb), for example?

The breaking up of education to fall within catchment areas of suburbs reinforces this trend by ensuring children of middle-class suburbs who attend public schools will attend with children of similar middle-income families.

The same could be said of children from poorer households and poorer suburbs who all attend the same schools, and so on. This trend is, perhaps, accentuated by the increase in children attending private schools for the middle class and the elite. This is a whole other subject matter, but the point is the same: the creation of mass-produced suburbs in the post-Second World War era created homogenous living arrangements, which have created social circles ranked according to income. This differs substantially from more traditional urban settings, where walkable environments

---

[97] Davison, G, *'Car Wars: How the Car won our hearts and conquered our cities'*, Allen & Unwin, 2004.

and compact towns meant people of different socio-economic groups often crossed paths on a daily basis.

The empathy that may have existed in society prior to the establishment of mass-produced suburbia, for example, which led to reforms in law and improvements in city planning and public health in the late 1800s, was a characteristic of the pre-automobile suburb. People of all walks of life in the past lived close to each other and, due to proximity, shared the problems that were common to society at the time. This created greater empathy across different socio-economic groups. The irony is that these reforms, coupled with history and economic circumstance, led to the creation of the suburban model, which has made it possible for people of different socio-economic groups to avoid each other and become immune to broader societal issues and concerns.

Unfortunately, segregation through living arrangement is self-perpetuating. A child growing up in a suburb of the same economic and social cohort is less likely to develop connections – and, in turn, empathy – for people from other social classes and is, therefore, less accustomed to or prepared for living in a diverse society. The 'other' person becomes somewhat the unknown, and experience of it is only witnessed through word of mouth or via social media, such as the radio or television. Accordingly, the more homogenous the environment, the less understanding there is of what is different in society, and this almost inevitably leads to a greater discourse between what occurs in the suburb and what occurs outside of it.

The onset of new social media, such as Facebook and Twitter, perpetuate this reality, as the majority of people's connections are friends from school or work, which, in suburban Australia, is often the same linear socio-economic group. This phenomenon is true for the rich and poor. A lower income earner may have little understanding of the middle class and the more wealthy, and the wealthy have little understanding of the poor, for they have little or no association with each other. After all, if you live in a wealthy suburb, go to a wealthy suburb's cricket club, attend a private school and attend social outings with peers of similar backgrounds, when do you run into poorer people – at the train station? Not likely, since wealthier people are more inclined to use a car and drive, rather than use public transport.

Has this always been the case, though? Not really. In older suburbs in Australian cities, their design and the mix of different types of housing ensured people from different economic and social backgrounds existed together. In these older suburbs, there are apartments, which have a mixture of renters and owner–occupiers; maisonettes, which are smaller apartment blocks; townhouses; a mix of single housing; and so on. This mix of housing creates the scenario where it is possible for wealthier managers and business owners, who are likely to own apartments and single-residential houses, to live closer to nurses and teachers, who may live in townhouses or rental properties. Unlike the suburban system of homogenous buildings driven by income levels, it does not isolate people from each other. The same parks and shops are used by the business owner, the managerial class or the teacher. By sharing the same public realm, these people have the same opportunities to interact and meet to discuss the differences in their lives and/or similarities. This discourse results in bridging the gap between people of different backgrounds, creating greater understanding, respect and, most importantly, empathy.

The House and Land Package

The creation of standardised suburbia has been made possible by the standardisation of the land and building industry in Australia. The manufacture of suburbia and the suburban home has spawned a massive building and land development industry worth billions of dollars annually, which represents some 5% of Australia's overall gross domestic product (GDP).[98] To put it another way: in 2018 alone, 221,877 homes were built across Australia to a value of $105.4 billion, employing 1.177 million people.[99] It is a beast of an industry. Everywhere you go, the land development industry and project home builders dominate, from newspaper marketing to electronic mass media. One only has to look in the local newspaper to see a multitude of advertisements associated with building magazines and promoting the home and dreams of bigger and better places to live. Once confined to a billboard on the edge of a new subdivision or estate, the creation of mass electronic media has meant advertisements now reach into our homes through the television set, radio and our mobile phones.

Unlike the United States, where land subdivision and home building are largely created together, Australia has developed a slightly different model of marketing and selling the Australian dream, with 'house' and 'land' essentially being two distinctly different industries that share a symbiotic relationship. In America, places like Levittown in Pennsylvania were built by the same developer who created house and land packages. This approach is the ultimate in mass production, where the developer assumes total control over the entire estate. This is why you see many pictures of suburbia in the United States resembling the same homogenous form. This approach has gained less popularity in Australia, with Australians tending to be more individualistic and different from their neighbours – albeit slightly.

The industry in Australia evolved slightly differently from that in the United States, to the point that the land developer is a distinctly different entity from the project home builder. Developers, such as Peet and Co, Stocklands and Lendlease, create land estates that subdivide land into single-residential housing lots that are then marketed and sold separately to an individual, who then selects their own

---

[98] 'Housings Contribution to Gross Domestic Product (GDP)', National Association of Home Builders, www.nahb.org.

[99] 'Window into Housing 2019', HIA, www.hia.com.au.

builder to construct the home, in what is distinctly two separate transactions. This gives the illusion of variety in the system, but, in reality, this is not the case. Because standardisation is the key to marketing and creating the house and land package, land developers create standardised block sizes designed to fit specific standardised house designs. Up until the late 1990s, this resulted in the creation of standard block sizes to meet typical house designs for three to four-bedroom households. Since the 2000s, this has slowly been changing, with a greater variety of block sizes creeping into new estates, not due to innovation, but more so through affordability. Since the price of land has continued to rise in most cities in Australia, estate developers have reacted by creating small blocks for cheaper house and land packages. This has brought some diversity to land estates, in terms of the ultimate house and land package, but all the other elements that make up suburbia have remained largely the same.

So far, we have talked about land developers, but we can't do this without considering their bedfellow: the project home builder. In Australia, most building companies are geared to create mass-produced housing, and the suburban culture that took hold in the post-war period created an industry whose sole purpose was to tell people what home they want. In the past, traditional builders focused on developing individualistic buildings that had a design that responded to the layout of the land and used architectural features and designs to distinguish the building from its surroundings, according to its function and the desire of the owner or its inhabitants. This is why, in traditional neighbourhoods – such as Highgate in Perth's inner suburbs – the architectural type and position of homes is varied and scaled to its surroundings, creating a sense of place, even for the humble home.

Instead, the mass production of standardised blocks aligns itself with the homogenous features of the building industry. Housing in suburbia then resembles the same two-car garage, three-or-four-bedroom, two-bathroom home, which is mostly single storey. Instead of spending time focusing on creating unique buildings that fit the topography of the land, the standardised subdivision created by the land developer leads to the standardised response in housing. What results is that project home builders, who own the home-building market, pre-design houses to fit standardised blocks, and then, through clever marketing and selling through a subordinate real estate industry, people are convinced they need a three-to-four-bedroom home, even if they are a couple without children.

What has resulted from all of this is that architecture is almost completely taken out of the equation, since you don't need an architect to design a standard home for a standard-level block. The most a designer in the industry does is adjust the setback line or garage to meet standardised planning codes; this ensures mass production of the Model T home is uninhibited.

The standardisation of home building has become so refined that, if a prospective purchaser wishes to adjust the standard house plan or come up with an entirely different house plan, they are often penalised financially for doing so. Out of affordable necessity, this forces most would-be property owners to stick to the standard house design.

The standardised approach to home building in Australia is best reflected by the number of players in the industry. While the consumer can be forgiven for thinking there is choice in the market, through the existence of a large list of builders, in reality most building companies are owned by only several parent companies. If you don't believe me and think there is a variety of choice in the industry, just look at the statistics. Over 80% of all housing constructed in Western Australia in 2017, some 20,000 homes, was through three main project home building companies: BGC, Dale Alcock and Alcock Brown Neaves Group (ABN Group), and the Julian Walters Group. These three building companies corner the market with construction through their various subsidiary building companies that are all pitched to different market segments. Remember what I was saying before about creating suburbia for different income groups? Well, building companies were created to achieve the same purpose. The tragedy of the home-building industry is that we are building monotonous standardised homes in standardised subdivisions that no longer differentiate from each other (other than price), cementing the homogenous nature of suburbia, and this has transformed our landscape into one big monotonous sprawl.

A Loss of Place and Time

As a professional town planner and former developer, I can vouch for the grip the automobile has on the fundamentals of planning in Australia and the legacy it leaves. While we should be thinking about people planning first in Australia, as advocated by Danish Architect Jan Gehl – who has spent his career and life's work promoting planning as a 'people first' profession, the reverse is true. The automobile and the transport framework based on it take centre stage when planning a new neighbourhood, suburb or town. The people element – i.e., where we would like people to gather, such as in public spaces, and the quality and usefulness of the public realm – is often overlooked or considered as an afterthought.

Working as a town-planning regulator for local government in part of my career, I can attest to the construct of the planning system and its bias towards automobile planning. It is by far the most prioritised element: how we are going to move people around the shapes the plans developed for places, which are, more often than not, faceless suburbs that have no heart and no elements that give the place a sense of uniqueness and quality. Often, the few elements that do give a place a sense of uniqueness, such as vegetation and heritage, are obliterated in place of standardised lots and a convoluted road network.

Perhaps as a testimony to the legacy of the automobile-planned living arrangement and an ode to the fall from grace of people planning in our planning system, we can turn to the rise of the place-making profession as a case in point. Because our planning system does not cater adequately for people planning, place makers – which is a relatively new profession made up of a hybrid of planning, architecture and landscape architecture professionals – are now required to come in to an established area to try to retrofit the place to promote community interaction and engagement, which is often lacking in the automobile-based places that the development industry is creating. It is a growing profession in Australia, and when you think about it, it's a sad one, since it highlights that we have lost the art of making places that are actually desirable for people, and this is because the automobile-based suburb has taken over.

The automobile suburb has driven Australians over the edge, as we spend more and more time now in a vehicle than we do with friends and family. This lost time cannot be recovered, and, for people who live further and further away from destinations, more and more time is being lost that could otherwise be spent engaging in activities that bring meaning to a person's life or assisting in a community endeavour. In the past, the Marchetti constant kept cities and towns in check, ensuring the distance between the centre of a place and its fringe would be within walking distance or a commutable distance by tram and train. But the explosion of the automobile and the urban form that comes with it has created cities that are no longer walkable and are difficult to travel to by train, or are limited at best.[100] The automobile might mean we have the personal freedom to jump in a car and drive to our heart's content, but, in reality, we are spending more and more time in cars, often on our own, and this is having unintended consequences on time and mental health. People being time-poor is causing stress in our society, and this is unique to the automobile-based city, the consequences of which we will be discussing later in this book.

---

[100] Newman, P and Kenworthy, J, *'Sustainability and Cities: Overcoming Automobile Dependence*, Island Press, United States, 1999.

3

KEEPING UP WITH THE JONESES AND THE HOUSING AFFORDABILITY CRISIS

What we have witnessed since the post-Second World War period, through a combination of economic, political and social trends, is the entrenchment of the suburban ideal within Australian society. With the suburban house and land model established in Australia as a significant and thriving industry, it is no longer the case of just getting people to purchase a modest place to call their own. The industry is now beyond that step and has moved towards satisfying consumer cravings to have bigger and better homes. It's difficult to ascertain which came first, the individual drive for a better home, with the housing industry responding to this drive, or the housing industry marketing bigger and better homes for consumers to buy. I suspect the latter came first, as it ties back to the ideological war that has been raging between the two global superpowers (United States and the Soviet Union) since the 1940s: to prove one ideology is better than the other. It also ties in with growing prosperity in Australia and the ability for Australians to accommodate bigger and better homes.

The house, which started out as a roof over one's head, has now become a major element of the consumption cold war, with industry and policymakers encouraging society to engage in the building and buying of bigger and better homes to satisfy growing wealth and prosperity in Australia, which has been on the rise since the end of the Second World War. This notion also aligns with the changing characteristics of Australian society since the war years, which has seen Australians leave behind being largely egalitarian and community-oriented people, to become more individualistic and self-absorbed. After all, the height of one's selfish ambition is one's home, and owning a little piece of Australia is considered – in the collective Australian conscience – to be one of the most important drives of personal ambition.

House Sizes

Since the post-war period's prosperity, house sizes in Australia have significantly grown. Since statistics commenced in 1945, Australian home sizes have been trending upwards from a modest 100sqm in 1950, to over 238sqm in 2020.[101] For over sixty years, home sizes have grown in an almost uninterrupted trend, to the point where the average home is now 2.4 times larger than the original post-war homes built for returning veterans. Perhaps symptomatic of Australia's suburban culture, combined with wealth, it is now not enough that Australians desire a home or roof over their heads, but instead this dream has become somewhat distorted and has morphed into a cringe-worthy desire to have the biggest and best home that money can buy.

As mentioned earlier in this book, at the same time that we have witnessed growing house sizes, we have also been experiencing a decline in household numbers – or persons per household. This complete inverse relationship appears to have grown unchecked for four decades, as the population per household has continued to decline since the 1960s, while house sizes have continued to increase.[102] Could this trend be a symptom of household size and desire with a lag effect? That is to say, more people lived in smaller households in the 1950s and 1960s, creating cramped quarters (five to six people per 100sqm-sized home), resulting in the perfect incentive to foster the desire for bigger homes to alleviate the cramped conditions. This is one possible explanation. Because this takes time and favourable economic conditions, it is not inconceivable that the trend for larger homes began to accelerate in the 1970s and 1980s as economic circumstances improved, and other factors, such as availability of land and increasing access to credit, became more widely available. After all, we are shaped by our experiences. If we experienced cramped conditions in small houses when we were young, this imbeds in our psyches, and, therefore, it is conceivable that growing up we would aspire to a better lifestyle that included a larger home – money permitting.

Wealth appears to have been a major factor for the growth of house sizes as we progress on this journey of discovery, but consideration of wealth in isolation would be a misnomer, as there are other factors that influence homes sizes, such as social trends, lifestyle and ideology, which collectively conspire to create a part of what has become the ever-growing Australian Dream.

---

[101] *'Average house sizes in Australia'* Economic Insight, Commsec, Dec 2020.
[102] *'Population and households'*, Australian Institute of Family Studies, aifs.gov.au.

Keeping Up with the Joneses and the Housing Affordability Crisis

1950s	
Melbourne	
Average size – 100sqm	
Average price - $1,050	
Sydney	
Average size – 100sqm	
Average price - $1,950	
Perth	
Average size – 100sqm	
Average price -$1,550	
Brisbane	
Average size – 100sqm	
Average price - $950	

1960s	
Melbourne	
Average size – 125sqm	
Average price - $4,060	
Sydney	
Average size – 125sqm	
Average price - $8,000	
Perth	
Average size – 125sqm	
Average price -$6,000	
Brisbane	
Average size – 125sqm	
Average price - $4,200	

1970s	
Melbourne	
Average size – 155sqm	
Average price - $12,800	
Sydney	
Average size – 155sqm	
Average price - $18,700	
Perth	
Average size – 155sqm	
Average price -$17,500	
Brisbane	
Average size – 155sqm	
Average price - $11,800	

1980s	1990s	2000s	2020s
Melbourne Average size – 165sqm Average price - $39,500	**Melbourne** Average size – 195sqm Average price -$131,000	**Melbourne** Average size – 235sqm Average price - $191,000	**Melbourne** Average size – 238sqm Average price - $835,000
Sydney Average size – 165sqm Average price - $68,850	**Sydney** Average size – 195sqm Average price -$194,000	**Sydney** Average size – 235sqm Average price -$287,000	**Sydney** Average size – 238sqm Average price - $1.16m
Perth Average size – 165sqm Average price - $40,350	**Perth** Average size – 195sqm Average price - $101,125	**Perth** Average size – 235sqm Average price - $156,250	**Perth** Average size – 238sqm Average price - $562,000
Brisbane Average size – 165sqm Average price - $35,475	**Brisbane** Average size – 195sqm Average price - $113,000	**Brisbane** Average size – 235sqm Average price - $170,000	**Brisbane** Average size – 238sqm Average price - $759,000

Figure 3.1: House sizes and prices – then and now[103]

---

[103] *'Images of Suburban housing'*, courtesy of WA State Library and archives Sergio Famiano, 2022.

Generating Wealth

Statistics show that Australians have steadily become more affluent over the past seventy years since climbing out of the Great Depression and the end of the Second World War. This has seen a rise in the general standard of living in Australia, with people being able to purchase a home, educate their kids, drive a new car – for the most part – and, importantly, feed their families. This version of Australia includes a healthy middle class that ties in with the 'fair go' attitude that has become synonymous with our country – that is if you give it a go you can make it.

But what has allowed Australians to become more affluent and successful as a society? Are we now rewarded for harder work? Are we now rewarded by higher incomes? The statistics would say otherwise. For most Australians, the single biggest economic indicator of wealth and living standards is the average income. Changes in average weekly earnings in Australia have been tracked since the 1960s.

Since the Second World War, it appears that wages have been growing, albeit with some bumps caused by global economic conditions in the mid-1970s and late 1980s, which in turn have had their influence on the Australian economy and standard of living. To illustrate this, in 1969, the average weekly take-home pay was around $529; this has since increased to $1257 in 2022. This represents an approximate 2.5 times increase in average weekly earnings since the late 1960s. This sounds promising, as a 2.5 times increase in wages seems a lot, but, in truth, it is not all rosebushes. When properly considered, this increase over a fifty-year period is actually low, especially when you factor in the cost of living or, in other terms, the inflationary impact on wages. If you take this into consideration, the average weekly wage has barely increased over the fifty years since 1969, with wages, in real terms, only growing by a few percentage points. This means the average worker in the 2020s isn't much better off than their counterpart in the 1960s.[104]

Since the 1970s, we have also noticed another trend: wage growth in Australia is slowing. Between 1969 and 1991, the average wage increased from $529 to $893. This near doubling of wages took twenty years to achieve; it took a further thirty years for them to double again in 2022. With real wages barely growing and average wages slowing since the 1990s, what does all this mean for the average Australian, and, more importantly, what is causing this slump? The answer may lie in comparing wage growth in Australia to productivity.

Since the recording of statistics began in 1948, wage growth in Australia has been tracking side by side with productivity. So basically, when the company made more money through increased labour productivity, so did the worker, and this was reflected in matching increases in wages to productivity. Between 1948 and 1973,

---

[104] *'Average Weekly Earnings, 1969-2019'*, Australian Bureau of Statistics, May 2000.

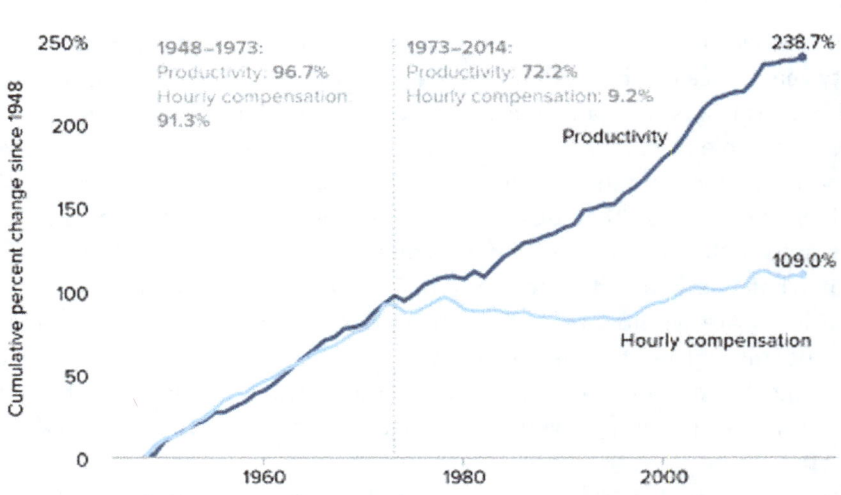

Note: Data are for average hourly compensation of production/nonsupervisory workers in the private sector and net productivity of the total economy. "Net productivity" is the growth of output of goods and services minus depreciation per hour worked.

Figure 3.2: Disconnect between productivity and a typical worker's compensation (1948–2014)[105]

the percentage increase in wages almost matched that of productivity at 91.3% and 96.7%, respectively.[106] This is healthy for an economy and a society, as it shows the average worker is sharing in the spoils of increased productivity, and the additional money earnt through increased productivity is not just going into the expanding pockets of business owners and stockholders (if a publicly listed company). This also seems fair, right? If you are earning more for your boss, why wouldn't you get a greater share of the spoils? Well, after the Second World War, Australians did.

It's not surprising then when people reflect on the 1950s and 1960s, they choose the term "the good old days". During this period, the average household in Australia was comprised of the nuclear family: two parents with two or three kids. Within this typical household type, the father was generally the bread winner, and the wife had the option to stay home to look after the house and kids or to work part-time. At the time, household incomes were high enough that many families could afford to purchase a home, send their kids to school, purchase a new car every seven years and take a family holiday, and the wife could choose to work or not. "The good old days",

---

[105] 'Labour Productivity versus Compensation 1948-2014', ABS 2014.
[106] 'Labour Productivity versus Compensation 1948-2014', ABS 2014.

as my parents often refer to it, was when life was simpler, and issues such as stress and anxiety were uncommon.

As a reflection of these good old days, household incomes rose steadily in the post-war period, and there seemed to be a healthy balance between work, having what you needed – and most of what you wanted – and, importantly, having time for family and friends. This, however, all changed in the mid-1970s, when we started to see a new trend emerge. Instead of wages matching productivity growth, there was a dramatic slowdown in the growth of real wages and a growing trend of the labour market not sharing in the spoils of increased productivity.

Between 1973 and 2014, productivity grew a staggering 72.2%, while real wages only grew by 9.2%.[107] This meant that, as labour became more productive and the earnings of companies began to rise, the spoils of this gain were not flowing equally to the employer and employee, but instead flowed to the employer and the stockholder. This divergence is concerning, as it shows a growing divide between the take-home pays of CEOs, managers and stockholders and those of the average worker in Australian society. It also reveals that wage growth during 1973 to 2014 was relatively subdued, and this is a concern for households, as it directly affects their disposable income.

So, are the capitalists in our society stealing all the cream? The answer is yes, with trade unions that have diminishing negotiating power to set a fair wage complaining that workers are getting a raw deal when it comes to sharing the profits. In economics, there are two main factors of production: capital and labour. Workers pocket their income as wages, and the owners of capital pocket theirs as profits. According to statistics, during the 1960s and early 1970s, wages as a share of total income scaled highs above 60%. During this period, industry led by unions was widespread, and wage inflation was constant. This ensured the average worker got a fair share of the pie. This gradually changed from the mid-1970s onwards, as the effect of unions on bargaining power began to decline. In perhaps a watershed moment, it is ironic that in 1983 the Hawke government, a Labor Government, embarked on an accord with the union movement to bring wage claims and wage-driven inflation under control. Since that time, the decline in the wage share as part of overall profits has accelerated, and, as a result, more and more money has been flowing one way to business owners, stockholders and the managerial class in our society.

There are plenty of theories for why labour's share of income has declined since the 1950s and 1960s, which is a trend evident around the developed world. Some theories blame the declining bargaining power of labour on declining unionism and successful attempts by predominately right-wing governments to weaken unions. Others claim that the globalisation of world capital has meant capital can now move more freely, forcing countries to be wage competitive or risk having businesses shut

---

[107] 'Labour Productivity versus Compensation 1948-2014', ABS 2014.

down and moving to a more 'competitive source' – in other words, cheap labour. Since the 1970s onwards, this has seen the growth of economic powerhouses such as China, Taiwan and Japan at the expense of countries like Australia, which has lost most of its manufacturing base, which was gained in the 1950s and 1960s and lost in the 1980s and 1990s, to overseas countries.

Economic conditions also play a role, as every time there is a recession there is capital flight that moves to more competitive countries, which is especially true in the era of globalisation. Just ask the British people, who lived and worked through the Thatcher years (1979 to 1991). Great Britain, like Australia, witnessed a couple of severe recessions at the beginning and end of the 1980s. These recessions saw manufacturing suffer in Australia and Britain, with manufacturing moving offshore to countries like Japan and Taiwan, largely for short-term profits. The news isn't all bad though. If you are a CEO, member of the managerial class or stockholder, your income during the 1970s onwards exploded – so much for a 'fair go'.

If wages have been subdued and profits increasingly concentrated within a few professions in our society, how has Australia managed to maintain a good standard of living? Well, the answer, for a lack of a better way of putting it, is women.

While economic conditions can play a factor in slowing income growth – as seen in the recessions of 1982–83, the late 1980s and early 1990s, the "recession[s] we had to have", as quoted by the then prime minister Paul Keating – Australia's growing participation rate in the economy has had the most profound impact in generating wealth, while restraining the growth of average weekly earnings for the average Aussie at the same time. Noticeably, female participation in the Australian workforce began to accelerate in the 1970s and 1980s, with women joining the labour force ranks, which had previously been dominated by men. This occurred not just in terms of secretarial and administrative positions, which were the traditional domain of women in the workforce, but also in other professional fields, such as management and even executive positions, which had previously been unheard of.[108]

One of the social revolutions, which has occurred over the last fifty years, is the increasing recognition and acceptance of women's rights to engage in the workforce and to have the same opportunities as men. This revolution, which had its origins in federation, when women were given the right to vote, has been growing in momentum and has seen a steady increase in women participating in the workforce. This was especially true during the two world wars, when women replaced men on the factory floors, putting together tanks, trucks and clothing for the war effort. This period was brief, however, and after the Second World War men resumed their traditional duties, and women returned to the household. This began to change in the 1960s.

---

[108] *'Changing role of women in the workplace'*, The Drum, October 2012.

The gender revolution brought with it a new push for human rights for women, and this emerged into a movement that pushed for equality for women in general. This led into the 1970s, when laws were passed ensuring women received equal pay and working conditions. While the landmark years of the 1970s brought with them positive changes for women, it still took some time for the reality of the workplace to catch up, with women today still fighting for the right to equal pay in some industries. Needless to say, it has been a slow process but a growing one, which has seen women enjoy increasing benefits in the workplace throughout the 1980s, 1990s and 2000s.

Figure 3.3: The modern women's movement in the landmark years of the 1970s[109]

The revolution, which started in earnest in the 1960s – remember Germaine Greer, anyone? – brought with it many benefits for women, to the point that, today, women have increased their participation in the workplace and can compete with men as equals, with most women enjoying equal pay and similar conditions to those of their male counterparts. The growing female participation in the economy has raised household incomes by generating, in most cases, two-income households, which has been a noticeable and important side benefit to the growth of women in the workforce.

The table below reflecting labour participation rates (Figure 3.4) shows the steady rise of women in the workforce, particularly from the 1970s onwards. This trend has had a profound influence over the average household income, which has grown significantly, as single-income households were steadily replaced by one-and-a-half and two-income households.[110]

The growing female participation rate has arguably increased the overall pool of participants in the workforce, and this explains, in part, the slowing in average weekly

---

[109] Arrow, M, *'The Radical 1970's and the Royal Commission Australia forgot'*, Macquarie University, 2020.
[110] Australian Bureau of Statistics (6202.0), 2020.

earnings for the average person, as the labour pool has grown, putting downward pressure on wage growth.

So, what we have seen since the 1970s in Australia is an increase in women participating in the economy, which has had the effect of increasing overall family incomes, but, at the same time, the growth of individual earnings of each labour force participant has slowed to a standstill. This is due in part to the dilution of the labour market and the labour market becoming more competitive as a result. This is good news for business owners, since they have a wider range of people they can employ in their businesses, which puts the shoe firmly on their foot when it comes to wage negotiations. This certainly shifts the balance in favour of big businesses, as we have seen that, since the 1970s, real wages have barely grown as a result.

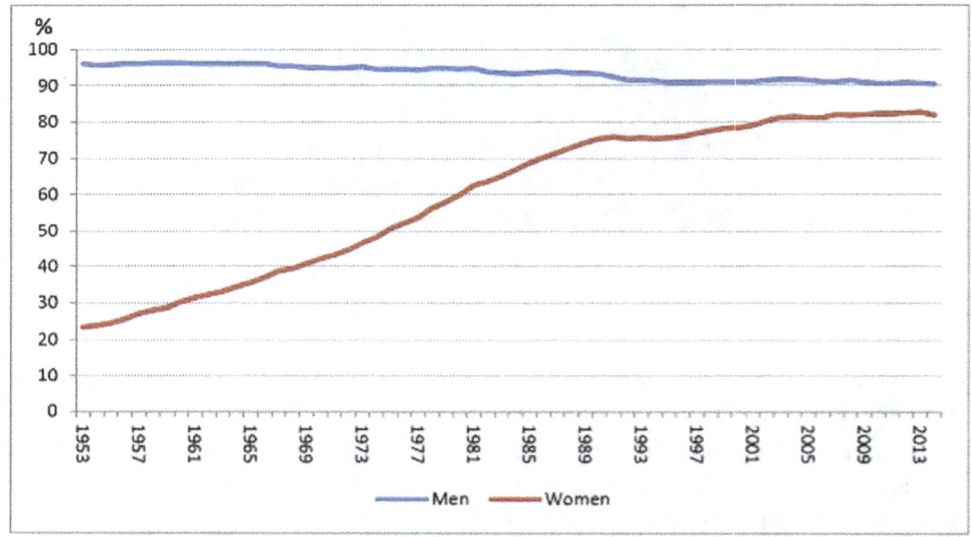

Figure 3.4: Long-term labour force participation rates[111]

So, if real wages have plateaued but overall household incomes have increased, this could only mean that the overall household income rise has been caused not by the real growth in average weekly earnings, but by the growth of one-and-a-half and two-parent household incomes in a climate of diminishing wages in real terms. You may be thinking "so what? Both parents have a right to work". This I agree with, but my concern is with the plateauing of the real average wage and the impact this has on labour market dynamics, the economy and, more broadly, on society in general. For example, it poses a strong question: are both parents choosing to work

---

[111] 'Long Term labour force Participation Rates', ABS, 2020.

on a discretionary basis because they want to and because the growth in the rights for women, in particular, warrants taking up new opportunities, or is it more out of economic dependence, because real wages are plateauing, so a second income is needed to make ends meet? I think it is a bit of both. There is an element of women choosing to work because they would like to, and this has certainly been welcomed for many reasons, such as diversity and different perspectives, but I also think there is an element of necessity, since the cost of living has greatly outstripped wages.

The shift between choice and necessity of both parents working has had a significant impact on Australian society. If both parents are having to work to make ends meet, then this puts strain on the family unit: it raises questions about how children are managed and what is, in turn, sacrificed as a result of two parents having to work.

My parents didn't reflect on the 1950s and 1960s as the good old days for nothing. There was good reason to reflect with fond memories. During this period, there appeared to be greater balance in society between work and leisure and, importantly, greater participation in community activities. Only one income was needed for middle-class families to buy a house, educate their children and go on holidays. At the time, women didn't have to work if they didn't want to and, therefore, could spend more time raising children, meeting with friends and volunteering at the local sports club or community centre. If these circumstances were true today, the choice would be available for either parent of a household to stay home and look after the children. But that is not the case, and, in most circumstances, this choice does not exist for families.

With both parents having to work now just to make ends meet, think about what is sacrificed. In most cases, out of necessity, children are placed in childcare, raised in unfamiliar surroundings and at great financial cost. Parents have less time to socialise, since they are spending their limited free time connecting with their children, whom they see less of during the day, and community groups and social institutions suffer, as there is less and less time to participate if you are working all day long. It is no wonder we have seen a decline in participation rates in community groups and events in more recent times – everybody is too busy working. Another symptom of this economic and social circumstance is that stress is on the rise, which we will discuss later in this book.

I would like to be very clear on this point so there is no misunderstanding. I am very supportive of both parents having the right to work. Men and women should enjoy equal opportunity to work and excel in society and make their contribution. This makes for a healthy society overall. My concern is that it appears, in more instances than not, that both parents are *required* to work out of necessity to pay the bills. I would like to see a society that offers families the option for either parent to take time off work to look after their children, especially in the early years of the child's growth – the really important years where character is developed and shaped. I would like parents in Australia to have the option to work without the overarching threat that they are going to lose their home or not make ends meet. When I reflect on the good old days of the past, that is what I mean – the choice for either parent to take time off work to look after their children, if they so choose. The reality is, however, that under the current circumstances Australian families find themselves in, in relation to housing affordability, most families don't have this choice, and I think that is a shame.

So yes, Australians may be wealthier now than ever before, but it has come at a cost. Wealth hasn't been generated by the labour market getting a fair go; instead, corporate greed and the diminishing power of unions has resulted in subdued wages with company and stockholder profits soaring, with this money being funnelled into the top 10% of the wealthiest people in Australia. The average person, by contrast, has only been able to maintain their standard of living by giving up personal freedoms, meaning more and more families, in particular out of necessity, have two parents that work. The egalitarian society that Australian is known for around the world is slowly dying, as we are now known as one of the hardest-working nations in the OECD.

Standard of Living: 1970s and 1980s to Today

So, if more and more people in our society are working just to make ends meet, what is costing so much, and what has changed from the 1970s to today? Could it be consumer items?

For the older generations... remember that record turntable you had to have, which sat in the hi-fi cabinet along with your long list of vinyl records? That colour TV that replaced the black and white with a large overhead cabinet that was big enough to double as a viewing platform for family photos? How about the cake mixer every kitchen just had to have? And of course, by the 1980s, you could add juicing machines, microwaves, video cassette recorders and home gaming systems, such as the Commodore 64 or the Amstrad 464, to that list, which goes on and on. Combined, this made up your cost of living.

It all started in the 1970s, when life's 'necessities' started to include a whole lot of expensive gadgets that, until then, had been considered luxuries for the rich and famous. And, back in the day, they were much more expensive (relatively) than they are now. Take for instance the colour TV set. In 1977, this would set you back around $800 – that's a lot when the average weekly paycheque in Australia at the time was around $550 a week. How about the video recorder? In the 1980s, a Beta or VHS Recorder would set you back $450, when wages were around $625 per week. Today, a small TV can be purchased for around $200, and the video recorder's successor, the CD player (also obsolete now), can be purchased for as little as $30.

Vinyl records, like *Rebel Yell* by Billy Idol, which I purchased in 1984 for around $10, are a thing of the past, with whole digital albums being available for purchase from iTunes or Amazon for around $12 – meaning the price of music, in real terms, has gone backwards. Or alternatively, these days you pay Spotify or Apple Music a monthly subscription to listen to what you want, when you want, for a fraction of the cost of the old vinyl records. Game changing technology, such as Apple Music, means that for some expenses in the thirty years since the 1980s it is difficult to compare like for like.

Even petrol isn't as expensive as one first thought. Despite going up in value and the risk of 'peak oil' looming, petrol prices at the bowser have been relatively subdued – that was until COVID-19. Generally speaking, and COVID-19 aside, petrol has gone up; for instance, the price of petrol just before the first Gulf War in 1991 was an average of 79 cents per litre, and the average wage was around $650 per week. Just prior to COVID-19, petrol hovered around $1.40 per litre, which is just under double the pre-Gulf-War rate, but wages since then have also doubled. With the recent Russian–Ukrainian war, petrol has gone up to just over $2 per litre. COVID-19 and the Russian–Ukrainian war aside, despite what most people think, when it comes to the price of petrol, it has remained stable relative to wages over the last thirty to forty years, with some exceptions, such as the First and Second Gulf Wars of 1991 and 2003–2004, when there were spikes in petrol prices that exceeded average inflationary rises in the cost of living.

What about food? By and large, food prices have been relatively stable, increasing slightly from year to year, and generally below the average rise in wages. A kilo of rice, for instance, was around 83 cents in 1984, and by 2021 it is only around $2–3, which is comparable to wage increases. Coffee, a core staple of the household, was a whopping $3.30 in the early 1980s – yes, instant coffee was that expensive – and it is now around $6, when wages have more than doubled. Alcohol, however, is perhaps one of the few items I can recall that has increased disproportionately to wages. A middy at my University Bar in 1993 was around $1.50, when the average wage was around $650. Today, a middy will set you back around $8/$9, depending on the beer you purchase and the place you go. This can be explained by the level of tax that has been added to alcohol and cigarettes, which have also increased disproportionately to wages.

You are probably asking "what is the problem?". While there are more and more temptations entering our lifestyles, such as new gadgets, by and large they have dropped in price (in real terms) dramatically since the 1970s and 1980s, in most cases, when compared to today. However, there is one staple, compulsory item that outshines the lot and is the trump card of affordability when we think of the cost of living: the home. The housing market is where cost of living changes are really out of proportion with the past. In 1984, the average mortgage size in Australia was $37,500, which is roughly twice the average annual salary of about $19,000 at the time. Today, the average mortgage is about ten times the average wage, which would be the equivalent of having an average annual wage of $180,000 per year. Sadly, the average annual wage is significantly less, at $90,000.[112]

---

[112] *'Selected Cost of Living Index'*, ABS, September 2021.

So, if food, transport and gadgets are cheaper, and we are earning more money than ever before, where is it all going? Well, it's clear – it is in housing. The only other competing factor is the cost of university. Believe it or not, up until the late 1980s, the cost for a university degree was free – that's right, free. Chances are, if you have a baby boomer for a boss, they got their degree for free. Since then, the price of a degree has been on the up and up. Today, a standard degree will set you back $40-50,000. Add that to you housing costs, and it is enough to give you goose bumps if you are nineteen years of age and looking towards the future.

Deregulation of the Banking Industry and Negative Gearing

As we enter the 1980s with real wage growth plateauing, there is another major shift in the economy, one that had a profound impact on the Australian Dream and plight of the working-class Australians: the deregulation of the finance industry.

The structural changes Bob Hawke and his side-kick treasurer Paul Keating instituted around the banking and finance industry during the 1980s can't be underestimated.[113] Prior to the deregulation of the financial system, the banking industry, which was based on a savings and loan structure, was geared around providing loans to owner–occupiers. To purchase a home, you had to have a significant deposit, and interest rates were more favourable if you were buying a house to live in. In contrast, if you wanted to purchase a house for investment, aside from needing a large deposit, you paid significantly higher interest rates. It's interesting that, prior to the 1980s, investment properties were largely for the super-rich. Investment in properties has always existed, but it was mainly for very wealthy people. They were the group in society that had millions of excess dollars, so they put it into commercial and residential properties, but they were only a small segment of the population.

In the 1980s, with the deregulation of the finance and banking industry, all of a sudden, we saw deposit requirements starting to decline for both owner–occupier and investment properties, and we also saw the interest rates begin to equalise. Owner–occupiers have always received a more favourable interest rate, even today this is true, but the difference now is only small. This is thanks to the deregulation of the banking industry. In the 1980s and 1990s, there was a fundamental shift in the way homes were viewed by Australians. No longer were investment properties just for the super-rich, but they could now be obtained by the growing middle class.[114] Properties were no longer viewed as just a place to stay – a necessity, a way to have a roof over your head – but instead a commodity, with properties being purchased for their exchange values and, therefore, used as leverage as a vehicle for wealth creation, especially for the wage-earning middle class.

---

[113] Christopher K, and Debelle G, *'Trends in the Australian Banking System'*, RBA, 2014.
[114] Christopher K, and Debelle G, *'Trends in the Australian Banking System'*, RBA, 2014.

The elephant in the room, which gave rise to the eventual boom in property investment, was the advent of negative gearing tax laws in Australia in 1985, where property owners who had investments running at a loss were able to offset that loss against other income earnt, such as wages for the average worker. This made property investment viable and attractive as a vehicle for wealth creation. Combined with lower deposits and interest rates for investment properties when compared with the past, negative gearing makes property investment very attractive indeed. To give you a sense of how much of an impact negative gearing has had on the tax system, negative gearing reduced personal income tax in 2001 by $600 million.[115] This has since increased to $3.9 billion in 2004/05, and $13.2 billion in 2010/11.[116] Massive numbers, which means the government has to find $13.2 billion somewhere else to plug the tax gap. This means increasing taxes elsewhere in the economy. I have to say this to be fair: Bob Hawke tried to reverse negative gearing tax laws in the late 1980s but was subjected to a significant backlash from big business and the middle class, so Bob Hawke and Paul Keating reinstated negative gearing before the end of the 1980s. How different ownership and property values might have been if they had stuck to their guns!

So why is this a problem?

Well, because of negative gearing, deregulation of the finance and banking industry – combined with Australians' general love affair with home ownership – we see for the first time in our history an explosion of investment properties during the 1990s and 2000s. This brought owner–occupiers in direct competition with an increasing group of investors for property, driving up property prices to the unsustainable level they are today. So, in the 1950s to the 1970s, we see home ownership as a democratic ideal: a dream for everybody, arguably to placate the growing wave of socialism and communism creeping into the world during that time. Now from the 1980s onwards, properties are seen as not just a must, but as a vehicle for wealth creation, and this has had a profound impact on the Australian Dream.

Spending Wealth: The Housing Trap

As it stands, Australia has experienced one of the longest periods of economic growth in the history of the developed world, with Australia experiencing twenty-nine years of consecutive economic growth, although this has been temporarily halted due to COVID-19. If looked at in isolation, Australians, on average, should be better off overall, as rising incomes and a growing economy are synonymous with a rise in the standard of living. Accordingly, Australians should be putting their feet up and relaxing, as greater income means more money to pay bills, service the mortgage and go for

---

[115] Wright, D, *"Policy Check: Negative gearing reform"*, The Conversation, 26 February 2017.
[116] Wright, D, *"Policy Check: Negative gearing reform"*, The Conversation, 26 February 2017.

holidays. But, as we will see, this isn't necessarily the case, as Australians are finding themselves entrapped in a consumption spiral that is driving a wedge between real income growth and debt. With steady but sustained wage growth, combined with favourable economic conditions, one could ask the question: what are Australians doing with their extra wealth?

As can be seen by looking at the graph below (Figure 3.5), Australians have been spending at a rate well above their ability to earn. At the same time that Australians have been experiencing household income growth, the economy has grown and both parents have entered the workplace, house prices have taken off and have obliterated all the gains in disposable income as a result. House prices have more than doubled in real terms over the last twenty years, with cities such as Sydney and Melbourne feeling the increases more than most other capital cities. In what appears to be a perfect storm of rising incomes and falling interest rates, house prices have risen significantly, with Sydney recording a 70% increase in house prices since 2012 and Melbourne 50%. Wage growth, on the other hand, has lagged significantly behind. With sustained low interest rates, people have been able to acquire larger homes, and house prices have increased significantly as a result. With negative gearing, we are also seeing more and more people investing in property, driving up prices. This is leading to bigger and bigger mortgages, which are soaking up the economic benefits of having a two-income household.

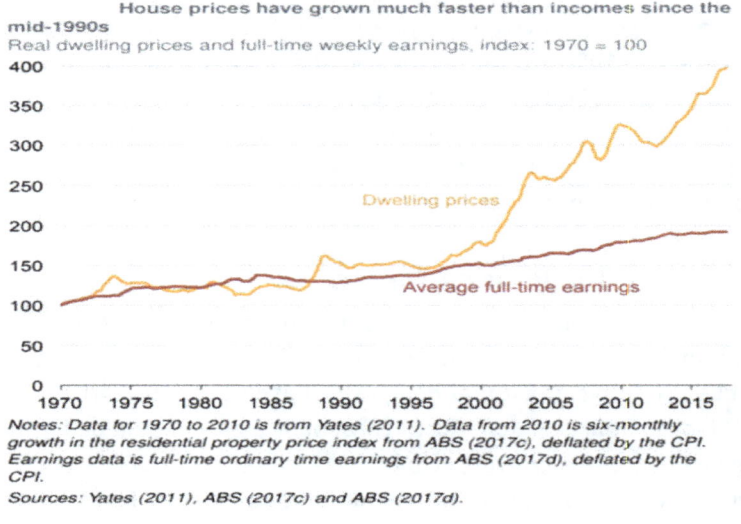

Figure 3.5: House prices growing much faster than wages[117]

---

[117] 'House Prices versus Incomes', Australian Bureau of Statistics, 2017.

The question of motive to work can be seemingly an endless question, right? There are so many factors that combine to create the reasoning behind an individual's choice to work. In this day and age, people can be motivated by wanting to take more holidays or contribute to society through work. Some people just want to be able to buy what they want when they want, such as a better car or nice clothes, or like to go out and eat on a regular basis with friends. But, if we look at the statistics, it is becoming more apparent that necessity is the biggest driver of employment choice, and housing appears to be the main culprit.

If we look at mortgages since the early 1990s, the average home loan in Australia has increased significantly from just under $100,000 in 1993 to $400,000 by 2018: a staggering 400% increase in the size of the loan.[118] Now, in 2022, the average mortgage size in Australia has grown to a staggering $618,729.[119] No surprises that Victoria and New South Wales lead the way when it comes to average mortgage sizes, with $804,675 and $652,187 being the respective averages as of January 2022.[120]

State	Mortgage size
NSW	$804,675
VIC	$652,187
ACT	$640,827
QLD	$516,686
SA	$457,493
WA	$463,844
TAS	$427,701
NT	$400,000

Figure 3.6: Average mortgage sizes per state (2022)[121]

Housing costs appear to be the main driver of people's choice to work. Because housing has become a major driver of consumer culture, people want a bigger and better piece of the Australia Dream. This is driving consumer spending patterns

---

[118] ABS Housing Finance, 2018.
[119] Bristow, M, 'What is the average mortgage around Australia', RateCity (using ABS lending indicators), March 2022.
[120] Bristow, M, 'What is the average mortgage around Australia', RateCity (using ABS lending indicators), March 2022.
[121] Bristow, M, 'What is the average mortgage around Australia', RateCity (using ABS lending indicators), March 2022.

towards bigger and more costly homes, which in turn drives the price of housing up further and further. This is exacerbated when you consider the incentive to invest in property through negative gearing, which further pushes the price of housing up. This perhaps explains why housing prices have far exceeded household earnings. It appears Australians are caught in a housing trap, where their love affair with owning a bigger and better home – multiple homes, if you are an investor – is driving up prices and mortgages faster than they can pay them. This has significant consequences, as we will see moving forward.

Debt

Do you feel you are carrying a lot of debt these days? Chances are you are not alone. Debt is becoming a common word in the vernacular of households in Australia, as Australians are fast becoming some of the most indebted people in the world. Once considered the 'lucky country', Australians are now paying for their lifestyles, and perhaps the best term to describe Australia is not the lucky country, but the indebted country. The most common measure of debt is household debt to disposable income: how much debt the average household is carrying as a percentage of their overall yearly income. In 1988, when the Reserve Bank of Australia began measuring debt ratios to household income, household debt was sitting at around 64% of household income, which was a fairly sustainable and serviceable debt level. That is to say if a typical household had an income of $100,000 per annum, total household debt would be $64,000. This debt level is considered reasonable and allows households to easily service their debt, while at the same time participating in the economy through normal consumption spending.

Since 1988 however, this ratio has grown significantly, and, as of 2021, the household debt to income ratio now stands at a staggering 203% of household income, representing a threefold increase in debt to household income since the 1980s. That is, if the average household is earning $100,000 a year, the debt levels are now sitting at $203,000. The consequences of this are obvious. With greater debt levels you have greater servicing costs, especially through loans and credit cards, and this takes an increasing proportion of money away from consumer spending. Australia now has one of the highest household debts in the world, ranked fifth in the world, behind Switzerland, the Netherlands, Norway and Denmark.[122]

---

[122] *'Household debt as a percentage of disposable income – globally'*, OECD data, 2021.

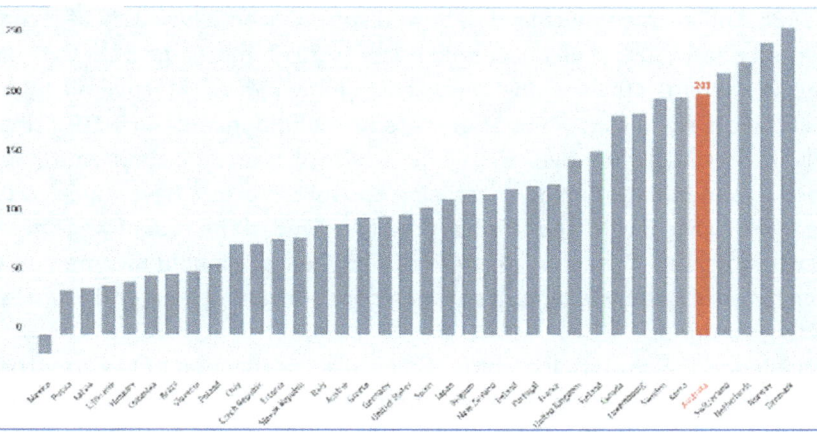

Figure 3.7: Household debt as a percentage of disposable income[123]

When we look closely at what is causing this extraordinary growth in household debt, it is clear that the cost of the average home is the main culprit, rather than personal debt, with mortgage debt rising significantly above personal debt, as can be seen in the graph below (Figure 3.8).[124]

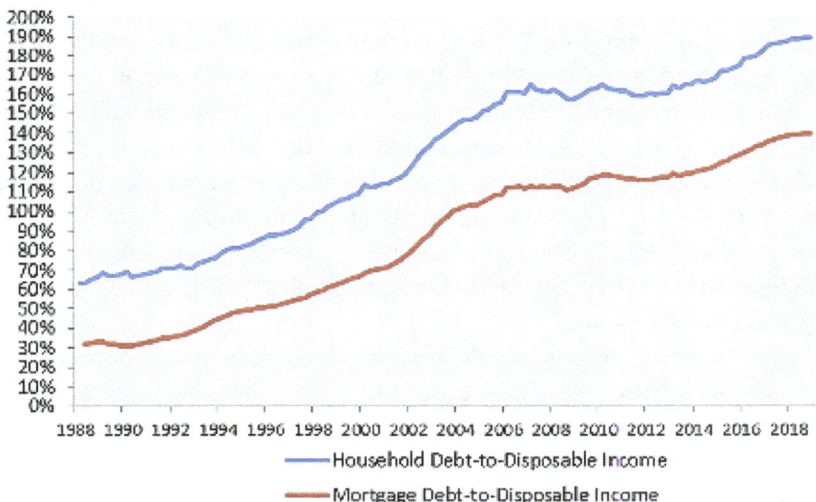

Figure 3.8: Household debt to disposable income and mortgage debt to disposable income[125]

---

[123] *'Household debt as a percentage of disposable income – globally'*, OECD data, 2021.
[124] *Reserve Bank of Australia – Australia's household debt comparison, RBA, 2020.*
[125] *Reserve Bank of Australia – Australia's household debt comparison, RBA, 2020.*

In 1988, the average mortgage debt to disposal income was 32% of income and represented nearly 50% of all household debt. By 2019, mortgage debt to disposable income had risen to 140% and now represents nearly 75% of total overall debt. While personal debt is significant (49% of average household income in 2019), this figure has only increased slightly over the years, while, at the same time, mortgage debt expanded exponentially. Rapidly increasing household prices have much to do with the rise in mortgage levels, and this has greatly exceeded the rate of wage growth, as we discussed earlier. This rising divergence between household income and debt is worrying for an economy reliant on consumer spending, and greater debt means less money to go around.

This exponential growth in debt is mirrored as a reflection of the country's GDP, with household debt growing from an average of 40% of GDP in 1988 to an extraordinary 130% of GDP by 2020.[126] This means the total household debt in Australia is equivalent to a whopping 130% of the value of Australians' total gross domestic product.

The massive expansion in household debt during a period of growing prosperity and wage growth via women working is a worrying sign. As debt soars, an increasing proportion of household disposable income has to be directed towards servicing debt, which means there is less disposable income to purchase the basic essentials, such as food, education and clothing and managing one's health. What has resulted from this trend is the creation of a new term, 'mortgage stress', which is starting to take hold in Australia. This terms stems from the level of household income devoted to servicing a mortgage on a home, and it is said that if a household has more than one-third of its disposable income devoted to servicing their mortgage, the household is considered 'under stress'. Once the mortgage servicing exceeds one-third, the household is under 'financial stress', as there is less money to provide for other basic essentials, education and bills, which take up the other two-thirds of income. In Australia, it is estimated that there are over 1,400,000 households currently at risk of defaulting on their mortgage, the highest level since records began in the 1990s. This is a staggering amount, which appears to be growing.

The areas in the country most affected appear to be in new suburb locations on the fringes of main cities, where new builds are accompanied by small deposits, leaving households with large mortgages. Some of the worst suburbs in the country have up to 1 in 5 households suffering mortgage stress. Suburbs such as Wollert in Melbourne and Edmondson Park in Sydney have in excess of 20% of properties in the suburb in mortgage stress. The worrying sign is that mortgage stress appears to be growing, and this is despite record low interest rates, which traditionally provide relief from mortgage repayments.

---

[126] *Reserve Bank of Australia – Australia's household debt comparison, RBA, 2020.*

So, what does all this mean? Debt has been rising uninterrupted now for decades, so are we reaching a point where the credit card is maxed out? It appears we are getting close to this point. One of the greatest problems affecting the global financial crisis in 2007 and 2008 was global debt. In 2008, the collapse of the US banking giant Lehman Brothers was one of the catalysts for a freeze on global capital markets and caused the world's biggest financial catastrophe since the Great Depression in the 1930s. Countries such as the United States suffered extraordinary unemployment (10%), while Eurozone economies were decimated, with countries like Greece declaring sovereign bankruptcy. At the heart of the global financial crisis were debt and the ability for people to service debt. If people are unable to service debt, then loans default, leading to losses and bankruptcy. Lending also becomes more difficult, making refinancing harder, which compounds the malaise.

Since the global financial crisis, global debt has increased by nearly 50%. Global government debt is now sitting on $93 trillion, while global corporate debt is even higher at $101 trillion. Combined, the world is looking at $200 trillion in debt and rising.[127] Should global economic growth and credit continue to deteriorate, a new bout of financial stress could erupt, and the global financial markets could again become vulnerable, leading to further bank failures and possible sovereign failures, like what happened in Greece. In Australia, the big concern is household debt, which is 203% of household incomes, and this has grown significantly since the global financial crisis, leaving Australian households far more at risk of default should there be a downturn in the global economy.

The result of all this rise in debt has meant that a new term has been coined, one that surpasses mortgage stress: 'over-indebted households'. This refers to households that have debt three or more times their annual disposable income. Remember the example before of the average household having debt equivalent to nearly 200% of annual disposable income? Well, over-indebted households are households that exceed this average. Because debt growth has outpaced income growth and assets during the past twenty years, the number of households that are now over-indebted is up from 21% in 2003 to 29% in 2019 of all mortgage stressed households.[128] That is 1 in 4 mortgage stressed households in Australia. Sydney and Melbourne have the highest number of over-indebted households, with 407,000 and 419,600 households falling into this cat-egory, respectively.[129] Most of this, as we have seen above, is to do with mortgage levels. Most over-indebted households – approximately 77% – lack sufficient liquid assets to cover a quarter

---

[127] Mbaye, S, Moreno-Badia, M, and Chae, K, *"Global Debt Database: Methodology and Sources,"* IMF Working Paper, International Monetary Fund, Washington, DC, 2018.

[128] Laine G, *'Australian Mortgages holders take on risky levels of debt'*, Rate City, December, 2021.

[129] Laine G, *'Australian Mortgages holders take on risky levels of debt'*, Rate City, December, 2021.

of the value of their debts. Liquid assets are assets that can be easily converted to cash; they include bank accounts, shares, businesses and superannuation. A lack of assets may place over-indebted households at risk of defaulting on their loans if their income is not sufficient to meet repayments. This risk appears to be increasing in Australia, certainly for 1 in 4 households, and is a worrying sign for the economy.[130]

Perhaps what is scarier is that not only are Australians heavily in debt, but we are also heavily in debt at a time when interest rates are at historic lows. Traditionally, monetary policy used fluctuations in interest rates to increase or decrease spending in the economy. For example, if interest rates are sitting at around 7%, lowering them to 5% over a period of time reduces the servicing level of the mortgage, resulting in increased money that can be used to reduce mortgage debt, increase savings or be used to engage in additional consumption that stimulates the economy. What appears to be happening now is that Australians are heavily in debt and interest rates are low, leaving the government with very little opportunity to influence the economy through monetary policy. With low interest rates, there is very little left that can be done to reduce mortgage repayments and/or free up money to stimulate the economy. With historic high debt levels, low interest rates, plateauing wage levels and plateauing housing prices, a perfect storm appears to be developing, which could see consumption spending and wage growth continue to decline, allowing a vicious cycle of deflation to take hold.

Now, returning to our previous question: have we reached our spending limits? It appears the credit card is maxed out with little room for more credit to help stimulate the economy. The only way Australia can now maintain inflation and prevent the devaluation of assets is by pump-priming the economy through government stimulus. In other words: borrow money to spend to keep inflation going. This is exactly what has been occurring in Australia, with the Federal Government borrowing billions to stimulate the economy and prevent it from going backwards. In 2000, the Federal Government's debt was equivalent to 13% of GDP. By 2020, it was 44%, representing a massive 221% increase, or debt binge, in just twenty years. This increase in terms of a percentage of GDP is higher than any other country in the world, including the United States.

Overworked Australians

This dire predicament Australians find themselves in is having a profound impact not only on the economy but also on our lifestyles. With Australians now having the world's fifth-largest household debt levels, it is affecting our behaviour, and there is increasing evidence that it is changing our way of life. Hovering at around 203% of the GDP, Australia's household debt is only behind four nations – Switzerland, Norway,

---

[130] Laine G, *'Australian Mortgages holders take on risky levels of debt'*, Rate City, December, 2021.

Denmark and the Netherlands – and Australians are spending more time working to pay debt off.

There is a link between rising house prices and household spending, as we have seen previously. Many Australians are electing to spend more money and are doing so by borrowing from the equity they have in their homes. Homeowners are willing to increase their spending via borrowing against their home loans. This is resulting in mortgages increasing significantly.

Rising mortgage debt is affecting everything from employment to spending in the Australian economy and is having a profound impact on lifestyle, as Australians are finding that the larger debt they have, the longer they will be working to pay the debt off. Statistics show that Australians are now finding themselves working longer into retirement due to rising debt. Mortgage levels among Australians have soared from 36% to 71% for people between the ages of 45 and 54 years from the 1990s to 2015. In other words, Australians between the ages of 45 and 54 are 71% more likely to be carrying a mortgage debt. From the ages of 55 to 64, the incidence of Australians in that age bracket carrying a mortgage has increased from 14% to 44% – nearly half the people in that age bracket.[131] There is no doubt that a majority of the debt is from higher mortgages, as we have seen previously, but Australians are also willing to borrow more for their lifestyles, which is adding to the debt burden.

Australians working longer to pay off debt has had profound impacts on society. Firstly, higher house prices and mortgages are resulting in a decline in home ownership for younger people, and those who brave taking out a mortgage are doing so later in life and are taking on debts bigger than ever before. And so, the spiral begins. As house prices increase, people tap into their mortgage to fund their spending habits. This ultimately leads to a growing economy and further increases in house prices, which is what we have seen in Australia – in particular in cities such as Melbourne and Sydney – over the last twenty years. The bigger debts are leading to longer working lives, not by choice but through necessity.

Greater mortgage debt has important economy-wide effects through interactions with consumer spending and labour markets. Ageing is often associated with lower labour participation rates, due to declining physical and mental health, which reduces productivity growth. If Australians are extending their working lives to repay higher mortgage debts, this could have a positive impact on mitigating some of the productivity consequences of population ageing – albeit at the expense of greater exposure to debt in later life and consequently a constraint on lifestyle.

Interestingly, when house prices are rising, homeowners and investors are able to borrow more against their home to finance their spending, which is what we are seeing as a trend in Australia. In the short run, this can help offset the effect of

---

[131] 'Australia's Welfare – Work- Life balance', AIHW, 2017.

stagnant wages and thereby sustain growth momentum in the economy by allowing spending to continue, despite wages being frozen. If real wages continue to fall, though, people are left with higher levels of debt, and this ends up being a drag on growth – the notion that the credit card is maxed out leaving no room for further borrowing.

With borrowing restricted and stagnant wages, it is pretty hard to continue fuelling economic growth. As looked at previously, this is further exacerbated by low interest rates in the economy, which effectively neutralise the government's ability to further influence credit-based spending in the economy. The only avenue left is through government-debt-fuelled spending or stimulus packages, which have medium- and long-term implications on the economy, as debt needs to be paid back at some point – usually through higher taxes. We are seeing this happen now, as the Federal Government and state governments navigate the financial problems caused by COVID-19.

So, what happens when we approach the maxed-credit scenario, which is defined by the parameters of stagnant wage growth and impotent monetary policy? Well, the opposite occurs. Not only do we have a predicament where higher debt levels mean people have to work longer into their retirement or golden age, we have a scenario where the economy begins to go backwards. If wages fail to pick up, high levels of indebtedness will increase exposure to house prices and the possibility for interest rate increases, which will pose a threat to macroeconomic stability. "How?" you might ask. Well, if we can't spend our way through growth – that is, if wages are stagnant, and debt levels are high with interest rates at all-time lows – what is going to stimulate the economy to expand further? What will happen is spending will start to dry up, resulting in a reduced demand for consumer goods and housing, resulting in a fall in prices or deflation. This could be catastrophic for Australians carrying a large debt, as falling house prices leads to a greater risk of negative equity and ultimately housing default.

Have we learnt much from the global financial crisis? Not really. All we have done is continue spending through borrowing against our homes. We are now at the inflection point, where we have inflated house prices, large debts, stagnant wages and cautious consumers, since most consumers realise their debt is too high and it needs to be paid off. What this leads to is recession, which could have dire consequences for Australia, after experiencing twenty-nine years of economic growth and inflated asset prices.

The longer working hours and managing of debt is starting to affect Australians profoundly. In what was once described as the laid-back country, Australians are finding themselves more stressed, overworked and reluctant to take holidays. The proportion of Australians dissatisfied with their work-life balance is increasing, with more and more Australians reporting work is negatively impacting on the rest of their lives, causing stress and less time for themselves, their family and friends. In a study completed by the Australian Work Life Index, nearly a quarter of full-time working women and one-fifth of full-time working men feel extremely dissatisfied with their work–life balance, and two-thirds of full-time women and half of full-time men frequently feel rushed and pressed for time.[132] Further, more than 20% of Australian workers spend fifty hours or more a week at work, and 60% do not take regular holidays.

Working longer hours leads to lower work–life scores, higher absenteeism and lower productivity. Those who work the longest hours include workers in construction and mining, health, education, retail, hospitality, and managerial and professional consultant workers. Three-quarters of people working long hours say they would like to work fewer hours, even if that means less income, and most workers would take two extra weeks of holiday over a pay rise.

Sixty percent of workers stockpile their leave, even though not taking a holiday is associated with lower work–life satisfaction. In most cases, work pressure is what prevents them from taking their holidays. Women in full-time work suffer worse work–life interference than their male counterparts, and working mothers are particularly hard hit, as they attempt to juggle the demands of work and family. Poor work–life outcomes are associated with poorer health, higher use of prescription medications, more stress and more dissatisfaction with close personal relationships. These are growing factors and matters we will look into in the coming chapter.

Summarising the Crisis

In summary, we can see from key points in history, particularly through the steady growth in globalisation and the expansion of the workforce since the 1970s, that wage growth has stagnated in a real sense, with families and couples increasingly having to rely on two incomes. The deregulation of the finance industry and the advent of negative gearing in the 1980s have also seen the rise in the use of housing as an investment – a vehicle for wealth creation, with investors competing with owner–occupiers, driving up house prices and creating the housing affordability crisis. Growing house sizes, as an expression in the way in which Australians have chosen to spend their money, have also contributed towards the housing affordability crisis, with bigger houses increasing the cost of the Australian Dream.

When we reflect on the 'good old days' of the past – 1950s up until the 1970s – the term has been associated with the combined social and economic conditions in Australia experienced during this period, which have enabled Australians to have one parent working with a second parent having the option to do so if they choose, but not as a necessity. The traditional nuclear family of the day (two parents and three

---

[132] 'Australia's Welfare – Work-Life balance', AIHW, 2017.

kids) could also afford a house, put kids through education and go on holidays without financial stress.

Fast-forward to 2022, and the circumstances are vastly different, with real wage growth stagnant, housing prices outstripping annual wages many times over and parents and couples both having to work out of necessity to make the monthly mortgage repayments. Today, many singles, couples and families are enduring mortgage stress, having to deal with excessive housing costs, as well as other cost of living pressures, such as rising education costs, which together are conspiring to create a financially stressed household. It is not surprising that we have seen a rapid decline in overall home ownership in Australia since it peaked in the 1970s at 72% of all housing, to today where it has dropped to 63%.

Housing and Cost of Living - 1975	Costs	Housing and Cost of Living – 2022	Costs
Housing			
Sydney	$28,000	Sydney	$1,499,126
Canberra	$28,650	Canberra	$1,074,167
Melbourne	$19,800	Melbourne	$1,037,923
Perth	$18,850	Perth	$598,601
Brisbane	$17,500	Brisbane	$702,455
Adelaide	$16,250	Adelaide	$667,888
Hobart	$15,200	Hobart	$698,212
Cost of Living			
University fees	Free	University fees	$50,000
Loaf of bread	0.24 cents	Loaf of bread	$3.15
1 litre of milk	0.30 cents	1 litre of milk	$2.00
Newspaper	0.12 cents	Newspaper	$3.00
1 litre of petrol	0.57 cents	1 litre of petrol	$2.05
Average yearly wage	$7,618	Average yearly wage	90,000

Figure 3.9: Cost of housing and cost of living – then and now[133]

---

[133] 'House Cost and Household debt', ABS, 1975 and 2022.

4

THE GROWING SHADOWS

As we saw in the previous chapter, expanding house sizes, increased mortgages and increased debt are impacting our economy and lifestyles to the point where they are unsustainable for many Australians. But, as we will see, debt and the economy aren't the only factors of our daily lives at risk. Our love affair with the large house and suburbia is contributing to other 'shadows', such as growing environmental and health problems, as well as our dependency on cars, which is impacting our lives, our economy and, more importantly, our ecosystem.

Physical Activity

Physical activity is very important for a normal healthy life. Whether it be walking or cycling to work, taking time to attend a gym or trekking parts of our natural environment, all health experts say that a minimum level of daily physical activity is essential to ensure a healthy lifestyle. Campaigns promoted by the Federal Government, such as the Find Thirty program (30 minutes of unplanned walking daily), have helped to cement into the collective Australian conscious the importance of physical activity in our daily lives and the positive impact it has on our physical and mental wellbeing. But does where you live have an impact on how much physical activity you do in a day? Like with everything, the engagement with physical activity is determined by opportunity, and there is a growing body of evidence that suggests where you live helps to determine how much opportunity you have for physical activity.

This evidence suggests neighbourhoods characterised by low density, poor connectivity and poor access to shops and services are associated with low levels of walking and physical activity. "How so?" you may ask. As we establish more and more residential suburbs in new 'greenfield areas', the more distant these residential enclaves are to places of work, shops and places of interest. The notion of urban sprawl, which we have previously discussed, has been associated with isolation, and, as an urban form, it has a defining characteristic: it is car-dependent.

The environments we create, aesthetically and functionally, have profound consequences on our emotional connectivity to the people around us and to our physical settings, affecting both our quality of life and the manner in which we interact with the cities we live in. In addition to psychological effects, research is increasingly showing there are links between the type of built environments we live in and human behaviour as it relates to non-discretionary travel and leisure. With suburbia being where the majority of Australians now live, it is important that we pay close attention to the way people move in this environment and how it impacts the level of physical activity they engage in.

Australians are finding that, as more and more of us are choosing to call suburbia our home, more and more of us are finding ourselves in a travel pattern that is car focused, rather than using other forms of movement, such a walking and cycling, that involve physical activity. It has been proven in many studies that low levels of physical activity result in major risks of chronic health conditions. People who do not engage in sufficient physical activity are at greater heath risk, while people who engage in physical activity are shown to experience improvements in mental and physical health.

Australia's Physical Activity and Sedentary Behaviour Guidelines makes a set of recommendations that outline the minimum levels of physical activity required for health benefits, as well as the maximum amount of time a person should spend engaged in sedentary (inactive) behaviours to achieve optimum health outcomes.[134] The guidelines make different recommendations, depending upon age group, which are summarised below (Figure 4.1).

Upon closer examination of the guidelines and studies that have been paired to examine how Australians meet or don't meet these guidelines, there are some concerns that Australians are presenting as a nation of inactive people. Among children aged 2 to 5, statistics show that, in 2011, a total of 17% of children met the required physical and sedentary guidelines, while about 6 in 10 (61%) children aged 2 to 5 met the physical activity guideline, and one-quarter (25%) met the sedentary screen-based

---

[134] 'Physical Activity and Sedentary Behaviour Guidelines', Department of Health, 2017.

	Age 2–5	Age 5–17	Age 18–64	Age 65+
Physical activity	At least 180 minutes per day with at least 60 minutes of energetic play	Several hours of light activities with at least 60 minutes of moderate to vigorous activity per day	Be active on most, preferably all days with at least 150 minutes of moderate to vigorous activity per week	Be active on most, preferably all days with at least 30 minutes of moderate activity per day
Sedentary or screen-based activity	Should not be restrained for more than 60 minutes at a time. No more than 60 minutes of sedentary screen time per day	No more than 120 minutes of screen use. Break up long periods of sitting	Minimise and break up prolonged periods of sitting	Be as active as possible
Strength	N/A	Vigorous and muscle-strengthening activities 3 times a week	Muscle-strengthening activities 2 times a week	Incorporate muscle-strengthening activities

Figure 4.1: Physical activity and sedentary behaviour guidelines[135]

behaviour guideline.[136] For children between the ages of 5 and 11, and 12 and 17 years of age, the majority of children and adolescents were not meeting the physical activity and sedentary behaviour guidelines. In 2011, around 1 in 10 children aged 5 to 12, and only 2% of children aged 13 to 17, met the required physical activity and sedentary guidelines.[137] This is an alarming statistic, as behaviours that are formed at a younger age tend to carry into adult years. So, if the majority of children in their teenage years are inactive and spending too much time in front of a computer screen or TV, it is likely this behaviour will set them up for their adult years.

In terms of adults, the statistics are of equal concern, with just over 1 in 2 adults participating in sufficient exercise each day, with these levels determined in 2017/18. After adjusting for age, there was a slight decrease in the proportion of adults who were insufficiently active between 2007–08 and 2017–18, decreasing from 69% to 65%. The figure, however, is still high, with over 65% of adults simply not exercising enough daily.[138]

---

[135] *'Physical Activity and Sedentary Behaviour Guidelines'*, Department of Health, 2017.
[136] *'Physical Activity and Sedentary Behaviour Guidelines'*, Department of Health, 2017.
[137] *'Physical Activity and Sedentary Behaviour Guidelines'*, Department of Health, 2017.
[138] *'Physical Activity and Sedentary Behaviour Guidelines'*, Department of Health, 2017.

Inactivity can be caused by a number of factors, e.g., a lack of time or lifestyle choice, but increasingly it is more to do with a lack of time, which is a direct result of where you live and what your daily routine consists of. As Australians are working longer and longer to make ends meet, there are simply fewer hours in the day to devote to undertaking exercise in a formal sense. So, in order to get a minimum level of activity – say thirty minutes of moderate activity a day – Australians need to build this into their daily routine.

For many adults, this simply isn't possible. Because most Australians live in suburban environments, which are usually far away from where they work, it is less likely that people have the opportunity to exercise in their daily lives. After you add in the daily commute to and from work, the routine of coming home, making dinner, undertaking household chores and looking after children (if you have them), suddenly time for a run or walk is looking thin. Once you factor in all the typical daily work and home routines, there is little time left for enough exercise to keep fit and healthy.

Conversely, if you live closer to work or in the inner suburbs close to the city centre, where more of the traditional neighbourhoods are established, you are likely to spend less time commuting and, therefore, to have more disposable time to engage in exercise, family time or personal time. In the inner neighbourhoods, because work is usually located closer to home, people fortunate enough to live in areas such as Subiaco in Perth are able to build exercise into their travel routine, whether it be walking directly to work or walking to public transport.

A study undertaken by the Australian Catholic University's Institute of Health demonstrated the majority of suburbanites are spending too much time in their cars commuting to and from work, and this is associated with gaining weight. The study has found that time spent driving each day is associated with waist circumference, BMI, blood glucose levels and cardio-metabolic risk. People who spend an hour or more a day in their cars are, on average, 2.3kg heavier and 1.5cm wider around the waist, compared with those who spend fifteen minutes or fewer in their cars. This is significant, given that approximately 80% of Australians travel to and from work in their cars, with the average commuting time each day being an hour, while approximately 20% of people who drive are spending more than ninety minutes in their cars daily.[139] Spending such huge amounts of time in the car is contributing significantly to inactive behaviour.

Where you live is a major factor in how long you spend sitting in the car, and studies have shown that the further in the suburbs you live, the more likely you are to travel longer distances to get to work and back. The research shows that car commuters are

---

[139] *'Obesity in the Suburbs'*, Australian Catholic University's Institute of Health, 2018.

more likely to be overweight or obese, compared to non-car commuters or people who commute in a car for only short distances. No surprise really.

The reality is that the further away from the city centre you are, the less likely there is to be access to public transport, so people have to rely on their cars and spend a larger proportion of their time commuting in vehicles and less time engaging in physical activity. Car use is a common sedentary behaviour among adults and is a major contributor towards the time spent by adults engaged in sedentary behaviours rather than active physical engagement. As we will see in the next section, the decline in physical behaviour can have a profound impact on physical health and wellbeing.

Obesity

Australia is increasingly presenting as a nation of obese people. Statistics generated by the Heart Foundation show that, as recent as 2015, approximately 6 million Australians aged 18 years and over were considered overweight, representing a staggering 36% of the Australian adult population. As if this weren't alarming enough, the number of Australians aged 18 years and over who have now entered the obese category is almost 5 million, representing nearly one quarter of the entire adult population, and these figures are trending upwards. Statistics show the waistlines of Australians have been expanding since records started in 1995, with 18% of adults recorded as being obese, compared to 27.9% in 2015 (see Figure 4.2 below), reflecting an overall 49% increase over the period.[140]

Obesity is most commonly measured using the body mass index (BMI). BMI is a weight-to-height ratio and is considered to be a reasonable reflection of body fat for most people. BMI is calculated by dividing body weight in kilograms by the square of height in metres (kg/m2). Among adults, a person with a BMI greater than 25kg/m2 is considered overweight, while a BMI greater than 30kg/m2 is considered obese.[141]

	1995	2007/08	2011/12	2014/15
Obesity (total)	18.7%	24.8%	27.5%	27.9%
Obesity (males)	18.6%	25.6%	27.5%	28.4%
Obesity (females)	18.9%	24.0%	27.5%	27.4%

Figure 4.2: Level of obesity over time[142]

---

[140] *'Obesity in the Adulthood'*, Heart Foundation, 2015.
[141] *'Obesity in the Adulthood'*, Heart Foundation, 2015.
[142] *'Obesity in the Adulthood'*, Heart Foundation, 2015.

Australia appears to be in the grip of an obesity epidemic. Reports are starting to identify an acceleration of obesity among children in Australia. This is of great concern to the health and wellbeing of Australians, as being overweight when you are young usually leads to being overweight when you are older. Measured over a longer period of time, rates of overweight and obese children are alarming, as the statistics show. Based on a report by the Australian Institute of Health and Welfare, the percentage of boys and girls who were overweight in 1985 was 9.3% and 10.6%, respectively.[143] By 1995, this had Increased to 15.3% for boys and 16% for girls. By 2017, the same organisation reported that this figure had reached 1 in 4 young Australians being obese, with girls ranking just slightly higher than boys.

When compared internationally, Australians are fast becoming some of the most overweight and obese people in the world. Compared to similar developed nations, only the United States shows levels higher than Australia, with comparisons with Canada and the United Kingdom being similar, and Australia being well in front of France and Japan. Perhaps there is a connection, since the United States and Australia share very similar urban growth patterns, with suburbia and car dependency being key factors in defining American and Australian suburbs.[144]

Overweightness and obesity are currently major health issues both in Australia and internationally. The prevalence of overweightness and obesity is high and has been increasing over the last few decades, as statistics have shown. In Australian adults, the rate of overweightness/obesity is around 49%, with obesity being a major risk factor for many diseases, including type 2 diabetes, stroke, certain cancers and ischemic heart disease, and a risk factor for all-cause mortality.

The built environment in Australia plays a significant role in influencing overweightness and obesity levels, as the way in which our built environment is arranged has a profound impact on the low levels of physical activity engaged in by people who live in places like suburbia, and this inactivity is strongly linked to levels of obesity in our population. Environmental factors, such as well-maintained walking surfaces, residential density, public transport accessibility, public open spaces and mixed land use, are important correlates for higher rates of walking for recreation and transport, which tend to influence levels of daily physical activity and, in turn, the level of overweight and obese people.

Urban environments with higher walkability, access to public transport and access to services within walking distance of people's homes tend to be more associated with higher physical activity through walking and cycling. In other words, if your urban environment is based more on the traditional 'compact' urban environment,

---

[143] *'Tracking obesity in children'*, Australian Institute of Health and Welfare, 2017.
[144] *'Prevalence of overweight and obesity in selected countries'*, Australian Institute of Health and Welfare, 2002.

which was discussed in Chapter 2, you are more likely to walk and cycle and, generally, engage in physical activity as part of your daily routine. This lowers the incidences of obesity, since people are more active and engage in exercise as part of their normal daily routine. Typically, this tends to occur in the older and wealthier suburbs of our capital cities (such as Subiaco, Highgate and Como in Perth and Carlton in Melbourne), which are all neighbourhoods based on the early compact planning model of mixed housing types, with close proximities of shops, places of work and public transport.

The advent of urban sprawl, spurred on by the Australian love affair with big houses, presents a very different urban form from the traditional compact neighbourhood. These are areas defined as "metropolitan areas", where large percentages of the population live in low-density residential areas, which are car-based with low walking access to parks, shops, workplaces and public transport. These areas are shown to be associated with large concentrations of overweightness/obesity due to the higher levels of physical inactivity. Urban sprawl encourages car use and discourages physical activity, such as walking and cycling, leading to increased incidences of overweightness/obesity.

In a study undertaken by the Australian Catholic University's Institute for Health and Ageing, the physical activity level, weight and location within the city of 2,000 adults living in suburban and urban areas in Adelaide were tracked over four years.[145] The study found that those who lived in areas twenty kilometres or further from city centres experienced, on average, a 2.4cm increase in waist circumference over four years, compared to those living nine kilometres or fewer from the city, who experienced, on average, a 1.2cm increase in waist circumference.

The study found that, on average, people who lived in inner neighbourhoods closer to the city centre exercised more than people who lived further away from the city centre. The findings suggest that people living in suburban locations are more prone to putting on weight, and this can be partly attributed to their lifestyles. If you are further away from places of interest, the chances are that you are going to drive your car more, as opposed to walking or cycling, and this could be a contributing factor to higher weight gain through reduced physical activity. Certainly, there are other factors, such as diet and socio-economic factors, but the chances are that where you live contributes, since a person's level of physical activity is a major factor in overall health and wellbeing.

Essentially, when you live in a suburban location in one of the urban sprawl belts that characterise most Australian cities, expanding the urban growth boundaries without accommodating amenities, such as local shops, open spaces and public transport, can pose a serious threat to public health over a person's life. But, if you

---

[145] *'Where you live matters'*, Australian Catholic University's Institute for Health and Ageing, 2018.

live in suburban locations, the low-density nature and the economics that come with reduced population density makes it nearly impossible for local amenities and public transport to be established and to be viable.

Several explanations of this association have been proposed. Suburban residential locations increase the distance between home and destination (e.g., job), this increases the reliance on automobiles and minimises walking. Lack of sidewalks and bicycle trails, as well as the cul-de-sac street layouts that are typical in suburban areas, may decrease physical activity. In addition, the greater presence of large retail stores (i.e., big box stores) in the suburbs, concentrated in selected locations, means only a few people have walkable access to such centres. This results in more people having to drive their cars, reinforcing the poor physical activity experienced by people who live in suburban locations. Essentially, the large home, and the urban sprawl that comes with it, reduces the likelihood of a walkable lifestyle, and this leads to less physical activity. Increasing evidence shows that this is being linked to greater health issues.

If you think the correlation between where you live and weight gain is questionable, think again. As the percentage of people who have entered the overweight and obese categories in Australia has increased, so has the level of sprawl and suburban developments in our cities. Since 2005, Melbourne, for example, has added no less than fifty new suburbs, with 100,000 of the total 150,000 people in the growing city finding their way to the suburbs annually. This is roughly two-thirds of the population growth. This is not dissimilar to other cities, such as Sydney, Brisbane and Perth, except with different population growth rates. New suburbs in Perth's south-east growth corridor, such as Wungong and Byford, are set to provide housing for 250,000 people in the coming twenty years, mostly in a suburban setting. This far outweighs any of the gains to growth in inner-city locations through urban renewal, which sends the message that urban sprawl is set to stay for some time yet.

Suburbia can only be described as one of the biggest ironies in town-planning and public-health history. The town-planning movement was born hand-in-hand with public health through the Industrial Revolution, with housing and industry located close to each other, resulting in a myriad of health and sanitary-related issues. However, as town planning has matured, land use has been separated and taken to its extreme, producing urban sprawl. Things have turned full circle. Once seen as the panacea of all health issues in our cities, the way we are currently planning our cities in Australia through the suburban model is actually generating a myriad of public health issues, just of a different kind. While before, people were dying of pollution and unsanitary conditions, Australians are now confronted with physical inactivity and obesity, which are leading to a range of twentieth century health issues.

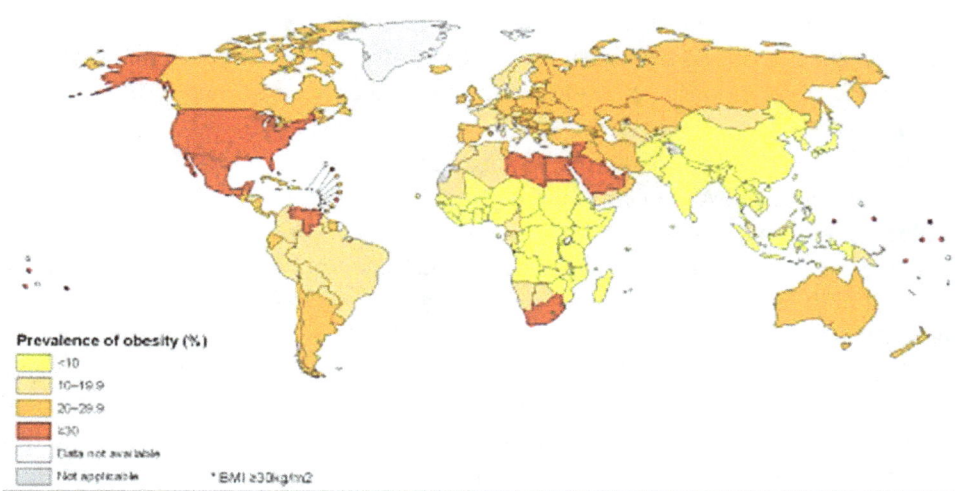

Figure 4.3: Obesity is a global problem, and Australia is one of the leading countries[146]

Mental Health

There is an ever-growing public sentiment that certain suburban locations create places where people suffer harm through mental distress; this includes anxiety, depression and a general lower satisfaction with life that affects self-esteem. Films such as *American Beauty* and *Edward Scissorhands* epitomise the isolation that may be associated with a suburban lifestyle, and this dramatisation works hand in hand with a growing body of literature that suggests that where you live can impact your overall mental health and wellbeing. As we have seen previously, a person's level of physical activity and wellbeing can be influenced, in part, by where they live. This can also be true of mental health, which has links to a person's level of physical activity and their overall physical condition.

Examining mental health in Australia has been a hot topic in recent years and is garnishing increasing focus from federal and state governments in terms of understanding mental health and its causes in modern society. This growing issue is being increasingly monitored, and the scale of the problem is perhaps summed up by the Australian Bureau of Statistics's National Survey of Mental Health and Wellbeing, which, in 2007, examined the level of mental health disorders experienced by Australians over a period of twelve months.[147] The survey found that approximately 45% of Australian adults had experienced mental health concerns, with 20% having experienced it in

---

[146] 'Obesity in Statistics', BBC News, Januaury 2008.
[147] 'National Survey of Mental Health and Wellbeing', ABS, 2007.

the twelve-month survey period. More recent estimates by the Australian Bureau of Statistics reflect that approximately 4.8 million Australians experienced mental health or behavioural conditions in 2017–18, which shows that reported mental health issues remain high.

Mental health concerns are increasingly presenting themselves in our younger population, with the Australian Child and Adolescent Survey of Mental Health and Wellbeing reporting that, in 2014, approximately 14% of younger people aged 4 to 17 years old (or 560,000 people) have experienced a mental health disorder during the twelve-month survey period. This is concerning, as poor mental health is associated with suicide, which is on a steady rise in Australia.[148]

If the enormity of the problem isn't self-explanatory when you look at the human impact of mental health in Australia, then perhaps the economic cost can provide a more sobering reality. In a report by the Royal Australian and New Zealand College of Psychiatrists in 2014, it was estimated that the total cost of severe mental illness arising from health and other associated services and lost productivity was $56.7 billion per year. To put things into perspective, the annual cost of mental health is equivalent to twice the Federal Government's annual budget for the Defence forces ($23 billion). In terms of direct costs, the Australian Federal Government spent $1.2 billion on Medicare for mental health services, and $511 million on mental-health-related prescriptions under the Pharmaceutical Benefits Scheme in 2014.[149] This figure has been growing since.

The rise of mental health conditions in the Australian community can be attributed to a number of factors, including socio-economic circumstances and genetic predisposition, but, increasingly, the construct of our built environment is being seen as an ever-growing contributing factor. While the majority of studies exploring the relationship between the built environment and the health and wellbeing of people is related to the extent to which the built environment impacts physical health and wellbeing, new studies are beginning to emerge that reflect on the impact of the built environment on mental health and wellbeing. From a physical health perspective, the built environment is often reflected upon in terms of how 'walkable' a neighbourhood is – or how pedestrian friendly a place is.

As we have already discussed, those who live in more walkable places are characterised as having more transport-related walking, greater physical activity and lower body mass indexes than people who live in less walkable neighbourhoods. Other urban factors, such as the level of public open space, the presence of trees and relative perception to safety, all contribute to higher levels of physical activity in a place. But physical health and wellbeing and mental health and wellbeing are linked, as a declining physical condition generally leads to mental health issues, such as anxiety, stress and depression.

---

[148] Australian Child and Adolescent Survey of Mental health and Wellbeing Report, 2014.

[149] *'Economic Impacts of Mental Health'*, Royal Australian and New Zealand College of Psychiatrists, 2014.

In a study undertaken by the Centre for the Built Environment at the University of Western Australia, the linkages between the factors that influence physical and mental health outcomes were examined in the context of the built environment and other associated factors.[150] The study examined socio-demographic factors (i.e., age, gender, education, etc.), built environment factors (walkability, transport options, physical barriers, etc.) and socio-environmental factors (i.e., group membership), together with behaviours associated with these factors, such as the level of sedentary behaviour, physical behaviour and nutrition. This was done to determine immediate outcomes, including body weight, cholesterol, hypertension, and general health and reported physical and mental health outcomes. Using data provided by the Department of Health in Western Australia, who surveyed four age groups between the ages of 0 and 15 years, 16 and 24 years, 25 and 64 years and adults 65 and above. The study spanned seven years between 2003 and 2009 and included 16,000 participants – a link between physical health, the type of built environment and mental health was found. In terms of the built environment, the study considered key factors, such as the level-of-land-use mix, street connectivity, road exposure, residential density, level of vegetation and overall walkability of the neighbourhood. The study found that, for suburbs characterised as car dependent, which lacked amenities and walkable access to parks and shops, the incidence of poorer physical health and mental health was higher than suburbs characterised as being walkable with higher accessibility to public transport, shops, and passive and active recreational amenities.

Where you live can have an impact on your mental health, because, depending upon the structure of your neighbourhood, it can either assist in reducing stress or add to stress. For example, for people who live close to shops, civic uses, places of work and public transport, it can be easier and less time consuming to move between places. This can reduce travel time in a car, or present alternative options, such as walking and cycling, which generally contribute to better health and wellbeing. Less time spent travelling also allows for more time to engage in other activities, such as meeting with friends and family, undertaking household chores, participating in community and civic engagements or engaging in fitness activities, which can all contribute to a sense of belonging and overall physical and mental health and wellbeing. On the other hand, when people are time poor – i.e., because they are spending a greater proportion of their time travelling to destinations – they have less time for other activities that can improve physical health and reduce stress, as a greater portion of their time is spent engaged in sedentary activities.

Piecing It Together

But what makes suburbs distinct from other places? As discussed in chapter 2, the mass segregation of land use drives a road between places, forcing people to almost

---

[150] *'Physical Activity and Mental Health'*, Centre of the Built Environment, University of Western Australia, 2009.

exclusively commute by private motor vehicle. Because this takes time and effort, and is usually a solo affair, not only is it entrenching bad habits, such as a lack of physical exercise, but it is also making people time poor; they are able to reserve less time to do things that may enrich life, such as walking in the park or catching up with friends or family. The list goes on. What can be known for sure is that living in a place that induces greater social isolation contributes significantly to mental health. This is counter-intuitive to human behaviour, which is characterised more as being gregarious in nature and in need of human interaction. Suburbia seems to create an environment that reduces the possibility of human interaction, and Australians are steadily presenting as being more depressed for it.

The truth is environmental factors play a significant role in shaping the health and wellbeing of people, and where we live, work and recreate directly influences our mental health. A study undertaken by Domain with Deloitte Access Economics and Tract Consultants looked at the health opportunities provided by suburbs in Sydney, Melbourne and Brisbane to develop a comprehensive overview of the key elements that determine the liveability of a place and the factors that act to detract from the liveability of a place. The focus was on both physical and mental health and wellbeing, given that the two are closely linked. The study identified place-based factors that either promoted or hindered the ability to lead a healthy lifestyle.[151]

Working on the notion that there are core factors that support the physical and mental health and wellbeing of a person, the study identified a total of ten indicators that make up a healthy suburb score. These are grouped into three broad categories, which are based on the type of influence each indicator has upon an individual's health. They are listed below.

1. Recovery indicators: To help an individual recover from a bout of illness or injury.
2. Hindrance indicators: To measure elements of a place that hinder an individual's ability to maintain a healthy lifestyle.
3. Promotion indicators: To promote a healthy lifestyle and possibly encourage residents to engage in healthy practices.

The suburbs were then given a star rating from 0.5 stars (poorest score) to 5 stars (best score) depending upon how they responded to the above criteria for the neighbourhoods that tick all the boxes. Each suburb in the cities of Sydney, Melbourne and Brisbane were examined with startling results. The study clearly showed that suburbs located along a main transport or train line and positioned in the inner circle of the

---

[151] *'Mapping Suburb Health'*, Domain, Deloitte Access Economics, Tract Consultants, 2017

city centre fared much better than the outer suburbs, which lacked the same level of amenity and public transport access.

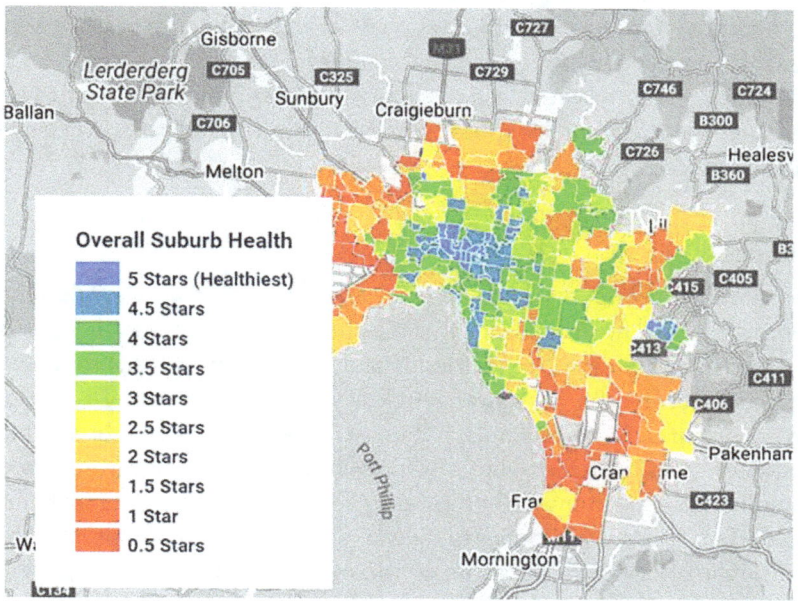

Figure 4.4: Suburb health results: Melbourne[152]

The neighbourhoods that fared better than the suburbs with a lower score had the following key elements in common as distinguishing factors.

Walkability

The notion of a place being 'walkable' highlights the capacity of a place to fulfil a person's daily needs, be that employment, shopping, access to services, education or public transport, combined with an underlying urban environment that facilitates a safe, efficient and enjoyable walking experience. Suburbs with walkable features, not only have the right infrastructure – such as pathways, sidewalks and connected networks – but quality walkways, such as tree-lined streets to provide shade and respite from the elements and to improve general aesthetic, both of which are conducive to encouraging walking. Many suburban environments in the outer suburbs lack basic infrastructure, such as a connected network of pathways and tree-lined streets and have longer distances to travel, making walking an unviable option for an increasingly time-poor population.

---

[152] *'Mapping Suburb Health'*, Domain, Deloitte Access Economics, Tract Consultants, 2017.

Transport Options

It is important that successful urban environments have options for 'active transport' to and from work. Active transport means the option for people to travel to and from work via a form of transport that includes physical activity, such as walking and cycling. Building in physical activity for travelling to and from work is very important for time-sensitive people. Suburbs with close proximity to large employment centres or access to established walking and cycle routes scored well for this indicator, while car-dependent suburbs scored poorly.

Open Spaces

The areas defined as 'open space', be they parks, plazas or urban-style piazzas, are a key promotor of a healthy lifestyle, since they provide places where people can reflect, exercise and meet up with friends and family in public environments, often without cost. Places such as sporting fields, which allow healthy participation in children's sporting clubs, for example, not only create a healthy environment for active engagement in physical activity, but also provide the forum to be part of a club and form community connections. So, it's not only active physical and mental benefits that are reaped, but also passive benefits by way of relaxing and socialising. Areas with excellent public open space are some of the most sought-after real estate in a city, which highlights its importance to human engagement and activity.

Tree Cover

It's not unusual to find the level of tree cover to be an important factor in the health and wellbeing of a place. Strong evidence exists that tree cover has mental health benefits, due to its association with nature and the natural environment, which has a calming influence over people. There have been many studies undertaken that link the property values of one street to another due to the level of tree cover. Trees also have the practical benefit of reducing air pollution and lowering urban temperatures – or the heat island effect, which has been studied extensively.

Access to Fresh Food

While exercise and overall physical activity is good for mental and physical health and wellbeing, it is also important that diet play a role in maintaining a healthy lifestyle. This is why access to fresh food via corner stores, supermarkets and local producer retail outlets is considered important. Having readily available access to fresh food increases the incidence of people purchasing fresh food, and this is why, in a healthy suburb, it is important not only that these outlets be established, but that they preferably be within walking distance of people's homes.

Volunteering/Community Engagement

An important hallmark of a successful community and a contributor to strong mental health and wellbeing is the level of community engagement and volunteering that a group of people engage in. Looking after one's own community not only is good for one's soul and provides a sense of purpose, but also has broader benefits for a community, especially when people are on the receiving end of volunteering and community giving. This often-underrated aspect of human behaviour is extremely important in building a sense of community and belonging by engaging in something that is beyond oneself. Joining a local environmental group, book club or elderly volunteer group, for example, all provide personal and community benefits that help build a sense of community and improve one's self-esteem and self-worth. While it can be complicated to measure exactly the benefits derived from volunteering or engaging in community activities, the common notion is that a community that is more likely to engage in volunteering and community activities is more likely to be better connected as a community and therefore be more cohesive.

Hindrance Factors

Fast Food

The predominance of and access to fast food in a community is being linked to a whole array of poor-eating habits and obesity. Documentaries, such as *Supersize Me,* dramatise the unhealthy impacts of consuming a fast-food diet, so it is natural that a community with a high number of fast-food outlets has greater access to poorer food choices, and this impacts overall physical and mental health and wellbeing. Accessibility is determined by the number of fast-food outlets found in a suburb, with a higher number meaning greater accessibility. As fast-food outlets are well known to be successful businesses, one can only extrapolate that, if there are more fast-food outlets in a suburb, then there is a greater likelihood that the residents and commuters in those suburbs would consume greater quantities of fast food.

Liquor Stores

Similar to fast-food outlets, liquor stores also contribute towards poorer diets, since alcohol contains significant sugar levels, and there is a link between sugar consumption and obesity. The consumption of alcohol also has the potential to cause other health-related issues from over drinking, including anti-social behaviour and addiction, both of which can lead to poor mental and physical health outcomes. Similar to fast food outlets, liquor stores as businesses are fairly successful; accordingly ,the more liquor stores within a suburb, the more likely there will be greater consumption of alcohol by the population in the suburb.

Promotional Factors

Hospitals

Access to key services, such as hospitals, is considered important, not only for the recovery period of an injury or illness, but also for peace of mind and mental health and wellbeing. Access to a hospital is not the only important factor, but also the number of beds in a hospital, as the larger the hospital, the greater the service provided to the community. Distance from a hospital and the number of beds are considered important factors for consideration when determining a healthy suburb.

Access to Medical Services

Perhaps more important than hospitals, access to medical services is a key factor in determining the health and wellbeing of a suburb, since people generally access health services, such as a general practitioner, physiotherapist or psychologist, more often than attending a hospital. The close proximity of support medial services and pharmaceutical shops play a key role in both the prevention of and recovery from illness and injury. Similar to other services, the more medical services located within a suburb, the greater the general accessibility to them by residents.

Community Services

The provision of and access to community services, such as community buildings for club meetings, organised sports or for civic-type activities, is a very important indicator of access to community facilities and engagement, since the more of these facilities that are provided in a suburb, the greater chance that people will participate in community activities. These types of uses support mental health outcomes via the provision of social connectivity for more isolated members of the community. In the case of organised sports, they can also provide benefits in improving physical activity and health and wellbeing.

Collectively, the list of common features and promotional factors that support a suburb are typically found in traditional 'built-up' neighbourhoods, which share a combination of public and private transport and are positioned close to the centre of the city. Outer suburbs that are car dominant are more dispersed, lack amenities and are high in hindrance factors, such as fast-food and liquor stores. Where you live does matter – not just for physical health and wellbeing, but for mental health and wellbeing.

The Urban Footprint

The one thing about big houses, suburbia and urban sprawl is that they are land hungry. It takes a lot of land to build suburbia, given its low-density nature; you need more land to house fewer people. When we looked historically at the urban forms of the past, the traditional walkable neighbourhood was compact, and its growth was limited to the walkable distance of an individual and horse and cart, which was typically around four kilometres from the centre of the city. These early European settlements, as an example, housed thousands of people in apartment quarters over four to five storeys in height. The centre of Paris is a good example of this type of living, with its walkable streets, human-scale apartments and buildings, and the ease at which everything from civic uses, community buildings, shops, education facilities and places of employment are within walking distance.

As we have discussed previously, walkability in cities changed slightly with the advent of the train and tram, which spread cities along transit corridors, with walkable nodes located around train/tram stops. It changed even more dramatically when the automobile became popular. These first two modes of urban form were not land hungry. The walkable city is contained within a four-kilometre radius, the transit city spreads along tram and train routes – but development is contained around the train/tram stops. Examples are illustrated below.

Figure 4.5: Paris (walkable city)[153]

Figure 4.6: Sydney (transit development)[154/155]

---

[153] *'Footage of Paris'*, Google earth and Sergio Famiano's private collection, 2015.
[154] *'Footage of Paris'*, Google earth and Sergio Famiano's private collection, 2015.
[155] *'Archival footage of Sydney'*, Battye Library, Perth, 2020.

This all changed when the so called 'freedom' of the automobile came along. The reach of the automobile meant the city could expand in all directions simultaneously, allowing development to go from compact apartment buildings to low-density, single-storey, detached homes in suburbs made exclusively of residential housing, as the images below reflect.

Figure 4.7: Suburban Sydney[156]

Of course, automobile cities aren't just made up of suburbs of residential housing, business parks and shopping centres; they also include distributor roads, freeways and a network of smaller roads to make it possible to move long distances between places. This all takes significant land. Our urban footprint is so extensive that some cities have sprawled a ridiculous distance that was incomprehensible just one hundred years ago. Perth, for example, from the norther suburbs of Yanchep to Mandurah, stretches over one hundred kilometres along the coastline and has an overall area of 6,400 square kilometres, for just under two million people. Similarly, Sydney stretches over one hundred kilometres along its coast and inwards, with an area of 12,000 square kilometres for over five million people. Every year, as these cities expand their suburban footprint, they encroach further and further into arable land for farming, bushland and ecological areas, which are coming under threat due to this encroachment.

To give a sense of the impact automobile-based development has on the urban environment, let's look at the growth of Perth, Melbourne and Sydney in the 2018/19 financial year. Alone, Perth expanded its urban footprint in 2018 by generating an additional 9,683 residential lots with a combined area of 345 hectares.[157] In terms of industrial and commercial space, it expanded by 505 lots and a further 134 hectares in area.[158] Combined, this is an urban footprint expansion of 479 hectares in one year alone – and the 2018/19 financial year was a slow year, as Western Australia grappled

---

[156] *'Archival footage'*, Battye Library, Perth, 2021.
[157] *'State of the Land'*, UDIA, 2020.
[158] *'State of the Land'*, UDIA, 2020.

with a slowing economy and slower population growth of less than 20,000 people per annum.[159] To put things into perspective, this is equivalent to roughly five square kilometres of new development or, better put, the equivalent of a new modest local government area.

While Perth's growth rate may be slowing, on the other side of the country things are different. Take Melbourne, for example. In 2018/19 alone, the urban footprint expanded by 18,470 residential lots, equivalent to 740 hectares.[160] When you combine commercial and industrial land, which included 782 lots amounting to 205 hectares, the total urban foot print expansion is 945 hectares, or the equivalent to nearly 10 square kilometres or five new suburbs.[161] This, of course, doesn't include infill development (development on existing lots), but, combined, Melbourne in 2019 grew by a whopping 150,000 people – and that was just one year. Sydney experienced a similar population growth to Melbourne but experienced much higher rates of infill development. Despite this, lot production was still around 7,190 residential lots established, which is equivalent to 272 hectares, and a combined commercial and industrial lot expansion of 140 hectares.[162] Combined, this is equivalent to approximately two new suburbs. I think you get the picture.

For relatively small population increases, the urban footprint is expanding significantly, and this is resulting in losses of bushland, habitat and fertile soil along our coastal regions. You may think then, "why don't we just put a limit on the amount of land that can be zoned for urban development and be done with it?". The truth is we do that. In every state, there is a zoning scheme that sets the urban footprint for a city: in Perth it is the Metropolitan Region Scheme, in Melbourne it is the Urban Growth Boundary. These act as urban growth boundaries, limiting the amount of new greenfield development. The problem is that we keep expanding it from year to year, through political pressure, self-interest or, in some circumstances, out of necessity. One thing is for certain: each time we expand the boundary of the urban footprint, more and more irretrievable arable land is lost to urban development, since our cities are located in coastal regions, and it is our coastline that has our best land.

Australia's population is unusually concentrated in two primary cities: Sydney and Melbourne, which have 5.3 million and 5 million residents respectively. The bulk of Australia's remaining 14 million people is found in the remaining capital cities of Brisbane, Perth and Adelaide, which have 2.4 million, 2.14 million and 1.32 million, respectively.

With the majority of Australia's population located within urban centres, you would think our cities would be fairly dense in population, but they aren't.

---

[159] *'State of the Land'*, UDIA, 2020.
[160] *'State of the Land'*, UDIA, 2020.
[161] *'State of the Land'*, UDIA, 2020.
[162] *'State of the Land'*, UDIA, 2020.

Melbourne, for example, is Australia's most dense city, with 497 people per square kilometre.[163] This is followed by Sydney, with 423 people per square kilometre.[164] When you compare this internationally to cities such as London or Vienna, which have densities of 5,590 and 7,030 people per square kilometre, respectively, it appears that Australia has some catching up to do.[165] This all means that the more Australian cities expand to accommodate suburbia, the more land area that is lost to the urban footprint, since densities in Australian cities are significantly below other cities in the world.

In Australia, most of the areas that experience strong population growth are in the fringe areas of the major cities. For example, the last five years have seen suburbs such as South Morang, Point Cook and Craigieburn-Mickleham in Melbourne experience the most significant growth across the country, all on a low-density-based model. These are areas that have significantly lower densities of people per square kilometre. In other parts of the country, such as Perth, suburbs such as Baldivis, Ellenrook and Harrisdale experienced the greatest growth, all on a low-density suburban-based model. The story is similar across the country. To gauge the impact this is having on the environment, one just has to look at the diminishing grassland areas in Melbourne.

In Melbourne, which has experienced extraordinary suburban growth to accommodate the Australian Dream, some 55% of 1,200 native plant species are threatened with extinction.[166] That is over half. If growth continues at a similar rate as in 2018, it is predicted that a further 21% of Melbourne's native plant species over the next 100 years will join the 'threatened with extinction' category.[167] This is a staggering predicament and is similar across other cities in Australia.

In Perth, ecological systems are disappearing as the Metropolitan Region Scheme boundary continues to expand. A common example is the diminishing habitat for the Black Cockatoo (Carnaby, Baudins and Red Tail). For hundreds of years, this species of bird has been roaming the coastal plains from the hills, with significant habitat found all over the Perth metropolitan area. Over 100 years of urban development, however, has seen a rapid diminishing of habitat in the coastal plain area, which is being matched by reduced habitat inland of Perth, where habitat is being removed for farming. In the city's north-east, a significant pine plantation established over fifty years ago served as a substitute for diminishing habitat, with the Black Cockatoo foraging through the pinecones. The rapid expansion of new suburbs such as Ellenbrook, however, has resulted in the mass clearing of these

---

[163] Nedad, F, *'The Cities of Australia'*, ID informed decisions, August 2019.
[164] Nedad, F, *'The Cities of Australia'*, ID informed decisions, August 2019.
[165] *'Population density for the United Kingdom'*, Office of National Statistics, May 2020.
[166] *'State of the Environment Report'*, Commissioner for Environmental Sustainability, 2018.
[167] *'State of the Environment Report'*, Commissioner for Environmental Sustainability, 2018.

pine plantations, meaning that even the substituted habitat for the Black Cockatoo is being removed in place of rooftops and roads. This is resulting in a massive decline in the species in the area, which appears to be a familiar story in other parts of Australia. Urban expansion needs to be checked in order for this environmental trajectory of decline to be arrested, which will take some convincing – both at a commercial and political level.

No Homes among the Gum Trees

If you are really honest with yourself, regardless of whether you consider yourself a greenie or not, you must be concerned about the level of clearing occurring in our major cities. Each year, large areas of bushland, which provide an ecology for a variety of unique flora and fauna, are giving way to low-density housing for the Australian Dream. What makes the situation worse is that current planning practices and economic expediency demand whole areas are cleared with little vegetation retained. This is because modern developers prefer to create flat readymade blocks, fully retained for the building industry to roll out its predesigned Model T-type homes on. The fact that this is being done en masse would make even the most hardened capitalist cringe at the absence of vegetation being retained when developers move in with their bulldozers and ready the land for development.

This isn't a story specific to any one city in Australia, but it is universal in its approach and refers back to the symbiotic relationship between the land developer and the project home builder – as we discussed earlier. The truth is, it is cheaper and more expedient to clear land and start from scratch than retain vegetation and work around the contours of the landscape. In what is an ironic twist on the whole scenario, the developers often name their new estates based on the natural feature that once adorned the landscape before the developers and builders moved in to obliterate the landscape – I should know. For ten years, I grew up in a middle-fringe suburb in Perth called Tuart Hill, named after the once abundant quantity of mature Tuart Trees that used to dominate the landscape. These trees accommodated a variety of bird life, not to mention a pleasant microclimate. but, when the developers moved in, they removed most of the Tuart Trees, with the landscape now dominated by single-residential housing and townhouses. The name Tuart Hill is a reflection of what was once there and is a reminder in case people forget. James Howard Kunstler in his book *The Geography to Nowhere* makes a similar description of development in the United States, which appears to name its new suburbs after the landscape it obliterated.[168] As mentioned previously in this book, what happens in America appears to find its way to Australia, one way or another.

---

[168] Kunstler, J, *'The Geography to Nowhere'*, Touchstone and Simon & Schuster, New York, 1994.

Few subdivisions these days retain large areas of vegetation. This creates an unnatural landscape devoid of any human connection to the environment. To show that I am not a total cynic, there are some developments bucking this trend, and I don't want to be seen as putting down the industry. However, if we are honest, developments such as Warralily in Melbourne and Parklands in the Gold Coast are few and far between, with most new suburbs preferring a cut and slash approach to subdivision. Figure 4.8 shows an example of this type of development in Perth's northern suburbs but, in truth, if I took the heading away it could be anywhere in Australia. What makes matters worse is that many new suburbs don't even place trees within the verge areas anymore, either due to a lack of space, conflict with underground services or concerns with maintenance. Take suburbs like Clarkson in Perth's northern corridor, or Harrisdale in Perth's south-east, all you see are rooftops. This is creating suburbs largely devoid of trees. This is a far cry from the 'home among the gum trees' notion that spurred the great home ownership and Australian Dream in the first place.

Figure 4.8: New subdivision in Perth's northern suburbs [169]

The Australian environment is under pressure, and new subdivisions of low-density housing are contributing significantly towards habitat loss. Many new subdivisions around the country are not only removing the majority of vegetation on-site before building commences, but are also leaving no room for new vegetation to be planted. In the 1950s, when housing was more modest – being around 100sqm on a block of land that averaged 700sqm – there was ample yard space to provide areas

---

[169] *'New Suburbs in Perth's north'*, courtesy of Sergio Famiano's private collection, 2011.

for recreation, a vegetable garden and trees to soften the impact of Australia's harsh environment. But, as the Australian Dream has evolved into smaller lots and larger homes, the large backyard, and excessive tree canopy that goes with it, has been lost. These days, many backyards are just 20sqm. This is a fundamental shift with dire consequences for the environment and the amenities of the people living in these households. For a classic example of this juxtaposition of old suburbia versus new, see Figure 4.9.

Figure 4.9: Older traditional suburbs (Joondanna, circa 1947 – 1955) versus new suburbs (Harrisdale, 2004 onwards) – where are the trees?[170]

The notion of site coverage – i.e., the percentage of a block that can be covered by a building – was once modest, being around 30%, but over the years this has increased to 50%, and, with much smaller lots, the percentage is as high as 70%. When you take into consideration paved areas for walkways and courtyards, along with driveways, up to 95% of the block can be covered by hardstand. This is a disturbing trend, which is not only occurring in new outer suburb developments, but also in the inner suburbs, where infill development is underway. In suburbs like Kelmscott and Armadale in Perth's south-eastern growth corridor, these suburbs are transitioning from single-residential housing on large blocks to two and three-unit developments, with each dwelling squeezing every inch out of the block to maximise the building footprint. A typical example of a before and after is illustrated in Figure 4.10.

---

[170] *'New Development in the Suburbs'*, Sergio Famiano's private photographic collection, 2014.

Figure 4.10: New infill development: before and after[171/172]

This trend is contributing significantly to the notion of the 'heat-island effect', which is where urban areas become significantly hotter than their surroundings, due to the loss of vegetation and mass expanse of hardstand, such as roofs, roads and paved areas – all of which absorb heat. The result is higher temperatures, which can have a significant knock-on effect to energy consumption, through increased use of air-conditioning, for example. The altered climate also makes for more difficult living conditions, affecting the health of people living in these environments, and also impacts nearby ecosystems, such as parks and foreshore areas, which provide refuges for animals.

Governments and industry practitioners have begun to recognise this problem and are starting to consider ways to reduce tree-canopy loss in new subdivisional developments and individual lot development. It is a slow and difficult process, since reversing this trend involves undoing a well-entrenched industry practice, which has become accustomed to rolling out standard homes. A change to this approach may now require developers and homeowners to consider more individual designs that work around environmental factors so trees can be retained.

The environment is critical to the longevity of much of Australia's flora and fauna, but it is also critical to creating hospitable environments for human habitation. The current trajectory of subdivisional development to accommodate the Australian Dream is having its impact on the environment by removing rare and unique ecological environments; this is devastating unique flora and is reducing the breeding and foraging habitats of our unique fauna. The Federal Government's expanding endangered and critically endangered list of flora and fauna is the canary in the coalmine for our environment.

---

[171] *'Aerial Photograph of Joondanna, Perth'*, Google Earth, 1950's and Harrisdale circa 2015.
[172] *'Archive footage of Armadale and recent circa 1960's and 2000's'*, Google Earth, 1964 and 2016.

The loss of tree cover and biodiversity is also affecting human habitation by creating warmer microclimates and reducing aesthetics, which is critical to the health and wellbeing of Australians. Remember, it is unnatural for humans to live in densely populated cities devoid of the natural environment. Prior to cities en masse, which took off after the Industrial Revolution, people lived in largely rural communities for thousands of years, surrounded by the environment, and this is ingrained within our DNA. It is, therefore, important that humans maintain a connection to the environment, for our wellbeing, if nothing else. It is clear, however, that the current form of the suburban experiment is not meeting this need, and drastic measures need to be taken to consider reversing this trend, so we can maintain our connection to nature – and save our precious ecosystems in the process.

Traffic and Gridlock

What inevitably comes with suburban sprawl and the Australian Dream is traffic. Because of the ease with which the automobile covers vast expanses, city suburbs, business parks, industrial areas and shopping precincts are connected by an intricate web of roads that start from freeways. Freeways are like the main arteries in the human body, connecting industrial areas with business parks and providing a regional connection to towns and outer suburbs. This is then followed by main distributor roads, which take vehicles from main areas to individual suburbs and local neighbourhoods, then, like capillaries, they form into individual streets, which service the common home, shops and local businesses. As mentioned above, this web of roads is land hungry and can constitute up to one-quarter of all land contained in a city.

Each road has an in-built capacity that is based on its level of service; in other words, each road is designed to take a certain capacity of vehicles, usually expressed as the number of vehicles per day, with acceptable limits defined by waiting times at intersections. The theory goes that the shorter period you have to wait at an intersection to cross, the greater the serviceability of the road. As an example, a typical local road within a suburb is designed to take up to 6,000 vehicles per day before the street becomes too congested, impacting not only the movement of vehicles but pedestrian and cycle movements across the road and the amenities of nearby residents and homes via noise and congestion. Most local roads do not reach anywhere near capacity, such is the sprawled nature of our suburbs, but the main roads, such as freeways and district distributor roads, are a different story altogether.

Because Australian cities are car based and are characterised by land-use segregation, most people have to commute long distances from home to work, usually by travelling on district distributor roads and highways. This is when things get tricky in the automobile city. Because work start and finish times are largely uniform across the city – i.e., most businesses and schools start between 8am and 9am and finish between 4pm and 5pm – you have mass hordes of vehicles moving, largely, in the same direction at one specific time of day. We call this the morning and afternoon rush, which generates the popular term 'traffic'. I call it the insane hour where many people – myself included – spend at least an hour in the vehicle going to and returning from work; that is two hours in the day gone, just by commuting.

In traditional compact cities, where people live close to where they work, much less time is spent moving from home to work. In cities such as Prague or Paris, people often spend less than thirty minutes travelling to work, and, in many instances, a car is not required, because public transport and other viable and healthier alternatives, such as cycling and walking, are available. This is not possible in most automobile cities, which require cars to fulfil the most basic errands, such as getting the newspaper or a litre of milk. In Australia, an inordinate number of trips are completed by the automobile.

Take Melbourne, for instance, which, at its core, has a good public transport system via an extensive network of trams. Despite having good public transport in its core city centre area, because of the nature of the sprawl which has engulfed Melbourne the last three decades, public transport to the broader suburban areas has some catching up to do. In Melbourne, the modal share is heavily in favour of the private automobile, accounting for over 76% of all transport movement. Public transport accounts for 19% and walking and cycling 5%, and Melbourne is one of the better cities in Australia in terms of promoting public transport use and walking and cycling.

Perth, which is a car-dominated city, has a more sobering modal share. Cars account for 84% of all transport movements, with public transport accounting for 12% and walking and cycling just 4%. Because of the car's dominance, Australian cities are more susceptible to increased traffic and the array of problems associated with it.[173]

Traffic has multiple major impacts to consider. The first is time. Time spent in the car results in an 'opportunity cost' – as the economists would put it – because this is time not spent doing other things, such as working, catching up with family and friends, exercising, etc. This opportunity cost is significant, given that the average Australian spends at least two hours in a vehicle on a daily basis, adding up to approximately thirty days per year of your life in a car. Time lost in a car has been measured in terms of its dollar value as an equation of a loss of productivity. In Australia, in 2014–15, this equated to $16.5 billion: $6 billion in private time costs, $8 billion in business time costs, $1.5 billion in extra vehicle operating costs and $1 billion in additional air pollution costs.[174] Imagine if we all had an extra one and a half hours in the day? Think of what we could achieve or how much healthier we might all be if we could use thirty minutes of that time to exercise.

Traffic in Australian cities is getting worse. The problem is with capacity constraint, which is built into a road network during construction. Freeways, for example, are built

---

[173] *'Urban Mobility Trends from Melbourne'*, Trans urban, 2021.
[174] *'Urban Transport Crowding and Congestion'*, Infrastructure Australia, 2019.

to handle a certain number of vehicles per day. One such road, the Mitchell Freeway, which runs through the heart of Perth, has a capacity constraint of around 200,000 vehicles per day. The busiest part of this freeway is between Cedric and Vincent Street, which sees approximately 180,000 vehicles per day. Even at 180,000 vehicles per day, congestion occurs during the peak periods, and time is lost sitting in bumper-to-bumper traffic.

As the suburbs expand and more and more people have to travel along a north-south trajectory to get to work, this capacity will eventually reach its 200,000 vehicles per day limit, which will result in significant time delays, particularly during the peak morning and afternoon periods. What can be done then? Well, there are only so many times you can widen the freeway until you reach a natural barrier and can't extend any further. This means increased congestion on the freeway will be the norm of the future. The alternative is to shift the modal share: introduce new public transport to shift usage from the private automobile to public transport or other means of transport. This is expensive and takes significant effort to change people's travel behaviours.

Traffic carries another major cost, and that is to our tax dollar. As cities expand, more and more roads need to be built to accommodate low-population suburban growth so people can move from place to place as freely as possible. Local roads, which service individual homes, are usually paid for by the developer of the suburb or industrial estate and are accommodated in the purchase price of the lot. So, if a residential lot retailed at, say, $100,000, the cost of the road as a portion could be up to $10,000, when you include all the drainage infrastructure required. These roads are then maintained by the local government, and landowners pay for this through their rates. The same is true for suburb distributor roads.

Higher-order roads, like district distributor roads and freeways, are usually funded by state governments via individual road boards, which are major service departments for state governments. In Western Australia, this is Main Roads WA, Victoria has VicRoads, and so forth for the other states.

State Planning also helps to maintain roads, such as significant distributor roads, which are in between local roads and highways in terms of significance. These state roads are funded through an array of taxes, such as the Metropolitan Improvement Fund, which is a tax levied on vacant land and investment properties to support state planning in Western Australia for maintaining, acquiring and developing selected state roads.

The establishment of new main roads is subject to political cycles, but the maintenance of existing state roads is a recurrent budget expenditure. Take, for example, Victoria. In the 2017–2018 financial year, VicRoads spent 3.4 billion dollars on a combination of administration, capital works for new roads and maintenance of existing roads.[175] This comes from a variety of funding sources, including taxes and

---

[175] VicRoads Annual Report, 2018–19.

levies (i.e., licenses), state expenditure to support capital works and federal government expenditure on significant 'congestion busting' projects. This is an ongoing commitment and appears to be increasing every year as our cities grow and require more infrastructure to support development. This money could be better spent funding hospitals, schools and other essential community activities.

Pollution

Sprawl and the accommodation of the automobile also bring about a significance cost through the pollution of the environment. Increased development, car usage and production of consumption items to fill our big homes lead to increased pollution in our built and natural environments. Pollution, in its many forms, can lead to human and ecological health issues associated with the quality of air, water and land, which are all essential to human and animal habitation.

One of the biggest impacts of urban sprawl is its effect on the creation of solid waste. In Australia, solid waste that is not reused or recovered ends up in large landfill sites across the country. There are 1,168 landfill sites across Australia, which take in approximately 20 million tons of waste each year, with around 90 landfill sites across the country – such as Werribee landfill, which is 212 hectares in size – accepting up to 75% of this waste.[176] This extraordinary figure exists even with the Australian state and local governments making significant efforts to reduce solid waste going into landfill sites by putting a strong focus on recycling.

Hazardous waste is a particular concern, because of its potentially harmful effects on the environment. Waste products include asbestos, chemicals, plastics, oils and other non-biodegradable products. Hazardous waste in Australia rose from 4.6 million tonnes in 2010 to 5.7 million tonnes in 2017.[177] This is projected to increase significantly to over 9 million tonnes by 2030. Solid waste often comes from construction activities, such as the redevelopment of former industrial areas and the redevelopment of new areas for residential purposes.

Building suburbia is contributing significantly to solid waste, with building products, such as chemicals and paint, being by-products of development. Also, building suburbia in former industrial sites requires significant soil remediation, which often leads to the mass removal of contaminated soil to special landfill sites for storage. This is an area that is growing in Australia, as the land that is easy to develop is being consumed, leaving old 'brown field' redevelopment sites to take up an increasing proportion of the slack. Traditionally, these existing brown field sites are former industrial sites and contain contaminated material from their historic uses.

---

[176] 'Australia's Waste and Resource Recovery Infrastructure', National Waste Report, 2013.
[177] 'Australia's Waste and Resource Recovery Infrastructure', National Waste Report, 2013.

Figure 4.11: Werribee landfill site in Victoria[178]

Air pollution continues to be a significant by-product of the Australian Dream. Given the known respiratory and cardiovascular effects and carcinogenic properties that constitute air pollution, sensitive individuals, such as children, the elderly and people with respiratory and cardiovascular diseases are particularly susceptible to air pollution. Mortality attributed to air pollution is on the rise across Australian cities, with approximately 2,200 deaths identified in Sydney, Melbourne, Brisbane and Perth in 2017 alone.[179]. This doesn't include the high number of hospital admissions, particularly of the elderly and children, for respiratory dysfunction as a result of air pollution. The biggest impacts on air pollution come from nitrogen dioxide and sulphur dioxide coming from car exhausts.

There a several factors that increase air pollution in Australian cities. The first is population growth. Australia's urban areas are continuing to expand at a rapid rate to accommodate an increasing population. As mentioned previously, in 2018 alone, Melbourne grew by a staggering 150,000 people.[180] Population increase will drive increased air pollution from both domestic and industrial sources, unless there is a significant decline in the per-person level of pollution. The nexus is simple: as the population grows, so does suburbia, since the majority of new development to house a growing population is occurring on the fringes of our cities.

---

[178] *'Australia's Waste and Resource Recovery Infrastructure'*, National waste Report 2013.
[179] *'Health Impacts of Air Pollution'*, Australian State of the Environment Report, 2016.
[180] *'Regional Population Growth in Australia'*, ABS, 2018–19.

Urbanisation is another significant factor contributing to growing air pollution in Australia. By 2061, it is estimated that 74% of all Australians will be living in capital cities, such as Perth, Melbourne, Sydney, Brisbane and Adelaide. This compares with 62% in 2011.[181] This will lead to increased development in our cities, not just for residential and industrial development, but also for roads, which are likely to be heavily trafficked, resulting in increased congestion and population.

Increased transport and energy demands will be the third significant factor affecting air population growth in the future. The Australian transport sector is growing and will continue to rely heavily on oil as its primary source of fuel for the next twenty years. Diesel as a source of fuel is also growing and is also a significant polluter. The growth in the use of transport fuels can be attributed to the general growth in industrial activity, more suburbs and a reliance on cars as the primary source of transportation.

With an ageing population in Australia, it is expected that deaths related to air population will rise, especially as the percentage of the population above the age of sixty-five is expected to double by 2050.

Increasing suburbia to accommodate the Australia Dream involves transforming our natural landscape, which allows water to pass through soils, into impervious landscapes, such as bitumen and concrete, which block water from moving. When water cannot move freely, its movement needs to be managed through drainage systems.

Water that enters waterways from road surfaces or drains can have a significant impact on natural ecosystems and wetlands, given the pollutants (i.e., topsoil, chemicals, oil and grease), which are generally picked up through the drainage cycle from road surfaces and then dumped into wetlands or drainage areas that usually form parks and reserves. This is polluting waterways and disrupting ecosystems for a variety of animal and birdlife in our natural environments.

Increased hard surfaces are also resulting in increased volumes of water with increased velocities entering watercourses, which is creating capacity constraints, particularly when unseasonable events occur (i.e., floods that occur in 1-in-10-year and 1-in-100-year events). When these un-seasonal events happen, they often result in the flooding of watercourses and treatment trains, which spill over into roads, walkways and, in some instances, homes.

Transport-related surfaces, such as roads, driveways and carparks, comprise of up to 70% of impervious surfaces in urban environments. As suburbia expands, so does the impervious environment. The pollutants that find their way into watercourses have a variety of sources, including vehicles, construction activities, erosion and surface degradation. Oils and litter also have ecological impacts on watercourses, in addition to their immediate aesthetic impacts. Heavy metals and polycyclic hydrocarbons are two common pollutants in urban stormwater that can have negative impacts on human health. Exposure or human contact with these pollutants can lead to headaches, hypertension, skin cancer, lungs and bladder dysfunction.

---

[181] *'Australian State of the Environment Report'*, 2016.

Figure 4.12: Air pollution caused by vehicles, industrial development and fires is growing in Australia[182]

The Environmental impacts of residential development

An often acknowledged but overlooked impact of suburban development is the impact it has on the environment. Often, environmental impacts are accepted as a necessary cost of building to house our growing population. But it shouldn't be like this.

Environmental impacts are traditionally considered in the context of the loss of habitat and ecosystems, which are literally removed to make way for suburban development. This has been looked at by state and local government and academics, and, unsurprisingly, suburban development leaves a nasty footprint by removing what was once an ecosystem and replacing it with and expensive and detrimental urban form.

I would like us to turn our attention towards the other environmental impacts suburban development causes: water consumption, energy consumption, embodied energy consumption and carbon dioxide emissions.

Researchers Bill Randolph, Darren Holloway, Stephen Pullen and Patrick Troy undertook a study in 2006. Their research was developed in collaboration with Landcom (NSW's state land developer) to examine the water and energy consumption of households in different developments undertaken by Landcom since its establishment in 1976.[183] The purpose of the study was to understand, where similar developments are concerned, if progress had been made in reducing energy and water consumption, and also how larger-scale high-density development in inner-city areas performed against more traditional low-density development in suburban areas, in terms of energy and water consumption and overall impacts on the environment.

---

[182] *'Australian State of the Environment Report'*, 2016.
[183] Randolph, B, Holloway, D, Pullen, S, and Troy, P, *'The Environmental Impact of Residential Development',* 2006.

The study used a number of parameters to define the research, including water and energy accounted for in terms of kilolitres of water and gigajoules of energy, with energy measured in terms of operational energy which includes energy, such as electricity and gas used on a day-to-day basis. The second aspect of energy consumption was measured in terms of embodied energy, which refers to the energy used in the production of building materials as part of the construction process. A final parameter includes measuring the amount of greenhouse gas emissions, measured by annualised carbon dioxide production. The research parameters were measured across eleven estates: four were Landcom estates and the other seven were private estates.[184]

In respect of the average annual water consumption for all the case study areas, the following table (Figure 4.13) details the findings, with a comparison made between low-density estates from the 1970s to late 1990s and a comparison between these estates and high-density or infill estates.

	Average Water Consumption Per Dwelling 2003 (kl)	Average Water Consumption Per House 2003 (kl)	Average Water Consumption Per Multi-Unit Dwelling 2003 (kl)	Average Water Consumption Per Capita 2001 (kl)
Low-Density Estates				
Late 1970s				
St Clair	291	291	NA	95
Cambridge Gardens	265	264	NA	96
Early 1980s				
St Andrews	271	271	NA	89
Raby	284	286	195	98
Early 1990s				
Glenhaven	414	415	NA	133
West Pennant Hills	385	387	243	121
Late 1990s				
Narrellan Vale	261	263	173	92
Harrington Park	281	281	NA	89
High-Density Estates				
Kings Bay	188	NA	180	84
Abbotsford	184	NA	183	88
Cabarita	224	248	194	99
Liberty Grove	202	NA	200	79
Total	297	305	191	102

Figure 4.13: Comparison of water consumption between different estates[185]

---

[184] Randolph, B, Holloway, D, Pullen, S, and Troy, P, 'The Environmental Impact of Residential Development', 2006.
[185] Randolph, B, Holloway, D, Pullen, S, and Troy, P, 'The Environmental Impact of Residential Development', 2006.

The results of the investigation into the eleven estates revealed, firstly, that in all cases – except one (Glenhaven) – government-sponsored projects through Landcom all achieved lower water-consumption rates than the private sector developments they were compared with. This is due, in part, to the approach taken by government developer agencies to push for more innovation and sustainability in their projects; this includes measures to reduce water consumption through the use of more water-efficient appliances and the creation of landscapes that are less reliant on scheme water. The key finding that is relevant to this book, from a comparative sense, is that higher-density estates performed significantly better than lower-density estates, from the perspective of water consumption. This is understandable, since smaller lots, with more efficient designs, mixed in with apartment development, means less landscaping and, therefore, reduced water consumption.

Promoting a development form that reduces the consumption of scheme water is very important for the environment, since water is a fairly scarce commodity in Australia, with many capital cities now reliant on scheme water, which is manufactured through desalination plants. This shows that fresh water is in decline. Reducing water consumption is key to the future of Australia, as climate change is having an overall negative impact on Australia's fresh-water supply, so Australia needs to find ways of tackling this issue in a twofold approach: by reducing consumption and increasing the manufacturing of drinking water through desalination. This becomes even more important when you consider the increase in irrigation for food production. In the future, greater water resources will need to be diverted towards irrigation, rather than consumption for households.

When we turn our focus towards operational energy consumption (electricity), the results are similar; however, we do see some differences in consumption between estates (Figure 4.14).

One of the main distinctions between the estates in the study is the observation of the Glenhaven and West Pennant Hills estates, which, together, registered significantly higher energy consumption than the other estates. This is largely accounted for by the socio-economic differences between the estates, with Glenhaven and West Pennant Hills having a significantly higher median household income than other estates. This demonstrates the sensitivity between median household income and electricity consumption. However, setting these estates aside, Landcom's low-density estates performed better than private estates on energy consumption, and, once again, Landcom's high-density estates performed significantly better than low-density estates and other high-density estates in terms of energy consumption. Energy consumption in Landcom estates shows clearly that government initiatives to reduce

	Electricity Consumption Per Dwelling 2004 (kwh)	Electricity Consumption Per House 2004 (kwh)	Electricity Consumption Per Multi-Unit Dwelling 2004 (kwh)	Electricity Consumption Per Capita 2004 (kwh)
Low-Density Estates				
Late 1970s				
St Clair	7.708	7,708	NA	2,241
Cambridge Gardens	8,686	8,686	NA	2,757
Early 1980s				
St Andrews	7,523	7,522	NA	2,193
Raby	8,032	8,100	6,873	2,426
Early 1990s				
Glenhaven	13,061	13,062	NA	3,842
West Pennant Hills	11,848	11,907	10,438	3,309
Late 1990s				
Narrellan Vale	6,293	6,295	6,214	1,973
Harrington Park	6,900	6,900	NA	2,066
High-Density Estates				
Kings Bay	3,740	7,540	3,152	1,685
Abbotsford	8,724	NA	8,688	3,966
Cabarita	8,505	8,445	8,610	3,259
Liberty Grove	5,480	NA	5,392	2,030
Total	8,375	8,524	6,679	2,553

Figure 4.14: Electricity consumption – comparison between different estates[186]

energy consumption through the installation of photovoltaic cells, in particular, have had a significant impact in curbing energy consumption, when compared to private estates, which do not mandate such energy consumption measures.[187]

The investigation into embodied energy, or the energy spent to manufacture the materials that go into the construction process, takes into consideration a lifecycle estimate of the energy consumption in different dwelling configurations across the estates. The total embodied energy per dwelling, which is measured in gigajoules, was again highest in the higher-income estates, such as West Pennant Hills and Glenhaven, while the lowest embodied energy was measured in the high-density case study areas, particularly the Landcom estate of Kings Bay. The main findings relating to embodied

---

[186] Randolph, B, Holloway, D, Pullen, S, and Troy, P, *'The Environmental Impact of Residential Development',* 2006.
[187] Randolph, B, Holloway, D, Pullen, S, and Troy, P, *'The Environmental Impact of Residential Development',* 2006.

energy are that, with the exception of the Liberty Grove estate, high-density developments generally performed better than lower-density suburban areas in having a lower embodied energy.

The anomaly with Liberty Grove was that there was a high level of reinforced concrete used for basement parking throughout the development, more so than in the other comparable estates. Taking into consideration household size, higher-density development is not a predictor of embodied energy patterns. While the low-density developments of Glenhaven and West Pennant Hills still have the highest total embodied energy, largely due to the large size of the houses in these estates, the high-density areas of Carabita, Abbotsford and Liberty Grove have total embodied energy per capita values generally higher than the four oldest lower-density estates in the study, showing modern standards have not improved or reduced energy consumption. Once again, government projects have provided a better demonstration of sustainability, with the Kings Bay estate rating significantly lower for embodied energy than the other estates.[188]

	Electricity Consumption Per Dwelling 2004 (kwh)	Electricity Consumption Per House 2004 (kwh)
Low-Density estates		
Late 1970s		
St Clair	2,420.6	704
Cambridge Gardens	2,463.9	782
Early 1980s		
St Andrews	2,547.6	743
Raby	2,212.8	669
Early 1990s		
Glenhaven	4,421.9	1,301
West Pennant Hills	4,874.8	1,362
Late 1990s		
Narrellan Vale	3,027.7	949
Harrington Park	3,540.8	1,060
High-Density Estates		
Kings Bay	1,424.2	642
Abbotsford	1,762.4	801
Cabarita	2,337.1	895
Liberty Grove	2,984.9	1,106

Figure 4.15: Electricity consumption – embodied energy[189]

---

[188] Randolph, B, Holloway, D, Pullen, S, and Troy, P, *'The Environmental Impact of Residential Development'*, 2006.
[189] Randolph, B, Holloway, D, Pullen, S, and Troy, P, *'The Environmental Impact of Residential Development'*, 2006.

The final criterion examined in relation to environmental impacts included a complete review of annual carbon emissions across electricity, gas and embodied area consumption across the eleven estates. The findings below (Figure 4.16) demonstrate again that the highest carbon dioxide emissions in the case study area were recorded in the higher-socio-economic suburbs of Glenhaven and West Pennant Hills. Two of the higher-density case study areas had high carbon dioxide emissions, which were similar to most other lower-density suburban areas. Despite this, the high-density development of Kings Bay by Landcom had the lowest level of carbon dioxide emissions. Except for Glenhaven, all the Landcom developments had lower carbon dioxide levels, compared with other estates in the study area. Overall, the study identifies, once again, that higher-density development is generally more environmentally sustainable as a built form and highlights the importance for policymakers to consider more compact forms of development for the future, rather than relying on lower-density housing, where sustainability is concerned.[190]

	Annual CO_2-e Emissions Electricity	Annual CO_2-e Emissions Gas	Annual CO_2-e Emissions Embodied Energy	Annual CO_2-e Emissions Total (Per Dwelling)	Annual CO_2-e Emissions Total (Per Capita)
Low-Density Estates					
Late 1970s					
St Clair	25.4	1.9	3.1	30.4	8.8
Cambridge Gardens	28.6	1.8	3.1	33.5	10.6
Early 1980s					
St Andrews	24.8	2	3.3	30.1	8.8
Raby	26.4	2	2.8	31.2	9.4
Early 1990s					
Glenhaven	43	2.5	5.5	51	15
West Pennant Hills	39	2.4	5.6	47	13.1
Late 1990s					
Narrellan Vale	20.7	1.9	3.9	26.5	8.3
Harrington Park	22.7	2.2	4.6	29.5	8.8
High-Density Estates					
Kings Bay	12.3	1.6	1.7	15.6	7
Abbotsford	28.7	1.9	2.2	32.8	14.9
Cabarita	28	1.7	2.8	32.5	12.5
Liberty Grove	18	1.8	3.8	23.6	8.7

Figure 4.16: CO2 emissions by estate[191]

[190] Randolph, B, Holloway, D, Pullen, S, and Troy, P, 'The Environmental Impact of Residential Development', 2006.
[191] Randolph, B, Holloway, D, Pullen, S, and Troy, P, 'The Environmental Impact of Residential Development', 2006.

The study, taken as a collective, highlights the importance of examining the environmental footprint of different urban forms.

The Financial Cost of Urban Sprawl

One of the biggest shadows of suburban development in Australian cities is the growing financial cost burden of building suburbia, especially when compared to other forms of development in existing urban areas. To create suburbia, everything has to be built from scratch – this includes roads, servicing and a variety of community services. This is expensive and requires significant administration in planning and coordination, draining the resources of state government planning, state government servicing authorities and transport agencies, as well as local governments.

The cost of different urban forms of development is becoming an increasingly relevant topic, as federal, state and local governments are competing with an ever-widening scope of priorities resulting from a growing population and are faced with the dilemma on where limited financial resources should be employed to ensure maximum investment impact and optimisation.

The economic assessment of infrastructure costs associated with urban sprawl has been the subject of investigation by various state and territory bodies, as well as universities, which have attempted to understand the differences in infrastructure costs to consider the economic sustainability and real development costs associated with the two forms of urban development in Australia. This is very important for urban planning professionals who grapple with policy to encourage infill development in existing suburbs and to curb new development in suburban locations.

It is very important for me to make this point, and I want to be very clear: suburbia is subsidised by taxpayers across the metropolitan area. When you go to purchase a lot from a new estate created by a Stocklands (land developer), for example, the lot price you pay does not take into consideration all the costs associated with creating the new suburb. This may be a shock to some people, but the reality is that the cost you pay for a lot on the urban fringe only includes the cost associated with developing the lot itself and some of the estate's amenities, such as local parks and local roads. It does not include the costs associated with the construction of major distributor roads, freeways, public transport, wastewater treatment, community facilities and essential services (police, health, education and fire), to mention a few. All this is paid for by the taxpayer, who is subsidising the cost of suburbia. It is very different for redevelopment in existing urban areas, because most of this infrastructure exists already.

In existing urban areas, there are major benefits that infrastructure – such as main arterial roads; public transport; and amenities, such as shops, employment areas and parks – already exist. Therefore, when residential land in existing areas is redeveloped, there is no need to replicate the infrastructure mentioned, because it already exists. For redevelopment in existing areas to occur, there may need to be some service upgrades, such as electricity, telecommunications and water and sewerage, to cater for more intense development, but other infrastructure traditionally provided by government, such as education, main roads and public transport, are already established. This compares significantly with new suburban areas on the fringe, where all forms of infrastructure, such as transport, education, fire and emergency, etc., need to be established, as well as supporting development services, such as electricity, water, wastewater treatment, gas and telecommunications.

A study undertaken by Roman Trubka, Peter Newman and Darren Bilsborough in 2010 sheds light on the true cost of urban sprawl in Australian cities. The study examines two alternative approaches to urban development. The first includes the redevelopment of more traditional, walkable, transit-oriented development neighbourhoods that involves redevelopment to create more residential density and mixed-use development supported by transport options. The second form of urban development is defined as new development on the suburban fringe of our cities, which generally consists of low-density residential housing in what are commonly defined as car-dependent suburban areas with limited transport options and reduced walkable access to amenities and places of employment. These two urban forms are referred to as the 'infill urban development' and 'suburban development'.[192]

The research, which draws upon a number of historic studies, examines the economic costs associated with these two approaches to urban development: firstly by examining the planning costs associated with transportation and infrastructure requirements, such as services, gas, electricity and sewerage, and secondly by examining the cost of 'externalities' produced from the type of urban development, such as greenhouse gas emissions and activity-related health costs. As a base, the project study area includes a number of existing suburbs within ten kilometres of the Melbourne and Sydney CBD and compares this with new suburban developments located forty or more kilometres from the Melbourne and Sydney CBD.

A sample of inner-urban areas includes the local government areas of Port Phillip and the Yarra in Melbourne and Melbourne Council (CBD), and South Sydney and Leichhardt in Sydney. In respect to outer-suburban areas, the study includes the Yarra Ranges, Cardinia and Mornington Peninsula in Melbourne, and Penrith, Camden, Gosford and the Blue Mountains in Sydney. The basic parameters of the study are identified in the tables below, which the authors of the study have derived from a number of sources linked to transport, mobility and accessibility to services and amenities.[193]

---

[192] Trubka, R, Newman, P and Bilsborough, D, *'The Cost of Urban Sprawl – Infrastructure and Transportation'*, Environment Design Guide, April 2010.
[193] Trubka, R, Newman, P and Bilsborough, D, *'The Cost of Urban Sprawl – Infrastructure and Transportation'*, Environment Design Guide, April 2010.

Criteria	Inner-Urban Development	Suburban-Fringe Development
Daily per capita greenhouse gas emissions from transport (measured in CO_2-e)	0 to 4kg	8 up to 10kg
Distance to CBD	Less than 10km	More than 40km
Activity intensity (measured by population and jobs per hectare)	>35	<20
Transit Accessibility	More than 80% with >15min service	Less than 15% with >15min service

Figure 4.17: Study parameters – cost of inner and suburban development[194]

The study draws upon a number of previous bodies of work undertaken by sustainable transport professors Peter Newman and Jeff Kenworthy, who have pioneered studies on automobile dependency within Australian cities, in addition to using investigations into the economic cost of different urban forms identified in a study titled Future Perth, which was commissioned by the Western Australian Planning Commission in Perth in 2001. Future Perth identifies the economic cost difference between developments in inner, middle and fringe areas.[195]

The Future Perth study, which was formative for its time, reviewed information produced by twenty-two studies across a number of countries, including Australia, America and Canada, and collated the findings into three urban areas: inner, middle and outer. The countries selected were chosen because the urban forms in all three follow very similar suburban-based urban morphology. The compiling twenty-two reports the study reviewed spanned between 1972 and 2000, with costs adjusted to reflect 2007 prices for comparative purposes, and using Australian Bureau of Statistics data to ensure economic anomalies, such as the 1999 - 2007 'mining boom' in Perth, were removed and therefore did not skew the cost of labour and materials during that extraordinary period. The costs aggregated were then applied to the development scenarios identified in the study area, including the inner and outer-suburban locations in Melbourne and Sydney, and then averaged to come to a cost per suburb.[196] The study's findings are detailed below.

---

[194] Trubka, R, Newman, P and Bilsborough, D, 'The Cost of Urban Sprawl – Infrastructure and Transportation', Environment Design Guide, April 2010.
[195] Trubka, R, Newman, P and Bilsborough, D, 'The Cost of Urban Sprawl – Infrastructure and Transportation', Environment Design Guide, April 2010.
[196] Trubka, R, Newman, P and Bilsborough, D, 'The Cost of Urban Sprawl – Infrastructure and Transportation', Environment Design Guide, April 2010.

Infrastructure	Inner-Urban Areas	Outer-Suburban Areas
Roads	$5,086,562	$30,378,881
Water and sewerage	$14,747,616	$22,377,459
Telecommunications	$2,576,106	$3,711,851
Electricity	$4,082,117	$9,696,505
Gas	$0	$3,690,843
Fire and ambulance	$0	$302,509
Police	$0	$388,416
Municipal services	Not Reported	Not Reported
Education	$3,895,458	$33,147,274
Health	$20,114,867	$32,347,327
Total	**$50,502,726**	**$136,041,065**

Figure 4.18: Infrastructure costs – inner versus suburban development[197]

As can be seen from the table above, there is significantly greater cost associated with infrastructure in outer-suburban areas when compared with inner-urban areas. This is not unexpected, given that in existing suburban areas infill development, or redevelopment, only require upgrades to some infrastructure; in some cases, services such as police, fire and ambulance can be maintained under existing services and are, therefore, sufficient to cater for the change in development in existing areas. This compares more favourably than outer-suburban areas, where whole new infrastructure is required to cater for new communities. Accordingly, from an economic perspective, it is significantly more efficient and effective to encourage redevelopment of existing areas into more intense land use, drawing upon existing services and infrastructure, rather than requiring whole new infrastructure in new suburban areas.[198]

While the study makes an interesting comparison between inner and outer-urban development forms, in terms of infrastructure costs, it also examines the operating/maintenance costs associated with the infrastructure required to support the two different urban development forms. The costs also look at the monetary impacts of

---

[197] Trubka, R, Newman, P and Bilsborough, D, *'The Cost of Urban Sprawl – Infrastructure and Transportation'*, Environment Design Guide, April 2010.
[198] Trubka, R, Newman, P and Bilsborough, D, *'The Cost of Urban Sprawl – Infrastructure and Transportation'*, Environment Design Guide, April 2010.

externalities, such as pollution, injuries, property damage and noise pollution, associated with the two different forms of development. After taking all this into consideration, the costs were then aggregated across 1,000 dwellings in each urban development form, for comparative purposes. Once again, and perhaps with no surprise, the study found a significant cost bias associated with newer outer-suburban areas, when compared with inner-suburban areas.[199]

Cost Associated with 1,000 Dwellings	Inner-Urban Areas	Outer-Suburban Areas
Capital cost of car ownership	$2,990,802	$8,628,654
Fuel costs	$1,203,925	$3,255,349
Other operating car costs	$1,476,392	$4,259,675
Time costs (total) Private transport Public transport Walking and cycling	$6,158,348 $3,116,810 $3,041,538 $0	$8,210,448 $8,210,448 $0 $0
Road costs	$1,216,597	$3,508,806
Parking costs	$2,184,489	$7,709,869
Externalities (total) Fatalities Injuries Property damage Air pollution Noise pollution	$243,731 $73,368 $23,627 $38,549 $90,777 $17,409	$703,250 $211,693 $68,172 $111,228 $261,925 $50,232
Transit costs (capital and operating)	$3,136,540	$470,481
Total	**$18,610,824**	**$36,746,532**

Figure 4.19: Cost of maintaining inner- versus outer-suburban development[200]

---

[199] Trubka, R, Newman, P and Bilsborough, D, *'The Cost of Urban Sprawl – Infrastructure and Transportation'*, Environment Design Guide, April 2010.
[200] Trubka, R, Newman, P and Bilsborough, D, *'The Cost of Urban Sprawl – Infrastructure and Transportation'*, Environment Design Guide, April 2010.

In summary, new suburban areas are costly. They are nearly three times more expensive to set up than using existing urban areas and are nearly twice more expensive to operate on an ongoing basis. This represents a significant cost burden and a very inefficient form of development and is arguably a more destructive form of development when compared to redevelopment in existing urban areas. Putting on my economist's hat, if we were to internalise all the costs associated with producing a lot on the urban fringe – i.e., include all the other costs subsidised by taxpayers and then charge them to the person purchasing the lot on the fringe – suburban land would very quickly be significantly more expensive than inner-urban land.

To think of the numbers in a different way... if we were to build forty new suburbs on the fringes of Sydney or Melbourne, rather than building the equivalent housing in existing urban areas, the cost difference would be enormous – approximately $3.4 billion. That doesn't include the ongoing costs. These are the sorts of numbers we are talking about, and our cities are each planning within their growth boundaries for more than forty extra suburbs. If we developed within existing urban areas instead of spending money on maintaining new and unsustainable suburbs, the money saved could go towards essential things like better public transport, health and education – all of which contribute to a healthier, smarter and more sustainable society. Instead, billions of our tax dollars are poured into an unsustainable, environmentally damaging and, at some level, socially isolating suburban environments. It's nuts.

For the past fifty years in Australia, billions of dollars have been pouring into building a car-dependent suburban-growth model, which is costly, bad for our health and environmentally unsustainable. So, why do governments and taxpayers fit the bill for subsidising suburbia? Well, part of the answer is affordability. The government pours billions of taxpayer dollars to subsidies for suburbia because if it had to be funded by the land developer in full, they would pass this cost on to land buyers, which would double housing costs overnight. New suburban development is also a big business, and there are many players in the market, which have lobby groups that put their hooks into the government to ensure suburban development is supported, subsidised and continues indefinitely. I am certain most people don't know how much suburbia is being subsidised by taxes; if they did, they would think very differently about promoting new estates as 'good' places to live.

The truth is that the tide needs to turn on new suburban development, and, as I mentioned previously, while it won't completely stop, it needs to be significantly reduced, with more attention directed towards the redevelopment of more sustainable inner-suburban locations, where infrastructure exists and servicing costs are much lower.

The Growing Shadows 119

The Cost of Suburbia

Suburbia is subsidised by the taxpayer...

Update of existing infill areas versus new suburbs: $50m versus $136m

Figure 4.20: What's not included in the price of land in new suburbs? [201] [202]

---

[201] *'Suburban Melbourne and Freeways'*, Google earth, 2021.
[202] *'Picture of Public Transport, Police Station and Fire Station, hospital – Perth'*, courtesy Sergio Famiano 2021.

Vulnerability: Car Dependency and Peak Oil

Australian cities are car dependent, with approximately 80% of trips taken by private automobile in Australia.[203] This is significantly high, with the remaining 20% of trips accounted for through public transport (bus and train), walking and cycling.

Much has been written about car dependency in cities, which is a subject that has been pioneered by Australia's own Professor Peter Newman and Jeff Kenworthy in their book *Sustainability and Cities – Overcoming Automobile Dependence* and numerous books and articles thereafter.[204] Australian cities are particularly car dependent, with most cities expanding significantly following the Second World War, when transport planning shifted from public transport to the private automobile. As explained in Chapter 1, in cities such as Perth, influential transport planners, like Gordon Stephenson, travelled to the United States to observe the new wave in transport planning based around the car. This relatively new transport philosophy was imported to Australia, thus severing ties with traditional public transport planning.

The mass expansion of freeways that resulted from Stephenson's epiphany has created suburbs and facilitated urban sprawl based on the car as the primary method of transport. Today, Australian cities rank as some of the most car dependent in the world, with the graph below (Figure 4.21) showing Australian cities are tied with the United States.

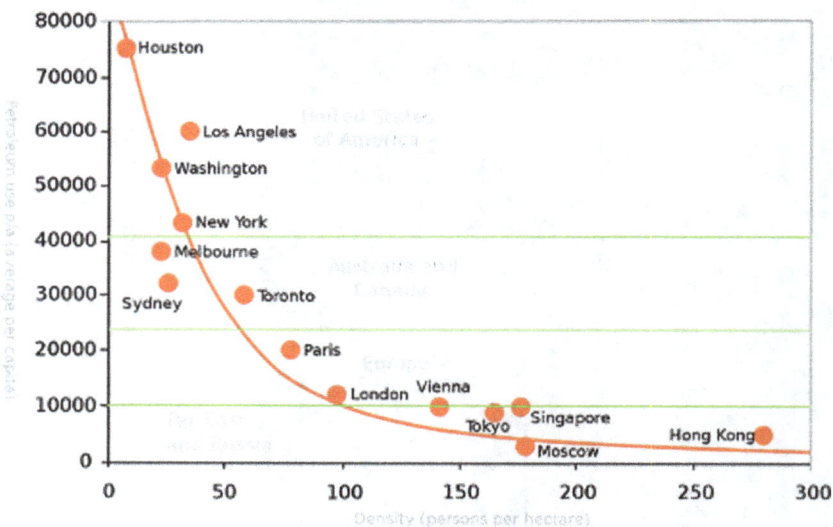

Figure 4.21: Car dependency worldwide[205]

---

[203] Dodson, J and Sipe, N, 'Unsettling Suburbia: New Landscape of Oil and Mortgage Vulnerability in Australian Cities', Griffith University, 2008.
[204] Newman, P, and Kenworthy, J, 'Sustainability and City's: Overcoming Automobile Dependence', Island Press, 1999.
[205] Newman, P, and Kenworthy, J, 'Sustainability and City's: Overcoming Automobile Dependence', Island Press, 1999.

As a whole, Australians are car addicted, but there is wide variation in automobile dependence, which is directly dependent on where you live. For instance, households in inner-city locations of Australia's major cities are less car dependent than outer-suburban locations, primarily because inner-city locations are based on a more walkable urban fabric. Accordingly, there is greater access to public transport, and neighbourhoods are based on a walkable catchment to amenities (shops, parks, etc.); therefore, walking and cycling often substitute the car for modes of travel. Because inner-city areas are also more compact, there is a tendency for car trips to be shorter, with more destinations being in closer proximity to where people live. As mentioned previously, inner-suburban areas are characterised as having more pedestrian-friendly infrastructures and are more abundant in amenities, which facilitate alternatives to car dependency.

The study by Domain mentioned previously illustrates this point. Outer suburbs, on the other hand, are based on an urban fabric centred around the automobile; this means land uses have deliberately been dispersed so people can only travel to them via car, thus reinforcing the notion of car dependency. Middle to outer suburbs make up the bulk of Australian cities, which accounts for why Australian cities register as some of the most car dependent in the world.

The underlying facilitator of Australia's car dependency has been the abundance and relatively easy access to cheap oil. Oil has been around for centuries and has been used for a variety of purposes, but it wasn't until the invention of the combustible engine in 1859 and its refinement into the common automobile that oil took on a more mainstream purpose.[206] Since then, the world has been mad on finding oil and has expanded its use across not only energy, but also into lubricants, plastics, pesticides and a myriad of synthetic materials used for a variety of household items. Such is the importance of oil that it has long been considered the cornerstone ingredient of the modern economy. If you don't agree, then perhaps being reminded of who the biggest corporations in the world are today will change your mind. In the top ten are five oil companies: Sinopec, China Natural Petroleum, Royal Dutch Shell, BP and Exxon Mobil. If you add Toyota and Volkswagen, which are primarily vehicle-producing companies, seven out of ten of the world's biggest companies are oil and car related. This is despite the rise of technological giants Amazon, Google, Apple and Microsoft over the last twenty years. The dominance of oil in the world economy is paramount, and countries like Australia rely heavily on its easy distribution and abundance.[207]

Lucky for Australians, oil has been abundant throughout the nineteenth and twentieth centuries, with world production expanding from approximately 100 million barrels annually, in 1900, to 33 billion barrels annually today.[208] But questions have

---

[206] Newman, P, and Kenworthy, J, *'Sustainability and City's: Overcoming Automobile Dependence'*, Island Press, 1999.
[207] *'Worlds Larges Companies'*, Global Finance, 2022.
[208] Heinberg, R, *'The Party's Over'*, New Society Publishers, 2005.

long been raised as to how sustainable this growth is, given an ever-growing global population and expanding global economies, particularly in the developing world, such as China and India, which is resulting in increasing demands for oil.

The American geophysicist King Hubbert published a theory in 1956 that examined the temporal evolution of oil production, which takes the shape of a bell curve. Oil production starts at zero and then rises to a peak, which can never be surpassed. Once peak production has been reached, production declines and prices go up until oil resources are depleted – or are too costly to have a widespread use. While his theory was largely ignored at the time, Hubbert predicted oil production in the United States would peak between 1965 and 1970, which attracted strong criticism, and even ridicule, from the oil industry. However, his assumption turned out to be correct, and oil production in the United States peaked in 1971.[209] Thus, the notion of 'peak oil' was born and highlights the frugality of oil and the problems that come with reliance on it in modern society.

There have been many predictions associated with the peaking of oil production, and there is an ever-growing list of countries that have reached peak oil, including significant oil-producing countries such as Venezuela (1970), Iran (1974), Nigeria (1979), Indonesia (1991), Norway (2000) and, more recently, Qatar (2007).[210] As a result, oil production is increasingly being concentrated in a few countries found in the Middle East, such as Saudi Arabia, Iran and Iraq, which are traditionally unstable economically and politically, leading to the potential for 'oil shocks'. This was experienced in the 1970s, when Arab member-states of the Organization of Petroleum Export Countries (OPEC) decided to quadruple – overnight – the price of oil to almost $12 a barrel by cutting global oil production and restricting exports to the United States, Japan and Western Europe. This was in retaliation for Western support of Israel against Egypt and Syria during the Yom Kippur War and in response to a persistent decline in the value of the US Dollar, which eroded the export earnings of OPEC countries.[211] The impact of this price shock subsequently had a destabilising effect on countries such as Australia and the United States, which are dependent on stable oil prices. Indeed, many countries, including Australia, suffered economic recessions during this period, driven by a spike in energy costs and the economic restructuring required as a result.

Similar oil shocks have occurred since, including an oil shock in 1979 that occurred as a result of a revolution in Iran, which had the impact of damaging the Iranian oil industry, causing output to be reduced and a rise in prices – which was made worse by the subsequent outbreak of war between Iran and Iraq in 1980.[212] The impact contributed to economic recessions in Western countries during the early 1980s, including Aus-

---

[209] Hubbert, M, *'Nuclear Energy and the Fossil Fuels'* Presented before the Spring Meeting of the Southern District Division of Production, American Petroleum Institute, Plaza Hotel, San Antonio, Texas, 1956.
[210] Andrews, S, and Udall, R, *'Oil Production by Country'* Oil and Gas Journal, June 2010.
[211] Heinberg, R, *'The Party's Over'*, New Society Publishers, 2005.
[212] Heinberg, R, *'The Party's Over'*, New Society Publishers, 2005.

tralia during 1981 to 1983. It was only due to efficiencies in car manufacturing and an industry resulting in less fuel consumption that the late 1970s' price shock was abated.

As if increasing in greater regularity, a further oil shock occurred during the 1991 Iraq War, following Saddam Hussein's invasion of Kuwait and the subsequent conflict, which disrupted oil production in these two countries, impacting the price of oil at the bowser significantly. In Australia, this was one of the factors that prolonged "the recession we had to have" in the early 1990s.[213] More recently, the war in Iraq and Afghanistan from 2003 and the rapid growth in demand by developing nations, such as China and India, has resulted in a similar price shock in oil during the 2000s, driving prices up as high as $144 per barrel of oil in 2008.[214] This, again, negatively affected economic growth in Western countries, in particular the United States, which suffered not only from rising energy costs during the mid-2000s, but also from the sub-prime mortgage crisis, which also spread to other countries, namely those in Europe. While not the only factor, the significant spike in oil prices in the mid-2000s played a role in one of the biggest global financial crises experienced since the Second World War – one of which we are still feeling the aftershocks of today.

Recently, we have had another oil shock: this time resulting from the Russian invasion of Ukraine in 2022. This has had the impact of disrupting gas and oil supplies around the globe, raising the price of a barrel of oil to nearly $120. This has pushed petrol prices up in Australia to record highs of $2.30 per litre. These shocks are only going to get worse as oil stocks start to deplete across the globe.

Obviously, car-dependent cities are particularly sensitive to oil-price shocks, which are occurring more frequently due to collusion or conflict, and this is set to only worsen as oil production globally begins to peak, resulting in more sustained higher prices over a longer period of time. People living in poorly designed suburban locations not only rely on importing everything, since they are remote from key service areas, agricultural areas and manufacturing, but are also often isolated geographically from their social contacts, their places of employment and areas where they conduct their shopping and recreation. People, therefore, must drive long distances for virtually everything they need. Such dependence has created a commuter culture, with the daily roundtrip commute taking on average an hour a day in Australia.

When I think of my own travel behaviour, I think this makes sense. I spend 1.5 hours a day just getting to and from work and spend most of my trips in the car, and I live in the middle suburbs of Perth. Taking on a new job, I used public transport for a while, but I found it challenging relying on infrequent public transport that pushed out my travel time to 2.5 hours per day. But I am one of the lucky ones, as I at least have access to public transport as a substitute for the car. For suburban locations, which are further out from the CBD and, therefore, more isolated and reliant solely

---

[213] Yerrigan, D, 'The Prize – The epic quest of oil, money and power', Paperback, 2009.
[214] Yerrigan, D, 'The Prize – The epic quest of oil, money and power', Paperback, 2009.

Figure 4.22: Energy wars – our addiction to oil

on the car for transport, the daily commute can be upwards of 1.5 to 2 hours, just to get to work and back home.

This dependence on the automobile leaves people living in suburban locations particularly sensitive to rises in transport costs, since driving a vehicle, and for longer periods, means the cost of fuel features more prominently in the household budget. What makes this reality worse is that people who live on the fringes of cities are also some of the most disadvantaged in the economy, which adds further pressure and sensitivity to the reality of the home in the suburbs and exacerbates this trend. People who live on the urban fringe also tend to have higher rates of car ownership, which increases transport expenses.

Where you live and vulnerability to oil prices aren't the only relationships affecting household budgets. Where you live is also likely to determine if you have a mortgage or not. As the premise of this book suggests, home ownership is strongly desired by Australians and is a major economic and lifestyle factor influencing all of us. A large portion of Australians still purchase their homes via a mortgage, and, because household income largely determines borrowing capacity, lower-income households often find their opportunities for home ownership in middle to outer suburbs, where house and land is generally more affordable. For instance, most first-home buyers more than likely find themselves purchasing a home on the outer fringes of Australian cities because of the initial affordability of the house and land, and constraint in lending. The reality is, though, that the initial affordability found in the purchase price of the house and land is offset by the indirect costs associated with the location on the fringe – mainly with transport costs being a main factor, with residents in outer-suburban areas more likely to be travelling longer distances by car to destinations. People in these areas also tend to find themselves more time poor, which has costs associated with stress, mental health and overall health and wellbeing.

The predicament of people living in the middle to outer-suburban areas of Australian cities, therefore, leaves them more exposed than their inner-city cousins to changes in transport costs and mortgage-servicing levels over time. In a measure of how much a household would be impacted by fluctuations in fuel prices, inflation and interest rates for mortgages, a ground-breaking study undertaken by Jago Dodson and Neil Sipe in 2006 and 2008 examined the sensitivity between inflation, mortgage servicing and fuel prices on the household budgets of Australians in all major capital cities. In what became aptly known as the VAMPIRE index (Vulnerability Assessment for Mortgage, Petrol and Inflation Risks and Expenditure), the study focused on four key variables: car dependency (proportion of people working who undertook a journey to work and proportion of households with two or more vehicles); income levels (median-weekly household income); and mortgages (proportion of homes being purchased through a mortgage or similar scheme). The car dependency variables indicate the extent of car dependence for travel and, thus, the household's level of investment in travelling costs. When combined, these factors provide an insight into the extent

126 The New Australian Dream

households are exposed to rising costs for transport. The mortgage variable represents the extent of mortgage tenure and, accordingly, exposure to interest rate rises. The income variable indicates the financial capacity for households to absorb changes to mortgage and fuel level rises.[215]

When combined and examined across the Australian cities of Brisbane, Sydney, Melbourne, Adelaide and Perth, the study ranked suburbs from those with a minimal vulnerability to changes in fuel prices and mortgage servicing to those suburbs that were highly vulnerable to cost changes. The results for Perth and Melbourne are detailed below (Figures 4.23 and 4.24) and speak for themselves.

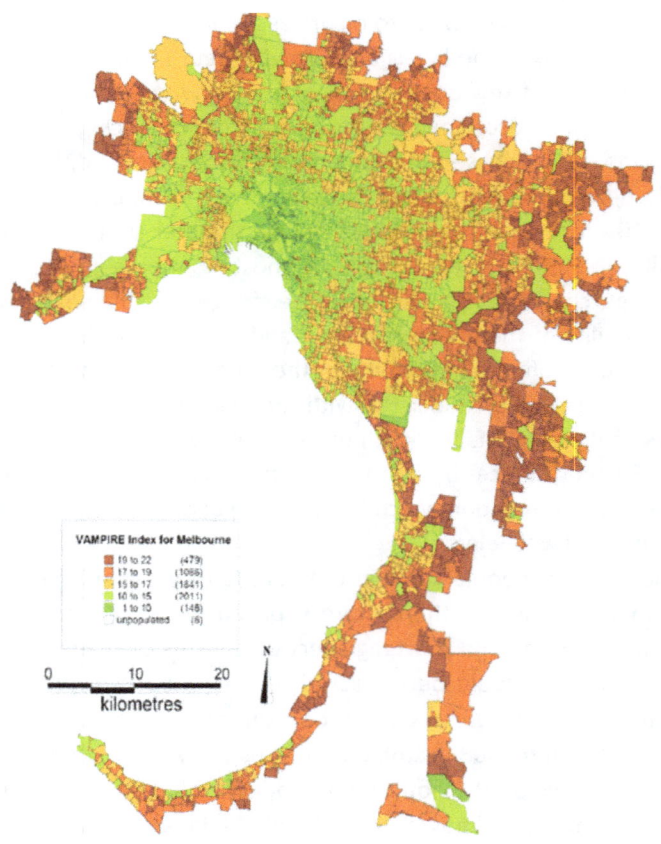

Figure 4.23: Housing debt and oil vulnerability for Melbourne [216]

---

[215] Dobson, J, Sipe, N, 'Shocking the Suburbs: Urban Location, Housing Debt and Oil Vulnerability in the Australian City', 2008.
[216] Dobson, J, Sipe, N, 'Shocking the Suburbs: Urban Location, Housing Debt and Oil Vulnerability in the Australian City', 2008.

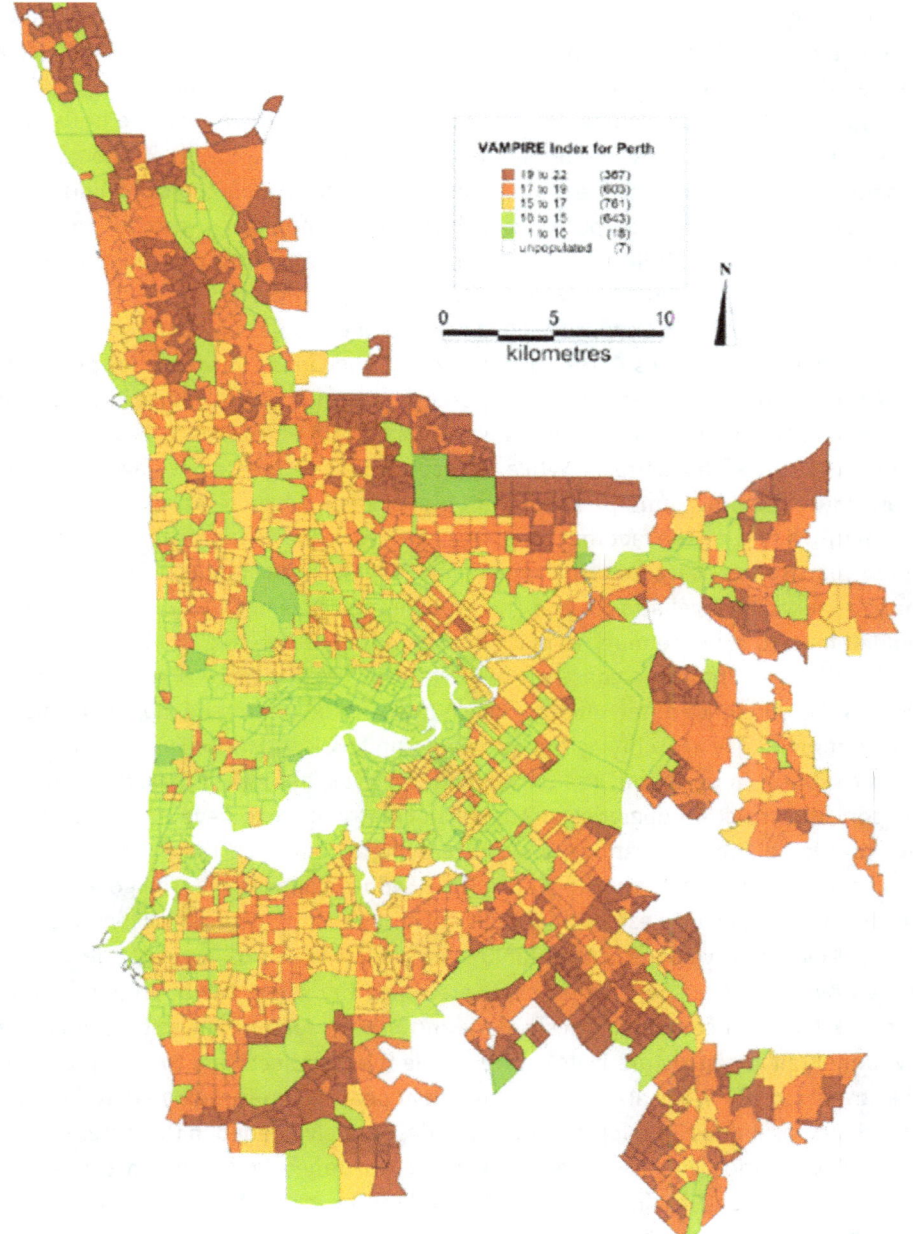

Figure 4.24: Housing debt and oil vulnerability for Perth (by location)[217]

---

[217] Dobson, J, Sipe, N, *'Shocking the Suburbs: Urban Location, Housing Debt and Oil Vulnerability in the Australian City'*, 2008.

The study showed fairly consistent results, with higher and lower vulnerabilities concentrated in different sections of Australian cities. Despite there being some local variation to this trend, higher vulnerability tended to be found in the middle to outer-suburban locations, where cheaper housing attracts lower-income households and where transport systems are highly automobile dependent. By comparison, households located within the inner sanctum of our cities typically had higher incomes, greater access to public transport, lower mortgage spread and lower reliance on the automobile for travel. Accordingly, changes to mortgage rates and fuel prices placed them in a less vulnerable position financially.

The household 'stress' experienced in Australian cities has a geographic and socio-economic bias to the outer suburbs, and this stress is becoming an increasing problem as fluctuations in fuel and increasing mortgage levels impact household budgets. A growing trend in household foreclosures in Australia suggests both of these factors are beginning to impact Australian households. While, in recent times, interest rates have dropped to historic lows, relieving some pressure from fuel prices – which remain stubbornly high at the petrol bowser – the fact that mortgage levels have increased significantly over the last ten years serves as a counterbalance to any relief in interest rates. With the average mortgage servicing level at 3.5% and the average mortgage at $618,729, interest rates wouldn't have to increase much to place households at severe risk.

What is clear about the construct of Australians cities is there is an inherit vulnerability to the middle to outer suburbs, which needs to be addressed. So, what role can the government play in rectifying this imbalance and assisting those living in the middle to outer suburbs in becoming less car dependent? Well, in recent times, the significant transport infrastructure upgrades in Australian cities appear to have been occurring in inner to middle suburb locations, which is serving to reinforce the advantages these areas have over outer-suburban locations. Take Sydney, for example. The government is investing over $6 billion in establishing light-rail infrastructure over a 12-kilometre route, which will largely service the central suburbs of Sydney – suburbs, arguably, already well serviced by public transport. Other cities are doing the same. Melbourne is spending up to $11 billion in combined government and private sector expenditure in creating new tunnel-rail infrastructure in its centre. While these projects add to the efficiency of public transport use in the areas they service, it appears counterintuitive to reducing car dependency, as it does little for infrastructure desperately needed in the outer suburbs.

Of all the cities, Perth – one of the most car-dependent cities in the world – is bucking this trend by investing over $4 billion in its METRONET project, which proposes to expand the heavy rail network into outer-suburban locations, such as Byford and Ellenbrook. The project aims to reduce car dependency and, therefore, vulnerability to oil shock for these suburbs. Initiatives such as METRONET need to become more of a feature of investment by government and the private sector in our capital cities if we are to tackle car dependency head on and reduce the pressure of oil vulnerability on the outer suburbs and the most vulnerable Australians in the mortgage belt. More will be discussed on this point later in this book.

5

THE CHANGING FOUNDATIONS OF THE AUSTRALIAN DREAM

As we saw in the last chapter, there are significant storm clouds brewing on the horizon for the Australian Dream. Rising debt and overworked Australians aren't the only issues confronting those who take the leap into home ownership. The growing shadows of poor public health, obesity, damage to the environment and peak oil all have links to the current form of the Australian Dream, which seems fixated on large homes on medium-to-large-sized blocks of land. Although we are seeing signs that this is changing, with some cities recording growth in smaller blocks and apartments, the majority of Australians are still calling the suburbs home. This raises the question: what is the future of the Australian Dream? Do the current conditions that have kept the Australian Dream stable over the last seventy-odd years remain the same, or are the fundamentals changing, and will this change the shape and form of the Australian Dream? What we will see in this chapter is that the conditions that have supported the current housing choice in Australia are beginning to change, and this will have long-term consequences for the current form of the Australian Dream.

As Safe as Bricks and Mortar

Everybody has heard the term 'as safe as bricks and mortar'. This is common in the Australian vernacular, as it refers to our trust in the stability of housing, not only as a 'real' asset that you can touch and feel, but as a reliable investment, which, in general terms, can always be trusted to provide positive and stable monetary gains in value over time. Real Estate agents will always refer to this phrase, using it as an attractive marketing ploy to engage the imagination of the Australian population when one considers where to put their hard-earned money. Because of this, we have come to believe property is more trustworthy than other means of investment. Is this true for the future though?

For most wage-earning Australians, there are three primary ways to invest money. The first is with the bank and financial institutions, earning interest. The second is through the various share and bond market opportunities. The third is through investment in real estate, whether it be purchasing your own home to live in, an investment property to rent or commercial property to support a business. For the better part of the last 100 years, real estate and interest have been the primary investment tools for most people, with shares really only becoming a mainstream investment tool for the masses since the onset of financial deregulation in Australia during the 1980s and the creation of compulsory superannuation.

The differences between these investment tools vary, with the level of the individual risk being the key driver of consumer choice. Shares and bond markets are traditionally risky and can fluctuate widely over short periods of time. Take, for example, the recent onset of the COVID-19 pandemic and the impact it has had on local and international share markets. In the space of two weeks, in March 2020, the All Ordinaries Index – one of the key market indicators for the Australian stock market – lost over 30% of its value. In the weeks that followed the outbreak, daily gains and losses were recorded in the 2 to 5% bracket, which shows just how volatile the share markets can be to external shocks. You can literally have $100,000 at the beginning of the week and finish up with $70,000 by the week's end.

On the other hand, however, the interest earned from having deposits in a bank and real estate have long been held as stable and trustworthy investments, hence the saying 'as safe as bricks and mortar'. These investments are generally not subject to the same wild short-term fluctuations experienced in the share market. This seems right, doesn't it? After all, everybody has to live somewhere, whether it be your own house or a rented place, we all need a roof over our heads. Housing, or 'shelter' if we consider it in its most basic form, appears as one of the core drivers of human survival, if you believe the American psychologist Abraham Maslow and his 'hierarchy of needs'. The need for shelter ranks up there with food and clothing as being essential to human survival. It is considered a necessity not a nice-to-have, which makes it a very attractive investment indeed. But is property today as safe as bricks and mortar from an investment perspective? Recent events in the Australian real estate market and globally would challenge this dictum.

Over the last thirty years, the Australian real estate market has been confronted by two major shocks that have impacted real estate prices. During the 1980s – certainly from 1982 onwards – economic growth, fuelled by population growth and the deregulation of the financial markets in the Hawke–Keating era, generated massive growth in the housing market, mostly in the form of suburbia, with house and land being the primary form of urban development across most capital cities, except

Sydney, which also enjoyed growth in the apartment market. The shock that brought this to a crashing end was a combination of the 1987 stock market crash and the exacerbation of interest rate pressures, in the "recession we had to have", which was enacted under Paul Keating's stewardship as treasurer of the national economy. During this period, we saw real estate prices spiralling out of control along with Australia's foreign current account deficit.[218] To put the brakes on the runaway current account deficits and the hot real estate market, Keating instituted a severe recession, prompted by the Reserve Bank of Australia who increased interest rates to the all-time highs of 18% and 19%.[219]

While debt levels at the time— about 3 to 1 (i.e., mortgage levels back then were equivalent to three years of gross wages) — were significantly different from those today, when considered as a ratio of debt-to-income levels, i.e., the high interest rates cut deep into households and put the brakes on the national economy, bringing the attractiveness to invest in the real estate market to an abrupt end. The result saw housing prices go backwards for a time but not severely, and, as interest rates began to ease in the early 1990s, real estate began to make a slow recovery, with small single digit growth annually. This shock to the system, albeit at the time challenging, did show the resilience of the property market to overcome the initial impact of monetary policy, with price recovery brought on by healthy population growth, the easing of interest rates and the relative affordability of housing — with the ratio of mortgage-to-income levels being relatively stable at 3 to 1. What happened in the 1990s, following the shock of the late 1980s, was slow growth in housing prices, but growth, nonetheless, which supports the safe as bricks and mortar notion.

But, from the late 1990s and well into the 2000s, something happened in Australia and across the globe that changed all this and created a unique property boom. On the other side of the globe, the deregulation of the financial industry in America, beginning with the Clinton administration's repealing of the *Glass–Steagall Act* over several tranches during the late 1990s, resulted in finance and access to money changing forever.[220] Enacted during the Great Depression to regulate the banking industry by dividing banking into two distinct industries — savings and loans, and investment banking — the *Glass–Steagall Act* ensured the United States did not have a repeat of the 1920s, where large commercial banks were engaging in risky investments to bolster their bottom lines.[221] This Act, which stood in place for over sixty years, resulted in a relatively stable financial system, which, because of regulatory checks and balances, has averted a repeat of the financial shocks experienced during the Great Depression era. With the repealing of this Act in the late 1990s, however, this all changed.

---

[218] Day, D, *'Paul Keating: The Biography'*. Fourth Estate, 2015.
[219] Day, D, *'Paul Keating: The Biography'*. Fourth Estate, 2015.
[220] Day, B, *'Paul Keating: The Biography'*. Fourth Estate, 2015.
[221] "Banking Act of 1933 (Glass-Steagall), Federal Reserve History", www.federalreservehistory.org, 2021.

The end of the Glass–Steagall era saw the mass deregulation of the world's biggest financial market, which resulted in unprecedented investment in the stock market and real estate industry by commercial banks. This had a global effect of increasing liquidity and access to money via cheap loans, which, at one point, allowed those from all walks of life in American society to access a loan for a house, even if they did not have a stable job or income. This was articulated beautifully in the Hollywood film *The Big Short*. The relaxing of lending checks and balances meant that, in the film, a pole dancer on casual wages was allowed to gain access to loan funds to support investment in five houses, with a minimum deposit – something that was unheard of in the decades prior. This widespread expansion of investment from the top to the lowest common denominator resulted in a massive expansion in investment in countries like the United States, and this had a knock-on effect globally. This involved financial institutions giving loans to people with low earning capacities and poor credit histories for 'sub-prime' mortgage bonds for initially low interest, followed by a reset into high interest rates after a few years.[222]

China, which was already developing rapidly during the 1990s and fast becoming the industrial workshop for the globe, enjoyed a massive stimulus in development as a result in the expansion of American-sponsored investment. This came in the form of mass demand for Chinese products and consumer goods. With much of the United States' manufacturing shifting to China in the 1980s, the unprecedented wealth and demand for consumer goods in the United States, due to monetary expansion, made China a hotbed for manufacturing, as it worked day and night to keep up with American and global demand. This, combined with the Chinese Government's own internal expansion policies to lift hundreds of millions of people from poverty to the middle class, saw China – the world's most populous nation – experience the greatest sustained economic expansion in human history.[223]

The extent of this expansion cannot be underestimated. The period between the 1990s and early 2000s witnessed China's economic growth expand yearly by 8 to 10% in GDP, and this resulted in the massive expansion of all major cities in China, with the equivalent of a new city being built every month, in what can only be termed as 'infrastructure expansion on steroids'. When the world's most populous nation expands at this rate, it has global implications.

Australia benefited from this expansion in three primary ways. Firstly, through the expansion in the demand for Australian raw materials, such as iron ore, copper, zinc and petroleum, to support the mass demand for steel, electronics and manufacturing in China. Secondly, through education: with more and more Chinese families seeking to educate themselves out of poverty, thousands flocked to Australian universities as a result. Thirdly, in the production and export of food

---

[222] Duca, J, *"Subprime Mortgage Crisis"*. Federal Reserve History, 2014.
[223] Naughton, B, *'The Chinese economy: transitions and growth'*. Cambridge, 2007.

to support China's insatiable demand, as more and more Chinese people lifted themselves out of poverty and into the middle class, which brought with it a demand for wine, milk, wheat and other staple commodities. During this period, Australian mining companies and universities suddenly became global household names. BHP and Rio Tinto, for example, emerged as titans in the mining world, with Australian universities entering into the global top 100 list for the first time. The knock-on effect would have a generational impact on Australia.

In the 2000s, this led to a once-in-a-generation stimulus in Australia's three primary industries: mining, education and farming, which created masses of jobs, population growth and wealth in Australia. Thousands flocked from across the globe, primarily from the UK, Italy, New Zealand, China and Malaysia, to seek a new life in Australia and take advantage of the unprecedented expansion of jobs in Australia's three primary industries. The only economic blip during this period was the twin towers disaster in the United States, which caused a ruffle in the share market and impacted, albeit only slightly, the United States and global economies. This event, however, prompted the US to respond by further deregulating its financial industry by introducing economic stimulus through lower interest rates and fiscal injections of billions of dollars into infrastructure and housing, which ended up expanding the scope of the boom that was already in motion as a result of the removal of the *Glass–Steagall Act*.

The downside – or upside, depending on your age – of this unprecedented growth period in Australia was that the conditions were set for a massive property boom, the likes of which Australia had never seen before, nor likely will ever see again. The perfect storm was set. Through a combination of relatively low interest rates (in the early 2000s it was around 6 to 7%); a commodity boom, which saw a massive expansion in mining infrastructure – particularly in states such as Western Australia and Queensland; and a prolonged economic boom in China, we witnessed a massive expansion in the Australian economy. The China boom, in particular, led to a massive demand for commodities along with demand for education and food, which saw populations across Australia grow to unprecedented levels as everyone wanted to get in on the job boom occurring. In Melbourne alone, the population grew to 150,000 people annually in 2017, and smaller cities, such as Perth, expanded by 50,000 to 60,000 people annually.[224] This was equivalent to literally two and a half times the normal growth annually. This collectively saw a massive boom in the housing industry, with record new housing stats reached in most states. Perth, for example, witnessed a growth rate of 26,000 new dwellings per annum in 2014–15 – up from a usual 16–18,000 new dwellings per annum.[225] This massive increase put significant strain on cities and the administration

---

[224] *'Regional Population Growth'*, Australian Cities, ABS, 2014–15.
[225] Flat out: Perth tradies in hot demand as building numbers rise, 2014 https://www.watoday.com.au/national/western-australia/flat-out-perth-tradies-in-hot-demand-as-building-numbers-rise-20141017-117v0y.html.

in general, which had to reorganise and geared up to deliver greater quantities of housing and infrastructure to keep up with demand.

Despite the reengineering of government agencies and the private sector, this explosion in the construction of new infrastructure and housing could not keep up with demand, and real estate prices exploded as a result. The graph below (Figure 5.1) shows that many state capitals experienced double-digit growth annually during the 2000s through to the early years of the next decade. Perth, for example, experienced a median house price increase from $160,000 in 2000 to $470,000 by 2008. Melbourne experienced a similar growth in median house prices, growing from $180,000 in 2000 to $390,000 in 2008.[226]

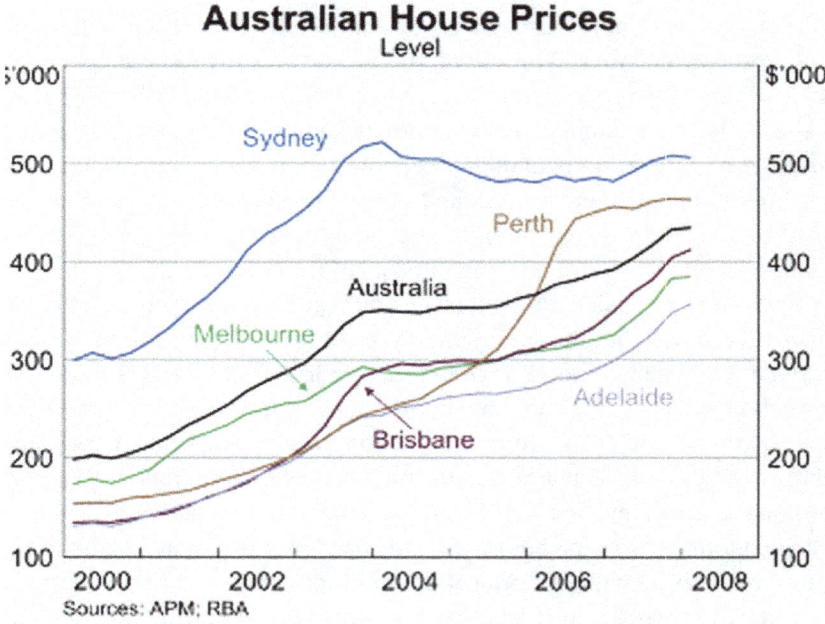

Figure 5.1: Australian house prices, 2000 to 2008[227]

What makes this boom unique is that, while wages increased with the boom – due to shortages in labour across all industries, wage growth still failed to keep pace with housing prices. The difference between the two was significant. This has occurred to the point now that, in most capital cities, the average price of real estate is many times the yearly wage of the average employee. While, during the 1980s, it was a ratio of around 3 to 1, this ratio exploded to 8 to 1 – meaning the average

---

[226] 'Australian House Price Growth 2000-2008', RBA, 2008.
[227] 'Australian House Price Growth 2000-2008', RBA, 2008.

price of a home in most capital cities is equivalent to eight years of the average gross wage. This changes the dynamic dramatically, since mortgages represent the biggest household expense.

The growth in housing prices has already been discussed at the beginning of this book and is very concerning when we think about property market fundamentals. It is concerning, because house prices that outstrip income levels cannot be sustained over time. There simply isn't the money available in the average household budget to continue paying exceedingly high mortgages in addition to other expenses, such as education, food and clothing, which typically constitute the household budget. This is why we are seeing, perhaps for the first time in our history, the term 'mortgage stress' (discussed previously) in households. The added tragedy of this set of circumstances is that the fundamentals that underpin the boom in housing prices don't last forever, and this can have a significant impact on households who bought during the price boom. The mining boom, for example, which commenced around 1999 and created thousands of new jobs, eventually came to an end in 2015. Now that the 'boom is over' and mining companies have moved from constructing infrastructure to production, the demand for jobs has dropped off, and, in many industries, it has gone backwards, which reverses pressure on incomes and employment growth.

This has been most significant in Western Australia, which is dependent on mining, agriculture and housing development to power its economy. Since the end of the mining boom in 2015, jobs in Western Australia have been drying up, and this has had a knock-on effect in reducing immigration to and population growth in the state, which has dropped from its highs of 60,000 annually in 2014/15, to 20,000 in 2020/21.[228] This 'slowing' has impacted all industries, in particular the construction industry, which at one point, was geared up to build 26,000 new dwellings a year and has now crashed to a new reality of 14,000 dwellings per year in 2020.[229] You can imagine in this industry alone the drop-off in demand for project managers and tradies.

The new economic reality in Western Australia resulting from the end of the mining boom has brought a crash to the housing market, as demand for new and existing housing has severely dropped off. You might think this is natural and has occurred before, but this boom is different, and the answer lies in the levels of debt carried by households. Aside from government stimulus, which supported the property market during the COVID-19 pandemic, the last few years in Western Australia have witnessed the 'big decline' in house prices. The drop in employment, prompted by a decline in economic activity, has released pressure off housing, and this has resulted in the deflation of housing prices. The other effect of this new economic reality is that the drop in demand has seen a massive drop in wage growth

---

[228] 'Regional Population Growth Australia', ABS, 2014–15.
[229] 'Number of new home building starts in Australia from financial years 2015 to 2019', Statista, 2019.

to the point it has flatlined. This is a worrying picture, because households being heavily geared with high debt and declining house prices combined with a flatline in wages puts households under severe economic stress. In many instances, property owners are confronted for the first time with the notion of negative equity – they owe more on their house than what it is worth. This is an escalating trend.

Remember, we have already discussed trends since the 1960s, where the typical household had one bread winner. This one income at the time could sustain the mortgage and household expenditure, and people lived comfortably because household incomes as a ratio to house prices were at a more sustainable level (i.e., a ratio of 2 to 1). But, as the 1970s turned into the 1980s and real wage growth began to lag behind house prices, we started to see a widening of the ratio and the growing necessity for two parents to work: one full-time and the other part-time to sustain the mortgage and household expenditure.

Since the 1990s/2000s boom, we have seen most households having two parents or couples without children who work full-time, because house prices have far outstripped wage growth, and the ratio of income to house prices has grown to well above 8 to 1 (on average). So, what does this mean? Well, it means that, for house prices to be sustained, the gap between house prices and income would have to narrow, preferably with wages outstripping house-price growth. For this to occur in the current climate, most workers would need to get a second job. This scenario is unlikely, not to mention unsustainable. Instead, we are experiencing a situation where job security is in question and wage growth has flatlined. Without wage growth and a buoyant economy, this only means one thing: asset prices will begin falling to a more realistic level. This is already happening, and Perth is the canary in the coalmine on housing prices, as the Western Australian economy and housing market have peaked before those of the other states.

In Perth, which has largely been in recession since 2015, property prices have been in steep decline. After having the boom of all booms, which saw the average property price rise from $160,000 in 1999 to $585,000 in 2014, there has been a sustained gradual decline as the local economy grapples with the unravelling of the once-in-a-generation mining boom. Population growth in the city was once sitting at around 60,000 people per annum and is now hovering around 20,000 – the slowest growth Perth has seen in decades. We are in 2022 now, and with population growth in Perth at a halt, due to COVID-19, property prices have risen slightly, only due to government stimulus. The average price for a home in Perth is now sitting at around $598,000, which is only slightly above 2014 prices.[230] For the first time in a long time, many households face the prospect of negative equity when the stimulus ends and interest rates rise. People in this predicament live in fear that they need to maintain

---

[230] *'Medium House Prices in Metropolitan Perth'*, Landgate, April 2022.

their increasingly unstable jobs just to meet the mortgage so they can avoid a default on their loan. Needless to say, these are stressful times to be living in Perth, but Western Australia isn't the only state confronted with this situation.

In Melbourne and Sydney, the stakes are much higher, since wage growth has also flatlined, but their real estate markets are much more inflated than Perth's market. In 2022, the median house prices for properties in Melbourne and Sydney are $1,050,000 and $1,500,000, respectively.[231] With the average wage sitting around $90,000, the ratio of income to house prices is a whopping 11.8 to 1 in Sydney and 9.7 to 1 in Melbourne.[232] These two markets have been propped up by significant foreign investment in real estate, mainly from China, and significant population growth, which I have already mentioned. The onset of COVID-19 in early 2020, however, has seen the unemployment rate double, with most casuals joining the unemployment queue, and population growth coming to a halt. The perfect storm is in place.

When we compare ourselves internationally, Australian cities are now up there as being some of the most expensive in the world. When we look at the top twenty-three most expensive cities in the world, five of them are Australian cities. It is no surprise that Sydney is ranked third in the world, with an income-to-household cost-ratio of 11.8 to 1.[233] Only Hong Kong and Vancouver are more expensive. This leaves Australian cities highly geared and highly exposed to financial fluctuations.

With wage growth having flatlined, properties enduring mortgage stress, and population growth and investment grinding to a halt, the real estate market is about to enter a very tough period, with property prices expected to drop by 10–15%. This would place unprecedented numbers of households in negative equity territory and could make the Perth property bust look like a scratch rather than an amputation. This is why the government's response to COVID-19 has been swift to bolster incomes for people who have lost work and for businesses forced to shut down. The government fears the deflationary impacts on the real estate market and what this would entail, especially if we start to see mass bankruptcies and foreclosures on loans. It could be Australia's Global Financial Crisis moment.

So, is property going to show its resilience as it has done before when faced with similar crises and start the slow climb upwards? Not likely. We have seen price increases, due to COVID-19, but, once this is over, we will likely see property prices decline. Why? For the alternative to happen, wages would need to increase, and this hasn't occurred in Australia for some time and is even less likely due to the COVID-19 crisis. For markets such as Perth, which has already suffered a downturn,

---

[231] *'Medium House prices Sydney and Melbourne'*, ABC, December 2021.
[232] *'Medium Income Earnings Australia'*, ABS, February 2022.
[233] *'House prices to income ratio – internationally'*, Australia Financial Review, 2021

any grassroots potential for growth in house prices after a five-year funk has been completely snuffed out by the pandemic, which has brought supply shocks to the local and national economies.

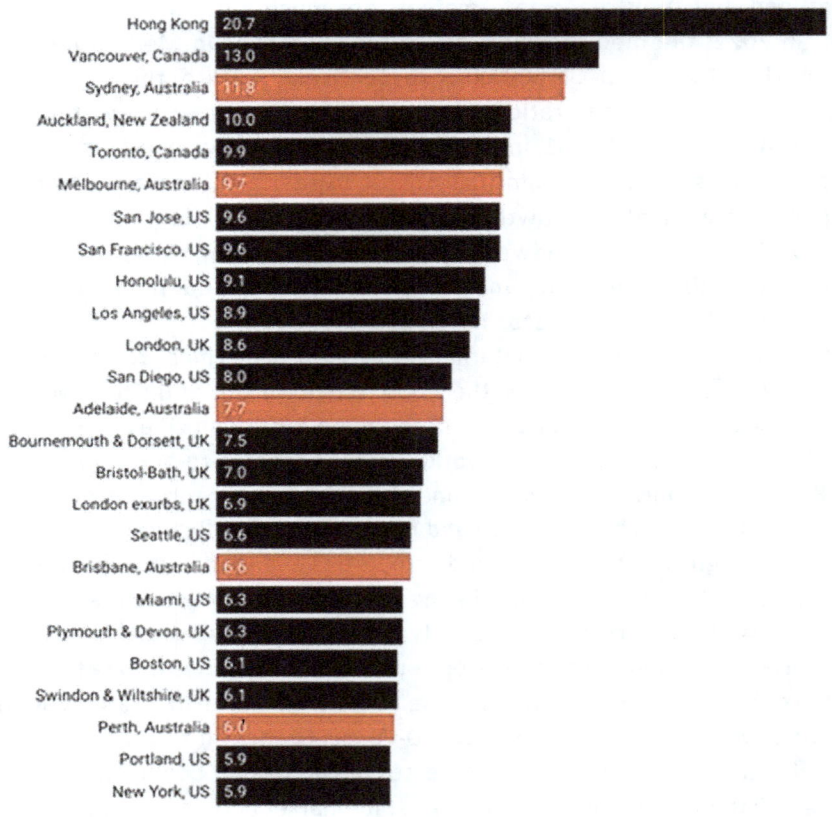

Figure 5.2: Median house price to income ratio[234]

As a result of this, property prices are expected to fall post COVID-19, and there is no reason to suggest this trend will be arrested, unless there is a massive government-debt-fuelled infrastructure boom, which follows fiscal messages by state and federal governments to stimulate the economy due to the COVID-19 disruption. These things generally take time, though, with shovel-ready infrastructure projects still requiring six-to-twelve-month lead-in times before construction commences. The effects also seem to be temporary, as we would soon come back to the same situation we are in now when the boom is over and wage growth flatlines.

---

[234] *'House prices to income ratio – internationally'*, Australia Financial Review, 2021.

So, what of the term 'as safe as bricks and mortar'? I am not so sure this is true anymore, as the fundamentals that underpin property price growth over the last 100 years have changed. Flatlined wages and declining housing affordability means we are maxed out. There is no more supply-side opportunity that can sustain property price growth into the future. Price growth over the last fifty years was sustained by the growth from one to two income earners per family. This has now reached its peak effect, with the only stimuli available being for people to get a second job or for wages to rise at a rate that exceeds house price growth so that there is a catch-up period and the income to property price ratio narrows, say from 10:1 to 7:1.

Neither scenario is likely, so, as a result, property prices will have to drop as a countermeasure. This process is likely to be slow, as governments, in tune with the impacts of deflation, throw everything they have to try and reduce deflation. This will see property prices slowly decline over time rather than rapidly decline, with the impact of COVID-19 being the exception. So, housing affordability is one nail in the coffin. Are there others? We will see.

Demographic Time Bomb

The housing affordability question and its impact on the ability for households to sustain the burden of paying high mortgages is a significant nail in the coffin for the safe as bricks and mortar notion, but it's not the only factor that may spell out its end. The demographic composition of Australia is also a fundamental element of the Australian Dream and change has been in the winds for some time now. Since the 1950s and 1960s, where most households were dominated by family groups, in more recent times the population has been ageing, and there is a greater number of households that feature only singles or couples without children. You may not think it, but the subtle change from a relatively young population in the 1970s, where the average age in Australia was 27.4 years old, to a more aged population, with an average age of 37.9 years of age in 2020, is having a profound impact on the property market dynamics, which will significantly influence the shape and form of the Australian Dream in the years to come.[235] This is because different age cohorts demand different housing, and, with an ageing population, this will affect the housing market on a seismic level.

The age group that offers the biggest potential to purchase property is between the ages of twenty-five and forty-five years, and then the sixty-to-seventy-year age bracket. In these population ranges, we find people buying their first homes (i.e., between twenty-five and thirty years) and second home buyers (between thirty and forty-five years), with the latter upsizing due to better financial circumstances and/or a growing family. The third age group, from sixty to seventy years, are the downsizers, moving from the family home to the smaller unit or apartment dwelling as the

---

[235] 'Australian Population Average', ABS, February 2020.

children move out to become renters or first-home buyers. These age groups have the biggest impact on the shape and form of the Australian Dream, because it is these cohorts who drive the shape and form of the housing market.

The baby boom that occurred post the Second World War, between 1945 and 1965, produced the biggest cohort ever in Australian history. During this period, approximately 5.5 million Australians were born or arrived in Australia as immigrants.[236] This period witnessed a massive explosion in what we know as the baby boomer cohort, which has dominated the housing market ever since. When this cohort matured to the ages of twenty and thirty years, between 1966 to 1995, and left home, they formed predominately three-to-five-person households, as most baby boomers followed the traditional family model of leaving their childhood home, getting married (in most cases, early in adulthood) and having two to three children. They are perhaps the last generation to follow this model. It is not surprising then that during the period between 1966 and 1995, when the notion of the Australian Dream really took hold, Australia witnessed an unprecedented explosion in suburban development, with the most popular dwelling type by far being the single-storey or double-storey house, with three or four bedrooms to support the traditional nuclear family of two to three children.

If we take Perth as an example, the statistics show that, during this period, the average household in Australia was dominated by the traditional family household and couples without children represented 74.7% percent of all households in 1991, with all other household types, such as singles and groups (blended families), only representing 20% and 5.2%, respectively.[237] Naturally, during this time, the property market experienced extraordinary growth in housing, as the biggest cohort in Australian history matured and entered the housing market as first- and second-home buyers. It's not surprising then that Australian cities such as Perth experienced a mass expansion of suburbia during the 1970s, 1980s and 1990s as a result.

The composition of housing types in most cities has followed a similar pattern to Perth. If you look at Melbourne, for example, the overwhelming majority of household types consist of single- or two-storey housing on suburban blocks, with three and four bedrooms. In Perth, as at 2022, the single house on a green title lot represents 79% of the total housing market. This makes sense, because the Australian Dream, which boomed after the Second World War, consists of a family block in suburban settings. This was the payoff, remember, for the war, and this notion has taken hold ever since. First it was the golden generation – those born in the 1920s who lived through the Great Depression and the Second World War who were sold the new Australian Dream of the house on a block of land with a car. This generation then on-sold this notion to

---

[236] *'Baby Boomers in Numbers'*, ABS, 2019.
[237] *'Perth Household Mix'*, ABS, 1991.

the baby boomers, which, because of the size of this cohort, put the Australian Dream as we know it on steroids.

As mentioned before, the baby boomers are the last generation to follow the traditional household pathway of leaving their childhood home, getting married and settling down with children early in life. They are also the first cohort who, by and large, rebelled against tradition and, through their formative years and early adulthood, lived through the mass transformation that took place in Western culture, such as the civil rights movement, the liberation of women and growing wealth, which came with the post-war period. Australia wasn't immune to this and was directly influenced by cultural changes occurring mainly in Britain and the United States during the 1960s and 1970s. Through a combination of increased opportunity for women in the workforce and changes to cultural norms and laws, baby boomers also have another title to their name: being the largest cohort to experience divorce. From the 1980s and 1990s, Australia started to see a change in society, with divorce being a viable option, when it was previously unthinkable, or even taboo, to even contemplate a divorce. What resulted was a change in different household types, with single households and singles with children growing significantly during the late 1980s and 1990s onwards. Some 60% of marriages ended in divorce for the baby boomers. This has had a significant impact on household types in response to this growing socio-economic reality.[238]

From the 1990s onwards, Australia started to see the traditional nuclear family household become less dominant. The rise of the single and single-with-children household has taken hold during the 2000s and now represents one of the most dominant households in Australian society. It currently makes up 30.6% of all households across Australian cities and is expected to grow to 40% by 2030.[239] Why is this? Well, we have already discussed one reason – high divorce rates for the baby boomers – but there are other reasons that are having an impact. The children of baby boomers, perhaps weary of the complications associated with marriage, combined with the greater economic opportunities both for men and women, have seen a fundamental change in societal norms.

The children of baby boomers are often referred to as Generation X and Generation Y. These are people born between 1966 and 1978 (Generation X) and between 1979 and 1999 (Generation Y). These two generations are children of less stable households (remember, 60% of baby boomer marriages failed), they have entered the workforce in relatively prosperous times (certainly true for Generation Y) and have witnessed unprecedented opportunities, especially for women, as Generation X and Y entered the workforce when equality and opportunities for women were more widespread, compared to previous generations. The circumstances for these two generations

---

[238] *'Talking about my generation'*, ABC, December 2018.
[239] *'Household Mix in Australia'*, ABS, 2019.

are vastly different from the baby boomer generation, who had family life and the traditions associated with it thrust upon them.

As a Generation X (born in 1975), I was fortunate to live in a stable household, but I grew up with many friends who didn't, and I witnessed how this impacted their life choices when they decided to leave the family home and go out on their own. I found Generation X and, to a similar degree, Generation Y to be generations who defer marriage until their late twenties and early thirties, with many forgoing marriage altogether. For example, the average age of marriage has increased from twenty-one years and twenty-three years for women and men, respectively, in 1976, to thirty years and thirty-two years for women and men, respectively, in 2018.[240] They are also the generations who have chosen not to have children or to defer having kids until career fulfilment is reached, usually in the mid to late thirties. Many are choosing to get married but not have kids altogether.

This has contributed to the very low birth rate in Australia, which is now one of the lowest in the developed world, at 1.74 children per childbearing woman, compared to 3.9 in 1960.[241] This is in significant contrast to previous generations and is impacting the property market. Collectively, the 'break up' of baby boomer households later in life and the impact this (and economic and social circumstances) has had on the next two generations has exacerbated the growth in the single and couples-without-children household group, which has now become the most dominate household group in Australian cities.

How does this affect the demand for property? Well, there is a fundamental shift away from traditional large family homes on large blocks to different types of household that fit the population make up. For example, smaller housing, units and apartment-type housing is growing in popularity. The ageing of the baby boomer cohort is also contributing to this trend, as baby boomers are becoming empty nesters, so they are downsizing from the family home to smaller accommodation. You may be thinking "so what?", but this change is significant. Remember, most Australian cities, perhaps except for Sydney, are predominately suburban cities. Perth's suburbs, for example, come right up to the city's CBD. So do Canberra's, Hobart's and Adelaide's, with Melbourne's not that far behind. This means there is a significant mismatch between the type of housing within Australian cities and the demand for housing types by the population. As mentioned previously, most households are composed of singles or couples without children. The housing mix, however, is still predominately single dwellings with three to four bedrooms on a large block. Take a look at all Australian cities, particularly their housing mix and household demographic.

---

[240] *'Average age of marriage – men and women'*, ABS, 2019.
[241] *'Australian fertility Rates – 1960 to 2020'*, ABS, 2020.

Household Type	Number of Households	Percentage of Total
Couples with children	2,687,377	30.3%
Couples without children	2,198,551	24.8%
One-parent families	919,133	10.4%
Other families	102,563	1.2%
Grouped households	354,925	4.0%
Lone person	2,023,544	22.8%
Other non-classified households	427,124	4.8%
Visitor only households	148,425	1.7%
Total	8,861,642	100%

Figure 5.3: Summary of household types in Australian cities [242]

Dwelling Type	Number of Dwellings	Percentage of Total
Separate house	7,042,759	71.1%
Medium density	1,769,161	17.9%
High density	898,371	9.1%
Caravan, cabins, houseboat	96,630	1.0%
Other	47,544	0.5%
Not stated	47,031	0.5%
Total	9,901,496	100%

Figure 5.4: Summary of dwelling types in Australian cities [243]

The Australia Dream, which was based fundamentally on the single dwelling with three to four bedrooms and dominates the housing type in most Australian cities, is suddenly out of step with the population, which is progressively changing. This means the dominant household type for the change in population is no longer single houses with three to four bedrooms, but smaller dwelling types to cater for couples without children, one-parent families or singles households, which collectively make up 58.1% of total households. This figure is also growing when you take into consideration the ageing population and also the greater number single and couples-without-children households for our Generation X and Y population, which are deferring marriage,

---

[242] *'Census of Population and Housing'*, ABS, 2016.
[243] *'Census of Population and Housing'*, ABS, 2016.

kids and, by and large, having fewer kids than previous generations. Will this trend continue for Generation Z (born 1997 onwards)? It is still too early to know, with the eldest of this generation just hitting twenty-five, but we won't have to wait too long.

The demographic transition that has been ongoing in Australia since the 1970s is now coming home to roost, with housing type lagging behind the population change in Australian society, which will profoundly impact the real estate market. What we will now see is the traditional three-to-four-bedroom home, which makes up 71.1% of all houses, falling out of favour with much of the population as being an 'extravagance' to the needs of most households. With the baby boomer population cashing out of their large three to four-bedroom households in ever increasing numbers, and fewer people in the market interested in buying them, we are likely to see a glut of three-to-four-bedroom single-storey and two-storey houses on the market for the foreseeable future. This is likely to restrain the growth of real estate prices for these types of dwellings for some time to come, especially given they have already been inflated in value due to the economic boom period in Australia during 1992 and 2022.

With declining demand for and increased supply of three to four-bedroom houses in the market, this will fundamentally change the Australian Dream and force a shift in the way we develop old suburbs and create new suburbs. We are likely to see an increase in demand and a lagging supply for smaller dwelling types in Australian cities. Smaller three-bedroom 'grouped dwelling' and 'townhouse' housing types are likely to grow in popularity, in addition to smaller dwelling types, such as two-bedroom units and apartments. Cities, which are more flexible in their planning and building regulations, are likely to fare better and see a take-up in these smaller dwelling types over traditional larger dwelling types (large three- and four-bedroom houses). For suburban cities, such as Perth, Adelaide and Melbourne, it means a fundamental shift in thinking for the way they consider and deliver housing, as there will need to be a significant transition from typical suburban homes to smaller dwelling types and apartments. For cities such as Sydney, which has a healthy balance in housing type, this transition is already underway.

One thing is for sure: the way we plan our cities will need to change if they are to adapt to the changes in Australia's demography, which is seeing a distinct shift from the family household to singles and couples without children. For the next twenty years at least, this will negatively impact the market for large family homes and generate significant growing demand for smaller household types. Are we seeing signs of this already? Household sizes have tracked virtually uninterrupted in growth for the last fifty years, but, as of 2017, it would appear household sizes have peaked. As demonstrated previously, Australia appears to have reached 'peak housing', with average households peaking in size at 238sqm in the 2010s and declining since.[244] This is a

---

[244] *'Housing size in Australia – Historic overview'*, ABS, 2018

product of changing demographics, with smaller housing demand gaining momentum, but it can equally be seen as an affordable housing issue, as Australia can no longer afford to build massive 220+sqm homes on large blocks.

The demographic time bomb for typical suburban development is ticking away and is reason alone for a change of the Australian Dream, but combine it with housing affordability, and we have a significant case to change the way we plan and develop our cities in the future.

Planning Theory and the Changing Market

It is perhaps not surprising that, with changes in housing affordability and demographics in Australia and other Western cultures, such as the United States, over the last twenty to thirty years, we have seen an explosion in new planning theory that promotes a change in the way we develop our cities. The most profound of the 'new planning theories' is perhaps best encapsulated in the 'New Urbanist' movement, which had its roots in the United States in the 1980s and 1990s through influential urban designers, town planners and architects, such as Andreas Duany, Peter Calthorpe, Elizabeth Moule and Elizabeth Plater-Zyberk. New Urbanism captures the zeitgeist of the time in recognising the flawed planning of car-based suburban development, while also recognising fundamental changes in demographics and affordability, which are also driving change. Contrary to the automobile-based suburban model, which focuses on movement and single-serving development that is dispersed in low-density and transport-focused development, New Urbanism focuses on land use and housing diversity developed around small town centres. This is then supported by the traditional main street, with public transport, such as railways, bus lines and pedestrian-friendly environments, taking primacy over the private automobile.

Key to this form of development is the town centre, which is clearly defined as a combination of a public space for gathering, similar to the European 'piazzas', supported by civic land use, commercial, retail and apartment-style residential and townhouse (higher-density) housing. Typically, other housing is mixed, in the form of apartments, townhouses and semi and single-detached housing that is within a five-minute walk from the town centre, therefore making alternative transport, such as walking, cycling and public transport, a better option than driving. The archetype of this form of development is encapsulated in the American developments of Seaside in Florida (remember the movie *The Truman Show*?) and Prospect Town in Colorado.

One of the defining characteristics of New Urbanist planning is the diversity of housing accommodated in their master planning. This includes a healthy mix of apartment development of all sizes, townhouses, micro developments, grouped housing, and semi and detached housing. This differentiates significantly from the development that prevailed in the United States and in Australia during the 1950s through to the 1990s, which was predominately mono-cultured suburban development.

In Australia, there have been some examples of 'master planned', 'New Urbanist' development, such as Harbour Rise in Perth's northern coastal suburb of Hillarys and Claisbrook Cove in Perth's inner city. Victoria Park in Sydney and Tullimbar Village in New South Wales are other examples. These developments have followed a very different type of built form and mix of land uses and have proven successful, as demonstrated in the take-up rates when new housing product are released to the market and the low transit population experienced in the development – i.e., when people buy into the area, they tend to stay. We will discuss some of these projects later.

While change is slow in Australia, the influence of planning theories, such as New Urbanism, is gaining momentum, partly because of their appeal to catering for more diversity and density, which reflects the aspirations of new generations and the general composition of households within Australia, which is moving away from the traditional family unit to smaller households. Even suburban planning is changing to cater for more diversity than previously contemplated. For example, the Western Australian State Planning Authorities' adoption of the 'liveable neighbourhood' community codes is not a perfect incarnation of New Urbanist principles, but it does adopt many of the core principles of New Urbanism – particularly by bringing back walkable neighbourhoods, housing diversity, grid-type road hierarchy and smaller scale retail and main street development principles. Similar design codes have been established in Queensland, Victoria and New South Wales, which, by and large, depart from the traditional neighbourhood planning that for almost fifty years has focused on a combination of semi-vehicular and cul-de-sac road planning, with singular housing supported by a primary school and small local shops, which are often unviable due to the low-density nature of the suburb catchment.

Part of this change has been precipitated by changing planning theory, but changing market circumstances have also played a role. With traditional family units reducing in numbers and other family groups growing in number, the market has had to adjust to reflect changes in housing demand. While the lure of having a three-to-four-bedroom home is still attractive to many household groups, an increasing number of people are shunning the large home and settling for smaller, carefree homes with minimal gardens and backyards to maintain.

We are starting to see this change in suburban developments across Australia, with increasing block sizes and variable house sizes coming into the equation. But, as mentioned previously, this is creating its own problems, with new suburbia being populated by increasingly small blocks with large houses, leaving no backyards or vegetation. This is creating 'heat islands' across our vast suburban areas, which is particularly concerning, given that Australia is confronted with a higher-than-normal-temperature climate that is likely to exacerbate in the years to come.

While our urban environment is changing, is it changing for the better? It's debateable. New Urbanism has many qualities that are worth adopting for Australia. Not only does it reflect a scale and type of development that is more fitting to the population that inhabits our cities, but it is also more sustainable. One thing I know is that change is slow in Australia. New Urbanist-type developments are few and far between in Australia, with most new developments following a bastardised version of suburbia, with the same sprawl-like design with large houses on smaller blocks. These large houses on small blocks are cutting out the few qualities that originally came from living in suburbia in the first place, such as its links to nature, big backyards and large amounts of vegetation. It is definitely fair to say a rethink of our approach to planning our cities is on the cards and needs to happen sooner rather than later to ensure our cities move with the people that inhabit them and not the other way around.

Time to Reflect

So, is the Australian Dream changing, or does it need to change? My thoughts are both. The Australian Dream is changing, as we are seeing limitations appear with housing affordability and demographics now starting to influence the size of Australian homes as we move from an average of 238sqm households, to a more realistic size that reflects human needs and scale. Most of this characteristic change in dwelling size is being played out in inner-city locations, with the growing popularity of apartments, which tend to be single or two bedroom and between 60sqm and 100sqm in area. This is balanced against the suburban home, which is still large in size – between 250sqm and 350sqm in area – being produced on ever smaller lots. This polarisation is skewing the numbers, because we are still seeing the production of large numbers of large single- and two-storey suburban homes.

What we are starting to see is a shift in the dominance of single-residential homes and a gradual increase in the popularity of apartments, which is influencing the look and feel of the Australian Dream. This is perhaps inevitable when we confront housing affordability and demographic shifts, but is it all that needs to change? Is the Australian Dream destined to be a bastardised version of the suburban experiment, with small islands of development that reflect New Urbanist principles and the influx of some apartment product, or will we see a fundamental shift in the way we plan our cities? I know if we progress on our current trajectory, it is likely that little will change. Suburbia will be developed, albeit with increasingly small lots and large houses, that will be devoid of any of the characteristics that made suburbia attractive in the first place, and we will see some ad hoc apartment developments near activity centres and in some of the inner-suburban locations of our capital cities. We will still be tied to the car, however, which will continue to be the dominant mode of transport, bringing with it all the problems we discussed in Chapter 4.

What is needed is a fundamental shift in the way we plan our cities from the top to the bottom – taking a very macro- and micro-economic-style approach that has been adapted to city planning. This contemplation is perhaps an interesting segue into the final two chapters of this book, which examine the pathways to changing the Australian Dream towards a more compact, dense, human-scale and transport-supported form of living: downsizing towards a new Australian Dream.

6

MACRO-PLANNING THE NEW AUSTRALIAN DREAM

When we ponder the challenges confronting the present form of the Australian Dream, one could be excused for contemplating that its future is limited, and change is afoot. The challenges are great, and the fundamentals that made the single house a stable investment are changing, notably with housing affordability and demographics being the core factors. As a positive, choice is always a variable that can change over time, and as circumstances change, so can consumer wants and desires. This is a simple notion, however, and, in reality, the type of housing provided to the masses is shaped by a number of factors, which include, most importantly, regulatory factors, governance and industry, which is controlled by relatively few people.

It isn't as simple as people going to a builder and asking for a particular type of house to be built. That sort of 'free market system' of 'free choice' exists in theory, but in practice is something else entirely. In most instances, consumers approach builders and are effectively told what house they can build. This is particularly true of the project-home-building industry, which dominates the housing market, accounting for no less than 85% of all houses being built in Australia. In Perth, for example, between the BGC group of companies – the Julian Walters Group and Alcock Brown-Neaves – they build approximately 70% of all houses in Perth. When we look at the remaining 30% of housing, its builders comprise largely smaller builders, which oscillate from standard home building to bespoke home construction. Because bespoke home building is unique, it is generally more expensive, and is therefore only a viable option for a small number of people in the market. These are usually unique builders such as Zorzi Homes in Perth, which builds between forty and sixty specially designed homes a year, usually for the wealthy among us who can afford the higher prices that come with unique house designs.

So, how can the Australian Dream change to fit the circumstances that confront it? Firstly, consumers can have some influence by demanding a change in housing typology. The industry itself can change; however, this has proven to be slow, as developers take comfort in what is proven and tested and tend to push their products onto the market, thereby shaping consumer demand and desires through clear and persistent marketing. This is the key area, I think, market control, not consumer ideas and wants. So, if builders are driving the industry, what can influence the builders? The answer is very simple: the government. The key area where change can be led, and perhaps is most controversial, is through the third tier of regulatory change. This involves the government of each state taking a lead in shaping housing and urban agendas through demonstration and regulatory changes that force the land and building industry to consider alternatives.

Now if you are a friend of John Maynard Keynes and consider yourself a 'Keynesian', in the economic sense – or, more radically, an advocate for greater state control through the soviet type of government intervention – then the government playing a greater role in driving change in the building industry could be your ideology of persuasion. However, if you are more of an advocate for the free market, as are economists like Frederick Hayek or his cousin Milton Friedman, then the very notion of government intervention into anything likely sends a shiver down your spine. This is an important notion in the housing debate, since our political parties, which are by no means extremists on the political spectrum, still sit on either side of the political ledge, with Labor leaning more towards the left, and the Liberal party leaning more towards the right. Hence, picking one over the other will tend to influence the level of involvement the government has in the building industry and ultimately the Australian Dream. That's all I will say on that, since I would prefer to be politically agnostic and leave you to decide which ideology takes your fancy.

If, as Australians, we are to downsize our housing and urban footprint in general, with the aim of presenting a new form of the Australian Dream to future generations, then we need to consider what influences can assist this transition as Australia moves from a predominantly suburban culture to development that involves urban consolidation and includes a smaller-housing built form. Since builders are slow to react, and consumers have little say, the answer lies in looking at regulatory factors through government, with the important distinction that it is the government's job to convince the private sector that change is not only positive on an environmental and social level, but also, more importantly, that it can be profitable. This is where the problem lies, since the prototype of anything new often does not have a strong history, resulting in reduced confidence, and is often more expensive than the more tried and tested models of the same product. In the housing context, this means more compact and often multi-level products, which can be more expensive and complex to deliver. To help solve this conundrum, we can look at how we plan our cities, drawing on both macro- and micro-planning factors to understand the underlying factors that influence the housing industry and simultaneously work together to drive change on the macro- and micro-level scales.

Macro-Planning Our Cities

When we talk about macro-planning in the context of the urban planning of our cities, we are talking about the regulatory factors that define the strategic framework that drives the planning and development of our cities. There are influences on a broad scale that shape our urban environment, similar to how macroeconomics shapes the broad structure of our economy. When we put this into the context of our cities, it conjures up the notion of key factors such as transport planning and urban morphology, which together shape the way our cities are designed and the way we move around our cities, in a manner that is similar to how the balance of trade and interest rates affects the broad trade and level of investment in our economies.

If the above is true for macro-level matters, it is also true for micro-level factors. In the context of our urban environment, this could include industry structure and attitudes (i.e., building industry in the context of our cities), which are influenced by macro factors that transpire to deliver on the ground outcomes. This is similar to microeconomic factors, such as the role of unions, which influence labour markets and wage levels in the economy. If we turn our attention to macro factors, in the context of city planning, the key macro-planning issues are associated with the driving influences that impact our overall urban environment and structure, and this includes strategic frameworks that influence the following key areas critical to our cities, which will be discussed in turn.

1. Growth boundaries
2. Transport
3. Places of interest – transit-oriented development
4. New growth areas
5. Strategic planning system and role of government

In all Australian cities, there are 'growth boundaries' that are set by the strategic planning framework established by each state government and the political system. The growth boundaries set the limits for how 'new greenfield' or suburban, rural and industrial developments can take place in a city and are the first place to start when looking at how we can curb suburban development and strive for a more compact city and urban form. It may be difficult for the layman to contemplate the notion of a growth boundary, since, to the naked eye, the development of our cities seems to be ever constant, but they exist and form an important restraint on how our cities can grow now and into the future.

By way of example, in Western Australia, the State Planning Department)the Western Australian Planning Commission) and its administrative arm, the Department for Planning, Lands and Heritage, set the strategic framework for the metropolitan area of Perth by establishing and administering the Metropolitan Region Town Planning Scheme. This scheme, which was set up in 1963, establishes the extent to which urban, industrial and commercial development can occur in the metropolitan area.[245] It does this by setting a boundary around the metropolitan area and, within that boundary, establishes a broad range of land uses through zones and reserves to control what can be developed. This includes zones, such as urban, industrial, rural and commercial zones, and reserves, such as parks and recreation, public purpose and major road reservations. In terms of where suburban development fits in, the scheme will zone land for urban development and urban deferred. By restricting the amount of land that is zoned as urban and urban deferred within the metropolitan area, the Western Australian Planning Commission can effectively control the extent of future suburban development by restricting (or expanding) the amount of land that is available for suburban-type development.[246]

This approach to land use control is not dissimilar across Australia, with similar metropolitan schemes in existence in cities such as Melbourne and, in a different way, Sydney. In Melbourne, it is called the Melbourne Metropolitan Planning Scheme, established in 1968, and is administered by the Department of Environment, Land, Water and Planning.[247] In Sydney, however, in place of a metropolitan-wide scheme, the planning framework has a metropolitan-wide strategy or policy, which is then delegated down to individual Town Planning Schemes operated by local governments in the Sydney metropolitan area. In short, the strategy is put together by the state government through the Department of Planning, Industry and Environment in Sydney and administered by individual local governments.

You would think that, once established, the Metropolitan Region Scheme – or its equivalent across Australia – could set the complete framework for urban development in a city from its inception, but, in reality, this isn't the case: it is a moving feast. The Metropolitan Region Scheme can be modified and works hand in hand with strategic planning documents established by state governments and set the 'vision

---

[245] Gregory, J, Gordon, D, *"Gordon Stephenson, planner and civic designer"*. Town Planning Review. 83 (2): 269–278, 2012.

[246] Gregory, J, Gordon, D, *"Gordon Stephenson, planner and civic designer"*. Town Planning Review. 83 (2): 269–278, 2012.

[247] Tsutsumi, J, Wyatt, R, *"A brief history of metropolitan planning in Melbourne, Australia"*, 2006.

framework' for each Australian city. In Melbourne, for example, the scheme is called 'Plan Melbourne – 2017 to 2050', and in Perth it's 'Perth and Peel @ 3.5 million'. These non-statutory documents (or, better termed, policy documents) set the strategic vision for the city and present the guiding framework for the Metropolitan Region Scheme to operate. For example, 'Plan Melbourne – 2017 to 2050' may set an infill development target (development in existing urban areas) of 50%, which means the metropolitan scheme in Melbourne will need to allow for at least 50% of all new development to occur within the city's existing urban footprint.[248] The other 50% will be delivered in the form of new suburban development in new growth areas – usually on the fringes of the metropolitan area, where urban development meets rural or bushland areas.

These strategic policy documents are very important and have been criticised somewhat for not pushing more infill development as part of overall development. For example, Perth's 'Perth and Peel @ 3.5 million' strategic planning document promotes only 47% of all new development as infill-type development (380,000 dwellings)– that is development in existing urban areas – meaning that 53% of all new development (420,000 dwellings) will need to be found in new growth areas, or, better put, new suburbs. Importantly, once these targets are set at the strategic metropolitan-wide scale through the Metropolitan Region Scheme, local governments through their own local town planning schemes (localised versions of the Metropolitan Region Scheme) are required to ensure that local own planning schemes conform with the Metropolitan Region Scheme. This process ensures continuity between state and local government planning systems.[249]

With strategic policy influencing the Metropolitan Region Scheme, and in turn Local Town Planning Schemes, it is therefore possible to seek amendments to the various schemes in order to expand the zones mentioned, and historically this has mostly occurred in the context of rezoning rural and urban deferred land to urban development land. This usually occurs on the urban fringe, where suburban land meets rural land. This process is almost constant and involves the steady encroachment and removal of rural land to make way for suburban land across our cities.

Often, as a result of political pressure, all amendments to metropolitan schemes require ministerial approval and support from the state parliament. Hence one of the biggest tussles in the urban planning industry is the, seemingly, four-way confrontation between people living in rural locations wanting to preserve their rural lifestyles and the web of government and industry groups that participate in the urban development industry. This includes the urban development industry and their lobby groups who push for change to support more urban growth; the regulatory authorities in the state

---

[248] https://www.planning.vic.gov.au/policy-and-strategy/planning-for-melbourne/melbournes-strategic-planning-history.
[249] Hamnett, S, Freestone, R, *'Planning Metropolitan Australia – Planning, History and Environmental series'*, 2020.

and local planning apparatus, which are responsible for regulating Metropolitan and Local Town Planning Schemes; and the fourth, and perhaps most influential element, the politicians. These are the ministers and members of parliament who are required to endorse or refuse recommendations to change metropolitan schemes based on advice received from regulatory authorities and lobbying from the industry.

While regulatory authorities, such as the Department of Environment, Land, Water and Planning in Melbourne, are guided by their strategic planning documents (Plan Melbourne – 2017 to 2050) to moderate urban development decisions and recommendations, in reality regulatory authorities can often be by-passed. Often what happens is, early in the regulatory process, government departments are by-passed by urban developers across Australia, many of which are nation-wide companies, using their connections with parliament and lobbyists through the Urban Development Institute to put pressure on governments to make changes to the metropolitan schemes, which can be aligned with the metropolitan schemes as they are or misaligned – as often happens. This pressure, which is ever constant, works collectively to ensure the wheels for the suburban bus keep turning.

I've mentioned previously that this often results in direct confrontation between people longing for the rural lifestyle and the urban development industry, but, more often than not, it is a one-sided battle, as the needs and wants of the individual seeking the quiet life are often outweighed by the power that land developers, and their equally powerful lobby groups, yield over the political system. It is also a difficult proposition to pass up the opportunity of land being rezoned from rural to urban, since land values tend to skyrocket when this occurs, presenting the rural landowner with a financial windfall. Hence, the suburban machine has all the elements to keep on churning, and this needs to change. It is also the place to start focusing on if we are to put the brakes on suburb development – or better, to slow down the urban sprawl – and refocus on developing our existing urban areas so that a more compact and sustainable version of the Australian Dream can evolve.

The machinations for supporting suburban development are clear in Australia: the Metropolitan Region Scheme dictates to local town planning schemes, and any change through legislation – that is, change in the former – leads to change in the latter. This, combined with an eager development industry, keeps the suburban train moving, but the same cannot be said when we consider the other side of the ledger: infill development (or better put: development in existing built environments). The zoning of land within infill areas is set solely by the local planning schemes of individual local governments who 'self-govern', when it comes to considering infill development targets set by the state government. The way it works is that the State Planning Strategy, such as 'Plan Melbourne 2017 to 2050', may set a target that 50% of all new development should be in existing areas, which local government should follow. The trick is that state governments are limited in their political will to force local governments to abide by these targets and adjust their local town planning schemes to ensure infill targets have a chance to be met. So, when various state governments release their planning strategies, technically local governments should be amending their town planning schemes to reflect the intent of the planning strategy. This often involves local town planning schemes being rezoned to enable predominately single dwellings to be developed into grouped dwellings, townhouses or apartments. The trouble is many local governments snub the density targets for fear that the resulting built form will change the character of existing suburbs, and what often results is a shortfall in infill development targets being met.

So, what do we have? On the one hand, suburban development has a clear run at success, given the complex web of the development industry, politicians and lobby groups that influences the creation of new urban land, with local governments consigned to comply by legislation. On the other hand, the state encourages new infill development but is reliant on local governments interpreting the targets and then implementing them through local town planning schemes. One approach is guaranteed, while the other requires greater negotiation to succeed. Hence why new growth areas tend to be more successful in reaching their targets than infill development.

Each state government has a Minister for Urban Planning, with legislation – such as the *Planning and Development Act 2005* in Western Australia – that enables ministerial powers to 'call in' local town planning schemes and force local governments to change their schemes to conform with state planning policy. This power exists in theory and could turn the tables in favour of infill development by the state, forcing local governments to meet infill targets through their local town planning schemes, but, in reality, this seldom happens, because infill development is a political 'hot potato'. To have a situation where a state government minister calls in a local government's town planning scheme, forcing planning changes through the local community, is political suicide, and it would take a very brave minister to use their call-in powers to force local governments to comply with state government targets. Changes to local government town planning schemes are, therefore, largely voluntary and incremental, at best, which hinders the transition that is needed to encourage higher-density living in our more traditional neighbourhoods, which are generally better serviced by amenities and transport. The way out of this conundrum is through legislation and political will, which could be difficult to count on in all instances.

Dealing with Our Suburbs

Across all Australian cities, the development form that contributes towards the greatest footprint on the environment is suburban development. This has been discussed previously in this book. The low-density nature of suburban development is the most land-hungry form of development in the world and contributes to between 75% and 80% of all new development footprints in our capital cities, such as Perth, Melbourne, Brisbane and Canberra; this is less the case in Sydney, as it has matured and has a greater focus on infill development or redevelopment of existing land for higher-density housing. Sydney is also constrained geographically.

As mentioned previously, strategic planning documents set targets for residential development, which are set through two broad categories: infill development and new suburban development. Perth's strategic planning document – 'Perth and Peel @ 3.5 million' and beyond – sets targets for infill development at 47% of all new development and new suburban development at 53% of all new development. The problem with this strategy is, firstly, -it is difficult to ensure infill development can be achieved, because it can't be forced, but also that the vision still allows for 53% of all new development to be suburban-type development (largely three- and four-bedroom housing). When we are talking about an additional 800,000 houses required, say between now and 2050, the allocation of approximately 420,000 new three- and four-bedroom dwellings on the urban fringes leaves a very nasty footprint. If each block averages 300sqm, this means a total area of 126,000,000sqm or 12,600 hectares or 126 square kilometres just for the lots. Then, you have to add all the roads and supporting infrastructure. Pretty soon, you are talking about 200 square kilometres of land.

It's just a number, right? But when you put it in perspective, 200 square kilometres is equivalent to two times the entire area of the City of Stirling in Perth's central suburbs, or, put another way, it is equivalent to approximately forty-five new suburbs. But remember – this just reflects residential housing and supporting infrastructure. You need to also consider the commercial and industrial land required to support 420,000 dwellings. That could expand the footprint to three City of Stirlings. It also facilitates a type of built form that is incongruent with what the projected demand is, with family-type housing forecasted to be less of a priority in the future.

If you look at the historic growth of Australian cities, there has been a predominant focus on the suburban model of development. As a result, you can see how fast the city area has been consumed by low-density development. This can be seen by looking at Perth, which has expanded enormously since the original Metropolitan Region Scheme was established in 1963, when Perth's population was around 500,000. Since that time, the population has expanded to 2.125 million people and is forecast to grow to 3.5m by 2050. This growth is significant, particularly when you consider that Perth's footprint is near the size of London. It raises the question: can we, as a city, afford to continue growing the way we have over the last fifty years?

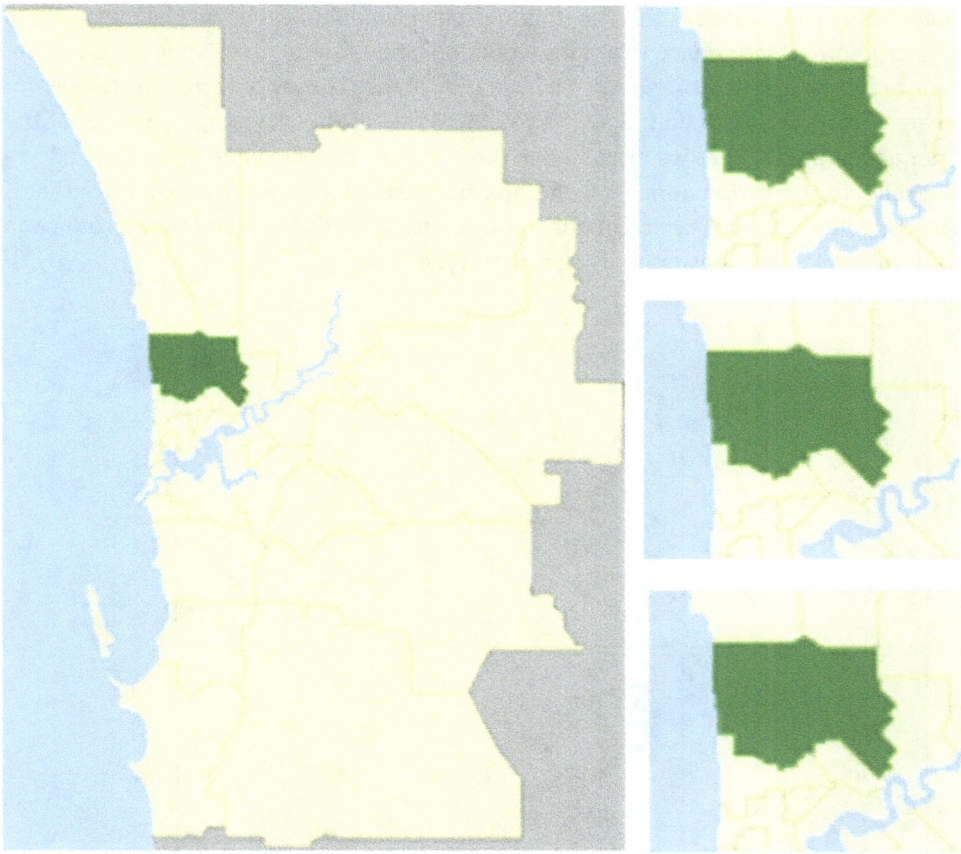

Figure 6.1: Growth equivalent to three City of Stirlings – can we afford this?[250]

If we want to start curbing the urban footprint, there needs to be a concerted effort by policymakers to turn the tables on new urban development and promote new infill development instead. Using Perth as an example, it's clear we can't keep expanding the size of the metropolitan area to the equivalent of two to three City of Stirlings every twenty or so years. It is clearly not sustainable, and the quality of life will suffer if we continue to expand the city, putting a strain on infrastructure and services to support further suburban expansion. Therefore, a new approach is needed, one where targets for infill-type development should be closer to 70% to 80% of all new development, with the less significant balance applying to new urban development.

---

[250] City of Stirling, Wikipedia, 2021.

Apart from being more sustainable, this approach would reflect a more efficient use of infrastructure, since service upgrades would only be required in existing areas, rather than brand new infrastructure in new growth areas. This approach, which calls for greater urban consolidation, would also better reflect the changing dynamics of the emerging population, as we discussed in the last chapter, by expanding a city in a form that reflects population demands. This approach would also reduce the crunch that is occurring on rural land, which needs to be set aside for lifestyle and food production but is instead being consumed by suburban-type housing.

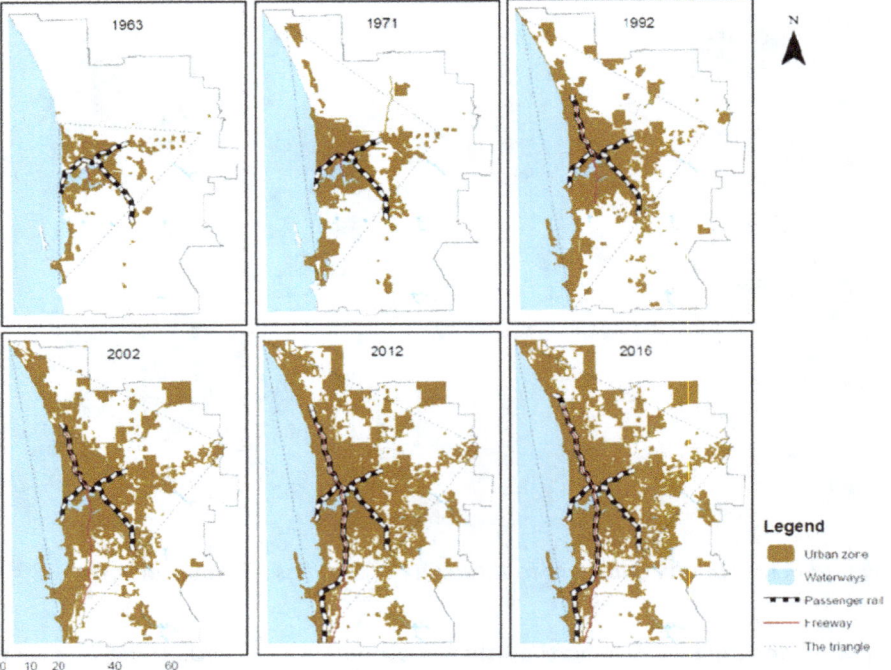

Figure 6.2: Historic growth of Perth, Western Australia 1963–2016[251]

By resetting the targets for infill and greenfield development, you do two things. First, you begin to change the narrative away from a focus on suburban development to infill development, including medium and high-density housing. This will force the development industry to shift its priorities, strategic focus and investment to a different built form. The other impact is that it will change the shape and form of our cities. Turning inwards and focusing on redeveloping existing urban areas will have a massive impact on improving metropolitan housing densities, which will support

---

[251] Kelobonye, K, *'Drivers of Change of Urban Growth Patterns: A Transport Perspective for Perth',* April 2019.

greater population numbers, businesses, places of interest and public transport viability.

The population density of Australian cities is low when compared to other more international cities. Australian cities should set targets to increase population densities to a more sustainable level, and it doesn't have to be on par with places like Paris, which holds 21,067 people per square kilometre, or London with 18,769 people per square kilometre, but a more modest population density of between 1,500 to 2,000 people per square kilometre.[252] Having said that, places like Paris and London are some of the most liveable cities in the world, and they are far more dense in population than Australian cities. I am being conservative in my suggestions, because it might come as a shock to most Australians if I suggest densities of 10,000 people per square kilometre and over. After all, increasing the density of Melbourne from 453 people per square kilometre to 2,000 per square kilometre is a quadrupling of the population density – any more and our policymakers and politicians may have a heart attack.

City	Density – population per square kilometre	Population
Melbourne	453	5,159,211
Adelaide	404	1,359,760
Sydney	400	5,367,206
Perth	317.7	2,125,114
Canberra	173.3	431,380
Brisbane	145	2,560,720
Hobart	125	238,834
Darwin	46	147,231

Figure 6.3: Population densities of Australian cities (2022)[253]

This change or reprioritising is significant and will take political will and courage to implement. The good news (for developers) is that this change will take time and, therefore, there is scope to refocus and reprioritise without having to make dramatic and disruptive changes over the short term.

Because our cities are starting from a very low population base when compared to international cities, it will take time for Australian cities to lift their population densities

---

[252] Nenad, S, *'The City of Australia'*, .id Informed decisions, August 30, 2019, https://blog.id.com.au/2019/id-news/fun-stuff/the-city-of-australia/.

[253] Nenad, S, *'The City of Australia'*, .id Informed decisions, August 30, 2019, https://blog.id.com.au/2019/id-news/fun-stuff/the-city-of-australia/.

to 1,000 to 1,500 persons per square kilometre. This makes it more important that governments across Australia work closely with the private sector to instil changes in practice, supported by political will. The Federal Government can also play a role through incentives to encourage state governments to rethink their current policies and back this up with strategic policy to encourage more infill development within our cities and to reduce the expansion of our cities' urban footprints. After all, with higher density comes a greater need for infrastructure, such as public transport infrastructure.

This has been done before; for example, in the early 1990s, with the Labor Government of Bob Hawke establishing the Build Better Cities Program.[254] The program was first funded in the 1991–92 Commonwealth Budget and had the overall objective of "promot[ing] improvements in the efficiency, equity and sustainability of Australian cities and increase[ing] their capacity to meet the following objectives: economic growth and micro-economic reform; improved social justice; institutional reform; ecologically sustainable development; and improved urban environments and more liveable cities".[255] The Commonwealth Government agreed to provide up to $816.4 million over the period of December 1991 to June 1996 in order to meet these objectives.[256] The program operated via formal agreements with individual state and territory governments and targeted twenty-six distinct areas throughout Australia.

The Build Better Cities Program is credited for the establishment of many model infill developments in the hearts of Australian cities, such as Claisbrook Cove in the eastern end of Perth's CBD, which was a ground-breaking project that demonstrated the benefits of higher-density inner-city living at a time when the development industry was almost completely focused on suburban development. Across Australia, the initiative resulted in the creation of numerous government redevelopment authorities, such as the East Perth Redevelopment Authority in Perth, which was the forerunner of today's Development WA, and similar organisations in Melbourne, such as Vic Urban, which was the forerunner of Development Victoria today. These organisations have set the benchmark for urban development and demonstration across Australia, which we will discuss in more detail later.

By providing policy support and funding opportunities, the Federal Government can greatly influence the future shape of our cities by promoting development that is infill focused and supports residential housing and urban design demonstration projects. The Morrison Government established the Department of Infrastructure, Transport, Regional Development and Communities to help guide federal funding for city building programs and established a funding arrangement called City Deals, which is a partnership between federal, state and local governments to channel money for city-scale

---

[254] Butcher, J, 'Australia under construction: Nation building, past present and future', ANU Press, 2018.
[255] Butcher, J, 'Australia under construction: Nation building, past present and future', ANU Press, 2018.
[256] Butcher, J, 'Australia under construction: Nation building, past present and future', ANU Press, 2018.

projects.[257] An example is the City Deal between the Federal Government and South Australia for Adelaide to invest money into the development of strategic government sites in the city to promote high-density residential and new commercial and civic precincts in East Adelaide. Initiatives such as City Deals can be channelled to those state governments taking bold strides to change their cities, focusing on redeveloping existing urban areas over new suburban areas. Starting from the top, with a focus on reshaping state government urban strategy, this is critical to changing the form of the Australian Dream as we strive for a more compact and sustainable urban form.

The other key reform necessary is the alignment of state planning policies with local planning schemes to ensure density targets for new infill development can be achieved. Legislative changes could be brought in to ensure all local government town planning schemes are reviewed within one to two years of state governments publishing their state planning strategies, with the aim that individual local governments need to demonstrate how they are adjusting their schemes to meet state planning strategy targets for new development. Those local governments that fail to comply with the review can have their schemes automatically 'called in' by the state planning authority and the review undertaken by the state government. This may seem harsh, but it is a critical and necessary measure to ensure that state and local governments see eye to eye on the future of planning for our cities. This requires a bi-partisan approach that goes beyond electoral timeframes, which is a big ask but one worth considering, since planning for cities takes years – and change even longer.

Figure 6.4: Less of this and more of this... Australian cities need to limit growth boundaries – targets of 70% infill and 30% greenfield should apply[258] [259]

---

[257] Adelaide City Deal, Department for Infrastructure, Transport, Regional Development and Communications website, https://www.infrastructure.gov.au/territories-regions-cities/cities/city-deals/adelaide.

[258] 'Urban fringe' Sergio Famiano's private photography, 2015.

[259] 'TOD development', Vic Urban, 2017.

Transport

Transport is perhaps one of the most critical factors that shape our cities. It is a legislative requirement that every property have access to a road, and, from a sustainability perspective, transport accounts for just over one-third of the carbon pollution in our atmosphere; accordingly, having a good public transport system goes a long way to achieving a more sustainable city.[260] Most modern cities around the world have excellent, well laid out and connected public transport networks. They are also diverse in their approaches to transport – i.e., they don't solely rely on movement by private vehicles or public transport but include cycling and walking as viable transport options. When you consider international cities such as Paris and Singapore, their public transport networks are extensive and connect deep into the metropolitan areas. In addition, they have dedicated cycle routes that offer safe and easy movement, and they are compact cities, which makes walking a viable option (remember the Marchetti principle discussed in earlier chapters?).

The key ingredient to support a diverse and well-functioning transport network in a city is density of population. This is a scary subject for Australians, who have gotten used to having large properties and big backyards, but it is a critical issue that Australians need to come to terms with, and fast. Since having a dense population means that urban areas are more compact, and this means land uses are brought closer together, it is essential that Australian policymakers tackle the issue with density head-on. It is important to have a denser population, because this means public transport becomes a more viable option, since there are more people per square kilometre to use the public transport network. Look at the difference between Melbourne, for example, with a population density of 453 people per square kilometre, and Paris, which has a whopping 21,067 people per square kilometre. It doesn't take a scientist to work out that a public transport system in Paris would be more viable than in Melbourne. Since infrastructure costs are similar, subject to servicing constraints, the variable is determined by how many people use the network.

In Perth, the southern suburbs railway line from Perth central to Mandurah, which is a 63-kilometre-long route, has approximately 30,000 to 40,000 people that board the train line on any given day.[261] This is barely viable in a global sense. In Paris, a similar train line would have between 250,000 to 300,000 people boarding per day. Similar infrastructure, but vastly different outcomes in terms of passenger numbers. This is because public transport in Australian cities reaches out like tentacles into the urban fringe to service low-density residential and suburban-type areas, with most dwellings consisting of single houses or grouped dwellings. This means the population catchment for each train station is small in comparison to other cities in the world.

---

[260] *'Opportunities for reducing greenhouse gas emissions in Australia'*, Climate Change Authority, 2012.
[261] *'Mandurah Train Line Boarding numbers'*, PTA, 2012.

In Paris, for example, it is vastly different. Their railway snakes through their version of the suburbs, which is constructed of mainly three-to-four-storey apartment buildings, bringing significant amounts of the population close to the epicentre of train stations. For Australian cities like Perth, Melbourne, Brisbane and Sydney to mature, there needs to be a significant change in density and, equally important, a focus on how public transport can capitalise on this change.

So, what of transport in our cities today? Predominantly, Australian cities are car dominated – a product of planning that took place in the 1950s and 1960s, which followed the United States Urban Model and resulted in the creation of vast freeways during the 1960s and 1970s. This set the cast for low-density suburban planning. In Australian cities such as Perth and Melbourne, the establishment of Metropolitan Region Planning Schemes resulted in the establishment of vast reserves for major and arterial roads to ensure land is set aside for major roads, rather than for urban development. This has facilitated the establishment of extensive freeway networks in our major cities and has also, through the Metropolitan Region Scheme Tax (which we pay on our land rates, for example), established a funding network for these roads.[262] Such is the commitment to freeway planning in our major cities that we have a planning scheme that sets aside the land, supported by a funding mechanism, so organisations such as Main Roads in Western Australia can have a budget to construct and extend freeways almost in perpetuity. In Perth, this budget exceeds two billion dollars annually.[263] Do we have such planning and funding for public transport? The simple answer is no.

Public transport infrastructure is neither sufficiently planned for in our cities, nor funded through some form of tax mechanism. Usually, public transport is funded through the consolidated revenue of the state government coffers, topped up by federal funding, usually granted as part of an election commitment. In most cases, it is ad hoc and by no means guaranteed. While state governments in recent years have published public transport plans for major Australian cities, which establish the strategic frameworks for the location and guidance of public transport expansion in our cities, there is no guaranteed funding plan or tax similar to what Main Roads receives for freeways and arterial roads on an annual basis. For example, the Perth Metropolitan Transport Plan prepared by the Barnet Government in 2015 is a wonderful document with pretty pictures and includes many interesting ideas, but it is basically sitting on a shelf unloved and unfunded.[264]

When the McGowan Labour Government came to power in 2017, the previous transport plan was tossed out and replaced with METRONET, a plan to expand the passenger rail program in the Perth metropolitan area. This program is partly funded

---

[262] 'Land Tax explained', ATO website, 2021.
[263] 'Main Roads Annual Budget 2020/21', MRWA, 2020.
[264] 'Perth Metropolitan Transport Plan – 2031', Department for Transport, 2013.

by the state government, with the balance (sum 80%) being funded by the Federal Government as part of a City Deal, and is a one off, rather than an ongoing year-by-year program of committed funds. This is a fundamental flaw of the state governments' system of funding for transport infrastructure. Clearly absent in Australia is a strategic bi-partisan strategy for public transport that transcends different governments. Rather, what exists is micro policy that can change depending upon the government in power, which is beholden to short-term election cycles. Right now, Perth has a pro-public transport government under Mark McGowan, who has released METRONET, but this could change in four years' time, and public transport expansion could be shelved as a result. This approach will need to change in future, if our cities are to become more sustainable and supportive of higher-density development, and if there is going to be a consistent approach to the delivery of public transport across our cities to support it.

How can planning for public transport in our cities change in the future? Well, unless there is a dedicated tax raised to fund the consistent and ongoing provision of public transport that binds successive governments to a bi-partisan public transport strategy, then the future for public transport in our cities will always be beholden to the government of the day and whether or not they are pro-public transport. What is needed is for each Australian city to adopt a public transport strategy that is binding to both the Labor and Liberal Governments and the creation of a tax to ensure funding is available for its ongoing implementation. Failing the installation of a new tax (it may be politically unacceptable to establish a new tax for public transport), state governments need to set aside a portion of consolidated revenue to devote to public transport implementation and expansion. This could be undertaken in concert with seeking federal funds through the Federal Government's Infrastructure Australia body, with the two combined to give long-lasting commitment to public transport infrastructure expansion in our cities.

On occasion, the Federal Government, as part of federal stimulus, sets aside money for the implementation of regional-type infrastructure. To assist in the distribution of federal funds, the government body Infrastructure Australia was established by the Federal Government to be used as a filter to help decide which state and territory receives funding from the Federal Government for key infrastructure investments. The way it works is the state government puts together an infrastructure project, commits a portion of state funds to its implementation and then puts it to the Federal Government via Infrastructure Australia to seek equivalent funding from federal government coffers. Infrastructure Australia isn't just set up for public transport, but rather for all types of infrastructure, such as regional roads, ports and commercial trains. Infrastructure Australia, therefore, acts as a filter, since there is not enough money going around for every project on the state government's wish list. As a body, it recommends the most favourable projects to the Federal Government to commit its limited funding.

Of course, this is not always equitable, and the government of the day often makes selections based on political favouritism – or 'pork barrelling', to put it another way. Still, it is the system we have, and nobody said it was perfect. To improve the chances of fairness, Infrastructure Australia should be bi-partisan and operate as an independent body whose decision is final on the allocation of infrastructure spending. While not perfect, it would somewhat reduce the amount of political influence on who gets the money.

In addition to changes to governance to engender change in our cities, the Federal Government should set aside a percentage of all federal funding solely for public transport infrastructure. This is critical to ensure that all funding in the pool doesn't go to roads or bias some other form of infrastructure, which is what often happens. Secondly, the Federal Government can insist, as a condition of obtaining funding approval, that each state government has an Infrastructure Australia-approved public transport strategy that is binding to successive state governments, with amendments to the strategy only approved following state government and Infrastructure Australia's approval. This would tie in state governments to Infrastructure Australia, will ensure a consistent approach to the allocation of public transport funding across the states and will also reward those states who are organised and have a plan.

It is also hoped that this approach would be equitable, with states receiving a fair share of public transport funding, rather than some cities receiving all the funding, while others receive little to nothing. Sydney, for example, has received its fair share of funding for public transport, with its inner-circle light-rail project being, perhaps, one of the most expensive light-rail projects in the world, at approximately six billion dollars.[265] As a biased Western Australian, I have to ask... when is Perth going to receive the equivalent federal funding for its mid-tier public transport network? It would be nice to see light rail in Perth sometime this century.

Figure 6.5: Sustainable transport – less investment in roads and more in public transport[266]

---

[265] *"Sydney's new light rail opens 14 December from Circular Quay to Randwick"*, Transport Info NSW, Archived from the original on 9 December 2019.

[266] 'Sydney Light rail' and 'Perth Freeway', Sergio Famiano's private photography, 2021.

Mid-Tier Transit

A lot is often said, but little done about mid-tier public transport. You are probably thinking "what is this, and why is it called mid-tier?". There are essentially three levels of public transport in Australia. The first tier includes fast or rapid public transport, and this comes in the form of heavy passenger rail. The passenger railways are on dedicated rail tracks, are unimpeded by other forms of transport and are reliable and fast. They also can't go everywhere and, therefore, are more suited to providing transportation between major destinations.

The second tier of public transport, or the mid-tier, supports heavier passenger rail and has traditionally consisted of light-rail or bus rapid transit; more recently, this includes trackless tram technology. This form of infrastructure is more nimble than heavier passenger rail and can be used to work through our urban environment, connecting passenger rail stations with major activity centres, shopping and office areas, and major employment hubs, for example. This form of public transport is more versatile than heavier passenger rail, but still has some of the advantages of passenger rail, such as light rail, which can operate in its own dedicated lane, ensuring reliability and speed. The technology is also versatile in that, at key points, this technology can be shared with road traffic, if needed.

The final tier of public transit is buses. Now, buses have been around for eighty plus years in Australian cities and are versatile, in that they can go places where passenger rail and light rail, for example, can't go – buses can pretty much go anywhere a vehicle can; however, this is also their Achilles' heel. Buses are traditionally less reliable than other forms of public transport and are also shunned by many people, with buses often being noisy, clunky and uncomfortable. Because buses also have to deal with traffic, most people would prefer to drive their own car rather than be stuck on a crowded bus – although a bus fare may be cheaper than driving and parking your car.

In most Australian cities, all three tiers of public transport exist and work effectively towards ensuring public transport is spread throughout our cities, providing a viable alternative to the private automobile and also providing affordable transport to those in our community who are less fortunate or unable to commute with a private vehicle. In my home city of Perth, however, this is not the case, and there is no mid-tier transit to speak off. This has long been debated in Perth, and there have been many discussions at the political and academic levels as to the importance of introducing a mid-tier transit system to increase the versatility of public transport and also to support infill development in established areas. As a local government employee, I know only too well the pressure that is applied from state governments to local governments to increase residential densities in established urban areas.

In Western Australia, the state government's Department of Planning, lands and Heritage administers its State Planning Strategy and prepares key documents, such as 'Perth and Peel @ 3.5 million', which it then imposes on local governments to implement. In a nutshell, the strategy document advises that, by 2050, the population of Perth could be 3.5 million (currently 2.125 million), of which a large portion must be accommodated in existing urban areas. The state government then, through its legislative powers, ensures that, when local government town planning schemes are reviewed, the residential density is increased so these strategy document forecasts can be met. This seems fairly simple, but the Achilles' heel of this strategy is transport. You see, our roads can't be widened anymore, and, in many cases, they are fixed. If you are asking local governments to increase residential density in existing areas that have fixed road capacity, what happens? Traffic congestion and lots of it. Traffic, and private vehicle usage in general, is one of the biggest contributors to greenhouses gases and is also one of the major disruptors to urban amenity – if you have lived near an arterial road, you would appreciate the noise it generates.

So, if you can't widen the roads anymore, but you are inviting more people (with cars) into an existing urban environment, what do you do? The answer is a modal shift: get more people out of their cars and onto public transport. Light rail, bus rapid transit and trackless trams, or a combination of the three, is the solution. By snaking mid-tier transit through our suburbs, you provide a viable and affordable alternative form of transport for people to use, and you can manage the crisis emerging from increased housing density and the question of how to move all these extra people without negatively impacting the amenities people enjoy in existing suburbs. Simple solution, but you would be surprised to know that it is anything but simple.

The organisation charged with the responsibility of developing a mid-tier transit strategy for Perth is the Department of Transport and the Public Transport Authority, and, at the time of writing this book, I was advised that "they are tinkering with a strategy" in the background. In other words, they don't have a mandate from the state government to work on this issue; therefore, there's limited funding or resources to prepare such a plan. However, such a plan is critical for Perth, as you can't have one state government agency asking for residential density increases, and then have another state government agency not being granted the ability to plan and deliver the infrastructure that is critical to support it. The department is trying; however, it is just not getting the political support needed. There is an obvious disconnect – one that needs to be solved.

At the time of writing this book, a group of colleagues of mine and I have been working closely with fifteen other local governments in Perth to lobby the state government for funding and priority to deliver a mid-tier transport strategy for Perth. The strategy is critical in giving confidence to local government and industry in planning for urban change. The development industry is also demanding such a plan, repeatedly saying it wants to deliver apartment developments but needs light rail to support it. All I can say is watch this space; we might get lucky and have mid-tier transport in Perth before I am sixty.

Public Transport Implementation

The implementation of public transport infrastructure can be tricky. Most metropolitan region schemes, when established, did not set up specific corridors for public infrastructure, since these plans were developed during the height of the car era, and, accordingly, major reserves were set aside for roads to access freeways, rather than specific public transport rail routes. The only rail routes that exist in the Metropolitan Region Scheme are historic – i.e., they predate the establishment of the scheme. When metropolitan region schemes were developed across most of our cities in the 1960s, it was assumed that buses would be the public transport of choice, and, accordingly, making road reservations for cars meant also making provisions for public transport. The thinking didn't exist that we should also have dedicated reserves for passenger and light-rail options, since these modes of transport fell out of favour in the 1960s and 1970s. So, there are very few dedicated reserves for public transport in our cities – other than historic lines.

For those cities that have Metropolitan Region Schemes, such as Perth and Melbourne, there is one advantage for having a car-dominated city: the widths of road reserves for freeways and arterial roads tend to be very wide, and this has meant passenger rail lines can be introduced within major road reservations, since there is usually room for both. This is why, in Perth and Melbourne, for example, major passenger rail lines follow a linear pattern within main arterial roads. In Perth, for example, the Mitchell Freeway accommodates eight lanes of motor-vehicle transport and the main northern suburbs railway line in its centre. The same is true for the southern alignment to Mandurah.

In fact, if you look at the public transport network for Perth, it has five major railway line routes, which reach deep into the suburbs. Three of these routes are historical train lines, such as the Armadale Line, Midland Line and Fremantle Line, which were established before the age of the automobile, and were subsequently easy to extend. The other two railway lines are the Clarkson Line, which services the northern suburbs, and the Mandurah Line, which services the southern suburbs. They both completely follow the north-and-south-bound freeway. In fact, they are formed in the middle of the freeway with bridges extending either side to link land use with the train station. It is not the best form of public transport network, since the integration of land use with transport is virtually non-existent; positioning the railway station in the middle of the freeway means there is a four-lane highway on either side, creating a great divide between the station infrastructure and land use. This is why much of the north- and southbound railway line train stations in Perth are dominated by a sea of car parking, rather than integrated mixed-use development, which is common in most European cities. While it's good to have this infrastructure, it is a missed opportunity in terms of transport and land use integration.

As a city, Melbourne is more mature than Perth, on a public transport basis, and operates similar to Perth, with a number of railway corridors following the freeway alignment. It also has a number of historical lines that predate the automobile, which have since been extended. Melbourne is more mature still, however, because it includes significant light rail in its public transport armoury, which supports the heavy passenger-rail network. In the Perth transit system, the five passenger rail lines extend out like tentacles into the suburb areas, but, because this is passenger rail, it follows a linear trajectory. In Perth, there are vast areas between the major passenger rail routes, which aren't serviced by rail; instead, Perth is reliant on buses, which have traditionally fallen out of favour with passengers, given that there is a perceived unreliability to road-based public transport.

Instead of a vast expanse of buses, they have filled the gap between linear passenger rail routes in Melbourne with high-quality mid-tier transit in their chosen form of light-rail infrastructure, which is fixed, dedicated and has a massive reliability factor. Having a car-based city with wide road reserves means the opportunity exists to have car space shared with light rail, given the streets of Australian cities tend to be wider than European cities, for example, which were developed predating the train and automobile. This is an advantage Australian cities need to capitalise on.

Capitalising on it, though, has been made difficult with the car lobby in Australia, which insists streets remain for cars only and not rail. Perth has had this battle, and it remains one of the main reasons why Perth is the only major city in Australia that doesn't have light rail in its public transport framework. In fact, it is completely absent of mid-tier public transport and, therefore, is totally reliant on buses, outside of fixed passenger rail. This is where political savvy and willpower is required. Light rail is considered a very successful form of public transport, because, as mentioned before, it is fixed on a dedicated route and therefore passes the pub test for reliability.

Light rail is found throughout European and major cities in the world and is seen as the next tier of public transport from large-scale passenger rail networks. Because light rail is characterised by shorter cars, the trains are nimble and, therefore, can work their way through tight streets and neighbourhoods where passenger rail can't go. They represent the classic public transport network that can work between the main passenger rail networks to ensure public transport can spread between main road and public transport corridors. Melbourne is a good Australian example of this, with most residential neighbourhoods within twenty kilometres of the CBD having access to light rail and/or passenger rail.

With Australian cities having wide road reserves, it should be easier than, say, in Europe to enable light rail to infiltrate the transport network. Yet, when you compare Australia with our European cousins, there is a gulf between acceptance and public opinion versus implementation of light rail in Australian cities. In European cities, despite the constraints of tight roads and sharing public space with cars and pedestrians, they find it easier to implement light rail than Australian cites. How is that possible? Well, the difference is in attitudes and standards. In terms of attitudes, there is a long-standing acceptance in Europe of the accommodation of light rail in their cities. They have had a long history with it, and Europeans have a very good understanding of the benefits it provides. In Australia, we have had over eighty years of 'car culture', which has transcended several generations, making it very difficult to convince people to share their roads with light rail.[267]

The truth is we have been so efficient at creating car-dominated environments that it is difficult to win the argument to have light rail as a partial substitute for the car, since it will take time for people to grow accustomed to taking fewer trips by the private automobile and taking more trips using light rail. It is a battle worth fighting, though, because the evidence shows that light rail is not only a more sustainable and efficient form of transport than the private automobile, but it also facilitates higher-density development, which is desperately needed in Australian cities.

Case Study: Sydney

This is a battle that Sydney is currently fighting within its streets, as it commits to the establishment of the Sydney Light Rail Project. For Sydney, which has no Metropolitan Region Scheme – therefore no 'higher mechanism' for the reservation of land for freeways, regional roads and public transport – implementing 'game-changing' public infrastructure is made significantly more difficult. The Sydney Light Rail Project commenced in the early 2000s, when it was used to establish the 5-kilometre inner-city-west light rail connection from the Central Train Station to Lilyfield, which picks up major landmark sites, such as the Exhibition and Convention Centre in Sydney's west. This project was followed by its 5.6km extension westward into the suburbs from Lilyfield to Dulwich Hill, following a former freight rail line corridor, rather than a tight street network.[268] The extension was completed after two and a half years of development and opened in March 2014. This project was rather simplified, due to its extension along a former freight rail corridor, which significantly reduced problems with congestion – a result of sharing road space with railway line.

Sydney's light rail program has now turned its attention towards the east of the city, with a project to extend the light rail network from the city's centre to the city's east in the works. The 12-kilometre route features 19 stops, extending from Circular Quay, along George Street and Central Station, through to Surrey Hills and Moore Park, and then on to Kensington and Kingsford via Anzac Parade, and Randwick via Alison Road and High Street.[269] The stops are designed to service major transport hubs and create easy interchangeable passenger transfer with buses, trains, ferries and the

---

[267] 'Davies,G, *'Car Wars – How the car one our hearts and conquered our cities'*, Allen and Uwin, 2004.
[268] O'Sullivan, M, *"Sydney's inner west light rail line out of action for up to 18 months"*. *The Sydney Morning Herald*, November 2021.
[269] O'Sullivan, M, *"Sydney's inner west light rail line out of action for up to 18 months"*. *The Sydney Morning Herald*, November 2021.

inner-west light rail line. The project, which commenced in July 2014, has been beset by problems associated with implementing light rail into an existing car environment, with significant cost blow-outs resulting from managing and relocating services, traffic and land-take requirements in sections to ensure the light rail network can function hand in hand with automobiles. The project's initial cost of $1.6 billion, or an estimated $134 million per kilometre (one of the most expensive light rail projects in the world), has blown out to $2.1 billion, or a whopping $175 million per kilometre.[270] The project was due to be completed early in 2019 but has only just completed in June 2020 – a year over the timeframe.

Despite its cost and delay, Sydney's commitment to light rail is a welcome sign that the city is maturing and recognising the benefits of diversifying its public transport options to ensure Sydney's suburbs are well linked by public transport to the city centre. This will create enormous opportunities for redevelopments to take place around the light rail stations to maximise transit-oriented development. Providing fixed and reliable public transport deep into suburban areas not only increases trip generation by light rail over the private automobile, but also opens up vast areas for redevelopment along transit-oriented principles. This will assist in transforming areas from low-density housing into medium- and high-density options, supporting the maturation of the city and the transition of the Australian Dream to a more sustainable urban form.

Figure 6.6: Sydney Light Rail network[271]

---

[270] O'Sullivan, M, *"Sydney's inner west light rail line out of action for up to 18 months". The Sydney Morning Herald*, November 2021.

[271] *'Sydney Light Rail Service Map'*, Sydney.com.au.

Implementing Light Rail

So far, we have discussed the importance of having a transport strategy that is supported by funding from both state and federal governments that has bi-partisan political support. We have also discussed the possible funding opportunities through Infrastructure Australia and setting minimum targets for public transport. The next factor that is critical to implementing light rail is understanding the Australian Standards and how they are inherently biased towards the provision of infrastructure for the automobile.

There are Australian Standards for many things, ranging from individual products to the provision of infrastructure. Australian Standards influence the implementation of infrastructure, as service providers such as Main Roads Western Australia look to implement Standards when planning for the establishment of roads of all types. In Australia, we are a conservative lot, and the provision of road standards can be such that it makes it difficult to implement other forms of infrastructure when a 'shared' approach is needed.

When implementing the Sydney Light Rail Project, part of the implementation process involved placing light rail down existing rail corridors. In these circumstances, there is a clear separation between rail and road. Accordingly, there is limited perceived or actual conflict between the infrastructure options. When light rail is shared with the automobile, however, the circumstances are different. The Australian Standards require minimum separation between light rail vehicle and automobiles, and this can sometimes make it difficult to implement light rail in a shared scenario. It has been done before, but it is challenging, and often accommodating the minimum standards results in cost blow-outs in requiring wider reserves or land-take to make sure minimum distances between vehicles and light-rail carriages are achieved. Often, transport authorities are reluctant to implement light rail and automobiles in a shared scenario, due to perceived risks of collisions, which has been a common theme in setting back light-rail implementation in Australia. If you look at Europe, however, they have no problems with implementing light rail in a shared infrastructure scenario. This is something Australian cities and administrators of public transport need to reconcile – i.e., there needs to be an acceptance that light rail can be shared with automobiles and safety and effectiveness can be maintained.

Australian Standards are just that, 'standards', and can be varied, but it takes political courage to modify or defy standards, given the legal implications should an accident occur, for example, and the Standards, or lack of following the Standards, are found complicit in the accident. The preferred approach is for public transport administrators and politicians to accept that light-rail vehicles and automobiles can share infrastructure, rather than deferring light-rail implementation until the perfect circumstances, such as a vacated rail corridor, come into existence. This is important, because, unless there is acceptance that light rail can be shared with the automobile, we will be reliant on extraordinary circumstances for light rail to be implemented.

The Australian Standards also need to change to make implementing light rail more favourable and give light rail priority over the automobile, when the two share infrastructure. This means accepting congestion as a reality when light rail is implemented and taking the perspective that increased congestion can be positive, since it will encourage more people to use light rail as an alternative, which is the whole point. Once again, this needs political will, and I ask politicians to step up to the plate on this issue for the sake of our cities and sustainability.

Case Study: Gold Coast Light Rail

A project recently completed in Australia that has had an immediate impact is the Gold Coast Light Rail Project. With the first stage completed in 2014, the Gold Coast Light Rail, or G-Link as it is known, is a 20-kilometre-long light-rail track that includes fifteen stations running from Helensvale Station in the north, to Broadbeach Station in the south. The origins of the project featured in the Gold Coast Council Transport Plan as far back as 1996. This project was followed up by federal and state funding in 2002 to consider its feasibility to extend the arm of the Gold Coast public transport response to what is one of the fastest growing areas in the country, with population growth hovering around 2-3% annually.[272]

In a sign of collaboration between local, state and federal governments, in 2009 the Queensland Government committed $464 million to the Gold Coast Rapid Transit Project, which was supported by $365 million committed by the Federal Government and $120 million provided by Gold Coast City Council.[273] Collectively, the near-one-billion-dollar commitment to build the first 13 kilometres of the light-rail system was awarded to Bombardier Transportation, Downer EDI, Keolis, McConnell Dowell and the Plenary Group, who constructed the line and have rights to operate it for eighteen years under a public and private sector partnership.[274]

After the extension of the line to accommodate the Gold Coast Hospital in 2017, there are plans to further extend the line by 6.3 kilometres to Burleigh Heights, again with local, state and federal governments stumping up the $640 million for the extension.[275] Patronage on the line has been a huge success, with initial estimates upon the opening of the line reaching approximately six million passengers per year in

---

[272] 'Gold Coast Rapid Transit Corridor Study', City of Gold Coast, Archived from the original on 11 December 2013, Retrieved 6 December 2013.
[273] 'Gold Coast Rapid Transit Corridor Study', City of Gold Coast, Archived from the original on 11 December 2013, Retrieved 6 December 2013.
[274] Moore, T, "Gold Coast light rail stage two and Brisbane link unveiled". Brisbane Times. Fairfax Media.
[275] Payne, K, "Gold Coast light rail stage 3A: $112m funding committed to Broadbeach to Burleigh tram extension". Gold Coast Bulletin, 2018.

2014/15.[276] This has since increased to 10.74 million in 2018/19.[277] The Light Rail Project has been so successful it now contributes 35% of all public transport use in the Gold Coast area and has dramatically improved pedestrian movement and reduced private vehicle use. The Gold Coast Council's 2036 Transport Plan has a further 68 kilometres of light-rail track across 4 lines.[278] Such is the faith and trust that the Gold Coast Council has in the success of light rail in its city.

Figure 6.7: Queensland Light Rail[279]

The project wasn't without difficulties, with resumption equalling $170 million to ensure the light-rail system fit within adequate rail and road reservations.[280] Many of these resumptions may not have been required if Australia Standards had been relaxed somewhat to accommodate the modal share between the light-rail system and private vehicle movement. Because we like to separate the two in Australia, this often results in wider reserves being required, leading to the resumption of land at key pinch points.

One of the key influential factors supporting the implementation of light rail on the Gold Coast came from increased traffic congestion, which was being caused by the 20,000-strong student population at Griffith University and the growing patient numbers at the Gold Coast University Hospital. From an environmental standpoint, the

---

[276] Payne, K, *"Gold Coast light rail stage 3A: $112m funding committed to Broadbeach to Burleigh tram extension"*. Gold Coast Bulletin, 2018.

[277] *"Light rail",* www.goldcoast.qld.gov.au. Archived from the original on 10 July 2018.

[278] *"Light rail",* www.goldcoast.qld.gov.au. Archived from the original on 10 July 2018.

[279] *'Government commits $351million to light rail'*, Top 100 Women, 2021.

[280] *'Government commits $351million to light rail'*, Top 100 Women, 2021.

project has been hugely successful in reducing carbon emissions on the Gold Coast, with light rail providing a greener alternative to the automobile. It is also a system that runs on electricity, so it produces almost no emissions. It is estimated that the light rail has reduced local greenhouse gas emissions by 114,000 tonnes over its first ten years of operation and has reduced the number of private automobile trips by up to 10%, representing a real mode shift from private automobiles to public transport.[281]

The success of the project lends itself to the importance of planning many years in advance and sticking to a plan to ensure the consistency and support of all tiers of government, which are essential in securing funding for its implementation. The fact that the Gold Coast Council was visionary enough to identify light rail as a real solution to growing congestion when it earmarked light rail in its 1996 transport plan cannot be understated. More importantly, it persisted with this plan and further expanded the vision for the network when the transport plan evolved. This consistency is important to build trust and momentum in government funding to support such a venture. This is a strategy other governments across Australia can learn from.

The Gold Coast Light Rail network is now extending into existing suburban areas, which presents opportunities for redevelopment and greater modal shift, as people can now set aside their cars and undertake trips via light rail. Development opportunities appear across the light rail's stations, many of which are already dense due to high-rise development that exists on the Gold Coast. This is perhaps a reverse example, where high-rise development was constructed first, followed by congestion, then the implementation of higher-order public transport came into effect to reduce the traffic strain. Evidence globally shows that the implementation of light rail early in a project can act as a catalyst to encourage high-density development.

New Technology: Trackless Trams

In 2019, I attended a presentation by Professor Peter Newman of Curtin University's Sustainability Institute on the potential of trackless trams to transform public transport in Perth. Trackless trams are a relatively new transport technology, originally pioneered in Europe in the 2000s, but it has its variants in China. Essentially, trackless trams are similar to light rail in that they have a purpose-built design to differentiate them from other modes of transport and have an all-door boarding system, but instead of running on tracks and overhead power cables, they run on tyres. Unlike light rail, trackless trams have significant advantages, in that they are less disruptive to install, cause minimal disruption to adjoining local businesses and communities and do not have extensive overhead infrastructure, which can be a visual blight to the streetscape of an area. Trackless trams also have the added advantage of being

---

[281] *"TMR Annual Report – Appendix 2 – Performance statements 2015–16"*, Department of Transport and Main Roads, 2016.

quieter than light rail and more environmentally friendly, because they are powered by lithium-ion batteries that can be recharged over a very short period of time, with charging points located at select pick up stations or depots.[282]

I first experienced this technology when I visited Metz in France, in 2015, and was amazed at its design, operation and capacity to mimic all the benefits of light rail without the disadvantages of being a fixed-rail system with overhead infrastructure. Metz, with a population of just under 120,000 people, has a similar challenge to Australian cities, in that population density and constraints to civic budgets hamper efforts to seriously contemplate light rail as a viable solution to encourage public transport use. As an alternative, Metz has elected to take on this new technology, and it appears to be a viable alternative to its expensive light rail cousin.

Unlike light rail, which can cost up to $120 million per kilometre to install (Sydney Light Rail has come in at $175 million), trackless trams are estimated to cost approximately $10–15 million per kilometre, which includes the trams themselves along with the tram stops.[283] They are not just cheaper; trackless trams can be implemented with relative ease. This is in stark contrast with light rail, which involves significant disruption to a community through the installation of tracks and overhead infrastructure. An example of the impact to business and traffic that comes with implementing light rail can be seen in Sydney's Light Rail project, which we have already discussed. Having been completed over budget, and nearly one year behind schedule, one of the downsides of the Sydney Light Rail Project was its disruption to business and traffic movement during its implementation. Many businesses reported that they had been struggling with the disruption associated with building light rail, noting that foot traffic and commerce suffered as a result of the extensive rail works over a two-to-three-year period.

This is in stark contrast to trackless trams, which can be implemented with relative ease and without major disruption to local businesses. In addition to having minimal disruption, trackless trams also have the latest technology. One of the technological innovations that sets trackless trams apart from other modes of public transport is their inbuilt stabilising technology. This technology is built into the vehicle's suspension and ensures all bumps and slopes on conventional roadways are moderated via the suspension adjusting, so that the cabin is maintained, in most circumstances, on an even setting. This means the cabin of the vehicle is maintained at a near consistent level, despite the topography of the road, allowing for a much smoother ride than light rail and bus technology. Having experienced trackless trams in Metz, I can vouch for their comfort and reliability.

---

[282] *'Why Trackless trams are ready to replace light rail'*, The Conversation, September 2016.
[283] *'Why Trackless trams are ready to replace light rail'*, The Conversation, September 2016.

The potential for this technology in Australian cities is seemingly endless. Having worked in Perth my entire career, I have seen a number of leading aspirational projects, such as the MAX Light Rail Project, the Knowledge Arc Light Rail Project and the Stirling Central to Scarborough Beach Light Rail Projects, be deferred or made more difficult by the enormous expense and disruption involved in committing to light-rail infrastructure. The emergence of trackless trams, however, offers a real alternative at a fraction of the cost.

There are many projects across Australia that could benefit from this new technology, and the beauty of it is that it can be implemented relatively easily and in a fraction of the time it takes to implement light rail. And, if trackless trams are given dedicated lanes like light rail, they can have all the reliability and certainty that comes with light rail. Think of all the dual-carriageway roads within our Australian cities. These could be adapted to accommodate trackless trams without major disruptions to the network. The technology has the potential to be a game changer for public transport in Australia.

Figure 6.8: Trackless tram (China)[284]

For just under nine years, I worked for LandCorp – The WA State Land Developer (now Development WA) – and was fortunate to have led the planning and delivery of the Cockburn Coast (Shoreline) Project. Located approximately 4.5 kilometres south of Fremantle, alongside the Indian Ocean and consisting of a development area of 98 hectares, the project aims to transform a former industrial area into a thriving residential and commercial community with up to 12,000 residents. The project, which is expected to take ten to twenty years to complete, includes the rejuvenation of the South Fremantle Power Station site into world class retail, commercial,

---

[284] *'Could trackless trams replace light rail'*, Curtin University, March 2019.

residential and tourist attractions. The project is aspirational, as it intends to create high-density living along the Australian Coastline through three distinct precincts: Shoreline, The Power Station and Hilltop.

During the planning phase of the project, an integrated transport plan was developed to ensure the high-density population would be accommodated through a considered transport solution, which includes the operation of a light-rail link from Fremantle Train Station to the Cockburn Coast Project. Further studies, which were done in consultation with the surrounding local governments (Cities of Cockburn and Fremantle) and the Department for Transport and Public Transport Authority, identified a preferred light-rail route that would commence at Fremantle Train Station and head to the core of the Cockburn Coast Project, including the South Fremantle Power Station redevelopment. The route has the potential to extend further from the Cockburn Coast development to Cockburn Central, which is located adjacent to the train station on Perth's southern suburbs railway line.

Figure 6.9: The Cockburn Coast – can't afford light rail but could afford trackless trams[285]

With the implementation of the Cockburn Coast Project commencing in 2015, progress has been slow – partly due to the mining downturn, but also due to a lack of commitment by the state government towards public transport infrastructure, which is necessary to underpin a project that is promoting predominately high-density living. State government commitment towards light rail for the project has been hampered by its cost, which is likely to exceed $100 million per kilometre. The advent of trackless trams, and their spread across Europe and China in recent years as a viable alternative to light rail, could prove to be a game changer, with a line from Fremantle to Cockburn Coast (stage 1 of a broader route) having the possibility of

---

[285] *'Cockburn Coast'*, from DevelopmentWA website, 2021.

being implemented for a fraction of the cost of light rail. For this to occur, broader commitment would be required from the State Government to further investigate the possibility of implementing a trackless tram link from Fremantle to Cockburn Central via Cockburn Coast. This shouldn't be a difficult task, as work for a light rail route has already started, and the route has been confirmed as being viable over the long term.

Figure 6.10: Artist impression on how trackless trams could work[286]

Cities like Perth and Adelaide, which are traditionally low-density cities, are in desperate need of a transport revolution, with the development industry reporting that the high-density aspirations of state governments across Australia, such as in 'Perth and Peel @ 3.5 million' (Strategic Planning Document for Perth), are constrained by a lack of infrastructure, including the availability and reliability of low-cost public transport. The establishment of trackless trams as a real alternative to light rail has the potential to revolutionise public transport in cities such as Perth and Adelaide and to breathe new life into these cites, which desperately need to move away from car dependency if they are going to grow more sustainably in the future. The uptake of these technologies in Australia has been slow, and one of the challenges confronting the use of this new technology is that state governments' transport departments are reluctant to try something new. I would suggest that the state governments of our capital cities consider this new technology long and hard, as it has all the benefits of light rail but without major disruption and cost.

---

[286] *'Farewell 2010's (aka a decade of transport in review – and a new decade in preview)'*, TraNZport, 2019.

Creating Places of Interest: Transit-Oriented Development

The Changing Australian Dream through Transport-Led Development

There is a catalytic effect when new transport infrastructure, such as light rail, is implemented, which enables other forms of urban development to be created. The New Urbanists call this 'transit-oriented development', which is a type of urban development that maximises residential development through higher density and commercial and public space opportunities that are within walking distances of train stations. As discussed previously in this book, this is not a new concept, as many of the earlier cities of Europe and North America that expanded in the 1800s did so along train lines, with development generally being denser as you approach a walkable catchment to the train station. The by-product of an area being serviced by high-quality public transport is that you get a completely different form of urban development from suburbia. Housing, in particular, is different, with most development in transit-oriented developments being higher-density apartment and smaller townhouse developments.

Transit-oriented development offers a real opportunity to change the Australian Dream, offering a different lifestyle from suburbia – namely a life that is more 'public oriented', with people living in transit-oriented developments having smaller properties but greater amenities, such as transport, shops and restaurants, at their fingertips. More and more Australians are preferring to be more connected within their neighbourhoods and to seek a more diverse lifestyle than that which can be offered by suburbia.

We will now turn our attention to a number of examples of transit-oriented development in Australia that are having a profound impact in creating a new form of the Australian Dream.

Case Study: Docklands Development Melbourne

Melbourne's Docklands Project is one of the largest urban redevelopments in Australia and is a prime example of a transit-oriented development. The project consists of 190 hectares, including 44 hectares of water, 3.7 kilometres of waterfront and nearly 4 hectares of new public open space.[287] Located west of Melbourne's CBD and positioned in a waterfront location, the Docklands development was a key industrial area that transitioned into a significant port to support the growth of Melbourne City in the nineteenth century.

Throughout history, as far back as the 1860s, the Docklands region was home to a number of industrial-type activities, including the Melbourne Gasworks, railway

---

[287] *'Docklands Project Summary'*, Development Victoria Website, 2021.

industry and military depots.²⁸⁸ The area was also home to noxious industries, such as abattoirs and tanneries. Seen as a working-class area of Melbourne, Docklands began to transition in the 1880s, when it was redeveloped into a port that was completed in 1892.²⁸⁹ The significance of the Docklands port can't be understated, and, by 1910, the Docklands area had expanded to handle close to 90% of Victoria's trade and was essential to the Melbourne economy. Docklands continued its expansion and, by the 1950s, was by far Melbourne's busiest dock, handling a wide range of cargo, including coal, steel, animals, wool and wheat.

By the time the swinging '60s came around, the fortunes for the Docklands area began to change, beginning with the Harbor Trust's decision to use cargo containers that required different storage space to the long sheds lining the docks.²⁹⁰ As a result, new docks and transport infrastructure were built west of the Victoria Dock in the 1970s, which had the effect of rendering much of the old Docklands redundant. The decline of the Docklands continued during the 1980s until it became a largely derelict and redundant area affected by crime, high vacancy and homelessness. It also became a home for the burgeoning rave scene that took hold in the early 1990s, utilising the large empty warehouses for rave parties.²⁹¹

In 1990, the Cain State Government identified the Docklands area as a blight on Melbourne and set about establishing a Docklands Task Force to review the feasibility of redeveloping the area and to consider its transition from historic land use to a new urban redevelopment.²⁹² In 1991, the Docklands Authority, which has since been renamed Development Victoria, was established to oversee the planning and regeneration of the Docklands area and its integration into the Melbourne CBD. A number of attempts to consider the future of Docklands in 1991 and 1992 failed, which included redevelopment associated with a failed bid for the 2000 Olympics.

In 1992, the Kennett Government was elected, ushering in an era of projects and redevelopment, which included a focus on kick-starting the Docklands Project. Rather than taking a traditional top-down approach to planning and development, the Kennett Government – through the Docklands Authority – initiated a process to have the development industry design and construct the vision for the Docklands Project. Subsequently, the Docklands area was divided into precincts that were separately tendered to the private sector for planning and development. Despite best endeavours, this process failed, and it was clear the government would need to

---

[288] *'Docklands Project Summary'*, Development Victoria Website, 2021.
[289] *'Docklands Project Summary'*, Development Victoria Website, 2021.
[290] Millar, R, *"Docklands a wasted opportunity?"*, The Age. Fairfax, 2006.
[291] Tomazin, F, Donovan, P, Mundell, M, *"Dance trance"*, The Age, Fairfax. December 2017.
[292] Dovey, K, *'Fluid City: Transforming Melbourne's Waterfront'*. Sydney: University of New South Wales Press, 2005.

play a role in coordinating infrastructure planning for the project.²⁹³ This led to the completion of the Docklands Village Precinct, which was originally intended to be for residential and commercial mixed development. This was set aside, and instead it became the preferred location for the new Docklands Football Stadium, which was seen – along with Spencer Street Train Station – as an anchor to the Docklands redevelopment.

In 1997, the Docklands Authority commissioned the preparation of the Docklands Masterplan, which was the first attempt at a coordinated plan for the redevelopment. Utilising its position relative to the CBD and the availability of nearby public transport in passenger rail and light rail in the city centre, the vision for the Docklands development was to create a transit-oriented development that would provide for significant retail, commercial and entertainment-type land uses, as well as significant residential development in the form of apartment development.

Construction of the Docklands redevelopment commenced in 1997, with the Docklands Stadium, set to house Australian Rules Football events, and the first of eight distinct precincts used for residential, commercial, retail, dining and leisure purposes. By early 2000, the Docklands Project began to gain momentum, with development being divided among a number of precincts that contained a number of significant developments, as described below.

Batemans Hill Precinct – Bordered by the Yarra River to the south, Spencer Street to the east, Docklands Stadium to the north and Victoria Harbor to the west, it consists of approximately 100,000sqm. This precinct is a mixed-use hub that includes land uses such as commercial, retail, residential and cultural heritage sites. By 2022, more than half of the precinct has been built and includes the Watergate/Site One apartments, office complex and tower development, which includes the home of the Bureau of Meteorology and Medibank and also the Melbourne headquarters of AMP, Kangan Institutes Automotive Centre for Excellence and the Fox Classic Car Museum. The precinct also includes a development that houses the Travelodge Hotel and other buildings that contain the home of National Foods. Further significant developments are planned for the precinct that will see its completion over the next five to ten years.²⁹⁴

Collins Square – This is a 2-hectare site within the Batemans Hill Precinct. The new development includes five office buildings, ranging in height from 12 to 50 storeys, with public space, 10,000sqm of retail floor space and the refurbishment of The Goods Shed, which was completed in 2018.²⁹⁵

Stadium Precinct – This precinct is located on the eastern edge of the Docklands and consist of the Docklands Stadium, Seven Network's Melbourne Digital Broadcasting

---

[293] Dovey, K, *'Fluid City: Transforming Melbourne's Waterfront'*. Sydney: University of New South Wales Press, 2005.
[294] Millar, R, *"Visionary architect set to transform Docklands"*. The Age. Fairfax, August 2007.
[295] *'Collin Square'*, Development Victoria website, 2021.

Centre, Victoria Point, Bendigo Bank offices and Quest Serviced apartments. Other proposed developments include 21- and 18-storey residential towers, supported by restaurants, bars and a retail plaza, in addition to 29- and 21- storey office towers, as well as three lower-rise buildings to house a 250-room hotel, pub, medical centre, retail, business club and gymnasium.[296]

Digital Harbor at Comtechport Precinct – This is a waterfront location that has an area of 44,000sqm, with development intended to expand to include 220,000sqm of commercial, residential, short stay and retail space. Three buildings have been completed, which are home to VicTrack, Australian Customs and Border Services, and the Telstra Learning Academy and Innovation Centre.[297]

Victoria Harbor – This area of Docklands is the centrepiece, with the precinct consisting of 280,000sqm, with 3.7 kilometres of waterfront. The project area consists of significant residential apartments, commercial office spaces, retail spaces, community facilities and public spaces – such as The Grand Plaza, Harbor Esplanade, Docklands Park and Central Pier. The area includes the headquarters of the National Australia Bank, ANZ, Ericsson, Lend Lease and Fujitsu, bringing thousands of employees to the area.[298]

NewQuay – This was one of the first residential and commercial developments in Docklands, opening in 2002, and includes six residential towers, and a number of townhouse developments.[299]

Yarra's Edge – This precinct is being developed by Mirvac and will consist of eleven apartment towers, once completed. The precinct is divided into three smaller precincts, including the Marina Precinct, comprising the marina and boardwalk, with six residential towers; the Park Precinct, comprising Point Park and two residential towers; and the River Precinct, comprising a mixture of townhouse developments and three high-rise apartment towers.[300]

Waterfront City – This precinct is a 193,000sqm retail and entertainment area, which consists of a shopping mall, Melbourne Star Observation Wheel, Icehouse Sports and Entertainment Centre, and numerous shops and cafés.[301]

Melbourne Central Studios - This is a significant film and television complex, which opened in 2004, and consists of 60,000sqm of area and includes five film and television studios.[302]

---

[296] *'Victoria, Development - Home'*, www.docklands.com, March 2017.
[297] Melbourneopenhouse.org, 16 July 2009 at the Wayback Machine.
[298] *'Victoria, Development - Home'*, www.docklands.com, March 2017.
[299] Development Victoria website, 2021.
[300] Liu, S, *"New reasons to visit Harbour Town"*. Docklands News, March 2018.
[301] Development Victoria website, 2021.
[302] Development Victoria website, 2021.

Figure 6.11: Docklands in the 1990s[303]

Part of the success of Docklands as a major transit-oriented development is due to its access to a variety of road, rail and water transport. It is well serviced by Docklands Highway, which provides road access to Westgate Freeway and links to the Melbourne CBD via Flinders Street, Collins Street and La Trobe Street. The project is supported by Southern Cross Train Station, which is a major passenger rail line, and also by Melbourne's light-rail network, including the City Circle Tram along Docklands Drive, and the waterfront and light rail stops have been extended within the project area along Waterfront City, Harbour Esplanade, Collins Street to Victoria Harbour, and routes running through Docklands via La Trobe Street. The infrastructure for Docklands also supports a number of main pedestrian and cycle corridors, as well as three ferry terminals that connect Docklands with the Melbourne CBD.[304]

Once completed (estimated around 2030), Docklands will be home to more than 13,000 people and provide employment to over 73,000 people.[305] The development also includes 1 million sqm of commercial office space and 9 hectares of parks and will also have attracted private sector investment of a whopping $14.6 billion.[306] Yearly construction on the precinct sustains approximately 2,500 to 3,000 jobs.[307]

---

[303] Development Victoria website, 2021.
[304] Development Victoria website, 2021.
[305] Development Victoria website, 2021.
[306] Development Victoria website, 2021.
[307] Development Victoria website, 2021.

Figure 6.12: Docklands 2020[308]

The success of Docklands has its origins in its setting and supporting infrastructure. Located west of the Melbourne CBD and blessed with a waterfront, the project has the setting to be a large-scale dynamic development that blends significant residential development with complementary public space, entertainment precincts and public transport. To support the Docklands development, light rail was extended into the project area to link it with the broader CBD and Southbank areas. The port also remains for recreational boating – supported by significant office development. While some cities have concerns that there isn't enough 'green space' in the project area to sustain the large resident and commercial workforce, the project is largely successful in offering an alternative to the Australian Dream, by combining smaller living with amenities in the form of transport, water, commercial, retail and entertainment opportunities, all within walking distance – something that is lacking in traditional suburbia.

Case Study: Yeerongpilly, Brisbane

While the Docklands is a project that has been evolving in earnest over the last twenty years, there are many new transit-oriented developments being planned that are in the early stages of their delivery. One such example is Yeerongpilly, in Brisbane's south, which is a 14-hectare redevelopment of the former Yeerongpilly Animal Research Institute located adjacent to the Brisbane River and is supported by the Gold Coast/Brisbane Railway Line.

---

[308] Development Victoria website, 2021.

Figure 6.13: Yeerongpilly redevelopment site[309]

Historically, the site was used for agriculture during the 1850s. Following the extension of the Southern Line Railway in the 1880s, the land transitioned to residential use. In 1909, the Animal Research Institute was established as a stock experiment station and was a centre for the control of diseases in livestock.[310] The site continued this function up until the early 2000s and also included a veterinary school. A Power Station was also built on part of the site in 1953 and operated until 1986, after which it was demolished. From 2008 onwards, the Animal Research Centre was gradually relocated to new facilities, eventually closing down in 2010.

During the 2007 to 2008 period, the Queensland Government conducted a competitive process to select a preferred developer for the site. The project was enacted in two stages, with the first involving the construction of a new regional Tennis Centre and 207 apartments west of the site, and the second being the redevelopment of the Animal Research Institute land for a transit-oriented development. In 2009, then-premier Anna Bligh announced that the redevelopment of the remaining site was to be fast-tracked to create high-quality residential accommodation, affordable housing, retail, commercial and entertainment-type land uses, leveraging off the existing Yeerongpilly Train Station east of the project site. After completion of concept planning and consultation in 2010, the land was put to market in 2011 for further project

---

[309] Sinclair, L, *'Everything you need to know about the Yeerongpilly Redevelopment'*, 2019.

[310] Sinclair, L, *'Everything you need to know about the Yeerongpilly Redevelopment'*, 2019.

development and commencement. After a tender process, the project development partner was awarded to Consolidated Properties Group, which included partners CVS Lane Capital Partners and Hutchinson Builders.[311]

Figure 6.14: Yeerongpilly Green Masterplan[312]

The project masterplan was approved in 2019 after an extensive consultation and review process, with marketing for the first development sites progressing to the market. The project, once completed, will comprise of 28,000sqm of commercial floor space, which will include a restaurant and café precinct comprising of 9,000sqm, as well as 1.8 hectares of public open space; it will also create over 1,200 new dwellings for an estimated residential population of 3,000.[313] It is anticipated that the development will attract $850 million in private sector investment and includes the retention of a number of heritage building for adaptive re-use for commercial and community purposes.

---

[311] *'Yeerongpilly Green masterplan maps out transformative Southside project'*, The Queensland Cabinet and Ministerial Directory, August 2019.
[312] *'Yeerongpilly Green masterplan maps out transformative Southside project'*, The Queensland Cabinet and Ministerial Directory, August 2019.
[313] *'Yeerongpilly Green masterplan maps out transformative Southside project'*, The Queensland Cabinet and Ministerial Directory, August 2019.

Figure 6.15: Artist impression of Yeerongpilly Green[314]

Yeerongpilly Green is just one of many new transit-oriented developments popping up around the country resulting from the redevelopment of underutilised former government land serviced by rail and the development of new sites resulting from the expansion of rail networks in the country. The accessibility to public transport enables mixed-used development to occur, supported by higher-density housing, creating an 'urban village' that differs significantly from suburbia, which is traditionally high density, singular in land use and poorly serviced by public transport. As more and more cities across Australia expand their rail networks, more and more opportunities exist to support transit-oriented development. This enables the Australian Dream to shift its focus from its low-density, large-house origins to smaller compact living supported by mixed-use urban villages.

Case Study: METRONET Perth

After years of chopping and changing its transport plan according to which government was in power, it appears, for the first time in a long time, that Perth has a stable public transport plan through METRONET. The program was the key election

---

[314] *'Yeerongpilly Green masterplan maps out transformative Southside project'*, The Queensland Cabinet and Ministerial Directory, August 2019.

platform of the McGowan Labor Government, which was elected in 2017, and promises to overhaul the public transport system in Perth and lay the foundations for its expansion. The plan is visionary in that it proposes the substantial expansion of the existing passenger rail network and the establishment of new passenger rail links to provide greater public transport reach into new and existing suburbs. The program calls for the expansion of the heavy passenger rail network, and also speaks to the potential of light rail in Perth. The program also has another key objective: to encourage transit-oriented development along existing and new routes and train stations.

The METRONET program is intended to be delivered over a three-term Labor government or over an eight-to-twelve-year period. During the writing of this book, Stage 1 is well underway towards delivery, and includes the following:[315]

1. Creation of the Perth to Forrestfield-Airport Link: A new passenger rail line linking Perth Train Station to Forrestfield via Perth Airport – $1.86 billion.

2. Thornlie to Cockburn Central: A new passenger rail line linking Thornlie to Cockburn Central – $1.25 billion.

3. Butler to Yanchep: Including the extension of the existing northern line from Butler Train Station to Yanchep, including the establishment of four new stations.

Planning for the extension of the Armadale Line to Byford is underway, as well as the delivery of the new $1.6 billion line from Perth to Ellenbrook. These projects are anticipated to be completed by 2025.

The METRONET program goes on further to propose the following post-2025.

1. The extension of the Armadale Line from Byford to Pinjarra.

2. The creation of a southern circular link from Perth to Forrestdale (Stage 1), then Forrestdale to Bibra lake, then Bibra Lake to Fremantle.

3. The creation of a northern circular link from Perth to Noranda, then Noranda to Stirling then back to Perth.

4. The creation of a new norther line from Perth Central to Wanneroo.

---

[315] METRONET Website, www.Metronet,wa,gov,au, 2021.

Figure 6.16: Perth's METRONET Plan[316]

In all, the METRONET program proposes the expansion of the public transport rail and the possible introduction of a light-rail network by an estimated 140 kilometres in total.[317] The steady roll out of the METRONET program is unprecedented in scale for Perth and shows a commitment by the Labor Government to invest in public transport for Perth's future. It also anticipates, for the first time since the 1950s, the contemplation of light rail as a possible future for Perth – although nothing is set in concrete. But METRONET isn't all rosy, and there have been some setbacks and missed opportunities that have come with a tight fiscal environment and the advent of COVID-19, which has also influenced the METRONET program's budget.

One of the program's key objectives is to integrate high-density land use and activity corridors into the rail expansion. This commitment to transit-oriented development comes from a good place, but its implementation has been somewhat thwarted by budget constraints and transport agencies who have focused more on

---

[316] METRONET Website, www.Metronet.wa.gov.au, 2021.
[317] METRONET Website, www.Metronet.wa.gov.au, 2021.

the provision of transport infrastructure, rather than the development opportunities that such infrastructure can bring.

The METRONET team comprises expertise from several state government departments to ensure an integrated approach to planning and development around train stations. Representation includes staff from the Public Transport Authority, Main Roads WA, Department of Planning, Lands and Heritage and expertise from the State Land Developer DevelopmentWA. The integration of expertise from a wide variety of government departments is supposed to ensure that new transport infrastructure can maximise redevelopment opportunities to create transit-oriented development. While METRONET creates a number of these possible opportunities – such as commercial and industrial development in Malaga and commercial and mixed-use development in Ellenbrook town centre – by and large the program falls short in developing significant transit-oriented development opportunities.

A classic example of METRONET falling short is its decision to snub transit-oriented development opportunities for the Armadale Strategic Metropolitan City Centre in Perth's south-eastern corridor. The Armadale Strategic Metropolitan Centre is one of eleven such centres within the Perth and Peel region, as identified in the Western Australian Planning Commission's Statement of Planning Policy 4.2: Activity Centres for Perth and Peel 2010 and also in the recently published 'Perth and Peel @ 3.5 million' Planning Strategy.[318] Positioned at the gateway of the south-east sector of the South Metropolitan Peel Sub-Regional growth corridor, this region is one of the fastest growing in Australia, with the population anticipated to grow from 196,340 to 455,770 people by 2050. During the same period, the labour force in the region is required to grow from 94,600 people to 223,740 (an increase of 129,140 jobs).[319]

As the primary multi-purpose centre for the South Metropolitan Peel Sub-Region growth corridor, the Armadale Strategic Metropolitan Centre is required to provide a mix of retail, office, community, entertainment, education and residential activities and perform as one of the primary areas for employment in the region. Armadale, however, is a predominately low socio-economic area; several attempts have been made in the past to support the area – notably during the Geoff Gallop Labor Government – but unfortunately with only limited success. As a result, the area is beset with a myriad of problems, including high unemployment and high mental health issues.

In anticipation of the METRONET project, and the extension of the Armadale to Byford Line, a forward-thinking local government in the City of Armadale embarked upon an extensive public and government stakeholder consultative process to prepare

---

[318] *'Perth and Peel @3.5m'*, WAPC website, www.gov.au.
[319] *'Perth and Peel @3.5m'*, WAPC website, www.gov.au.

an activity centre plan and business case for the Armadale Strategic Metropolitan Centre. In doing so, the City of Armadale considered the current condition of the city centre so that it could develop a future vision that would meet the expected population growth and required employment that would assist in arresting some of the social and unemployment issues confronting the region. Armadale found that, with 129,140 jobs needed for the south-east corridor by 2050, significant expansion of the city centre will be required, particularly in the areas of tertiary institutions (i.e., universities), government administration, retail and commercial diversity, and housing diversity.[320] With the city centre currently home to only 3,000 jobs, it was clear that it was underperforming, and, with the population expanding significantly in the corridor, it will be necessary for the city centre to grow significantly in both employment opportunity and diversity.

The City of Armadale learnt during early consultation with the METRONET team that the Armadale to Byford passenger rail extension will require, at a minimum, the grade-separation of at-grade level crossings at Armadale Road, Forrest Road/Third Road and Church Avenue. This requirement, which the city estimated would cost hundreds of millions of dollars, presented a once-in-a-lifetime opportunity to resolve a long-standing engineering constraint imposed on the Armadale Strategic Metropolitan City Centre, while at the same time seizing on the opportunity to create a new town centre for Armadale that is fitting of its Strategic Metropolitan Centre status. Currently, the passenger rail line dissects the Armadale city centre, causing an urban blight on both sides, as well as reduced pedestrian and vehicle connectivity, adding to the centre's woes.

Accordingly, as part of its planning, the City of Armadale came together with METRONET to consider three scenarios for the Armadale Strategic Metropolitan Centre that reflect different treatments to the grade-separation of the at-grade level crossings. These options included the following.

1. The undergrounding of the railway line as it enters the city centre, which involves sinking the Armadale Train Station to establish a new town centre, or piazza, around the train station. This would be supported by additional development for office, retail and residential structures and substantially improved connections east–west of the railway line.

2. Establishing a 'viaduct', which involves raising the railway line through the Armadale city centre, creating some additional development space and improved east–west connections.

---

[320] *'Armadale Strategic Metropolitan Centre Structure Plan'*, City of Armadale website, www.armadale.wa.gov.au 2021.

3. The final 'base case' option involves the grade separation of Armadale Road, Forrest Road and Church Avenue via bridge structures, with little to no improvement to the Armadale city centre.[321]

The city strongly supported the underground rail option and garnered support from the business community, residents and elected members for the proposal. This option formed the basis of the City of Armadale's Armadale Activity Centre Structure Plan and was seen as solving two major problems by resolving an engineering constraint to expand the Armadale to Byford passenger rail line and by providing a much-needed solution to rejuvenating the Armadale city centre. The critical components of the City of Armadale's Plan included the following:[322]

1. Extension of the passenger rail line from Armadale to Byford;
2. Undergrounding of the Armadale Train Station and creation of a new town square linking Jull Street Mall to the 'West of Rail' Precinct;
3. Expansion of the Civic Precinct by the City of Armadale, which will enable new modern civic buildings and high-quality office spaces to house local government and state government administration and private businesses;
4. Expansion of the retail, commercial and entertainment core from 50,000sqm to 300,000sqm, by 2050, to support a working population of up to 18,000 people (currently 3,000);
5. Creation of developable space to cater for modern tertiary education facilities
6. Expansion and diversification of housing (approximately 3,500 dwellings), which include apartments and short-stay accommodation, for a population of 7,000 people;
7. Creation of a legible, green and high-quality public realm throughout the city centre, enhancing place activation and recreational and entertainment opportunities; and
8. Economic multipliers that include $2.263 billion dollars in private sector expenditure over thirty years.

---

[321] 308 'Armadale Strategic Metropolitan Centre Structure Plan', City of Armadale website, www.armadale.wa.gov.au 2021.
[322] 309 'Armadale Strategic Metropolitan Centre Structure Plan', City of Armadale website, www.armadale.wa.gov.au 2021.

Figure 6.17: Armadale Strategic Metropolitan City Centre Structure Plan[323]

The City of Armadale's plan, which was approved in August 2018, was supported by a business case that considers a wide range of economic and social metrics to ensure a holistic appreciation of the long-term benefits associated with each of the three options considered. The business case concluded that, while more costly initially, the scenario detailing the undergrounding of the passenger railway provides far greater benefits from an economic and social perspective than the rival alternative options. Significant new development opportunities will be created in this scenario, which includes a town square, expansion of retail, commercial and residential opportunities, and additional office space that will cater for government administration and tertiary education institutions. This option also enables the superior integration of the development of land east–west of the current railway line.

Despite the clear benefits demonstrated by undergrounding the passenger railway line through the Armadale city centre and a spirited effort by the city to convince the state government to support its plan, the proposal was set aside, and the option to

---

[323] *'Armadale Strategic Metropolitan Centre Structure Plan'*, City of Armadale website, www.armadale.wa.gov.au 2021.

provide a viaduct through the Armadale city centre was selected as the solution. While there are some benefits to the chosen option, the preferred option to underground the railway line best optimises the transit-oriented development benefits of the new rail infrastructure. To me, this is a missed opportunity.

Figure 6.18: Artist impression of the new Armadale Train Station and redevelopment[324]

The Future of Transit-Oriented Development

Transit-oriented development has the ability to be a powerful catalyst for change in our cities and contribute significantly to 'place making', as shown in the case studies we have investigated as examples. Transit-oriented development creates places of interest and diversity, allowing the people who live in them to have walkable access to a variety of amenities, such as public transport, shops and civic places, that normally wouldn't be accessible via walking in low-density suburban environments. For transit-oriented development to be effective, it needs to have all the elements that make living in smaller dwellings, such as apartments and townhouses, more favourable than living in a large house on the urban fringes. This is generally the private versus public lifestyle debate, which we discussed earlier in this book. If you are living in a suburban environment, chances are your living arrangements will have all the benefits of living a 'private life': large house, backyard, etc. If you are asking

---

[324] *'Armadale Strategic Metropolitan Centre Structure Plan'*, City of Armadale website, www.armadale.wa.gov. au 2021.

people to substitute this convenience in place of an apartment or modest townhouse, then you have to offer the best that public life can bring as a fair trade off. Thankfully, we have seen enough transit-oriented development structures in Australia to understand the elements that make them successful and enjoyable places to live and work. The characteristics of a successful transit-oriented development must include a combination of the following:

Accessible Transport – This is fundamental and not only means having readily available high-quality and reliable public transport – such as passenger rail, light rail or trackless trams – but also means having pedestrian priority spaces, well connected walking and cycle pathways, and adequate vehicle access. The priority in movement must be pedestrian and cycling to encourage walking, which means having streets designed to slow traffic down and provide protection for cyclists and pedestrians, and, of course, it needs to be aesthetically pleasing and climate resilient.

Public Open Space – Adequate public open space that offers people living in an apartment or townhouse a viable substitute for the backyard. But this can't just be public space in a suburban sense, like a park. There needs to be a variety of public spaces: smaller pocket parks, urban open spaces and piazzas that encourage a variety of uses and opportunities to gather and celebrate.

Mixed-Use – Transit-oriented development shouldn't be single use places, like you see in suburbia, but should be 'hubs': places where people gather to engage in work, socialise, entertain and utilise services. They should include office spaces, shops, restaurants, cafés, pubs, human services (i.e., the hairdresser), medical centres, government services, supermarkets, retail outlets, theatres and cinemas, to mention a few. They should also include civic-type uses and community buildings. Development should be along main-street principles, where pedestrian-friendly design and smaller retail can flourish.

Variety of Residential Housing – One of the most important elements of transit-oriented development is the need to include a variety of residential housing, mainly townhouses and apartments, to ensure that residential densities within walkable catchments of the train stations are high. A high population ensures the mixed-use component of the transit-oriented development is successful, since more people within walkable distances of shops, for example, means more patrons, and therefore the shops would be less reliant on people coming from further away. High density also means the provision of public assets, such as public spaces, piazzas and entertainment spots, that are well utilised and maintained. Greater density in housing also means greater rates for local governments, which means they have more money to maintain public and civic assets to a high standard.

Transit-oriented development inspires a new form of the Australian Dream by allowing people to viably substitute their large homes in suburbia, which are often isolated and reliant on the automobile for access, and instead offers the opportunity to live a more contained and compact life. The benefits of this form of living include promoting an engaging lifestyle with housing that is better suited to the population (remember, by 2050 50% of all households will be single-person households), while offering all the conveniences that support smaller compact living within a walkable distance. A significant side benefit of this living arrangement is not only the conveniences that are offered by being close to work, places of entertainment and community facilities, but that this type of living arrangement also tends to enable people to build walking and cycling more into their lives, and, as a result, people tend to be physically and mentally healthier. After all, when you are more connected to a place, you feel more comfortable, safer and likely have a greater number of friendships and acquaintances that you can rely on for support.

I would like to reflect on my time spent in Paris, when I was nineteen years of age, back in 1994, and what I observed simply by regularly attending a local bakery/café...

When I was nineteen, I travelled to Paris and wanted to live (albeit, briefly) like a Parisian, so I regularly attended a bakery/café in Montmartre, where I had my coffee and breakfast daily. I observed most of the same people attending the café daily. When they arrived, the café owner greeted them and engaged in conversation. I'm not sure what they spoke about, as I had a limited understanding of the French language back then, but for me it was clear that people felt comfortable engaging in conversation and sharing life stories with the owner, like the regular bar attendees telling their life stories to Ted Danson in the TV drama *Cheers*. At the end of my first week of attending this café daily, I approached the owner to ask a few questions about his business, the people who attended and the café's general congenial atmosphere.

What I learnt was that it was a relatively successful family-run business that had been operating since the 1920s. The business's success hinged on the number of people walking past the café daily, and, because it was in a densely-populated neighbourhood, there was no shortage of people walking past. What occurred to me at the time was the power of density and mixed-use. You see, because there was a large number of people that lived in close proximity to the café, it was always well populated, and, as a result, the business thrived. The family could, therefore, operate the business for generations, and this had one major side benefit for the community: familiarity. Because the owners were always present, people became familiar with them, and friendships and acquaintances were formed. This isn't rocket science, just human nature. Think about whether this happens at your local café. Chances are, in Australia, most cafés move on or go bankrupt after five to six years, meaning there is an ever-present turnover of café owners to the point you don't feel tied to the place like our Parisians counterparts.

The business in Montmartre was so successful that a franchise wasn't necessary to make money, like it often is in Australia. There is a powerful lesson in this that goes beyond just economics – where business can be more viable – but also in a social sense, where people can build relationships or feel like part of the community. This was the power of village-type living, which you can also get in transit-oriented development, if it is done properly.

The success of combining mixed-use land, housing and population density with public transport can't be underestimated. The lifestyle generated through this type of living arrangement is why people in traditionally older villages in places such as Crete in Greece or Sardinia in Italy are known around the world to live the longest and also lead the healthiest lifestyles.[325] The secret is partly in the denser, more compact social environment these people live in, combined with other factors, such as diet, exercise and being part of a community. In these places, families of all generations meet in the public square on most evenings where they drink, eat, sing and dance. The young, old and middle-aged are engaged and feel a sense of worth and connection not only to family, but also to friends. This is why suburbia is so dangerous for people, because it doesn't promote human interaction or exercise, and, in most instances, people who live in suburbia live away from friends and family, whereas a village contains a wide spectrum of people in a society and brings friends and social groups closer together.

Lacking diversity in an area means less chance for friendships to develop with a wider group of people in society, and this could be challenging if you want to build empathy, respect and resilience in your community. For further reading on the evidence behind this, I encourage you to read *Blue Zones* by Dan Buettner. It offers a very interesting insight into the power of community-type living that Australia once had, which, when the automobile and suburbia became popular, was largely destroyed.

Transit-oriented development, which is the Anglo-Saxon response to obtaining a portion of the charm that many older European cities and towns enjoy, looks to be a growing opportunity in Australia, as policymakers and politicians alike begin to understand the benefits of combining easy, frequent and reliable mass rapid transit with an urban village lifestyle. Across Australia, as we see our cities expanding – and with the introduction of more rapid transit through passenger rail and light-rail vehicles – we are going to see more opportunities to create transit-oriented development and supporting urban villages, which will bring new opportunities for the Australian Dream, especially for people seeking a more engaging lifestyle.

While there will be more opportunities for transit-oriented development in the coming years, in reality, this won't be the only development form articulated in the years to come, as Australia struggles with a growing population and the aspirations of its predominately middle class. Development in the form of new greenfield areas will continue, and the question will be: should these areas develop as they have in the last seventy years? That is... should it continue to resemble a blanket form

---

[325] Buettner, D, *'Blue Zones'*, National Geographic, 2010.

of suburbia under a cloak of monoculture, low-density housing and divided land use, or should it take a different form? We will see in the next chapter that new growth areas will need to change their shape and form if Australia is to develop a more inclusive culture in our communities and respond to the growing demographic changes that will drive different housing choices from what we have seen over the last seventy years.

New Growth Areas

The new growth areas of the future represent an interesting space for urban development and the industry in general. Traditionally, these areas are the suburban, project home areas that are churned out en masse, replicated from suburb to suburb, with the same tier of school sites, commercial areas and blanket, monotype residential developments. Clearly, this model needs to adapt to a growing consumer sentiment that is demanding greater community benefits, amenities and diversity in housing. The latter is driven partly by changes in household demographics, with people being more comfortable living alone or in small family settings, which differs from the traditional nuclear family that dominated between the 1950s and 1990s. It is also driven by a real issue in housing affordability, which means, in many cases, people simply can't afford the house and land sizes that the baby boomers and Generation X were used to getting. With the typical three-to-four-bedroom house on a 450sqm block in Sydney costing upwards of $600,000 to $700,000 (circa 2022), this simply isn't within reach for most people, even with two incomes.

We saw earlier in this book the development industry's first attempt to respond to housing affordability in a suburban context, and we have witnessed the creation of small, narrow lots filled wall-to-wall with bricks and mortar, with an absence of greenery or outdoor space. It's an infantile form of suburbia, devoid of soul and spirit. If we are to create a more diverse and sustainable form of suburbia that responds to affordability and household diversity, we are going to have to be more creative, bold and long-term in our thinking. This can be difficult in an industry that is used to churning out suburban products, but, unless we go down a different pathway, we are condemning our new growth areas to becoming problem spaces for years to come.

A New Vision for Our Growth Areas

For new growth areas to change, there needs to be a form of development that reinvents itself. Development needs to stop consisting of a cookie-cutter abstract form of housing and subdivision and needs to embrace an approach that is characterised by diversity and integrated town and neighbourhood centres that are people oriented, rather than movement oriented. This means a fundamentally new way of planning, starting with putting people first, followed by amenities and then movement. It requires a new approach and focus to urban design, which, in Australia, has traditionally been about making way for cars first, then land use and then people last.

A prominent Danish architect named Jan Gehl brought a people-first approach to city planning in post-war Europe and transformed city planning in his home country of Denmark in the 1960s. Gehl was an architect who was schooled in modernism – you know the brutal architecture of concrete walls and flat roofs; it was his wife, a psychologist, who put the question to him: "why don't architects plan spaces for people?". You could say that was Jan Gehl's epiphany moment. This started him on the process of considering the "spaces between buildings" that are inhabited by people who become the key focus in planning urban environments.[326] In his role as a policymaker in Copenhagen, Gehl started by recapturing public spaces from the automobile. Post-World-War-Two Denmark was not that different from other countries in the world that were swept up in prosperity and a policy shift from public transport to the private automobile, which resulted in most of Copenhagen's beautiful public spaces being inundated with cars. Many were turned into streets, while others were converted to car parking lots, as people were pushed aside and cars brought in. Gehl started his journey of discovery by instituting a policy of removing cars from public spaces, allowing people to reclaim the streets and push the vehicle out of city centres.

Figure 6.19: Copenhagen in the 1950s[327]

---

[326] Gehl, J, Gemzøe, L, and Kirknæs, S, *'New City Life'*, Danish Architectural press, 2006.
[327] Gehl, J, Gemzøe, L, and Kirknæs, S, *'New City Life'*, Danish Architectural press, 2006.

Figure 6.20: Copenhagen today[328]

Jan Gehl's influence on policy has been profound, having been credited with transforming Copenhagen from a stark, car-oriented city to a people-centred city that introduced the outdoor café life to Dannes – something that was once thought only possible in Italian cities. Jan Gehl's theory is simple: plan places for people first – consider where you would like people to be, congregate, recreate, shop – and then build in the supporting elements that make this work. It is a fundamental focus on creating public spaces that are for people only, which is a profound amenity in itself and has massive health benefits – both psychologically and physically. It is also a theory that doesn't just apply to major world cities but can be brought down to small towns – even suburban settings – if designed properly.

Since the 1960s, Jan Gehl has delivered his theory and practice through work and literature, promoting a people-centric focus to creating new city centres and neighbourhoods across the world. His seminal book *Life Between Buildings,* which was first released in 1971, is a clear look at Gehl's theory and has been a guidebook to the 'humanistic planning' of our cities.[329] Gehl has since published many other books focusing on the importance of creating public spaces for people that bring a heart and soul to a place, rather than a mishmash of spaghetti roads and inadequate sidewalks, which push people to car travel as the primary form of transport.

---

[328] Gehl, J, Gemzøe, L, and Kirknæs, S, *'New City Life',* Danish Architectural press, 2006.
[329] Gehl, J *'Life Between Buildings'* Island Press, 1971.

Today, places like Copenhagen are now some of the most desired cities in the world: people focused, walkable and inclusive for all people. The planning of Copenhagen represents a holistic approach to urban planning that considers all the elements, rather than just the transport aspect, which has dominated city planning in countries like Australia over the last seventy years. You may think, though, that Gehl's approach can't be applied to Australia's suburban environment – well, if you think in terms of the way suburbs are currently planned, you would be right. But you have to think beyond what suburbia looks like today and instead reimagine what it *could* be. Over the past seventy years, the transport-dominated approach to suburban planning has created monotonous environments, which we have previously discussed. However, if we take a people-centred approach, we would get a vastly different outcome and place. We start this new vision by planning for our towns and neighbourhood centres first.

Creating People-Centred Town Centres

It's not surprising that, when we look at how to improve our new growth areas, we start at their core: the town centres. Traditionally, in new growth areas, there is a hierarchy of centres, these include: district centres (populations of up to 50,000 people), neighbourhood centres (populations of up to 20,000 people) and local centres (populations of up to 5,000).[330] The district centre, which represents the larger of the three in the hierarchy, presents the best opportunity to create a real town centre. In Australia, this typically takes the form of large, big-box retail centres and malls surrounded by car parking. They are typically designed with transportation systems for the automobile in mind, with the pedestrian and people focus way down the list in terms of priority. To create a proper people-oriented town centre, we need to take a fundamentally new approach to the designing and planning of these centres. We can break down the planning for new town centres by using the following four simple steps, each explained in turn and ranked in hierarchy of importance.

Step 1: *Where do we want people to be*?

Our starting point in designing our town centres starts with one question: where do we want people to be? It is a fundamental question, and the answer will shape the focus of the town centre and its design. If we look at successful traditional centres across Europe, America and parts of Australia and New Zealand, the starting place is the creation of a communal meeting place, such as a public square or piazza. This is a place which allows for a variety of uses, including as a place to catch-up with

---

[330] *'Liveable Neighbourhoods'*, WAPC website, www.wa.gov.au 2021.

friends, family and colleagues; a place to hold markets; and a place for events, such as concerts, movies and festivals.

Given that the focus of creating a public square is to create an environment that caters to the gregarious nature of humans, it is no surprise that public squares are often found in the centre of a place, where human activity is concentrated. If you look at examples such as Piazza del Campo in Siena, in Italy's Tuscan Region, or a more modern example in Rouse Hill – located thirty-five kilometres north-west of Sydney's CBD – you will notice they all have a town square positioned in the town's centre, where public activity is most concentrated. One of the core characteristics of public squares is that they are people focused and are almost reliant on foot traffic. This is fundamentally different from the way car-centric town centres have been designed in Australia over the last seventy years, where car parking dominates, and public spaces are squeezed into thin sidewalks and entries into 'internalised' shopping centres.

The public square doesn't just stand on its own as a place where people want to gather and enjoy spending time. These spaces work into a network of primary streets – or main streets – and then secondary streets, with each street having a specific role and function. People come to town centres for a variety of reasons:

- shopping (i.e., groceries, fashion, bakery, speciality),
- entertainment (i.e., café, pub, restaurant, fast food),
- services (i.e., real estate agent, physiotherapy, pharmacy, medical, post office),
- civic (i.e., library, community building),
- peripheral services (i.e., petrol station, fast food drive-thru), and
- living (residential).

Typically, a town square includes the type of uses that maximise the opportunity for daytime and evening 'place activation', including entertainment-type uses, such as cafés, restaurants, pubs; shopping-type uses, such as a supermarket; and civic-type uses, such as a library or community building. The town square is the most active space in the town centre and is seen as the primary place for gathering, entertainment and civic experience.

Adjoining the public square is the next tier of human space: the main street. This is the street that first introduces the automobile and bicycle; these are typically slow movement environments, allowing people to move freely across the main street without fear of being hit by a car. Designed typically for low speeds (i.e., 40 kilometres per hour), the main street is characterised by having trees on either side and a good balance between sidewalk and road. Main streets typically contain a variety of uses, which include restaurants and cafés that 'bleed' from the town square; a variety of shops, such as clothes shops, speciality shops and bookshops; and a variety of services, such as a post office, pharmacy and real estate agent.

Figure 6.21: Traditional public square in Siena, Italy[331]

Figure 6.22: Rouse Hill's Town Square[332]

---

[331] *'Piazza Del Campo'*, photograph from Sergio Famiano's private collection, 2001.
[332] *'Rous Hill Town Square'*, from Sergio Famiano's private collection, 2013.

Macro-Planning the New Australian Dream   205

The design of main streets is distinct, in that the automobile and bicycle are considered secondary forms of transport, with walking being the main form. Main streets must have the following elements, which collectively create a positive and inviting environment for pedestrians and slow traffic down without the need for excessive signage:

- single-lane road – one each way,
- small medium strip – 1 metre to 1.5 metres wide – containing a combination of hardstand and landscaping,
- car embayments that sleeve either side of the road,
- wide pedestrian pavements – approximately four metres in width (each side) – allowing for the inclusion of car bays, lighting, tree landscaping, alfresco dining and free-flow pedestrian movement, and
- activated shopfronts dominated by entries and windows for active 'people watching' and window shopping.

The design of the main street should create an intimate and well-scaled urban environment where pedestrians can easily cross the road. A typical cross-section of a main street design is detailed below and can be observed in practice using Scarborough Beach Road's main street in Perth's inner-northern suburbs as an example.

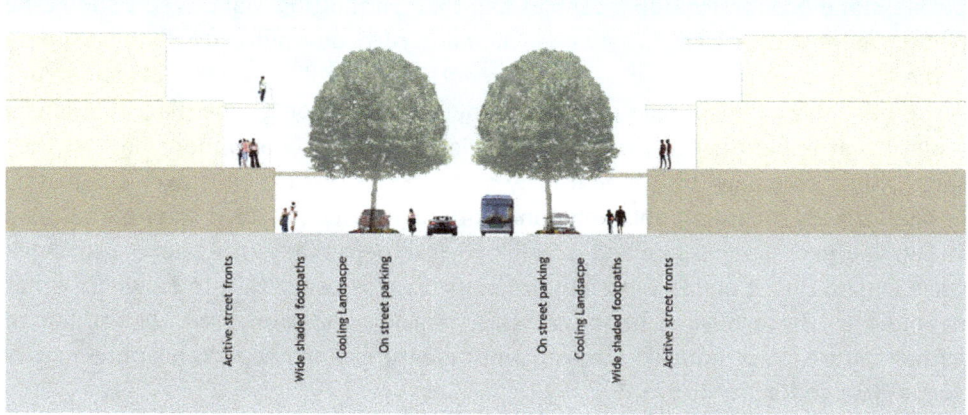

Figure 6.23: A preferred main street cross-section[333]

---

[333] Diagram by Insight Urbanism, 2022.

Figure 6.24: Scarborough Beach Road, Mount Hawthorn's 'main street'[334]

So, why are the public square and main street so important? Why not continue to build the box centre surrounded by car parking? The answer is as much to do with enhancing amenity and the 'people experience', as it is to do with supporting business and economics. Town centres and their supporting main streets should be places where people want to stay and linger and carry out multiple activities. Variety is the key, and creating the best environments that are filled with public amenities is the best way to encourage people to stay longer and enjoy the place. Designing a place that enhances the shopper's experience gives people options, in that they can do their shopping, visit a pharmacy and catch up with friends over a coffee all in one visit. By creating public environments that include a town square and main street, you're creating a safe and relaxing environment that entices people to linger. Once you do this, it builds a momentum of its own, as people like to be where other people are. These environments are safe, relaxing and, above all, well-suited to human nature, since humans are gregarious creatures and need stimulation, activity and human contact to thrive.

The box centre, on the other hand, which is filled with internal malls and air-conditioning, crammed with shops and surrounded by car parking, is a completely different place, which, therefore, fosters a completely different experience for people. The box centre is traditionally a crammed environment; they are noisy and

---

[334] *'Scarborough beach Road Main Street'* from Sergio Famiano's private collection, 2022.

unattractive places that, above all, are single-serving places. By this I mean, when people go to a box centre, because the experience is often tainted by the construct of the place (noisy/unattractive), they typically perform one, maybe two things, then get out quickly. Perhaps describing the experience will illustrate this further.

When you drive to a box centre, the first hurdle you face is finding a carpark. Often, the carpark is busy with traffic and finding a spot close to the shop you want to go to can be frustrating. Once the car is parked, you are then faced with walking through the carpark to get to the entrance of the box shop. Once you enter, you find that it is a completely manufactured environment, all internalised, air-conditioned and busy with people trying to negotiate each other by moving from shop to shop, with few places to sit. People aren't encouraged to stop and linger, since there is nothing attractive to look at. The internal environment is devoid of sunlight, amenities (trees, etc.) and people are busy rushing around. This is in stark contrast to the town square, where you could sit, read a book, have a coffee and people watch in a relaxed environment. The box centre is a place that dramatically lacks amenities, and, as such, you don't want to linger.

Why is lingering, hanging out and doing multiple activities so important? Well, it's healthy to start off with. When people are encouraged to slow down and enjoy the environment they are in, people are more relaxed; they catch up with friends and family and enjoy the natural environment – outdoors, rather than engaging in a space that is unnatural and confined, like a box centre. This is good for physical health and, more so, good for mental health. I can recall on many occasions visiting my local box shop with my wife. We had a choice of two very contrasting places to shop. The first was a traditional box centre. It was soulless and devoid of anything worth remembering, aside from the feeling of being rushed and wanting to get out. This was in contrast to visiting the Scarborough Beach Road main street, where my wife and I could relax, do our shopping at a slower pace and spend time having a coffee on the main street. Of course, we can do this at the box centre too, but there is something about being outdoors, amongst trees and people, that makes it a more pleasurable experience, compared to being in an enclosed and artificial environment.

The biggest benefit of encouraging people to have a nice experience at their town centre and linger around to do multiple activities isn't just a physical and mental health benefit, but also an economic benefit. You see, when people spend longer in a place, they tend to spend more money, and this is wonderful for the viability of businesses and the town centre as a whole. To show that it is not all fluffy humanistic benefits, traditional town centres also thrive as a place of commerce, and this alone should make retailers and developers of town centres straighten up and listen. Having been in the industry and involved in planning several town centres for over twenty-five years, I have often been confronted with the developer who is adamant that the box centre surrounded by car parking is the way to go.

I remember sitting down with one centre manager who outlined the case clearly: "If we secure a Coles or Woolworths, they [supermarket owner] want car parking immediately adjacent [to] the supermarket, with direct access from the shopping centre to the car parking".[335] This design technique was then followed by the inclusion of speciality stores that sleeve the shopping centre, facing the carpark. In the same conversation with the centre manager, they provided numerous examples of box centres that were ten years old and were struggling with high tenancy turnover, with the supermarket being the only business appearing to be doing well. My question to the centre manager was simple: "If your box centres are struggling after ten years, why do you continue to roll out the same design over and over again?" The response: "To appease the anchor tenant – the supermarket".[336]

What was evident to me following that conversation was that the developers of shopping centres are constantly thinking of short-term profits and the ability to immediately secure a key tenant in their centre, with little regard to whether or not other aspects of the centre would be successful over the long-term. It is my professional opinion that town centres are not a short-term proposition. That is, whoever is engaged in developing shopping centres should not be thinking in terms of short-term profits, but more the long game. Getting a traditional style town centre right might take a little longer to set up than a box centre – and may even take a little longer for it to be viable – but once up and running, the traditional centre becomes highly successful and a sought after place by the community, meaning thriving businesses and less retail and commercial turnover.

Rouse Hill in Sydney is a good example of this. Its design, which includes a town square in the centre supported by a main street, took careful planning and time for the proponent, GPT Group, to develop. Keeping true to the vision, GPT didn't cut corners and compromise the design and scale of the development; instead, it took its time to introduce the right uses and ensure the right mix to make it a successful centre over the medium–to-long term. Despite some early setbacks and careful negotiation, five years after its creation, the centre began to thrive and is now a major destination. Businesses are successful, business turnover is low, and management of the centre has improved as a result. It's a classic case of a 'hard-fought win', but one well worth it when you consider the longevity of our built environments.

The medium-to-long-term economic benefits in the town centre/main street scenario are clearly obvious, but the social benefits are subtler and often overlooked. Remember, if businesses are successful, they hang around longer. People then get to know the business owners and a social connection is struck between consumer and business owner, which is greater than just a superficial transaction. I know my

---

[335] Conversation between Sergio Famiano and anonymous Commercial Property Manager, 2016.
[336] Conversation between Sergio Famiano and anonymous Commercial Property Manager, 2016.

favourite café owner in the Scarborough Beach main street really well, because his business has been up and running now for eight years and is likely to continue on for many more years/decades. The same business in the box centre would have probably turned over once during that eight-year timeframe. It's very difficult to strike up an acquaintanceship with a business owner if the business turns over every three to four years. Naturally, in this scenario, you feel less connected to a place than if you'd gotten to know the business owner and become acquaintances over a ten-to-twenty-year period. This is what people often refer to as a 'sense of place'. It is a sense of knowing you are connected to the community; even if they are not your closest friends, they are still people you know and can have a conversation with and build up a rapport with.

Step 2: Mixed-Use Focus

The next step in the design process is getting the right mix of land use in the town centre. A town centre will not function effectively if it only has retail and commercial type land uses. There needs to be a mix of retail, commercial and residential land uses, with town centres being places with a mix of residential housing to encourage diversity in the population and alternatives to the typical suburb household. In big box centres, there is typically no residential housing whatsoever. There are simply 'houses of consumption', as mentioned earlier in this book, and have a single purpose: to sell products and services. These centres, which have proliferated over the Australian urban environment the last seventy-plus years, are typically dormant places that open during the day and close at night. The fact that there is no residential housing in the suburban town centres means there is no resident population to support other uses, and there is a lack of what town planners call 'passive surveillance', which often encourages anti-social behaviour and crime.

Mixed-use – mixing commercial and retail-type uses with residential – comes naturally to European and Asian cities. Because these cultures are older, they pre-date the automobile and therefore had to rely on walking and the horse and cart as a main focus of transport for millennia before cars came along and facilitated the spreading out of cities. It is, therefore, common in these cultures to have a multilevel building with a shop front downstairs facing the street or piazza, with residential housing in the form of apartments upstairs. This symbiotic relationship was the norm for centuries and is ingrained in European and Asian cultures. Take a look at the traditional town centre of Lucca, in Italy's Tuscany region.

Lucca has several public squares for people to gather; these places are supported by retail, entertainment and tourist-type uses at the ground level and then supported by three to five storeys of residential uses above. Historically, this was due to shop-fronts being owned by people living above, so there was a direct relationship between commerce and living arrangements. The close proximity of the residence to work was also a product of the Marchetti principle, which is the notion that people are only willing to travel between thirty minutes and one hour from place of living to place of work. In this pre-automobile era, which is reflected in the design of Lucca, this means people are only willing to walk no more than thirty to sixty minutes to work. This means a radius of around one to four kilometres – accordingly, people live close to where they work.

Figure 6.25: Mixed-use in Lucca's old town centre[337]

Places like Lucca are some of the most sought after places to visit in the world, with people enjoying the accessibility of places of work to living and not being dependent on the automobile to travel around the town. Lucca is one of those unique towns, which, on a weekly basis, closes the town centre from automobile traffic so that on weekends people can only move around the town centre by walking and cycling. This is made possible because the town centre is compact and everything is within a two-kilometre radius of the centre.

Re-establishing the art of building town centres like this is not only sustainable, but also adds many physical and mental health benefits for people who are privileged enough to live in such town centres. This art of creating mixed-use in the town centre has mostly been lost in the suburban town centres of America and Australia since the 1950s, but in Asia and Europe they have featured prominently and continue to be the

---

[337] *'Lucca's Town Square'*, from Sergio Famiano's private collection, 2001.

norm for most town centre developments, ensuring that traditional town centres – like the ones we see in Siena and Lucca, in Italy – are not lost but replicated, albeit in a modern form.

The notion of having a mixture of uses in town centres has started to gather some pace in Australian cities in recent times. If you look at some of the recent upgrades or redevelopments of large big box centres, they are starting to introduce restaurant and café strips, and also residential development, to create a village-type feel. A good example used previously in this book is Karrinyup Shopping Centre in Perth's northern suburbs. It was a big box retail and commercial centre established in the 1970s that was surrounded by car parking. The changing retail environment, which is seeing more and more retail being undertaken, has resulted in centres like Karrinyup Shopping Centre having to reinvent themselves as something like a traditional centre with a night life and resident population.

In 2017, the owners of Karrinyup Shopping Centre embarked on a significant redevelopment of a large portion of the car parking area around the centre to include a new 'eat street', cinema, entertainment precinct and residential apartments. The owners of the centre – Westfield – have recognised that big box centres are in decline, as consumers are becoming more demanding of a better experience. This represents a fundamental shift in the way we look at shopping centres, and we are starting to see them as possible town centres for the first time.

Figure 6.26: Karrinyup Shopping Centre; 'big box' retail surrounded by car parking (1980s)[338]

---

[338] *'Picture of Karrinyup – old'*, Media Tonic, 1986.

Figure 6.27: Karrinyup Shopping Centre in 2018; major redevelopment of the car parking into a new 'eat street', entertainment, cinema and residential complex, complete with a town square[339]

Figure 6.28: Karrinyup entertainment precinct today[340]

We shouldn't get ahead of ourselves though. Shopping centres cum 'entertainment centres' aren't quite Siena or Lucca in Italy's celebrated Tuscany Region. The spaces created are still privatised places and linked to commerce rather than treated as a 'public good', but it is a sign that the focus in Australia is changing, with a need to consider places of high amenities and mixed-use to support the future of these centres becoming more apparent. This growing diversification and creation of high amenities in redeveloping existing centres will pave the way for change in new suburban centres. Following this

---

[339] *'Picture Karringyup Shopping centre Stage 1'*, Proven project management, 2018.
[340] *'Photographs of Karrinyup Shops tod*ay', Artist impressions, Proven project management 2018.

new approach, we once again discover the importance of creating public space to support places for gathering and mixed-use, to support the viability of businesses and to support the creation of a holistic town centre that supports both shopping and living.

Step 3: Movement

It is only in Step 3 that we consider movement. In building the traditional car-based shopping centre, this is often one of the first steps considered in the development process: the need to set up the movement framework before moving on to land use, location and car parking. However, when we consider walking-based town centres, the movement network, while important, is third in the process and is seen as a faciliatory feature of development, rather than a dominate aspect of the design process. This is often the space where planners and architects clash with engineers, with the former seeing the creative process of 'creating space' and 'land use integration' as the most important part of the design process, while engineers tend to focus on the movement of cars and service vehicles as the dominant force. Personally, I think planners and architects should be in charge. Movement is an input into the 'spatial process' of design, rather than the driving feature, accordingly engineers should not lead. It must always be this way if we are to try to achieve sustainable walkable town centres.

After considering the core of our town centre supported by a main street and mixed-use/land use integration, we then start to build in the movement framework to connect the town centre with its surroundings and higher-order roads. Road design, where possible, should always be in a grid characterised by a series of interlocking streets at right angles. This was the general pattern of development in the 1900s, when the world witnessed a cross section of transport with the horse and cart, automobile and train all working together to create the movement network of the day. Most new subdivisions created during that era consisted of a grid, creating rectangular commercial and residential 'cells', as detailed in the figure below.

Traditional Grid Design (circa 1900)

Curvilinear Loop Designs & Beginning of Cul-De-Sacs (approx. 1930 – 1950)

Conventional Cul-De-Sac Design (since 1950)

Figure 6.29: Different road patterns[341]

---

[341] Kunstler, J, *'Geography to Nowhere'*, Touchstone and Simon & Schustler, New York, 1994.

The advantage of the traditional grid is that it is a permeable form of subdivision, allowing people to move easily within the grid. It is legible to the pedestrian, cyclist and automobile and, importantly, allows for land-use transition over time. If you look at all the traditional centres and surrounding suburbs of modern cities, such as New York and Melbourne, they are all characterised by this form of grid road and land-use layout. They are some of the most sought-after places to work and live and have the advantage of being able to transition or change with time, as seen in Perth's inner suburbs of Highgate and Mount Lawley. These suburbs were originally residential suburbs characterised by mostly single-residential housing on large blocks, but are now transitioning to 'mixed-use suburbs', with their main streets supported by high-quality public transport and diversity in land use and housing.

Fast forward to the 1950s and beyond, and we have the onset of the curvilinear and cul-de-sac street layout, which may have been successful in creating some nice and quiet residential suburbs but has dramatically failed in terms of permeability of movement and its ability to transition from one land use to another over time. While grid suburbs can transition from residential to mixed-use areas, cul-de-sacs are limited to only being residential suburbs, since the movement network in these suburbs is highly restricted. Many Australian cities, since the 1970s to early 2000s, have a ring of suburbs around them that, at the time of their development, were the periphery of the city but are now middle suburbs designed with the cul-de-sac layout. At the time, this was seen as a way of creating quiet and safe residential suburbs, but, in truth, they represent a dramatic lack of foresight, in that they are difficult suburbs to redevelop as the city expands and the pressure on land use changes within a city. It is, therefore, justified that, over the last two decades, town planners in Australian cities have seen the error of their ways and gone back to grid planning, with some curvilinear design creeping in from time to time to account for topographical issues.

Coming back to the design of town centres. In order to create high-quality town centres that facilitate walking and a variety of transport movement efficiently and effectively, the design of the centre must employ a grid design. The grid is critical to facilitating main street design and mixed-use development that is essential in the inner core of the town centre around the piazza and main street. It is also critical for the 'feeder streets' that link from the main street and secondary streets to the distributor roads that link surrounding suburbs with the town centre. In addition, it is critical to consider the type of streetscape one wishes to create, and this means considering where vehicle access and car parking will go. For the town centre core, or piazza and connecting main street, car parking is located in the rear of the property, away from the main street, so this area and the piazza is mostly for pedestrians. There may be some car parking in front of shops, in the form of embayment parking along the main street; however, this should only be allowed where rapid public transport (light rail or trackless trams) does not exist.

As we transition from the main street to the secondary street, we should encourage all car parking to be accessed from the rear of the property, with the primary street to serve as a main pedestrian, cycle and vehicle link. The secondary street is where land uses start to transition from mixed-use located in and around the piazza and main street to high and middle density residential housing in the form of two-to-three-storey walk up apartments, and two-storey micro-lot apartment developments. This mix in housing is critical to ensure we start to see townhouse developments, which tend to support couples without kids and small families, and apartment development in the core, which tends to provide housing for retirees and couples without children. This housing diversity is critical to supporting population variety in the community, in addition to enabling the establishment of a housing market that would enable residents to move from different housing typologies through the different stages of their life without having to leave the area where they have friends, family and links to community groups and associations.

As we have discussed previously, the movement network – while a critical component of the modern town centre – is seen as a facilitator of movement that supports land use and public areas, rather than being the core consideration that is supported by land use and public areas. The differentiation is deliberate and is fundamental to designing high-quality and high-functioning town centres. If we were to go back to considering movement first, we would design car-dominated town centres, with land use retreating to the centre of the street block and car parking surrounding buildings, supported by streets with high traffic volumes. This has been done to death in Australia, and the jury has delivered its verdict: no more.

Step 4: Public Realm Focus

The final (and yet one of the most important) layer of the design process, is the need to consider the quality of the public realm. This is tied to the first two steps in creating places where people want to gather. Steps 1 to 3 involve the creation of the framework for a robust town centre – a skeleton – for a neighbourhood, and this final step is like adding the muscle and skin to that skeleton to create the final body. The premise of the final step is a simple one: if we are to encourage people to move from a suburban housing setting (i.e., a big house on a small-to-medium-sized block) to small and medium-sized apartments and townhouses and encourage people away from shopping in big box centres to more traditional main streets and piazza-type retail and entertainment complexes, it is imperative we provide a high-quality public environment.

It goes with the theory that if we are trying to encourage people to engage in more of a public life by being out on the street, walking in the piazza or shopping down the main street, we need to make this an attractive proposition for them – one that makes the experience convenient, pleasurable and safe. This isn't just about providing trees and seating, but also needs to cover the entire spectrum of the public realm, from paving treatments, lighting, vegetation selection and the placement of seating and wayfinding public art. High-quality public environments need to be practical to encourage people to cycle and walk, sit and stay, as well as well designed to be safe environments that encourage people to visit the town centre at night and not just during the day.

The public realm quality is often forgotten when planning town centres, but thanks to the work by Jan Gehl and other architects and planners who have studied human nature and its relationship with the urban environment, it is increasingly being recognised as an important ingredient of a high-quality public environment. In the box centre surrounded by car parking, there is little attention paid to the quality of the public realm. It is just bitumen for car parking, with little to no pedestrian walkways or trees. The quality, if you want to call it that, is located within 'the box'. If we are going to turn this inside out and have people walk the main street and piazza, we must create a high-quality environment that makes people want to walk and cycle instead of drive and to be outdoors instead of trapped in a box centre.

The key is making the environment pleasurable, so that people want to get out of their cars and walk around, whether it be down the main street or within the piazza. Convenience stores all need to be close by, with parking tucked away, but not so far away as to discourage people from coming – after all, killing the car culture in Australia will take time. Putting car parking behind buildings but close to convenient walkways will ensure people will be comfortable knowing their cars are out of sight, but not too far away as to be a chore to reach. The high-quality public realm, with its bespoke pavement treatments, landscaping, lighting, seating and connection with land use, will ensure a person's experience is of high quality and will keep them coming back for more.

The use of public art can be seen as tokenistic, but is an important element in creating a sense of place and wayfinding. Sometimes, public art can be so abstract that only the artist themselves understands the art piece's meaning. In my career, spanning twenty-five years, I have seen plenty of twisted bits of metal passing as public art, and I think this is a wasted opportunity. When I was leading the Cockburn Coast Project, one of the historical facets associated with the project area was the 10th Light Horse Regiment that participated in the Gallipoli campaign in World War One.

Before the Gallipoli campaign, the 10th Light Horse Regiment used to undertake drills along the beach immediately adjacent to the project area. Accordingly, to build on this heritage, we commissioned the preparation of public art that reflected this history. This 'way finding' not only includes the naming of roads after the ships that carried the 10th Light Horse Regiment across the oceans to the future battlegrounds of Europe, but we also looked at building a sense of history relating to the First World

War theme into the pavement and the public art itself. The public art was as poignant as it was beautiful and included the Royal Service League in its planning and development. As you walk through the Cockburn Coast Project, there are markers, paving and art work that tell the story of our World War One history in a way that is simple and easy to understand. It represents a relevant and clever way to create a respectful reflection of the past and a sense of place for an area.

Figure 6.30: Public art at Cockburn Coast, Perth[342]

Lighting is also a key component of the public realm. Creating a vibrant and well-lit area during the night is key to generating a sense of place but also in creating awareness and a sense of safety. Lighting doesn't just have to be about lighting a space, but can also be a feature of the landscape, such as lighting an art piece. There are cleaver examples of lighting used to display images against walls or illuminate trees or other landscape features – I have even seen seats and tables that are designed to light up. Taken collectively, this creates a sense of presence or arrival in a public space and can also be used to create an interesting, attractive and positive atmosphere for a place.

Other key details of creating interesting places include the need to carefully select seating and tree planting. You think this is easy, but it's not. The selection of tree species can make or break a place, being an important element in providing shade but also needing to be aesthetically pleasing. Often, deciduous trees are used, like London

---

[342] *'Photograph of Public Art at Cockburn Coast (Shoreline)'*, DevelopmentWA website www.developmentwa.com.au.

Plains or Chinese Tallow, which have large canopies and are attractive but are also deciduous in autumn. Trees can also be used to help define streets and set them apart so you have a sense of arrival – a feature that tells you "*this* is the main street". I have seen many developments which have gotten this mix wrong, and it can sterilise a place and make it unattractive for people.

Figure 6.31: Key elements of public space (left to right, top to bottom): meaningful public art; quality shelter; quality lighting; quality trees; quality seating; interesting amenities; quality features; relationship with built form[343]

The choice and design of seating is just as important, as it can either be uncomfortable in design, detracting from people wanting to stay and linger, or it can be ergonomic and encourage people to linger. A good mix is required to make it attractive for people to stay and enjoy the space and to provide passive

---

[343] 'Various Photographs from Sergio Famiano's Collection', 2001, 2005.

surveillance, which builds a sense of safety. Nothing is worse than a public space devoid of people.

Summing It All Up

I have come across many developers in my time who feel a compromise in the design process achieves good outcomes and that the achievement of one or two of the above elements is enough to create a 'good town centre'. This is not true, however. It is a collection of all these elements that determines the success or failure of a place, so it's not good enough to provide one or two of the elements at a high quality at the expense of others. All of the elements determine the attractiveness and viability of a place and, importantly whether public spaces are adaptive to our climate conditions. For instance, if you are going to create a town centre that encourages walking and cycling, then you are going to need to provide a public realm that is well shaded in summer to create a hospitable micro climate that enables people to enjoy the outdoors, even in difficult weather conditions.

Because developers are often stuck in the past and can't resist the urge to design for the automobile in mind, it is imperative that the government – first through state government policy and secondly through local government implementation of that policy – sticks to its guns and requires developers to combine all four elements to create the desired town centre. If you have doubts or are feeling the pressure (and I am talking to state and local government planners), just remember what you plan will be around for hundreds of years or more. The built form may come and go, but the layout of the town centre will remain for a very long time, so if you have to dig your heels in to fight for the best outcome; adding a few months to the design and approvals process could save a lot of embarrassment and poor legacy through the creation of impoverished and poorly-designed urban environments. Remember, you want to create urban environments you will be happy to walk through and enjoy and not steer clear of when passing by.

Planning in Motion

If we combine the above elements in order, we soon develop a format for the creation of town centres that are people-centred and create a picture of how town centres should be developed and how they can look when they are finished. Below (Figure 6.32) is a simple diagram that shows the design process in sequence.

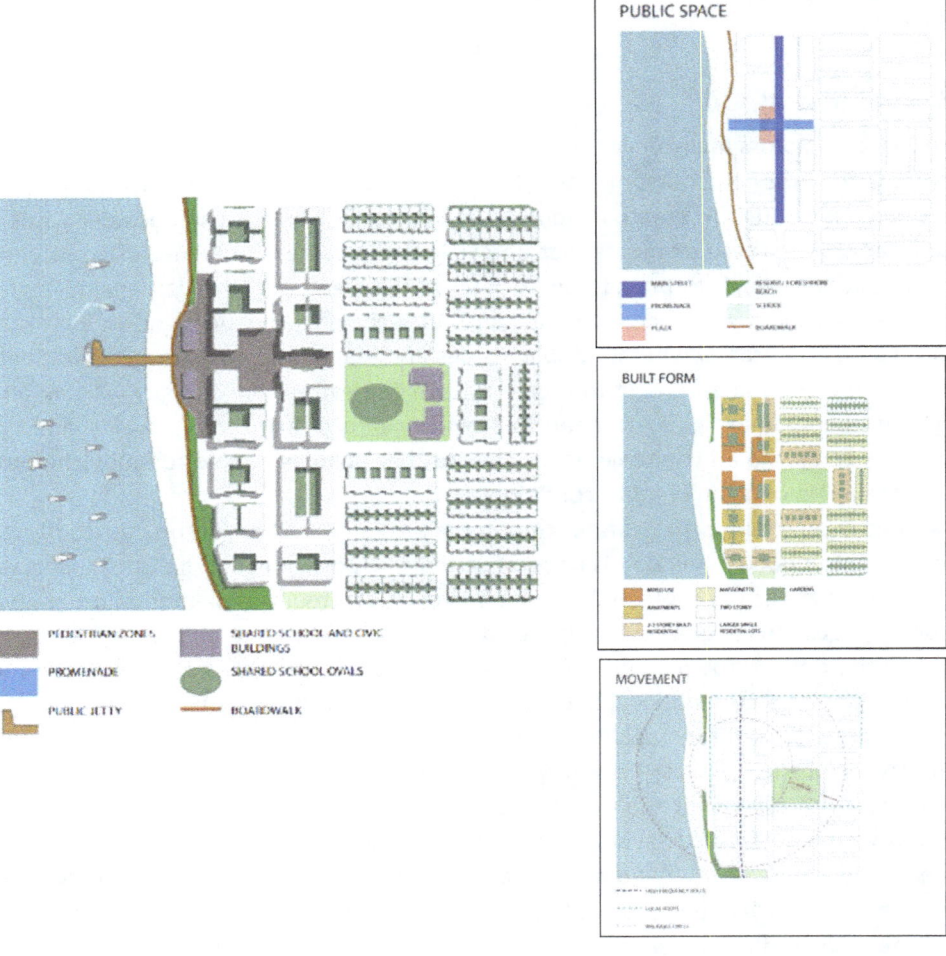

Figure 6.32: The design process combined[344]

When we break down the elements of the town centre as described above, we begin to paint a picture of what a town centre could look like and how it could function. An example of a sketched-up town centre is detailed below and comes from following the 4 steps described above.

---

[344] *'Diagram by Sergio Famiano with assistance from Insight Urbanism'*, 2022.

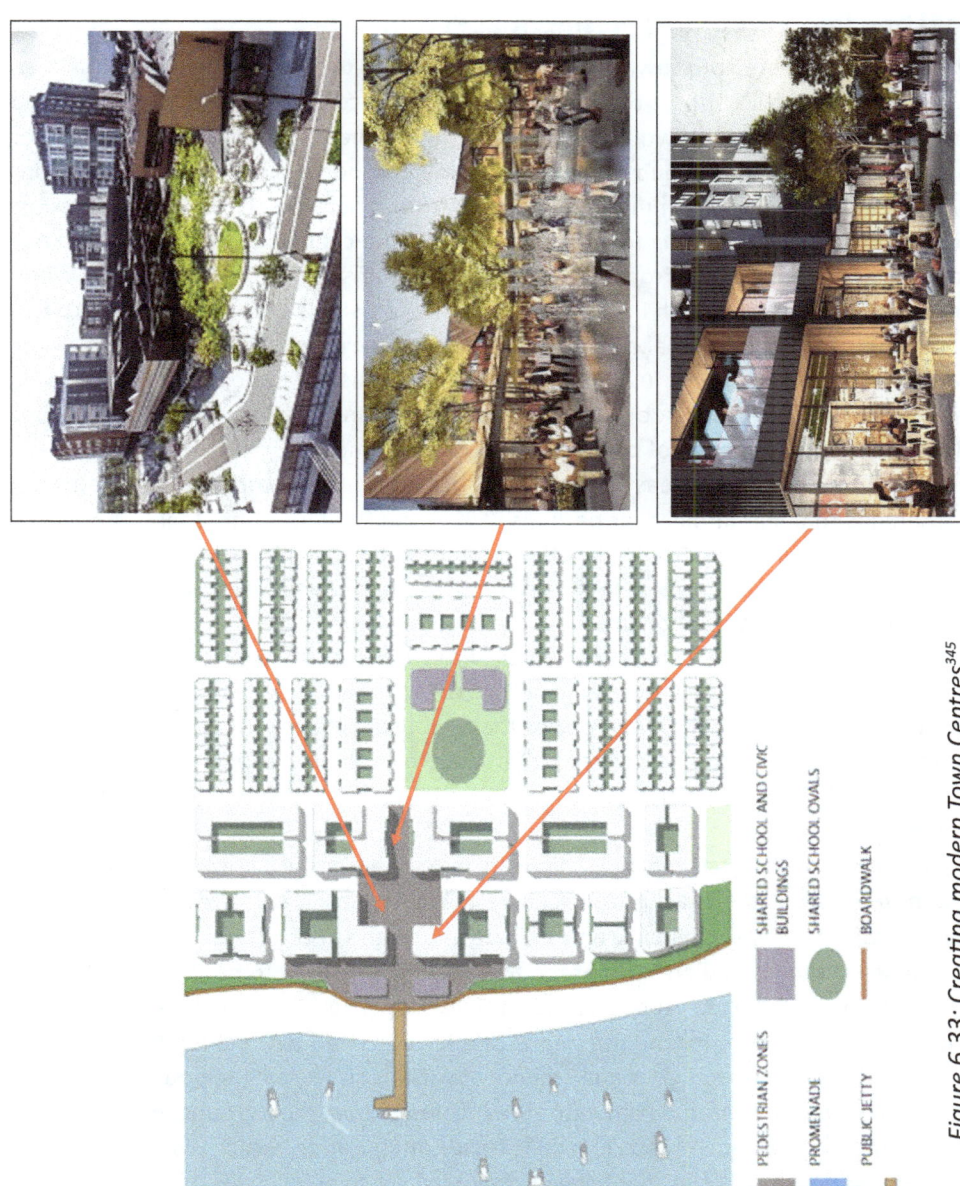

Figure 6.33: Creating modern Town Centres[345]

---

[345] *'Town Centre – ED Square'*, Fraser Property, March 2020.

Creating People-Centred Residential Precincts

Once we have created our town centre design, we need to focus on the residential area around it, which will support the function of the town centre and its viability. We also need to consider who we would like to live in the project area, and we should steer clear of having just one group of people, such as first-home buyers, and instead consider creating a diverse community of people from different socio-economic groups. This isn't just the 'right thing to do', it also reflects the changing demographics of our country, as we move away from a predominately family-household mix to a more balanced household mix, which includes singles, couples, single parents and aged households, which collectively make up nearly 70% of all new households. Designing new growth areas that cater for just one segment of the Australian population is not only problematic from a broad socio-economic and community building point of view, but also goes against the grain of prevailing population trends.

Our new growth areas should only contain large three-to-four-bedroom households that suit families for perhaps 25% of the total household mix. The rest of the household mix should cater for other groups, such as singles and couples without children. It's these groups who make up the majority of Australia now, and this is not likely to change anytime soon.

Diversity in housing also has one other major benefit: it means people can stay in an area for their lifetime. In the monoculture suburb that we have been creating since the 1950s, people have to move out of their suburb if they want to downsize. If we create suburbs with housing diversity, then we are enabling people to stay within the same suburb over their lifetimes. This is essential if we want to build and maintain a sense of community.

So, how do we *practically* build diversity in our new growth areas? Well, we made a start when we looked at our town centres. Since we are creating high-quality town centres with diversity in land use and a piazza and main street, it is fair to say that land-use values in the immediate core of the town centre are likely to be the highest priority, given the assembly of conveniences at your fingertips. This includes high-quality public spaces, diversity in land use and access to more frequent public transport. This is the area where you put your apartments of various sizes – single, double and three bedroom – so you have a mix to cater for different population groups and sizes. The apartments can be above shops in a mixed-use configuration, which would be located around the piazza and the main street, followed by selected two- and three-storey apartment sites that are adjacent to the main street and piazza.

As we move away from the main street and piazza, we start to introduce different built-form typologies: two-storey townhouses on micro lots (i.e., lots that are 100sqm in area). These properties typically cater for singles, retirees, couples and small families and represent density in a 'green title' or separate-lot built form. Remember, the key is to try and pack as many people in and around the town centre as possible. This is not only essential to ensure the safety and passive surveillance argument, but is also essential in densifying the residential catchment close to businesses to support their viability. We don't want to create a town centre that relies on a large hinterland to be viable. We want lots of people within walking distance of the businesses to ensure the hinterland is tighter and less reliant on people having to come from long distances to make the businesses viable.

This viability aspect has been totally forgotten in planning for town centres over the last seventy years. The rationale is simple and interconnected. If you have a low-density residential environment, the businesses in the town centre will rely on people having to travel long distances from the town centre to make it viable – that is, the viable hinterland is larger. Because the hinterland is beyond 800 metres away, and in some instances could be 3 to 5 kilometres, people will need to drive, and, when you are reliant on people driving to your town centre in order to make it viable, you need to design your town centre around the automobile. If you look at the inverse relationship to this – that is, you create a densely populated urban environment – then your viable hinterland for businesses is smaller, and if you can get this between 800 metres and 2 kilometres, then most people can walk, which means you can design your town centre around walking and not the automobile. This is a simple logic but one that has been lost in the way we have been building our new growth areas over the last seventy years.

If we recap, the core of the town centre is represented by the piazza and main street, supported by mixed-use, and the area immediately surrounding up to 800 metres (comfortable walking distance) should contain mainly apartments (various sizes) in mixed-use (commercial, retail and residential) and standalone apartment blocks (two and three-storey versions). It can also include some residential townhouse typologies on micro lots of two or more storeys. Outside of the 800-metre-walkable catchment, from say 800 metres to 1.5 kilometres, we can start to introduce larger lots between 100sqm and 350sqm in area that are of the two-storey and single-storey variety, which cater more for smaller and larger families, and therefore generally require larger living space for habitation. In this arrangement, we should be aiming for a population density of no less than 1,500 people within 800 metres to 1 kilometre of the town centre. This represents approximately 700 dwellings (mainly in apartment form), if we assume a density per household of around 2.3 people, which reflects the predominately single, couple (without kids), elderly (single and couple) and small family household configuration.

A key to linking the variety of household typologies and population is by using a legible street network that has a focus on facilitating walking and cycling and developing a street hierarchy to improve movement legibility. If you get the built form right, as described above, people – whether they are driving, walking or cycling – can understand that they are approaching a town centre, because the road layout is a grid and the land use intensity increases as you get closer to the town centre. However, this is not enough, and different landmark cues are required to support legibility. The easiest way you can do this, in addition to using a hierarchy of built-form typology, is by using streetscape design.

Similar to the way that main streets need a distinct design, the same applies to secondary and third streets and so on, so we create a clear and legible street hierarchy. This can be done by using specific street cross-sections and, more importantly, by using different vegetation or tree planting to help to distinguish one street from the others. How many of you have gone into a suburb in one of our Australian cities and the landscaping is all the same from street to street? Because the built form is also the same from street to street, it is easy to get lost as a driver or pedestrian, as every street looks the same. By designing streets differently, not just in terms of configuration via different cross-sections, but by also using different vegetation, each street can then make up part of a hierarchy, which provides visual cues to drivers and pedestrians that guide them to the town centre.

In recent times, we have started to see an interest in developing a hierarchy of streets to assist legibility. I know when I worked on the Cockburn Coast Project, south of Fremantle, we developed a Public Realm Guideline that identified a street hierarchy throughout the development, which reflected the intensity of the built form, land use and proximity to the town centre. This is something that needs to be developed for all projects, particularly for new growth areas where we are increasingly trying to diversify land use and break up the monotony that has characterised suburban development in Australian cities over the last fifty-plus years. We are also starting to see the introduction of 'green streets', which are characterised by additional tree planting and development, with vehicle access via a rear laneway to create a more pedestrian-friendly street. These types of streets are usually found as secondary streets to main streets, as they generally include more intense land uses that support walking as a primary form of movement into town centres. The combination of main streets, green streets and streets defined by a road and landscape hierarchy collectively add to the legibility of a new growth area and, in my opinion, are essential if we are going to challenge the traditional automobile suburb and its engineering-led design.

By combining the elements of land use, street hierarchy and legibility into the design process, we start to develop a very different type of new growth area to the ones normally created in Australia. If we start to combine these elements as an extension of our town centres, we start to see the creation of diverse and inclusive suburbs that are not only denser and provide housing for all ages during their lifetime, but also collectively act to support the viability of town centres. The neighbourhood is also more sustainable, as the hinterland for the town centre is smaller and therefore relies less on automobile travel to make the centre viable.

When we combine all the elements above, we begin to get a sense of what a new growth suburb could look like and how different it is from the traditional monotonous suburbs that are being rolled out at the moment. See Figure 6.34 below which reflects the possible new growth area if we adopt the urban design, socio-economic and demographic logic described above.

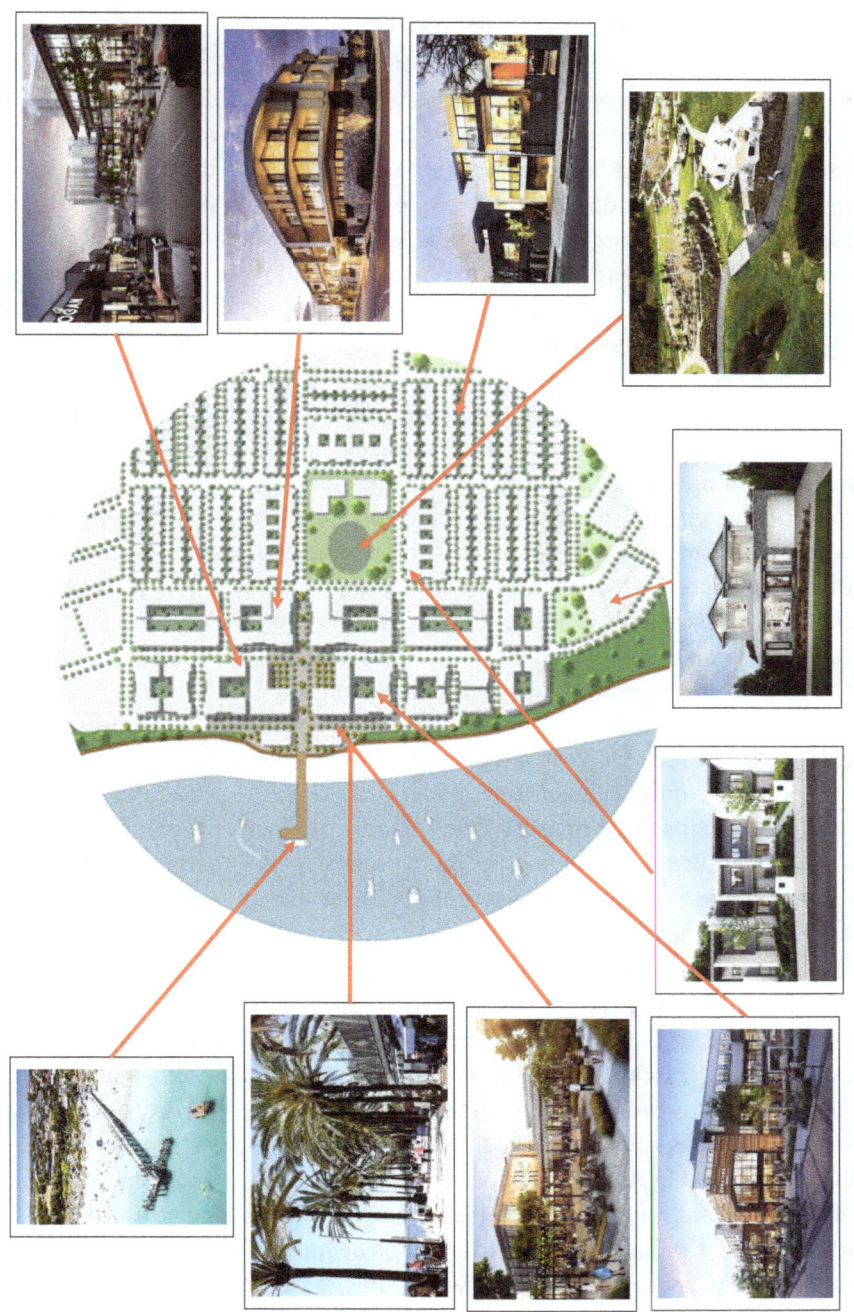

Figure 6.34: A vision for new growth suburbs[346]

---

[346] *'Diagram by Sergio Famiano with assistance from Insight Urbanism', 2022.*

Building Alternative Transport into Suburbs

Building a more diverse and denser version of new growth areas not only reflects the current state of demographics in Australia – with a particular need for diversity in housing type – but it also helps to support the viability of town centres, which we would like to see designed around the pedestrian. But this isn't the only advantage of a more diverse neighbourhood. They also support alternative transport and improved public transport services. For generations now, we have witnessed the proliferation of the low-density and monotonous suburb in Australian cities, and, because it is made up largely of single-residential housing, we have seen the steady diminishment of public transport as you reach further and further from the city centre, with public transport authorities saying that providing a service simply isn't viable at the frequency required to make public transport effective when you are creating suburbs with densities of less than 300 people per square kilometre. This can all change, however, if you change the composition of our new growth suburbs and build-in density from day one.

The density argument and its relationship to public transport service has been a long battle that I and my colleagues have been engaged in with public transport authorities since I entered the industry. At a very high level, planners (as a collective) have always argued that public transport in the form of rapid transit (passenger rail) or light rail, for example, if provided early in the development process, has the potential to lead to land-use diversification and density and facilitate the new urban form. The reason for this is that there is a strong correlation between public transport and land-use densification; so, if land developers can see that government is committing to public transport, this tends to build confidence, as there is an irrefutable link between density and public transport provision.[347] Put simply: the better the public transport, the higher the land-use diversity and residential density that can be supported. This seems to be a phenomenon that is well embraced around the world but has largely been ignored in Australia.

In the United States, for example, there are many instances where transport authorities have introduced light rail into new growth areas followed by development. There is an element of risk in doing this, since, for light rail to function, it needs a significant population catchment to support it. But history shows that when light rail is provided early in a new project, development follows, and not just any development, but mixed-use and higher-density residential development, which is critical for diversifying our cities. In Australia, however, there is such a reluctance to embrace this model, with state and federal transport agencies preferring to introduce light rail or other forms of rapid transit in existing areas where density already exists, and only then using light rail to replace buses with trams. With this logic in mind, to make alternative public transport viable in our new growth areas, we are going to have

---

[347] *'The renaissance of light rail'*, Australian railway Association, April 2021.

to build in density from day one. By changing the way we develop our new growth suburbs, this becomes a possibility.

But how do we ensure that the design of dense new growth areas is rewarded with better public transport? This is a valid question, because if we are going to ask land developers – who are largely made up of private sector firms – to depart from prevailing models of suburban growth and move from a low-density model to a medium-to-high-density model, they need to be assured that 'higher-order' public transport will support this type of development – sooner rather than later. Since public transport is the domain of the government, it is up to the individual state governments in Australia to develop a new transport plan that focuses on the planning and delivery of public transport to support future growth corridors that adopt the medium-to-high-density housing model. The first step in this intricate process is to ensure new development in new growth areas adopts a medium-to-high-density growth model. This is a hard but necessary first decision. The only way the government can do this is by using its state planning powers to develop guidelines that require new growth areas to be designed to support housing diversity and traditional mixed-use, piazza and main street town-centre designs.

In Perth, for example, the state government planning organisation (the Western Australian Planning Commission) has the state planning policy Liveable Neighbourhoods. This document, which is based largely on New Urbanist principles, provides the urban framework for the design of all new growth suburbs in Perth. The document was advanced for its day when it was first released nearly two decades ago, but the problem is the document doesn't go far enough in seeking the provision of traditional town centres and dense suburban environments. Accordingly, the document needs to be reviewed and re-written. The tale is likely similar in other Australian cities.

We have seen firsthand over the last two decades what the Liveable Neighbourhoods policy document creates in terms of new suburbs and centres: they are not diverse, and they are not dense places. Reviewing this document and its counterparts within other Australian cities would be the first step towards change – and it is a controversial one, since it will require a radical rethink in the way we plan our new growth areas and will need considerable engagement with the land and housing industry. This fundamental shift in urban planning will then need to be supported by the development of a new public transport plan that channels higher-order public transport to new growth corridors that follow this new line of development. This will be different for each city but consistent in the approach, with the transport network following the new urban planning form.

The next controversial, and indeed difficult, problem to solve is delivering the transport that is needed. As we have mentioned before, the problem is that passenger rail and light rail is inflexible and expensive to deliver. Developing transport plans for our cities is not the difficult part, it is finding the funding to implement mid-tier transport across our cities. There is no guaranteed funding for public transport in Australia. Instead, it is up to political parties – namely the state government. This can only be solved if there is bi-partisan support at the federal and state levels to devote funding to public transport, similar to there being funding for main roads in our cities.

The next crucial step is that, as a country, we need to embrace new technology to add to our mid-tier transport solution in addition to light-rail technology. This is why public transport authorities across Australia need to embrace new technology, such as trackless trams, as a more affordable – but equally effective form of public transport – solution for our mid-tier transport options.

Trackless trams are a relatively new technology and should be considered the public transport of choice for new growth areas and, similar to light rail, should operate on the premise of having a dedicated lane that provides a link between new growth suburbs, town centres and passenger rail lines, which tend to be linear in Australian cities. In Australia, we are good at developing linear-type public transport linkages, which, like tentacles, start from the centre of the city and spread out along linear corridors deep into suburban areas. This is great for moving people from the suburbs directly to a city's CBD but does little if you want to move horizontally across the city – say from one of the passenger rail stations to another on a different line. Assisting this east–west movement is where mid-tier transport comes into play in our cities.

Australia has traditionally been dominated by light rail, particularly in the eastern states of Australia, but it is increasingly becoming more difficult to afford and implement, as discussed previously. As a result, buses tend to be the backbone of lower-order public transport in our cities, but people generally don't like buses. With trackless tram technology, the problems with buses can be mitigated and at a fraction of the cost of light rail.

So, how can technology like trackless trams be built into our new denser suburban areas? Well, one advantage of trackless trams is that they are flexible – you don't need a fixed track for them to operate, so they can easily be transferred from one area to another. This flexibility is gold, as it makes it significantly easier to implement and also ensures a quicker process. The flexibility also means trackless trams can go just about anywhere. While the priority would be for trackless trams to have their own dedicated lanes, it is unrealistic for the entire route. This can be achieved, however, in key higher-order roads, where there are multiple lanes; this is critical to ensure speed and reliability. In other parts of a built-up area, however, trackless trams can share with traffic, for example, on a main street.

It is very important that trackless trams shouldn't be seen as being accommodated for in a separate corridor. In other words, for their implementation, the road reserve should not be widened to accommodate an extra lane. Why? This will create difficulties in land take and monetary compensation and would be nearly impossible to accommodate in existing built-up areas in Australian cities. It's what destroys public transport projects: the fact that they must be accommodated by expanding the road network, which is near impossible.

I say it is absolutely necessary that trackless trams be implemented by taking away a lane for traffic where multiple lanes exist. This may be seen as a disaster if you love your car, but there is good reason for doing so. Let me put it into context. To start with, you have a four-lane busy road (two lanes each way), which carries traffic of up to 20,000 vehicles a day. What I am suggesting is that we take away a traffic lane and dedicate it to public transport. This will mean that the single lane will be taking double capacity, which may seem unworkable at first, but I would say this is a temporary frustration that is required in order to change behaviours. If we keep accommodating traffic and widening our roads, guess what happens? We make it easier for people to drive cars and, therefore, our chances of modifying behaviours are nullified. However, if we reverse the equation and make it more difficult for cars to move around the city, then the pendulum shifts. People will start to see public transport as a more viable alternative that is cheaper, faster and more reliable – particularly if public transport has its own lane.

This is the only way we can shift travel behaviours. It is the same approach that Jan Gehl employed in Copenhagen. By taking away parking spaces and giving the space over to pedestrians, while at the same time improving public transport, Gehl was able to transform travel behaviours in Copenhagen from people predominately driving to people predominately walking or taking public transport. It sounds easy, doesn't it? But the reality is it's not. It takes incredible political will to make a decision of this magnitude. You are talking about asking the general public to not only put up with short-term frustration and deal with higher traffic, but you are also taking them out of their comfort zone of driving and instead having them rely more on public transport. It's a big shift, especially for the modern Australian, but it has to be done.

Taking this difficult path will not only promote more sustainable transport and achieve some of Australia's greenhouse reduction targets, but it will also prove to be cheaper for the average household. After all, if you can get to work using public transport, it may mean that many households could cut down to one vehicle in the family. This would represent enormous savings and also reduce our reliance on the fossil fuel economy. We will look at this in more detail later.

To achieve behavioural change, it takes time and commitment – bi-partisan commitment, which we don't have in Australia. Typically, the Liberals like roads, and Labor invests in public transport. This is a generalisation of course. Since climate change and reducing Australia's dependency on fossil fuels is a bi-partisan objective, and given transport is a significant contributor to both, there should be support for the promotion of public transport in our cities. One thing is for sure, there may not be total agreement across the major political parties on private versus public transport, but soon there may be no choice, given that our cities are becoming congested, and we are reaching limitations on how many lanes we can keep adding to our freeways, distributor roads and in our neighbourhoods. The decision may be forced upon both political parties before too long.

The Planning System and the Role of Government

We have seen in the various examples of transit-oriented development described in this book the powerful role that the government can play in leading the way in the demonstration of alternative development and driving change in the development industry. Transit-oriented developments are notoriously difficult to undertake successfully and require time and considerable upfront investment, in terms of both money and energy, to make them work, which is something the government is better placed to deliver rather than, say, the private sector, who are often beholden to stock owners who want guaranteed and consistent returns on their investments. It is for this reason I think there is a strong role for the government in the development industry, and governments from both political persuasions need to resist the callings of the private sector (acting on their own selfish desires) to divest the government of land and instead do the opposite: acquire and develop more land.

To understand how critical the government is to the land-development industry, we need to look at the two apparatuses via which the government operates in the land and housing game.

The Planning Framework: The Role of State and Local Governments

The planning framework the development industry operates within is set largely by the state government. This is purposeful, since urban development and housing is an essential ingredient for the welfare of a nation (remember Maslow's hierarchy of needs?); it is, therefore, essential that the framework be set by the government operating in the best interest of everybody and not just the few. Most state governments in Australia have a dedicated Ministry of Urban and Regional Town Planning. In Western Australia, you have the Minister for Transport and Planning. They have an administrative arm called the Western Australian Planning Commission, which is the governing body, and the Department for Planning, Lands and Heritage, which is the administrative function. Similarly, in New South Wales, the Minister for Urban Planning has underneath them the Department of Planning, Industry and Environment, and so on for each other state.

The names of the ministries and departments may change, depending upon the government of the day, but the essential service in providing a ministry and administrative department for urban planning is the same – such is the importance of town planning in our cities and regions. They have been a staple in the machinery of government since the early days when we had road boards, which formed into town planning boards and then into government departments as our urban areas have expanded. This gained greater significance after the Second World War, with governments investing heavily in housing and suburban development to support our returning war veterans.

These various ministries and state organisations are critical in setting the planning framework for each state in Australia that guides the redevelopment of existing brownfield or infill development sites and new greenfield or suburban developments. While the frameworks may vary slightly from state to state, most have the same or similar structure. In Western Australia, for example, the Western Australian Planning Commission, along with the Department of Planning, Lands and Heritage, are responsible for administering the Metropolitan Region Scheme for its major capital city: Perth. This scheme sets the administrative framework for broad land use and transport planning in Perth, allocating land uses, such as urban and strategic regional centres, to key commercial and residential areas within the city. This scheme also allocates classifications such as Primary Regional Road, Other Regional Road and Railway for significant movement networks within the city. Each of these is then controlled by different state government departments. For example, Primary Regional Roads are managed by Main Roads WA, and Other Regional Roads are managed by the Department for Planning, Lands and Heritage, while Railway corridors are managed by the Public Transport Authority. Other roads, such as Local Roads are all managed by local government.

The Metropolitan Region Scheme is deliberately broad in scale, providing a planning framework that captures all possible land uses within a city. Maps (e.g., Figure 6.35) provide a series of colours across the metropolitan area, which denote different types of land use and transport corridors. Green, for example, represents significant Regional Reserves; light red is Urban, allowing commercial and residential development; blue is Strategic Regional Centres, which is a higher-order employment and activity centre; purple is Industrial; and so on. See the Metropolitan Region Scheme for Perth Below.

The WA State Government, through the Western Australian Planning Commission, takes a strategic view on land use planning by assigning broad areas for key land uses. For this reason, the Metropolitan Region Scheme is 'king' in terms of setting the planning framework the populace has to follow. The Metropolitan Region Scheme doesn't stand alone, however; it is guided by key state-wide planning strategies, such as 'Perth and Peel @ 3.5 million', which highlights the areas where future urban development is to take place to support the growth in population from 2.25 million people, at present, to 3.5 million people, forecasted for the next twenty years. This, as mentioned previously, is partly accommodated for in existing residential areas through the redevelopment of existing areas and in the form of new development, which usually occurs on the fringes between urban-zoned land and rural-zoned land – basically rural land giving way to urban.

Supporting the 'Perth and Peel @ 3.5 million' strategic document is what the state calls the Sub-Regional Planning Framework. This essentially takes the overarching goals of the 'Perth and Peel @ 3.5 million' strategic document and divides the metropolitan area into regions or sub-regions where further detail on transport and land-use planning is provided. An example is the North–East Sub-Regional Planning Framework, which covers the industrial, commercial and residential areas located in Perth's north–eastern corridor, such as the local governments of Wanneroo and Swan. Collectively, the combination of the two groups of strategic documents form the framework for shaping the Metropolitan Region Scheme by making recommendations on transport and land-use planning, which are then carried forward to the Metropolitan Region Scheme through amendments.

In summary, state planning and strategic planning documents – such as 'Perth and Peel @ 3.5 million' – set the overarching goals and objectives of the Perth metropolitan area. This is then divided into five to six sub-regions, which look at a part of Perth or a corridor of Perth in more detail, setting goals and objectives for land-use planning and transport. The combination of the two then influences the Metropolitan Region Scheme, which is the operative statutory document that puts the theory into practice. But the planning doesn't stop there.

Supplementing the Metropolitan Region Scheme in Perth is a series of state government policies that provide the next layer of detail in the planning framework. This includes policy documents such as Liveable Neighbourhoods, which provides guidance to land developers on how to subdivide land and create town centres in a suburban context. This includes provision for public open spaces, the road layout design, the housing mix and the design of town centres. Then, there are other policies, such as *State Planning Policy 5.4: Activity Centres in the Perth and Peel Region*, which provide a hierarchy of activity and employment centres and guidance on how they are to be developed. Other policies, such as *State Planning Policy 3.7: Bushfire Planning*, provide guidance on subdivision and development in bushfire-prone areas and so on. To find a comprehensive list of state planning policies in Perth, all you need to do is access the Western Australian Planning Commission website: https://www.dplh.wa.gov.au/policy-and-legislation/state-planning-framework/state-planning-policies (accessed May 2022).

The state planning apparatus is enshrined in legislation. For example, in Western Australia the key planning legislation is the *Planning and Development Act 2005*. In Melbourne and Sydney, it's the *Planning and Environment Act 1987* and the *Environmental Planning and Assessment Act 1979,* respectively.

The state planning apparatus for town planning is key to the strategic planning framework for a city. I have talked about Perth, but it is similar in other states.

However, it doesn't stop there. In Australia, there is another tier of town planning: the local government. Local governments provide the final, yet critical, element to the planning system. Through legislation, such as the *Planning and Development Act 2005 (WA)*, the foundations are laid for state governments to set the strategic planning framework through the Metropolitan Region Scheme and state planning policies. This then flows down to the local governments, which, through the same legislation, are required to maintain a more detailed planning framework that aligns with the state government apparatus.

Similar in name to the Metropolitan Region Scheme, which covers the entire Perth metropolitan area, Perth is then divided into twenty-four local governments, stretching from the City of Mandurah, on the coast to the south, to the City of Wanneroo, to the north, and the Town of Kalamunda in the hills region. Each local government is required to establish and maintain a Local Planning Strategy (similar to 'Perth and Peel @ 3.5 million' but for a local government area only) and a Local Town Planning Scheme, which provides much greater detail on land use and transport planning. While under the Metropolitan Region Scheme there are broad zonings, such as 'urban', under the Local Town Planning Scheme these areas identified as 'urban' are then divided into separate residential, commercial, retail, local parks and recreational-type land uses. For residential, for example, there could be a variety of residential densities – referred to as codes – which determine the number of dwellings permitted on a residential block based on the size of the block and the residential density code that applies. For example, if your property is zoned R40, an average lot area of 220sqm is required, so if you have a 1000sqm block, you can, in theory, develop the lot for four dwellings. These minutiae of detail are within the purview of local governments, which can also have structure plans that guide subdivision and development, in mostly broad-acre areas, and local planning policies that may guide minor aspects of the built form, such as setbacks to lot boundaries and so forth.

The alignment between the state and local governments is essential, however, and this is mandated through legislation. For example, if in the Metropolitan Region Scheme there is a zoning change from urban to industrial land, say in the local government area of Fremantle, then the local government of Fremantle is required to amend its own Local Town Planning Scheme to reflect the new industrial zoning. Similarly, if the local government supports the preparation of a Structure Plan to guide the future subdivision and development of land in its jurisdiction, the Structure Plan needs to be prepared in accordance with the WA State Government's Planning Policy: Liveable Neighbourhoods. The nexus between the two is enshrined in legislation and is administered primarily through the two distinct Planning Schemes: the Metropolitan Region Scheme, which is administered by the Western Australian Planning Commission, and the Local Town Planning Scheme, which is developed for and administered by each local government. Below is an example of a Local Town Planning Scheme.

There is, therefore, an intricate and detailed link between the state government and the local government in the planning system, with the state government serving as the 'master' and the local governments as the 'servants'.

Figure 6.35: A section of a local government scheme[348]

So, how do you feel about the crash course in urban planning? Confused? Well, it's only scratching the surface. There are many policies, procedures and government agencies that work together to complete town planning for each state in Australia. I wanted to focus on planning, though, so that you could see the government has a significant role in determining the shape and form of our cities. This means changing planning practices often needs to start from the top, at the state government level, and to influence State Strategy, the Metropolitan Region Scheme and state policies, such as 'Liveable Neighbourhoods', which tell us how we develop our suburbs. If the state governments want to promote diversity in land use and promote different housing to reflect the demographic trends prevailing in our country, then they need to modify their strategies and the Metropolitan Region Scheme and look at key state policies.

This sounds simple but remember an appointed Minister for Planning, who is elected by the people, is at the top of the chain . Accordingly, elected members are governed by those who elect them and lobby for them the hardest. Often these are private sector organisations, which are generally less interested in community and environment benefits and instead are driven by short-term monetary gain. This is why we often see town planning reform focused on streamlining timeframes for approvals rather than focusing on quality – this is something Australia will have to address in the years to come.

There are also many instances where change can occur from the 'grass roots' (the local government) and rise to the top (the state government). We have previously looked at the example of the Gold Coast Council and its light rail push. It was the local government

---

[348] *'City of Stirling Town Planning Scheme No.3'*, City of Stirling website, www.stirling.wa.gov.au 2022.

who pushed the agenda, whence it was picked up at the state and federal levels. This is a significant example, but there are many smaller ones. In Western Australia, many local governments have raised concerns with the loss of tree canopy that occurs through infill development (knocking down an old house and developing three units). The *State Planning Policy 7.3: Residential Design Codes* enabled a built form that created 'battle-axe lots', where three to four units are squeezed on a block, with little open space area provided for tree planting and vegetation. For the R40 density code, for example, up until 2021 there was only a requirement to provide a 16sqm area for outdoor living space per dwelling. This barely fits in enough space for a table and chairs, let alone a tree and vegetation. In response to this, local governments began instituting separate local planning policies that required courtyard spaces to be increased to 30sqm and requiring a 'deep soil' zone for planting a tree. This had the effect of creating minimum spaces that could accommodate recreational activities and also allow for some landscaping.

Figure 6.36: Courtyard using RCodes[349]

Figure 6.37: Courtyard using local government policy [350]

---

[349] *'Pictures sourced from WAPC presentation on Residential Design Codes'*, WAPC, 2020.
[350] *'Pictures sourced from WAPC presentation on Residential Design Codes'*, WAPC, 2020.

The result of this minor furore by a local government has had a profound impact on the way we design our outdoor spaces and the links between indoor and outdoor spaces, so much so that, in Western Australia, the State government amended the *State Planning Policy 7.3: Residential Design Codes* to enlarge courtyard spaces in smaller units and townhouse developments and now requires deep soil zones and tree planting in courtyards. This is a small example, but it shows that local governments, through leadership and implementation, can influence state government policy and the development industry to create positive change.

To sum up, government has a big role to play in the urban development industry. Firstly, the minister sets the strategic direction for others to follow. Secondly, the state government department implements the minister's direction by setting the strategy for urban and transport planning and then cements this through State Planning Policy and the Metropolitan Region Scheme, which represent the operative arm of the strategy. This then flows down to local governments, which are required to prepare local planning strategies and local town planning schemes, which are approved by the Minister for Planning, following a review by the state government's planning arm. Because of this streamlined approach between the state and local governments, change for the better must primarily come from the state government. An example of reform by state government we can look at is the McGowan Labour Government's approach to planning reform.

Taking office in 2017, the Western Australian Government, led by Mark McGowan, instituted a rigorous planning reform process that had a two-pronged approach. The first was to streamline planning processes to reduce approval timeframes for key planning instruments, such as structure plans, town planning schemes, local planning strategies, local development plans, and subdivision and development applications. This reform included changes to planning legislation, such as the *Planning and Development Act 2005* and the supporting *Planning and Development (Local planning Scheme) Regulations 2015*, to enforce strict timeframes for accepting, advertising and approving planning applications.[351] This reform, no doubt, was a reaction to lobbying by the development industry, who are focused on streamlining the process and reducing the time that planning applications are with state and local government for assessment.

This reform process included taking away power from local governments for making determinations on significant commercial and industrial developments – an extension of the previous Liberal government's introduction of Development Assessment Panels, which can involve developments over $2 million in value determined by a separate body consisting of two local government councillors and three industry experts.[352]

---

[351] Planning and Development (Local Planning Scheme) Regulations 2015.
[352] Planning and Development (Local Planning Scheme) Regulations 2015.

This gradual whittling down of local government decision making is concerning, since it is the local government and its residents who bear the brunt of good and bad planning decisions being made by people who are miles away. The first tranche of planning reform has done nothing to improve subdivision and development quality but has sped up approval timeframes – a win for the development industry.

The second tranche of planning reform is involved in improving the design of largely significant built forms. The Design WA reform package consists of a dedicated team who is focused on instituting policy changes that greatly improve design in the planning process. These reforms include the creation of Design Review Panels at the state and local government levels to assess and provide advice on structure plans and development applications. Consisting of an independent group of town planners, architects and landscape architects, the panels are set up by local governments and provide design advice to applicants so built-form designs can be improved prior to formal assessment and determination. The new process has been a tremendous success, but it doesn't act alone, with policy reform also playing a key role.

The Design WA team has made significant reform by creating *State Planning Policy 7.3: Residential Design Codes (Volume 2)*, which provides a designed-based approach to the design and assessment of apartment developments.[353] In addition, Volume 3 (Medium-Density Housing) has been established to provide a design-based approach to the assessment of medium-density housing. These key reforms have shifted the planning pendulum away from pure statutory design to performance-based design. Working with the design review panels, the quality of development has lifted dramatically across the state, making it harder and harder to develop simple and poorly-designed dwellings, which Perth had been seeing over the last thirty years. It is imperative that the government, not just in Western Australia but across Australia, continues reform in town planning to lift not only design quality, but also design diversity to cater for an increasingly diverse population.

Some areas where I think there is a need for nationwide reform are detailed below.

1. Town centre development: Focus on creating people-centred places with a central piazza supported by a main street and a mixture of housing, including mandatory apartment development, townhouse, maisonette and small lot product. Minimum building heights of three and four storeys should be provided in the town centre's core, supported by key public transport links.
2. Continued decentralisation of government services: There needs to be a focus on supporting regional and district town centres by providing significant employment opportunities away from the cities' cores. This will support the role and function of regional, district and local centres, making the centres

---

[353] *'Residential Design Codes (Volume 2)'*, WAPC, 2019.

more viable, supporting commerce and population growth. They will also distribute transport movement away from the suburb to the centre, easing congestion during peak times.

3. Housing diversity: Minimum requirements for housing diversity and density in new suburban locations, including single-bedroom and two-bedroom homes, and aged-person housing. The latter is particularly significant, since we are moving towards an ageing population.

4. Transport planning and infrastructure planning: Greater coordination between the delivery of public transport and the provision of new land for development. This is needed to ensure public transport is delivered at the start or in the early stages of the development front to support dense development, rather than midway through or later in the development cycle, when it is difficult to achieve density.

The final point is critical in creating functional employment centres in a local context and is equally critical in creating diversity in housing in traditionally homogenous suburban locations. The traditional suburban model consists of a single house with three and four bedrooms and two carports. If we are to move away from this by encouraging apartment development, two- and single-bedroom housing on smaller blocks or in apartment configurations, and aged-person housing, then we need this to be supported by public transport, not just buses, but also light rail and trackless trams, which gives developers confidence that alternative housing can be provided for and supported by the necessary infrastructure.

The Role of Government Developers

As we have seen above, the government plays a significant role in setting the framework and 'rules', as it were, for the planning and development of our urban environments. The framework is followed not only by private developers from large national land development companies, such as Stocklands, Frasers and the Goodman Group, but also by our national builders, such as ABN Group, Metroplex and Pro Build. But it is not just the private sector that needs to follow the Planning Framework. State governments across Australia have vast landholdings in their possession too, and state governments have long been in the game of development – both in subdivision and estate planning, but also in housing.

The areas where the government traditionally plays a role in estate planning and housing are where the market has failed. In terms of estate-wide planning, this generally involves engaging in tough infill or brownfield development sites, which may be constrained due to contamination (i.e., historic industrial land) or are constrained due to a lack of services. There are also other projects, such as mixed-use and apartment developments in town centres, which aren't always viable for the private sector and are also places where governments own land.

You have all probably seen or heard of the ABC TV comedy *Utopia*. It tells the story of the country's NBA (Nation Building Authority), which is a newly created government organisation charged with overseeing the delivery of major infrastructure projects, including ports, urban development, rail, etc. The comedy value is that the bureaucrats who work at the NBA don't tend to operate in the most efficient manner, and, through blunder, self-interest and ridicule, they cause many grand projects to falter or stall. Combine this with the seemingly endless fads and ridiculous marketing ploys, what often results is the derailing of the staff's attempts at bringing projects from announcement to unveiling, with the projects typically becoming over-budget, delayed white elephants.

The point is, like it or not, the government is involved in urban development, and across Australia there are organisations who are responsible for – and have the form and function of the NBA in *Utopia* – planning and delivering difficult projects. Remember there has been a long history of government involvement in land development. During the pre-war years, state governments had held vast properties since the colonial period and created subdivisions to create land for housing, industrial and commercial development. Following the Second World War, this intensified, with state governments across Australia faced with the prospect of thousands of returning war veterans all needing a home. This gave rise to the State Housing Commissions, which not only subdivided land and created some of our cities' most charming inner-city residential areas, but also constructed housing. State Housing Commissions went on to play a key part in the delivery of social housing in Australia, from war veterans in the late 1940s and 1950s, to the least advantaged in our society today. This was a key part of the social housing program that swept through Australia during the 1960s and into the 1980s and beyond.

Like town planning, the provision of social housing – housing for those who can't afford housing – is a permanent fixture in our society, forming a key component of any government ministry. In Western Australia, it is called the Department of Communities, in Melbourne it is called Housing Victoria and in Sydney it is called the Department of Community and Justice. While the provision of social housing has been a cornerstone of governments past and present, the undertaking of subdivision and the creation of estates has been on and off for governments, depending upon the government of the day and the priorities they hold.

In Western Australia, the organisation involved in developing state land is called DevelopmentWA (formerly LandCorp). In Victoria, it is Development Victoria. In New South Wales, it is LandCom. Not all states have an organisation devoted to developing the land assets of the state government, but most do, and these are large and powerful organisations. These development agencies are charged with developing state land, which is often challenging and opportunistic – since many state-owned properties are fortuitously located in advantageous positions, such as adjoining railway stations, as previously discussed. Government land also contains some of the most difficult parcels of land to develop and includes contaminated land that requires significant intervention through remediation to make it ready for development – something that would prove impossible for the private sector to contemplate. We will look at a number of Perth-based examples to illustrate the role of government developers.

Case Studies: Perth Example
East Perth Redevelopment Authority – Claisebrook Cove

The area defining the East Perth Redevelopment Authority area in what is now known as Claisebrook Cove is approximately 137 hectares of riverfront land located east of the Perth CBD. In the 1800s, the area was part of the Claisebrook drainage network, which came from as far as Lake Monger, with the present site of the Claisebrook project area being the outlet for the drainage network, which, as the City of Perth expanded, began to flood, as more and more water was directed to this area.[354] It was not surprising that the Claisebrook area was swampy, with varying degrees of water pooling as drainage sumps as you approached the Swan River.

In the 1880s, it was possible to catch freshwater crayfish in the Claisebrook Drain, but as the population in the area expanded, the East Perth area became crowded, resulting in the expansion of the drainage network.[355] Two large open drains, with the broader Perth city centre as their catchment, flowed into the Claisebrook area, carrying significant pollution and rubbish dumped by residents into the drainage system. The area was often criticised for its stench, with the drain becoming a notorious dumping ground of noxious material from a variety of industries in the area, including a tannery, a soap factory, stables and sawmills. The area became synonymous with diseases and stench and became a 'no-go area' for much of the early 1900s.[356]

For most of the twentieth century, up until the 1980s, the Claisebrook area was primarily an industrial area, and it became the location of a number of large industrial uses, such as the East Perth Gas Works, East Perth Power Station (which was decommissioned and is being renovated for other purposes), the East Perth Railway Yard and engine sheds. Mixed in with the industrial uses from the early 1980s were a number of residential land uses and commercial enterprises, with housing consisting of mostly single or duplex housing for largely migrant families. By the late 1980s, and with the Gas Works in terrible condition and the value of land within the central part of Perth becoming more scarce, it was clear the area was in need of intervention for

---

[354] *'History of Claisbrook Cove'*, WA Achievers, wabiz.org 2019.
[355] *'The City sewerage'*. The West Australian, Perth: National Library of Australia, 4 June 1906.
[356] *'The City sewerage'*. The West Australian, Perth: National Library of Australia, 4 June 1906.

renewal and repurposing from a contaminated industrial area to a new residential and mixed commercial area.

Figures 6.38: Claisebrook Cove, circa 1950s[357]

In 1991, under the Labor Government of Peter Dowding and then, later, Carmen Lawrence, the East Perth Redevelopment Authority was established via the *East Perth Redevelopment Act 1991*.[358] The inaugural East Perth Redevelopment Authority was tasked with undertaking a significant urban renewal of the former industrial area and undertaking the redevelopment along the lines of the New Urbanism movement, which emerged in the United States in the 1980s. The East Perth Redevelopment Authority – with its own Town Planning Scheme, combined with redevelopment powers including powers of acquisition – became both a town planning regulatory authority and a redevelopment agency in one.[359]

Project Design

The key to the East Perth Redevelopment was the vision to create an inlet along the existing alignment of the Claisebrook Drain in East Perth to provide a focus and amenities for urban redevelopment in the area.[360] The inlet would be a canal waterway that provided an aesthetic and direct link to the Swan River, combined with publicly-owned facilities and amenities along its riverfront supported by dense development in the form of apartment, mixed-use, retail and residential townhouse developments. The

---

[357] *'Archival footage of Claisbrook Cove'*, circa 1950's, Department for Water.
[358] *'Australian New Urbanism – A Guide to Projects (Second Edition)'*, Australian Council of the New Urbanism, November 2006.
[359] *'Australian New Urbanism – A Guide to Projects (Second Edition)'*, Australian Council of the New Urbanism, November 2006.
[360] *'Australian New Urbanism – A Guide to Projects (Second Edition)'*, Australian Council of the New Urbanism, November 2006.

project included the remediation of contaminated land and the creation of unique 'containment cells' under the foreshore public open space.

One of the most challenging aspects of the project was realising its vision , which was the first in Perth that followed New Urbanist urban design principles, which introduced mixed-use, apartment development and townhouses as common forms of development in the one redevelopment area. At the time, Perth was very much a suburban city, with much of the development in the 1980s being purely single-storey housing on green title blocks. Because this built form dominated the industry, there were very few developers and builders who were in the 'space' of creating quality apartment and townhouse development. It is hard to believe today, but the East Perth Redevelopment Authority had to be a pioneer and actually work with the building industry to demonstrate alternative housing in the form of apartments and townhouses. The then-Planning Minister, David Smith, sponsored a design competition that drew on expertise across the country to design the early housing in the East Perth Redevelopment Area for the government to invest in, construct and display as a demonstration project for the local building industry to follow. Awards were given to Bruce James and Partners based in Sydney, Sharp and Ryan from Western Australia, and a team comprising of Shane Rothe, Paul Evans and Nigel Westbrook based in Victoria. The East Perth Redevelopment Authority constructed the successful designs on Constitutional Hill as a demonstration.[361]

Figure 6.39: Images of Claisebrook Cove today[362]

In East Perth during the 1990s and early 2000s, the new built form was brought to the Perth landscape in the form of two-storey and three-storey narrow townhouse developments, terrace housing that is rear loaded (garage from a real laneway), and a variety of three-to-five-storey mixed-use and apartment developments of different shapes and sizes. Narrow townhouse lots were also created (Brown Street, for example), which were five to six metres in width and two storeys in height, demonstrating an

---

[361] *'East Perth Redevelopment'*, DevelopmentWA website, 2021.
[362] *'Images of Claisebrook Cove'*, DevelopmentWA website, 2021.

alternative built form and use of space to create new and interesting ways of living. The project was also rewarded on several fronts for retaining some historical buildings, such as warehouses on Bennett Street, for restoration and conversion into apartment developments.

The high-quality built form is a testimony to the close working relationship between the government and the private sector to achieve new standards in built-form quality and design. The East Perth Redevelopment Authority not only broke new ground in driving diverse and superior built forms, but also achieved success in planning through the development of its Town Planning Scheme and Design Guidelines, which enabled new, diverse and quality developments.

The East Perth Redevelopment, which spanned twenty years, broke many barriers in the Western Australian – and indeed the Australian – housing industry. The project demonstrated a brand-new form of urban development – one filled with housing diversity and density, mixed-use, and significant amenities in the form of a variety of public spaces, including the Claisebrook inlet river reconstruction (along the original Claisebrook Drain) and green spaces of various shapes and sizes – that has created one of the most sought after places to live in Australia. The housing, in particular, brought life back to the potential for apartments and town housing to be a viable, and even a desirable, housing option in Australia, which had fallen out of favour in many Australian cities, with the exception of perhaps Sydney and Melbourne.

Figure 6.40: New built form in East Perth[363]

Subiaco Redevelopment Authority – Subi Centro

Not long after the establishment of the inaugural East Perth Redevelopment Authority, an opportunity presented itself in the suburb of Subiaco, in Perth's western suburbs, for a second redevelopment authority charged with the responsibility of redeveloping the train station and the industrial area immediately surrounding it. Subiaco

---

[363] *'Photographs of Claisebrook Cove'*, from Sergio Famiano's private collection, 2019.

was established as a largely industrial suburb in the mid-1800s, and the suburb was divided when the Perth to Fremantle trainline was developed.[364] This left a lasting legacy of blight and industrial development adjacent to the railway up until the 1990s, when land values in Subiaco were considered high enough to warrant the transition of industrial land to residential.

In addition to Subiaco, the *"neighbouring suburbs of Daglish and Jolimont were isolated from the Subiaco town centre, which centred largely on the retail 'main street' of Rokeby Road. Without an overall vision for Subiaco and its surrounding areas, the area was beginning to stagnate and beginning to blight due to the ageing industrial area being located in close proximity to the Subiaco town centre".*[365]

Figure 6.41: Subiaco in the early 1990s[366]

In 1994, the Subiaco Redevelopment Authority was formed via the passing of the *Subiaco Redevelopment Act 1994*. Like the case of the East Perth Redevelopment Authority, the legislation gave powers to the Subiaco Redevelopment Authority to prepare a Town Planning Scheme with the ability to enable town planning, land acquisition and redevelopment. The Subiaco Redevelopment was a major beneficiary of the Federal Government's Building Better Cities Program. This program granted federal funding to support major urban rejuvenation projects around Australia, with some several million granted to the project to support the main catalyst for the project: the sinking of the railway line around the Subiaco Train Station.[367]

It was eventually branded the Subi Centro Project and was beset by a number of challenges, including the significant engineering complexity associated with the undergrounding of the Subiaco Train Station, environmental remediation associated with cleaning up the former industrial sites around the train station, and – similar to the East Perth redevelopment – the desire to build a new form of development around

---

[364] *'Walking Subi Centro'*, City of Subiaco, 2017.
[365] *'Subiaco redevelopment housing strategy: discussion paper'*, Subiaco Redevelopment Authority, SRA 1996.
[366] *'Subiaco redevelopment housing strategy: discussion paper'*, Subiaco Redevelopment Authority, SRA 1996.
[367] *'Subiaco redevelopment housing strategy: discussion paper'*, Subiaco Redevelopment Authority, SRA 1996.

the New Urbanist design principles, which would challenge the market and the prevailing building industry at the time.

The redevelopment comprised of an area of approximately 80 hectares from the southern end of Subiaco's historic Rokeby Road retail main street, which is located approximately 3 kilometres west of Perth CBD. Subiaco has had a mixed history; the settlement was originally established in 1850, with Benedictine monks constructing a monastery and later a hospital to service the immediate area.[368] In the 1880s, the fortunes of the suburb increased with the gold rush in Western Australia, which resulted in the expansion of the suburb to accommodate workers to support the economic boom underway. It was during the 1880s and 1890s that the Fremantle to Guildford railway line was established, connecting Fremantle to Subiaco and Subiaco to Perth and the Guildford.[369]

The railway line has always had a profound impact on Subiaco: firstly by increasing accessibility to the area and the major port of Fremantle and the city's centre, and secondly by dividing the suburb into north and south. Built on a traditional grid pattern, the suburb of Subiaco developed from the train station, with Rokeby Road becoming the main retail main street and the areas immediately north and west of Subiaco being developed as more industrial type uses.

In the present day, Subiaco is considered a vibrant and successful mixed-use suburb, with an eclectic mix of historic and new residential buildings along a grid pattern of development linking to Rokeby Road as the mixed-use heart. All these elements link to the train station. It is also considered one of Perth's most sought-after entertainment precincts, with a mixture of quality cafés, restaurants and bars.

Subiaco also has some of the highest real estate values – a reflection of its success. It is easy to see this now, but Subiaco was a very different suburb in the 1980s, with an ugly train station dividing north and south, sleeved by tired industrial land to the south, with older residential and tired commercial and retail development. Economic stagnation beset the area, and many areas were rundown, blighted and vacant as a result.

The blighted condition of Subiaco prompted a grass-roots movement from Subiaco businesses to commence lobbying for intervention to turn around the fortunes of the Subiaco Rokeby Road and surrounding area. The Subiaco main street project emerged in 1993 and had the goal of uniting businesses owners, landlords and residents to promote a better and revitalised Subiaco.[370] While there was some momentum, the project eventually died off after a couple of years. There was a lack of agreement on project priorities and a lack of funding from business owners and the local government

---

[368] Bizzaca, K, *"City of Subiaco Thematic History and Framework"*, *City* of Subiaco, February, 2014.
[369] Bizzaca, K, *"City of Subiaco Thematic History and Framework"*, *City* of Subiaco, February, 2014.
[370] Bizzaca, K, *"City of Subiaco Thematic History and Framework"*, City of Subiaco, February, 2014.

to ensure the plan's implementation. While the movement itself was a failure, it did raise awareness of the area's ongoing plight, which eventually garnered the attention of the state government and, ultimately, the Federal Government.

The main premise of the Subi Centro Redevelopment focuses on the area immediately north of the Subiaco Train Station, which included the Jolimont industrial area and a vision for the project to create a transit-oriented development, with development leveraging off the benefits of accessibility to the Subiaco train line. The industrial area around the Subiaco Train Station was in economic decline, with many industries closing and relocating to new industrial estates emerging in the city. This led the state government to explore selling its land holdings in and around the train station. At the time, the state government explored the notion of raising the railway line to eliminate the Hay Street underpass, which had become a significant traffic bottleneck. However, the thought of having raised rail amidst a residential area was received with major objections from the community, who instead advocated for an alternative proposal to sink the railway line.[371]

As a result of the community objections, the City of Subiaco released a concept plan titled 'Subiaco 2000', which proposed the lowering of the Subiaco Train Station and the potential for the redevelopment of its surroundings.[372] To support the concept plan, the City of Subiaco enlisted the support of Murdoch University's Institute of Sustainability and Technology section to expand the scope of the proposal and develop an adjoining mixed-use development along TOD principles.

The concept developed from the grass roots of local government working in tandem with a university institution. It not only developed a possible vision for the area that was superior to the earlier incarnation developed by the state government, but it also presented a plan that aligned with the Federal Government's Better Cities Funding Program, which sought to provide seed funding for projects in urban infill areas that would be developed along TOD urban design principles.[373] After considerable advocacy by the City of Subiaco, the project was successful in receiving $5 million in seed funding from the Federal Government to support the sinking of the railway line.[374]

To achieve the vision for the new Subiaco, the City of Subiaco lobbied the state government to establish the Subiaco Redevelopment Authority in 1994 via supporting legislation. The premise of establishing the Subiaco Redevelopment Authority was to develop an independent statutory authority that would oversee the redevelopment of the project area. It would be self-funded using state and local government land

---

[371] Bizzaca, K, *"City of Subiaco Thematic History and Framework"*, City of Subiaco, February, 2014.
[372] *'Subiaco Urban Village 2000'*, City of Subiaco 1994.
[373] *'Subiaco Redevelopment Concept Plan Launched - media statement'*, Minister for Planning – Richard Lewis, 4th May 1995.
[374] *'Subiaco Redevelopment Concept Plan Launched - media statement'*, Minister for Planning – Richard Lewis, 4th May 1995.

within the project area for redevelopment and seed funding offered by the state and federal governments to establish the Subiaco Redevelopment Authority and to assist in funding the sinking of the train station.[375] The establishment of the Subiaco Redevelopment Authority was seen as essential for the project, as the City of Subiaco's council was too small to operate the redevelopment scheme and would have been beset with problems associated with divergent interests that could have convoluted the planning and development process. By establishing a dedicated state government entity with the power to plan and develop, the potential for smaller interests to subvert and stifle the project could be avoided. To ensure local interests were reflected in the overall vision of the project, a Project Board was established, which included representation from the City of Subiaco.[376]

The Project's Design

The project had a focus on transit-oriented development, i.e., urban design principles with a focus on establishing higher-density mixed-use and apartment development next to the train station, with new two-storey townhouse developments of various small block shapes further away from the train station. The Rokeby Road main street became the immediate focus, with the train station located immediately north on the alignment of Rokeby Road. This strong link was important to the development, as it reinforced the main street development and its link to the train station. With the undergrounding of the train station, this enabled the establishment of a public plaza immediately above the train station, supported by surrounding mixed-use residential development – approximately four-to-five-storeys in height. The concept included a strong 'green link' that was positioned east–west from the project area's western boundary through to the train station and then east of the train station to connect to the historic Subiaco Oval.

The intent of the project was to ensure the new commercial/retail area around the train station complemented and supported the Subiaco main street of Rokeby Road and included a variety of housing in the form of quality apartment development and new townhouse development supported by high-quality public open space. The project, therefore, was developed to support an additional 10,000 to 20,000sqm of new retail floor space and an additional 1,900 dwellings, with approximately 85% of all new development being medium to high-density housing.[377]

Project Development and Legacy

In 1998, the project reached a significant milestone in delivering Perth's first underground railway using a 'cut and cover' approach for the construction of the rail

---

[375] Bizzaca, K, *"City of Subiaco Thematic History and Framework"*, City of Subiaco, February, 2014.
[376] Bizzaca, K, *"City of Subiaco Thematic History and Framework"*, City of Subiaco, February, 2014.
[377] *'Courtesy of the former Subiaco Redevelopment Authority'*, Information document and Masterplan, SRA, 2010.

tunnel. The train station was established immediately adjacent to Rokeby Road and included a public plaza and surrounding mixed-use development up to four storeys in height. Following the sinking of the railway line, and due to a largely favourable property market, the Subi Centro Development accelerated over the next fifteen years to include the completion of the development around the train station, the redevelopment of former industrial land to the north and the redevelopment of the former Australian Fine China industrial site and TAFE site on Salvado Road.

It has taken twenty years, but the project is largely complete, with only pockets of development still to take place, and the project area has been largely normalised, which means planning control has been handed back to the City of Subiaco.

The project has been a big success in showing Australia the possibilities that come with applying New Urbanist urban design principles to an area that is supported by mass-transit rail. The project also demonstrated that a train station doesn't just have to be a place for departure and arrival or a means to gain access to a place, but instead it can be a destination in itself, with many cafés, bars, restaurants, retail stores and offices located around the train station. The project has been so successful many of the key development industry consultants are located in Subi Centro.

When the project took off, with the sinking of the railway line, there were no dwellings in the project area. Fast forward to 2022, there are now over 1,900 dwellings in the project area, with an additional 70,000sqm of commercial floorspace added (mainly offices) and 11,000sqm of retail space supporting approximately 6,500 workers in the area.[378] In addition to this success, property values in the suburb have increased dramatically from as low as $80/sqm in 1994 to $3,000/sqm in 2022. The project area has also attracted over $1.5 billion in private sector investment.[379]

Similar to the East Perth Redevelopment Area, the Subi Centro Project has been instrumental in reincarnating what the Australian Dream could look like by creating attractive apartments that have access to high amounts amenities, including a train station for accessibility and parks, plazas, retail and commercial areas. It popularised and paved the way for new apartment development in Perth and showed what could be achieved with proper planning controls combined with redevelopment support and funding. Again, this project was instrumental in transforming the housing industry by dramatically increasing the opportunities for alternative housing to the single-storey and double-storey homes on a 400sqm block by providing a variety of block sizes from 150sqm to 300sqm in area, and two-storey and three-storey housing that is largely rear-serviced by garages, creating very attractive streetscapes. This built form started the trend for laneway serviced blocks in Perth, which is now common in our new growth areas.

---

[378] *'Subi Centro and Australian Fine China Information sheet'*, courtesy of DevelopmentWA, 2021.
[379] *'Subi Centro and Australian Fine China Information sheet'*, courtesy of DevelopmentWA, 2021.

LandCorp – Cockburn Coast

The final government-sponsored redevelopment area I would like to look at in Perth is one I have mentioned previously, and is one close to my heart, as I was involved in the project's planning and early delivery. It is a project that embodies my sense of ideals, and those of many of my colleagues who worked on the project, in reflecting what a modern community in Australia could look like when we fuse together history, New Urbanist thinking, high-density and high-quality public realm, and transit-oriented design on a large scale, located next to a pristine water environment setting. When we talk about legacy projects, this is one that, if delivered properly and with patience, will be one of the key legacy projects in Australia and a showcase of demonstrating New Urbanism and transit-oriented development in a modern setting.

The Cockburn Coast has had a rich history steeped in industry, trade and the military, with the place serving as a training area for the legendary 1oth Light Horse in World War One. Going back as far as the 1870s, the area served as an industrial area with a meatworks being established that provided food for the local area and international markets. It endured for nearly a century, employing locals and migrants in the area. In the 1870s, to support the meatworks, the Robb Jetty was constructed to service the meat industry by providing a portal for cattle to be transported to the abattoir in the area.[380] To further support the meat industry, a freezing and chilling works was established, which supported the expansion of the abattoir and supporting industries in the area, such as a tannery and leather-preserving facility. The abattoir wasn't without its troubles and was plagued with financial difficulties and government bailouts, which resulted in the state government eventually taking it over in 1942 to ensure food supply for Australia's war effort.[381]

Post the Second World War, the abattoir expanded throughout the following decades but grew increasingly inefficient, and the decision was made to shut it down in 1992. All equipment was removed by 1994, and the building was demolished, with only the heritage chimney left standing as a reminder of the area's former industrial history. The Robb Jetty was also decommissioned, with remnants of the foundation still visible on the foreshore, together with a number of shipwrecks that litter the coastline as a historical reminder of its past. The area was distinct, and those old enough to remember will have the stench of the abattoir as you drove along Cockburn Road etched in their memory.

---

[380] *'Cockburn Coast District Structure Plan (Part 2)'*, City of Cockburn, Cockburn.wa.gov.au.
[381] *'Cockburn Coast District Structure Plan (Part 2)'*, City of Cockburn, Cockburn.wa.gov.au.

Figure 6.42: The abattoir and Robb Jetty (circa 1950)[382]

In addition to the variety of industries supporting the primary industry – the abattoir – the Robb Jetty was also home to one of Perth's largest and most significant power stations in the post-World-War-Two era. Needed to support the growth of Perth in the years immediately preceding World War Two, power generation in Perth during the 1940s was heavily reliant on a single 25-megawatt power plant at the East Perth Power Station, located in Perth's central north suburbs next to Claisebrook Cove (East Perth Redevelopment Area).[383] Because of this reliance, there were frequent power cuts in Perth during the 1930s and 1940s, prompting authorities to consider establishing a second power plant.

Following investigations by Russell Dumas of the Public Works Department, a 25-megawatt and 50-hertz generation site was purchased in South Fremantle alongside Robb Jetty in 1945. The selection of the South Fremantle Power Station site followed a number of factors; among them, it aligned with the ability to use an existing railway line for coal deliveries; it was located close to the shoreline to access sea water for cooling purposes; and it was also in reasonably close proximity to residential and commercial areas of Fremantle and the surrounding area of Cockburn. Construction of the power station commenced in January 1946, immediately after the Second World War, and took five years to complete, due to shortages in equipment and materials. It became fully operational in 1951, when David Brand, the Minister for Electricity, opened it.[384]

Power generation from the new power plant was achieved using a coal heating steam, which in turn spun two turbines that rotated the two 25-megawatt generators to create electricity, with the second generator coming online in September 1951. Two more generators came online in 1954, raising power generation at South Fremantle to 100 megawatts. To operate in conjunction with the 40-hertz East Perth Power Station, a frequency changer was necessary at East Perth until 1960, when the conversion of

---

[382] *'Cockburn Coast District Structure Plan (Part 2)'*, City of Cockburn, Cockburn.wa.gov.au.
[383] *"South Fremantle Power Station Register of Heritage Places Assessment. Documentation"*. inherit.stateheritage.wa.gov.au. Heritage Council of Western Australia, 2012.
[384] *'Cockburn Coast District Structure Plan (Part 2)'*, City of Cockburn, Cockburn.wa.gov.au.

the network to 50-hertz was completed. Coinciding with the opening of South Fremantle Power Station was a drastic rise in power consumption in Perth. Just before the opening, only 50% of homes in Perth required any conversion work to 50 hertz, but this number had risen to 94% by 1956.[385]

The South Fremantle Power Station forms a unique small group of power stations in the world. Firstly, the South Fremantle Power Station was one of only two power stations in Western Australia to be constructed as a steel and concrete structure with extensive glazing. The architecture type was stylised as an Art Deco-type construct with a cathedral-type reference, which reflected a symbol of the power of industry and functionalism. Sister power plants exist in London in the form of the Tate Modern and the Battersea Power Plant.[386]

Figure 6.43: South Fremantle Power Station (circa 1960)[387]

The South Fremantle Power Station has had an interesting history. It suffered damage as a result of a fire on the coal conveyor in 1954 – an event that prompted the conversion from coal to an oil-fired power station. This change was reverted again in the 1970s, when it became coal fired once more, due to the early 1970s' rising oil price. This conversion was not well received, with community concerns about emissions rising, as environmental awareness increased in the 1970s. The East Perth and South Fremantle Power Stations were subjected to new, more stringent environmental legislation in 1977.[388] With the expansion of the Muja Power Station at Collie, both the East Perth and South Fremantle Power Stations became uneconomical to operate, with the former closed in 1981 and the latter in 1985.

---

[385] *'Cockburn Coast District Structure Plan (Part 2)'*, City of Cockburn, Cockburn.wa.gov.au.
[386] *'Cockburn Coast District Structure Plan (Part 2)'*, City of Cockburn, Cockburn.wa.gov.au.
[387] *'Cockburn Coast District Structure Plan (Part 2)'*, City of Cockburn, Cockburn.wa.gov.au.
[388] *'South Fremantle Power Station Masterplan'*, City of Cockburn website, www.cockburn.wa.gov.au.

Some of my earliest memories are of the South Fremantle Power Station operating in the distance. For many years, two of my cousins lived on Thomas Street, which adjoins the Robb Jetty area, and, every time we visited in the later 1970s and early 1980s, I remember playing in the quarry next to the Robb Jetty area with the South Fremantle Power Station powering away in the background. The closure of the South Fremantle Power Station in 1985, after what was a relatively short life of thirty years, signified the beginning of the end of the Robb Jetty area, with the abattoir – the other main industry – closing in 1992. Between 1994 and 1997, most of the equipment in the power station was removed and some of the facilities demolished, leaving a shell of a building that has now become heritage listed (similar to the East Perth Power Station) due to its unique design and the representation it provides of the building of the inter-war and post-war eras.[389] In the late 1990s and early 2000s, the South Fremantle Power Station became an iconic venue for rave parties, and the building attracted much attention from graffiti artists, who have since left an indelible mark on the building.

Other historical value in the Robb Jetty area is marked through the influence of the Australian military. As part of Western Australia's contribution to the European campaign, the 10th Light Horse Regiment gathered in the Robb Jetty area and paraded and practised on the foreshore adjoining the Robb Jetty area. This military link continued into the Second World War, with the Beeliar Reserve – the regional reserve adjoining the Robb Jetty area – forming part of Perth's coastal defence from the Japanese, with gun emplacements positioned on the hilltops overlooking the South beach and Robb Jetty area.[390] These military emplacements remain in the area and form a key reference to the area's past.

In the late 1990s, the state government, through the State Land Developer (LandCorp), initiated a plan to redevelop the Robb Jetty area into a new industrial estate; this resulted in the creation of a number of lots north of the Robb Jetty area and on the Beeliar escarpment, which included Alba Oils (an edible oils manufacturer) and a variety of fishing companies, such as Sea Lanes. With the election of the Labor Government under Geoff Gallop in 2001 and the appointment of Alannah MacTiernan as the Minister for Planning and Infrastructure, the Labor Government changed tact with the Robb Jetty area and sought to repurpose it as a significant residential and mixed-use redevelopment – rather than a new industrial area – with the South Fremantle Power Station building being reactivated as an iconic tourist and mixed-use facility.

In 2005, the state government, through the Department of Planning and Infrastructure, initiated a process to consider the future vision for the Robb Jetty area, with a focus on phasing out the industrial use of the area and creating a residential and

---

[389] *'South Fremantle Power Station Masterplan'*, City of Cockburn website, www.cockburn.wa.gov.au.
[390] *'South Fremantle Power Station Masterplan'*, City of Cockburn website, www.cockburn.wa.gov.au.

mixed-use estate. Following a comprehensive process of engagement, the Cockburn Coast District Structure Plan was born in 2009, with the aim of achieving a new vision for the area and laying out the planning to guide the area's future redevelopment. The following key issues were identified for the project area:

- transitional arrangements for freight access, including continued freight movement along Cockburn Road, pending the future delivery of Cockburn Coast Drive to service existing industrial uses that will continue to operate in the medium to long-term future,
- staging of development in relation to the coordinated delivery of key infrastructure and services, including a light rail/rapid bus transit, key roads and transit routes, key retail, commercial and community uses,
- managing the interface between the existing industrial businesses and emerging residential and mixed-use during transitional phases of development,
- significant infrastructure costs associated with the power station precinct, including the relocation of the switchyard site, remediation of the south Fremantle Power Station building and site remediation,
- potential contamination in the project area as a result of its past industrial uses,
- fragmented land ownership in relation to the equitable distribution of infrastructure, public open space and with respect to the staging and timing of development, and
- Climatic conditions, particularly strong prevailing winds, and how they are addressed in the detailed design of the development.

In addition to identifying the issues with the Cockburn Coast area, the District Structure Plan laid the planning framework required to enable the transition of the project area from industrial to urban under the Perth Metropolitan Region Scheme. This included the need to prepare a more detailed planning framework for the project area addressing land assembly, project delivery and the location of key land uses and amenities, the preparation of a district-level water-management plan and an Infrastructure Delivery Strategy.[391] With over 40% of the Cockburn Coast land area under the ownership of LandCorp – the state government's land developer – they were selected to take the lead in undertaking the planning and delivery of the project.

---

[391] *'Cockburn Coast District Structure Plan (Part 2)',* City of Cockburn, Cockburn.wa.gov.au.

When I joined LandCorp in 2007, the Cockburn Coast Project was brought to my attention in 2008. I distinctly remember how nobody in the organisation was interested in taking on the project, advising that it was too complex and time consuming to take on. Sensing an opportunity to put into practice everything I had learned in planning, I took on the project as the sole development manager to undertake the planning and delivery of one of Perth's biggest and most challenging projects. In 2008, before the District Structure Plan was approved in 2009, I was already working on developing the Project Masterplan, District Water Management Strategy, Integrated Transport Plan and Infrastructure Strategy to enable the project to transition from industrial to urban under the Metropolitan Region Scheme. The City of Cockburn approved the masterplan and supporting technical documents in 2012 and supported the Metropolitan Region Scheme change that occurred that same year.

Figure 6.44: The Cockburn Coast District Structure Plan and Masterplan[392]

The Integrated Transport Plan, which took two years to develop in consultation with the Department of Planning and Infrastructure, Department of Transport, Main Roads WA, the Public Transport Authority, the City of Fremantle and the City of Cockburn, was pivotal for the project. In addition to identifying a high-density, mixed-use,

---

[392] *'Cockburn Coast District Structure Plan (Part 2)',* City of Cockburn, Cockburn.wa.gov.au.

village-type development, the project identified a potential light-rail or bus rapid transit route from Fremantle all the way through Cockburn Coast, including the South Fremantle Power Station, and then on to Cockburn Central, linking the Fremantle and Mandurah train lines.

Also developed in 2012 (and approved in 2014) was the South Fremantle Power Station Masterplan, which identifies the rejuvenation of the power station building and its immediate surroundings. The masterplan outlined how the Western Power switchyard site could be relocated and how the power station building could be restored and reused to create an iconic destination for Perth, which could include a marina in front of the power station building. The masterplan approval paved the way for the site to be changed from industrial to urban. The completion of the master-planning process for the project area paved the way for detailed town planning and project enabling to commence.

Figure 6.45: Images of the South Fremantle Power Station – what could be[393]

The Project's Design

The Cockburn Coast Project is located between South Beach and Port Coogee, approximately 4.5 kilometres south of Fremantle and 18 kilometres from the Perth CBD. It is one of Perth's most significant developments, with a project area of 333 hectares, of which 98 hectares is developable, and, over a twenty-year period, it proposes to transform an under-used former industrial area into a thriving residential and commercial community.[394] The project will comprise of three precincts: Robb Jetty (Shoreline), Hilltop and the Power Station Precinct. It collectively aims to achieve a residential population of 14,000 people in over 6,000 dwellings, supporting over 125,000sqm of commercial and retail floor space. When the project was developed, it was always intended to bring a portion of European high-density living to the seaside. A project of such scale, together with the power station development, will become a key destination for Perth.

---

[393] *'South Fremantle Power Station Masterplan'*, City of Cockburn website, www.cockburn.wa.gov.au.
[394] *'Cockburn Coast District Structure Plan (Part 2)'*, City of Cockburn, Cockburn.wa.gov.au.

The Cockburn Coast Project is designed to be a high-amenity development due to the high-density nature of the project and the need to provide a quality public realm to compensate for not having a large backyard. As a result, Cockburn Coast is designed to have an extensive range of community facilities and services, many of which will improve connectivity to the foreshore and provide an appealing destination for residents and tourists. These include:

- a beach piazza linked to the main street in the Robb Jetty Precinct (later called Shoreline),
- two new pedestrian bridges linking the project areas to the foreshore,
- improved foreshore facilities, such as boardwalks, kiosks, public toilets and a variety of uses associated with the foreshore area,
- opportunities for extensive uses within the power station precinct, including hotels, theatres, a restaurant and entertainment precinct, and possible marina, and
- an array of piazza-type and landscaped public spaces of various sizes to ensure the area contains a high standard of amenity.

From 2012 to 2014, the project entered its detailed planning and design phase. I spent a significant amount of time with my army of consultants and stakeholders building a project that was going to be a first for Perth on a number of planning and development fronts. During the three-year period, the Robb Jetty (Shoreline) and Hilltop Structure Plans were developed and approved. The Structure Plans were supported by a number of strategies, which included a Place-Making Strategy, a Public Realm Plan, an Affordable Housing Strategy and an Integrated Transport Plan, which were all a first for a LandCorp project. A Developer Contribution Scheme supported the two Structure Plans of Robb Jetty and Hilltop, which ensured the equitable delivery of key infrastructure, such as parkland, as well as the delivery of key amenity infrastructure and climate-change-mitigation infrastructure to support the future use of the foreshore area. All of this was met with significant support from ministers, local government elected members, landowners and key government stakeholders.

In 2014 and 2015, the project entered its delivery phase with the implementation of a $4 million decontamination package of works to clean up the Robb Jetty Precinct and make it ready for project delivery. Upon the completion of a $22-million detailed design package for Stage 1 in 2014, the project commenced delivery in 2015, with Stage 1 releasing a significant area for public open space and servicing and road connections to facilitate the delivery of over thirty three-storey townhouse sites and five apartment sites for the project, which yielded over $45 million in revenue.

From 2015 to 2021, the project underwent the release of a number of stages to create further apartment sites (large and small) and a mixture of two- and three-storey housing. An intensive place-making strategy has been employed over the project using a military theme to reflect the past history of the 10th Light Horse and the Second World War two-gun emplacements.

Also planned for the project, through the power station masterplan, is the rejuvenation of the South Fremantle Power Station, which is seen as the 'jewel in the crown' of the Cockburn Coast development. The area is proposed to be transformed into a major tourist, retail, entertainment and community centre, with new development in the form of apartments proposed above the existing building in the place of the former smokestacks. The building itself, which contains large void areas , is proposed to include approximately 5,500sqm of retail and commercial floor-space distributed across the ground, first and second floors and approximately 2,000sqm of retail and commercial floor space within the power station main street, providing retail in the ground floor and commercial floor areas. The building will also provide up to 150 apartments.

In terms of the wider power station area, two options were considered for the 54,000sqm of foreshore area in front of the power station. Option one was to have it as a protected area that could include a beachside pool, small retail and commercial buildings and recreational areas. Option two was to establish a world-class marina supported by over 800 dwellings made up of apartments and townhouses and an additional 8,000sqm of retail floor space and supporting commercial industries.

Heritage factors will be a key consideration throughout the project, which has involved direct consultation with the Heritage Council WA. The former power station is on the interim heritage register and is an excellent example of 1930s–1950s cathedral-style power stations built in Australia and the United Kingdom. The Cockburn Coast development is an opportunity to revitalise the building and create an iconic destination for Perth. Progress on the power station has been slow, however, with government agencies, such as DevelopmentWA, Synergy and Western Power, deliberating over the best way to deliver the project, including a possible joint venture with the private sector.

Figure 6.46: Artist impressions of Cockburn Coast[395]

---

[395] 'Cockburn Coast District Structure Plan (Part 2)', City of Cockburn, Cockburn.wa.gov.au.

Project Development and Legacy

The Cockburn Coast is a project in its early days of delivery, with a foreseeable twenty years until it is completed. Despite this, the project has demonstrated quality housing in all its forms through apartments, townhouses and medium-density apartment living. The 'missing middle' project at Cockburn Coast is a demonstration of how smaller dwelling types can be achieved in apartment settings over two and three storeys across a large footprint. This project has been successful, with sixty other dwellings sold between 2017 and 2020.

The project has much to give in terms of housing diversity and redefining the Australian Dream, with the project promoting largely medium- and high-density living, which has not previously been seen in Perth on this scale. As I write this book, further releases for apartment developments are being made in combination with maisonette-type housing and three-storey townhouses. This alternative living – one where Europe meets the sea – will define a special development, which can hopefully be emulated throughout Australia in the years to come.

Figure 6.47: Built form at Cockburn Coast[396]

Summary

Given the examples above, it is perhaps not surprising that state development organisations have been responsible for the majority of innovative developments across the country, such as Claisebrook Cove in Perth's east, Sydney's Victoria Park or Rocks Development in Circular Quay, which wouldn't have happened if left to the market to deliver. If you look at other redevelopments across Australia, such as Melbourne's Docklands Development or Adelaide's Riverbank Entertainment Precinct, they would have taken a different form had they been private land.

All these projects, and many more, have challenged the market by proposing apartment and mixed-use development and, in some instances, have generated new housing types, such as townhouse developments in Claisebrook Cove, which was defunct in Perth during the 1990s. If you look at government projects, they represent

---

[396] *'Images of Shoreline (Cockburn Coast)'*, courtesy of DevelopmentWA, 2021.

some of the most innovative, ground-breaking and most sought-after areas within the metropolitan areas of our cities. This is partly a product of their locations, often being in favourable inner-city locations, but also because they push the boundaries in urban development. If anybody in the development industry is honest with themselves, they would agree that this is a truism of our industry.

The Achilles' heel of state developers, however, is that they only control a small segment of the overall property market. State developers typically comprise up to 10% of all land in the development market, leaving the private sector with the majority of landholdings. While state developers can lead the way with innovation, they only have a small market share in their control, meaning that the government is limited in its influence when it comes to direct intervention in the market. From time to time, state governments come under pressure from the private sector to butt out of the land development industry. This happened during the Richard Court era in Western Australia, during the mid and late 1990s, where the government sold off significant areas of land to the private sector. This represents missed opportunities, since governments who generally don't have the burden of 'holding costs' with land can afford to take risks and push market boundaries.

Governments today manage the private sector's call for the 'privatisation' of government land by partnering with the private sector on a number of projects. This is popular in New South Wales and Victoria, with many governments playing a role in 'de-risking' land and preparing it for development, then either selling the land to the private sector or partnering with the private sector. Many developments have been undertaken this way and offer the opportunity for the government to engage in innovation with the private sector. This model has been more recently adopted in Western Australia, with projects like Alkimos – a large land and town-centre development in Perth's north–west corridor. The problem is the profit motive. While the government is driven by a multitude of factors, with making a profit just being one of them, the private sector is driven by profits, as it has shareholders to satisfy. Even in joint ventures, it is difficult to achieve innovation, since one half of the partnership is driven by profit. While there are some successful joint venture projects, if we are to be serious about change and innovation, the government has to go alone to lead the market.

So, what do you do with the other 90% of the market? Well, to influence the private sector's land-holding in the market, the government does have one trump card: it's the government state planning function that determines the planning framework for the wider market. By setting a clear policy direction and sticking to its guns, the government can force industry to change and introduce innovation in development, and, in many circles, this would be welcomed. I know there are many private developers who want to push the envelope and innovate, but going alone is risky. But if everyone has to do it, that de-risks it by ensuring everybody plays by the same rules. This is why the government is so important to the planning and development industry, and why I have focused on it so much in this book.

7

MICRO-PLANNING THE AUSTRALIAN DREAM

Up until now we have talked about the macro-planning of our cities and how this shapes our urban environments and influences the Australian Dream of home ownership. These are the elements that collectively come to define our cities, making them what they are today and what they could be in the future. Whether it be the modern planning framework, the form and function of transport, land-use planning or the role of the government and the private sector, these elements come together to holistically define the urban morphology of our cities as we know them today, and, if any one of these elements changes, we can see the influence it will have on the urban environment. If macro means 'big picture', correspondingly there are micro elements or 'finer grain' elements that exist and contribute to the urban forms of our cities. When we talk about 'micro matters' in the context of the Australian Dream, we mean the form of housing in our cities and the regulations that shape what we can and can't build.

What Does the Australian Dream Look Like?

When we look at the history of housing in Australia, size aside, we can see for the best part how little it has changed over the years. While housing sizes have increased – largely due to the growth of a wealthy and egalitarian society in Australia – suburban housing itself has changed little. The dominant form of housing in Australia is the single detached home on a green title (separate title) block. This has been the dominant development form in Australia and reflects the combination of Australia's vast landscape, which permits Australians to have a large block, and the desire to live in quarters that are separated or stand alone from other forms of housing, such as workers', tenants' and apartment housing that was common in Britain. The typical evolution of housing in Australian from the 1890s onwards can be seen below (Figure 7.1).

A short history of the Great Australian Dream...

Figure 7.1: A brief history of Australian housing[397]

---

[397] *'Various photographs'* from selected Famiano family archives, 2020–2022.

It has only been in relatively recent history, during the 1960s and 1970s and then from the 1990s onwards, that we have seen a change in the composition of housing in Australia. We are at an inflection point where the tide is turning, and we can begin to reimagine the Australian Dream, away from its traditional form of the standalone green title house. In the 1960s, largely due to mass immigration and also to the creeping influence of La Corbusier's Radiant City theory and its impact on the Planning Framework and architecture in general, we started to see the introduction of apartment living in Australia for the first time, which represented a significant departure from the standalone single-storey residential home that prevailed in Australia up until the 1960s.[398]

Figure 7.2: La Corbusier's Radiant City – better known as Towers in the Park[399]

This building typology resembled the uniform apartment complex that was springing up in Europe in the post-war era; it reflected little by way of amenities for the occupancies and existed mainly for the poorer segment of the population, who were unable to afford the house and land package prevalent in Australian cities. Examples of this type of housing, which came into existence between the 1960s and 1970s, can be seen across Australian cities and represent some of the worst housing in Australia's history. Cramped in design, often lacking amenities, such as balconies and common areas, and being large in scale, areas containing this type of housing, which was exported to Australia from Europe and Britain during the same period, became some of the largest hotspots of crime and dereliction in Australian cities. Part of the problem was design, but another, often overlooked, aspect is that it became a built form favoured by State Housing, and these buildings would often house up to 200 people, who came from poor state-housing backgrounds.

---

[398] Caves, R. W, *'Encyclopaedia of the City'*, Routledge, 2014.
[399] Caves, R. W, *'Encyclopaedia of the City'*, Routledge, 2014.

A classic example is the Brownlie Towers in Perth's suburb of Bentley, situated close to Curtin University. Built in 1971, the Towers were supposed to be an example of La Corbusier's Radiant City image, consisting of several ten-storey apartment blocks surrounded by parkland and car parking, in what should have been an ideal setting of La Corbusier's Tower in the Park image. Instead, the Towers became a "crime-ridden hell hole" (as described by residents) where many drug addicts resided, cars were stolen and set alight, and bullet holes peppered the stairwells. The Towers were finally demolished in 2019.

The Brownlie Towers resembled a similar story taking place around the world. In Britain, during the 1960s and 1970s, apartments became synonymous with rioting and civil unrest, which occurred during the late 1970s and early 1980s, especially during the Thatcher years. While rioting didn't happen often in Australia, the Australian incarnation of the La Corbusier masterpiece became host to crime hotspots and a multitude of ethnic and social class friction incidents that played out during the 1970s and 1980s. Examples of this type of housing can be seen below (Figure 7.3).

Figure 7.3: Perth's Brownlie Towers – The 'No Entry' sign is synonymous with resident sentiment[400]

It was this early incarnation of apartment development, which looked nothing like the charming mixed-use and apartment developments seen in mainland European cities that gave apartment development a bad name in Australia – one that would take years to lose. The early apartment developments resembled large office blocks and were often too large in scale and too uniform in design; they lacked common amenities, which made the house and land at the time a more favourable and acceptable built form. In most Australian cities, with the exception of Sydney, apartment development fell out of favour in the 1980s, and it wasn't until the 1990s that it made a resurgence – albeit in a new and improved form.

Apartment development continued in Sydney during the 1980s largely due to its expensive and unique property market, making apartment development a viable

---

[400] *'From nightly police raids to bullet holes in the stairwells: How a public housing experiment turned into a planning nightmare - as former residents say they can't wait for Brownlie Towers to be demolished'*, Daily Mail, 2019.

option due to different land/rent ratios when compared with other Australian cities. Still, apartments had their problems in Sydney, too, and those who lived in Sydney during the 1960s and 1970s would remember the near rebellion caused by Jack Mundey – the Australian union and environmental activist who went on to lead a successful campaign to protect the built and natural environment in Sydney from excessive and inappropriate development.

One of Jack Mundey's most famous and landmarked exploits was his challenge to the state government and private development industry in preserving The Rocks in Sydney's Circular Quay from mass redevelopment into apartments. Mundey joined Nita McRae's Rocks Resident Action Group, which targeted the Sydney Cove Redevelopment Authority.[401] In 1970, the state government gave the Sydney Cove Redevelopment Authority the responsibility of redeveloping The Rocks area. Recognising the historical significance of the buildings in The Rocks area and the proposal by the state government and the development industry to have it largely removed and replaced by 'modernist' high-rise apartment buildings, an unlikely partnership formed between the Sydney resident groups and the left-wing Builders Labourers Federation to halt the development of The Rocks against the wishes of the residents.[402]

The movement, which lasted several years, reached its zenith in October 1973 when residents and four members of the Builders Labourers Federation barricaded themselves in a demolition site and climbed onto the roof of condemned buildings in protest. What followed was a heavy-handed police intervention. A number of residents and Builders Labourers members – including Jack Mundey – who provoked widespread media coverage and attention to their cause of preserving The Rocks's historical buildings, were arrested.[403] What the demonstrations revealed was the lack of community participation in the land and building development process that was occurring at the time, and this led to changes to legislation that affirmed public consultation as an important part of the planning process. The other ensuing outcome of the events was that it delayed development until new legislation was created that gave greater protection to heritage conservation, which is why The Rocks today has large areas that are intact and have been preserved for future use.[404]

The Rocks is now a thriving mecca for artists and market enthusiasts and is one of the preeminent entertainment and heritage precincts in Sydney. It also influenced the architecture of modern development, which began to change in the 1970s from a brutalist form of modernism to the more palatable high-rise development we have come to appreciate today.

---

[401] Colman, J, 'Jack Mundey, the fight for The Rocks and Australia's urban heritage', May, 2017.
[402] Colman, J, 'Jack Mundey, the fight for The Rocks and Australia's urban heritage', May, 2017.
[403] Colman, J, 'Jack Mundey, the fight for The Rocks and Australia's urban heritage', May, 2017.
[404] Colman, J, 'Jack Mundey, the fight for The Rocks and Australia's urban heritage', May, 2017.

Figure 7.4: What The Rocks could have been and what it is today[405]

With the falling out of apartment development in the 1980s across most Australian cities, there was a mass resumption in the expansion of suburban development in our cities, largely based around the single-storey, single-residential home, with some variation in the form of the duplex development. The development, which is articulated below, set the tone for the 1980s, as suburban development became popular for the masses and also an affordable housing choice for the majority of the population.

The Original 1980s Duplex

While the majority of housing in the 1970s and 1980s consisted of single-residential suburban homes, some smaller housing also emerged in the form of the duplex. This dwelling is characterised by the creation of two, mostly single-storey houses side by side on what was a traditional large or standard block of between 600sqm and 900sqm in area.

The duplex tended to provide the more affordable housing market in Australia, with the dwelling and land being half the size of a traditional house and land block. They also catered for the singles and couples without children, as well as the elderly in our society at the time. This type of housing form was also a choice of housing for state governments, providing social housing for the less fortunate.

Aside from the duplex and some apartments, there were limited housing types in the 1980s outside of a single house on a green title lot, as this was when the baby boomers were beginning to have children and were focused on purchasing a family home. This type of single housing on a block of land made up nearly 80% of all new housing in Australia during the 1980s.

This single-minded pursuit to provide single-residential housing in Australia went hand in hand with the suburban experiment, which undertook a mass expansion in the 1980s across all our cities.

---

[405] *'Images of the Rocks Today'*, Sergio Famiano's record, 2011.

Figure 7.5: Typical duplex housing in the 1980s[406]

The 1980s Cul-de-sac

The 1980s was also synonymous with another ghastly creation: the cul-de-sac suburb. The French term *cul de sac* means a street or passage closed at one end. This incarnation had nothing to do with the French, though, and was largely an American invention that was imported to Australia as the latest and greatest way of designing residential communities. This form of subdivision created almost solely residential suburbs that are characterised as having a few distributor roads that traffic is funnelled into, while most residential properties are contained in dead-end streets. This abomination of design is not only difficult to navigate, as anyone who has tried driving through a cul-de-sac suburb can appreciate, but they are also fixed in design and nearly impossible to evolve. Unlike a grid-type subdivision, which has many points of access and allows land use to transition with time, the cul-de-sac suburb can only be residential, since the road layout precludes other forms of development from occurring.

"Why was the cul-de-sac created?" you may wonder. While the 'dead-end road' has been around for a while, the creator of the cul-de-sac, as we know it today, was Raymond Unwin, an Englishman, who did this in 1909.[407] The theory was that cul-de-sacs would create friendly and quiet residential areas and be a refuge from the growing bustle and influence of the automobile. While some do achieve this, they are also highly restrictive and lack flexibility.

They are also almost entirely dependent on the automobile for travel.

---

[406] *'Picture of a 1980's Duplex in Perth'*, from Sergio Famiano's photographic records, 2011.
[407] Marshal, S, *'Streets and Patterns'*. Spon Press, 2015.

Figure 7.6: The cul-de-sac suburb[408]

The 1990s and the Emergence of New Urbanist Housing

It wasn't until the 1990s that we started to see things change in Australian cities, with a wider variety of housing being introduced in the form of the townhouse and the re-emergence of the apartment development, particularly in the wealthier parts of Australian cities. The factor driving this change for smaller dwelling units was partly due to housing affordability, but it was also due to lifestyle change, which precipitated the coming re-emergence of the apartment – albeit in a more stylish form, which mainly catered for the wealthy 'downsizer' or early baby boomers, who were starting to move from large family homes into smaller apartment dwellings close to the city centre. A classic example of this shift can be seen in the City of Perth during the 1990s and the emergence of redevelopment authorities similar to Sydney two decades before, with development based on New Urbanist principles.

In the 1990s, in cities such as Melbourne, Sydney and Perth, Australia saw the emergence of government-led redevelopment authorities charged with rejuvenating inner-city areas and largely government owned and previously industrial areas, as well as transitioning to residential and mixed-use areas, due to higher land values. It was through these redevelopment authorities that we saw the re-emergence of the apartment and the diversification of housing from the single-residential house on a green title block, which dominated the 1980s, to the variable housing form through apartments of different sizes, to smaller townhouse products, rear-loaded garages and above-garage units or 'Fonzie Flats', as they are commonly referred to (a term from the sitcom *Happy Days*). Government intervention combined with New Urbanist thinking, which emerged in the late 1980s and 1990s, drove this change.

---

[408] *'Example of a Cul-de-sac Suburb, Perth'*, Courtesy City of Swan, 2021.

A classic example of the built form created in these new developments can be seen in housing generated by a number of projects in Australia, such as the East Perth and Subiaco Redevelopment Authorities in Perth (discussed previously), which were watershed projects that brought change in urban form and housing and have created some of the most sought-after areas in Australia. Some examples of the housing created during the 1990s and early 2000s as a result of developments such as Ascot Waters in Belmont (Perth) and Waterfront Green in Footscray (Melbourne) are detailed below (Figure 7.7).

Figure 7.7: New Urbanism brought new housing[409]

The creation of new forms of housing was not only good for people, in the form of actually providing housing that suited the demographic needs of our country, but also provided much-needed diversity of the built form to reinvigorate an industry that had grown stale on producing a homogenous built form for an increasingly diversifying population.

The 1990s Wasn't All Rosy: The Emergence of Group Housing

At the same time that we saw the emergence of New Urbanist planning in Australia combined with government redevelopment authorities to create new, diverse and interesting housing, the 1990s also saw the proliferation of another planning and building abomination: the battle-axe lot.

The 1990s was an interesting period. On the one hand, Australia witnessed the demonstration of new forms of housing that catered for many different types of groups in Australia, and, on the other hand, Australia saw the proliferation of the

---

[409] *'Examples of New Urbanism type housing'*, courtesy National Archive, 2022.

house-behind-a-house creation. The battle-axe duplex and triplex, as it is commonly referred to, would transform the building industry and many of our older suburbs – and not necessarily for the better.

Across Australia, in response to emerging changes in demographics and the creeping issue of housing affordability, we started to see planning changes at the state government level that effectively enabled the creation of the battle-axe lot. The battle-axe lot can be described as a house behind a street-front home, with vehicle access serviced by a short driveway that traverses down the side of the front home to provide vehicle access to the rear property. Initially, this form of development was created as an early response to an ageing population, with parents in older homes on large blocks transitioning from a five-person household to a two-person household, with their children leaving the property. The twin occupants suddenly found themselves in a relatively large home with a large backyard that was no longer needed.

The notion of the battle-axe lot, therefore, allowed the existing house to be retained for the original parents, and the rear backyard to be transformed from a 'green space' into a new dwelling. The approach was simple and genius, in that it provided obvious benefits for managing the changes in lifestyle of the original occupants by enabling them to remove an unnecessary backyard and also enabling them to invest in and develop a new home that would build on their retirement savings while they continued living in their original home. As time wore on, landowners were allowed to build two or even three homes on their property, often resulting in the original house being removed and three or four new dwellings being created on a block that was originally created for one dwelling. This was terrific for property investors, who could purchase a block with one house and then create three or four houses. Add this to negative gearing tax laws, and all of a sudden you have an industry created around this form of development.

The moderation of the number of dwellings that could be permitted on a property has had an evolution over time and has its roots with state government and local government planning changes. In Western Australia, for example, the original General Residential Codes (G-R Codes) were established in 1976 in response to local governments having different approaches to managing residential development.[410] The G-R Codes were brought in to create a more uniform approach across local governments, which supported the industry that, during the 1960s onwards, would experience significant growth due to mass migration. After a number of reviews, the Residential Design Codes (originally Residential Planning Codes) were established in 1985 and have since been updated four times, in 1991, 2002, 2008 and 2019.[411] The Residen-

---

[410] Hall, T, 'The Life and Death of the Australian Backyard'. CSIRO Publishing, 2010.
[411] 'Residential Design Codes', WAPC website, www.wa.gov.au 2022.

tial Design Codes are a State Planning Policy, which means, by law and through local government town planning schemes, all local governments are required to use and comply with the standards identified in the Residential Design Codes.

In terms of what determines the number of dwellings that can be permitted on a property, the Residential Design Codes contain a table that lists the relevant Residential Codes, with each code having a corresponding minimum-lot area requirement to enable development. So, for example, there are Residential Density Codes ranging from R5 to R180, with the lowest requiring greater land area per dwelling and the highest seeking less land area per dwelling. So, if you have a property that is identified as R20, this means you need a minimum area of 450sqm per dwelling. In order to create two dwellings on your block, you would need to have a minimum parent lot area of 900sqm. If a property is zoned R40, the area requirement is less, at 250sqm per dwelling; so, if you have a parent property that is 1,000sqm in area, then you could technically have four dwellings on the parent lot. I say 'technically', because you still need to comply with all the other requirements that come with the design of a dwelling, such as building heights, building setbacks, site coverage and minimum outdoor areas. This may result in you practically achieving three dwellings or four, if you choose to build two-storey houses.

In terms of implementation, each local government's Town Planning Scheme has a map, and every residential area within the scheme area is assigned a Residential Density Code – R20, R25, R40 and so forth. Aligning the designated Residential Density Code with the lot area determines the dwelling potential of your block. This is designed to be simple and easy to follow. This has been the yardstick of the development industry for over forty years now, and building companies are so in tune with the requirements of the Residential Design Codes that they have developed standard designs that meet the variable dimensions of lots that can be found in a metropolitan area. This entrenchment is a blessing in one sense but a curse in another. The blessing is that, like a Model T Ford, the development industry can roll out unit developments easily and cost effectively since all aspects of the design and construction process have been standardised. The flipside is that it has become entrenched in the building industry, and change, where it is needed, is difficult to achieve.

The Residential Design Codes have had a profound impact on urban development, particularly in older existing suburbs. You see, the careful and respectful implementation of residential densities would normally follow a pathway where there is diversity, which would allow for a different range of housing designs and mixes to be created in any given suburb. This is desirable, because it means people can stay in the same suburb their whole life, because if the large house on a block becomes too big, or the children have moved out, they can downsize into a small dwelling unit or an apartment. This makes sense, right? Wrong. This is not what has happened in many areas of Perth and other cities in Australia, where whole suburbs have been rezoned from

R20, for example, which only enables single-residential housing, to R40, which allows for three or four dwellings to be created on any given lot.

Since most traditional suburban estates were created with standard or similar lot sizes, this translates to whole suburbs moving from single-residential lots with large backyards, to areas with three or four dwellings on each lot. You may think that people don't have to develop three or four dwellings and can choose to develop two dwellings or just one, but, in reality, property prices adjust and force landowners to develop to the higher potential in order to maximise the value of the land. You see, when land is rezoned under a Local Town Planning Scheme from R20 to R40, for example, and you now have the potential to develop three dwellings instead of one, then the property value of the parent lot increases substantially.

You are probably getting the picture now as to why town planning is a highly contentious area and why, in state and local government circles, town planning attracts the most attention from press, business people and the community in general. Town planning deals with what you can do with property, and, since property is one of the biggest investments people will make in their lifetime, protecting property, in particular its value, can be a high priority.

While medium-density housing, or battle-axe lots, has many benefits, in that it is generally an affordable form of development and relatively easy to build, it does have a lot of downsides. Anybody who is genuine about housing can't go past the design implications of these types of dwellings and their impact on liveability, which is a troubling aspect of battle-axe subdivision. This form of development has been beset by many pitfalls. First and foremost is its impact on the environment. As previously mentioned in this book, the biggest and most notable impact of this form of development is tree canopy loss. When the original house and land was developed, there was significant space for a backyard and trees and vegetation. What typically happens when a decision is made to redevelop the site for two or three dwelling units is that the block is completely cleared and replaced by three dwellings and a driveway. This often leaves no trees left on the private property and no room for future planting.

Tree-canopy loss is a serious issue, since tree removal is resulting in the loss of biodiversity and shade and is contributing significantly to the heat island effect – the warming of the suburbs. In my native Perth, I live in the City of Stirling, which has taken the issue of tree-canopy loss seriously and, in doing so, has mapped the tree-canopy loss from 2000 to 2021 using historical aerial photography. The results are astounding, with over 15% of tree-canopy loss across the local government boundary occurring over a twenty-year period. This is despite the City of Stirling having an active tree-planting program that aims to replace the trees being removed. Even with a goal to plant over one million trees in the next thirty years, the City of Stirling still expects to have a net tree-canopy loss across its local government boundary. If you multiply this by twenty-four local governments, which account for the entire City of Perth metropolitan boundary, the outcome can shock even the hardest developer and critic of climate change.

One of the other unfortunate downsides to unit development is that it tends to result in very small outdoor courtyards. Under the original Planning Codes back in the 1980s, minimum outdoor areas of 40sqm were required to ensure adequate outdoor space for entertaining and space to accommodate key functional amenities, such as bins and clothes-drying areas. However, because it is becoming increasingly difficult to achieve a 40sqm (5m x 8m) outdoor area, especially when the property market is falsely demanding small dwellings have three and four bedrooms, the development industry has applied pressure on state and local governments, and, as a result, the Residential Planning Codes turned into the Residential Design Codes and undertook several changes – one of which resulted in the reduction of the minimum outdoor courtyard area to 16sqm. Can you believe that? That is an area that is no bigger than 4m x 4m.

The brainiacs who agreed to these changes have presided over a period of development that has created some of the most cramped and dysfunctional built forms. Town planning was created to improve amenities and public health, but creating outdoor living spaces that are no bigger than a bedroom is hardly providing quality amenities, in my opinion. It gets worse though. In many instances, these spaces are almost completely covered, leaving little opportunity for sunlight. I'm not sure how this is a step in the right direction.

The third, and perhaps the most impactful, aspect of the battle-axe form of development, is that, in the race to ensuring each dwelling is a monotone of three and four bedrooms and two bathrooms, designers have crammed more onto a smaller lot, more often than not in a single-storey configuration. The designs have become so tight that aspects of the design are compromised, such as bedrooms, which are often provided in an area that is less than 7sqm in area (2.5m x 2.5m in configuration). I have seen some really small bedrooms and living rooms that barely fit a small dining table and four chairs. The biggest space in the entire dwelling is the garage, which takes up a whopping 36sqm (or nearly 40%) of the dwelling, given our obsession with having our cars better looked after than our own selves. It is a fair comment to say that these dwellings, I think, are the ghettos of the future.

The above issues of amenity and tree-canopy loss have been growing in the consciousness of the town planner and house designer alike and have prompted positive industry changes. In the most recent iteration of the Residential Design Codes in Perth (2021) for example, changes to standards have been introduced that require minimum bedroom spaces and have increased outdoor courtyard spaces to ensure there is enough room to accommodate trees. There have been many other changes that reflect a step in the right direction, but the immediate casualty of doing all this will be housing affordability, sincemany new dwellings will now have to be two storeys in height in order to meet the new standards. It's either build up or build less. Either way, it has to be done, and the industry and consumers will need to adjust.

Housing Since the 2000s: A Mixture of Success and Failure

Since the success of government-led projects across Australia from the 1970s to the 2000s, which included redevelopment authorities such as Docklands in Melbourne, South Bank Redevelopment Authority in Brisbane, and the Subiaco and East Perth Redevelopment Authorities in Perth, the form, shape and size of the Australian Dream has changed dramatically. These government-led projects have had a profound influence in demonstrating New Urbanist planning principles, creating new housing diversity and a new urban form that is more sustainable than the urban form that prevailed during the mass of suburban growth during the 1970s and 1980s. If we look at new suburban development today, it is no longer comprised of the standard single storey on a 500sqm residential lot, but now includes significant diversity, which has its origins in New Urbanism and the demonstration projects that brought these new housing options to life.

New Growth Areas

Over our short history, we have seen a dramatic change in the size of our new lots in our capital cities. In the pre-war period, we saw lots being created that were between 900 and 1,000sqm in area. In the post-World War Two period, this began to mix with lots being created between 700sqm and 1,000sqm in area. By the time we reached the 1960s and 1970s, the industry was creating lots between 600sqm and 700sqm in area. As we turned to the 1980s and 1990s, we witnessed the creation of lots between 600 and 500sqm in area.[412] The steady reduction in lot sizes since the post-war period is as much to do with land affordability and immigration as it is to do with changing practices in town planning.

From the 1950s through to the 1980s, Australia witnessed households decline from five (two parents and three kids) to four (two parents and two kids). Australia also witnessed an explosion in immigration during this time, meaning that state governments had to fit more people into cities than before, and they responded by reducing lot sizes. As the 1980s and 1990s came around, we also started to see the divorce rate climb and the creation of many fractured households of two and three people. At the same time, we started witnessing lot and house prices increase significantly

---

[412] *'Household make up'*, ABS, 2016 Census.

– although not to the levels from the 2000s onwards. All these factors conspired to reduce the household lot size.

By the time the 2000s came along, serious changes to household mixes and housing affordability and the demonstration of New Urbanist planning started to see land and house products change dramatically. In the last twenty years, we have witnessed the creation of a large range of house and land products, including large lots between 500sqm and 400sqm in area, narrow lots between 350sqm to 225sqm in area and micro lots between 200sqm and 100sqm in area. The overriding driver for the reduced lot sizes is undoubtedly affordability. "Why is this?" you may ask, because most of the house and land packages described have three bedrooms, despite being small lots. We have seen very few house and land products over the last twenty years that have fewer than three bedrooms, which is surprising, given the Australian Bureau of Statistics states that nearly 50% of households only contain between one and two people in the dwelling.[413]

The race to the bottom by the industry has been driven by affordability, with house and land packages ranging between $350,000 to $500,000 on average in Western Australia and a whopping $600,000 to $800,000 in Sydney. Other cities, such as Melbourne and Adelaide, are somewhere in between the two examples. Imagine paying $400,000 for a small house on a small block. It's heartbreaking for today's youth, who will be the first generation confronted with smaller housing that they will be paying significantly more for.

I have to say I am in awe of marketing and propaganda. In Australia, we have a demographic that suggests 50% of housing should only have one or two bedrooms, but instead we have an industry that incessantly continues to market and propagate the need for housing to have a minimum of three bedrooms, two bathrooms and a two-car garage. Whether the house is on a block that is 400sqm or 200sqm, developers and the building industry are still pushing the three-bedroom, two-bathroom house with a two-car-garage design. If you try to think otherwise, you are immediately confronted with an industry that says "the resale value of your house will be compromised". For this reason, we have witnessed a most disastrous outcome in our new suburban areas: a small lot with almost no backyard, no planting or vegetation and only a minimal courtyard. This was discussed earlier in this book, with many examples of concrete suburbs being built across new suburbs in Australia, which result in a heat island effect that will last for generations, since there is little to no opportunity to retrofit the situation unless you demolish the house and start again. Somehow, this form of housing passes code for quality living. Many of these places don't even have street trees.

---

[413] *'Household make up'*, ABS, 2016 Census.

276   The New Australian Dream

Figure 7.8: New suburbs that have the best of nothing and worst of everything[414]

Despite the above being the norm for most of our new suburbs, there are some shining lights that bring hope to the industry. In some cases, micro lots have been created that defy the norm and are two storeys in height with single garages; this enables the house and land to be designed to have less of a building footprint and more land set aside for a courtyard and tree planting. Examples of these two-storey micro lots can be found in Perth's north–east development of Ellenbrook in the 2010s and have since become popular and spread their wings to other estates. While this is a step in the right direction, it is still the minority, and one of the fundamental barriers to this form of development proliferating is building affordability, with two-storey housing in Australia being costly. Trying to do the same thing on a similarly-sized lot using a single-storey configuration doesn't work and results in a house completely covering the block, as we can see in the above example (Figure 7.9).

Figure 7.9: Some light at the end of the tunnel[415]

So, how do we sum this all up? Well, we have seen dramatic changes to our suburban environments that have resulted in dramatic changes to house and land and,

---

[414] *'Pictures of new suburbs in Perth, circa 2010's'*, from Sergio Famiano's photographic collection, 2021.
[415] *'New Housing in suburban Perth'*, from Sergio Famiano's photographic collection, 2019.

importantly, amenities. The housing context hasn't changed much, with the majority of housing still created with three bedrooms, two bathrooms and a two-car garage, but the sizes of the dwellings have changed. We have seen bedrooms reduced from 20sqm in area (5m x 4m) to as low as 6.5sqm (2.5 x 2.5m). We have seen living rooms reduced in area from 40sqm+ to as little as 12sqm. We have seen courtyard spaces reduced from 60sqm+ to as little as 16sqm. We have seen whole suburbs go from averages of 500sqm per lot to 250sqm. We have seen once-leafy suburbs turned into concrete jungles. The list goes on. The figure below perhaps best summarises the dramatic changes witnessed in our suburban areas over the years, which, for me, are cause for concern, but you be the judge for yourself, since I am a biased and concerned town planner.

Figure 7.10: A short history of suburban development in Australia[416]

The Question of Affordability

Housing affordability is the so-called driver of innovation in the housing industry and, as we have seen, does not always produce good housing or urban environments. It is based on supplying a basic home to a market of people who are increasingly finding themselves 'priced out' of the market. So, if you are hoping to see more quality housing in a broader sense, then you might be disappointed. Housing affordability in Australia is at an all-time low, with the price of housing increasing significantly above inflation, and well above the average income. Even while writing this book, which has taken me more than a year, housing prices across our major cities have increased significantly, and I don't know about you, but I haven't had a pay increase in four years.

---

[416] *'Various subdivision forms'*, courtesy Google Earth, 2021.

The most recent CoreLogic data, as of 2022, indicates the following median house prices in Australian cities (Figure 7.12).

City	Median House Price
Sydney	$1,499,126,
Canberra	$1,074,167
Melbourne	$1,037,923
Brisbane	$702,455
Hobart	$698,212
Adelaide	$667,888
Darwin	$640,068
Perth	$598,601
Combined capitals	$994,579

Figure 7.11: Median house prices across Australia, 2022[417]

It is difficult to comprehend that there are now three cities in Australia where the median house price is above one million dollars, and Sydney tops it off with a median house price of $1,499,126 million and climbing. The combined capitals' average median house price is just below one million dollars. This is astounding when the average wage in Australia is just above $90,000.[418] This situation has only gotten worse during COVID-19, which has witnessed house prices increasing significantly, despite migration into Australia dropping dramatically due to COVID-19 restrictions. This is very much counterintuitive, I believe, since immigration drives housing demand, and, with immigration on hold, we should have seen house prices stabilise or even fall slightly, but this has not occurred, and, for the short-term at least, this situation is only going to get worse.

The price of housing construction during COVID-19 has also increased significantly, largely due to supply shocks in materials and supplies. Everything, ranging from steel, timber, windows and cabinets – most of which are imported these days – has increased in price significantly due to manufacturing and transportation chaos caused by COVID-19. For example, steel, which largely comes from China, has had production disrupted, which has forced prices up, as well as the cost of transportation, which in

---

[417] *'Australian Housing Market Update'*, CoreLogic, 2021.
[418] *'Australian Housing Market Update'*, CoreLogic, 2021.

some cases has increased four times over. This has all filtered back to builders, who have been forced to increase the cost of construction as a result.

It is not just materials, but also labour costs that have gone up. Many labourers come from the United Kingdom, China, Indonesia, Malaysia and New Zealand; however, with the borders being shut, it stopped labourers coming from overseas, drying up Australia's labour industry. This has resulted in significant cost increases. The cost of laying a brick pre-COVID-19, for example, was approximately $1.20 per brick, nowadays it's nearly $4 per brick, which is what we call hyperinflation in the building industry. Across Australia, the cost of new housing has increased between 30% and 40% over the last two years, which is completely unsustainable and is contributing towards housing inflation; if people can't afford to build, they will buy existing homes, which is also contributing towards the general overall price increase. This has started to abate as border protection across Australia has relaxed, and we are starting to see the situation stabilise. It will take some time, however, for the cost of construction to begin to decline to more acceptable levels.

Even when things settle down and we learn to live with COVID, as immigration resumes, we are going to see a resumption in price pressure as new migrants, whether they be from overseas or interstate, look for a place to live. Despite this, I ultimately believe prices will plateau and eventually start to decline, as I have mentioned previously in this book, due to an ageing population and limitations around affordability. If house prices continue to rise, eventually large segments of the population seeking a house will simply be priced out of the market of buying a house and will be forced to rent for the better part of their lives. This is not an ideal scenario, since I believe it is a given right for people to own a home. Like the United States, where the wealth of the nation is increasingly being concentrated in the hands of the few, which is seeing the middle class shrink away, so too will Australia follow this trajectory if things don't change. With young people being priced out of the market, their only chance of owning a house is if their parents pass away and bequeath their property or properties to them in their wills.

While the passing down of wealth will certainly happen for many Generation X and Generation Y couples and singles, there will, of course, be many who don't receive a significant bequest, since baby boomers have less superannuation than other generations and may have to downsize so they have spending money. In Australia, this will result in wealth being increasingly concentrated in the hands of the few who own property or properties, while those priced out of the market won't have anything and will be forced to rent.

Housing affordability, not sustainability, will be the fundamental driver of the housing market in the years to come (it already is!), so we are likely to see a continuation of small-lot products in new urban areas and smaller units and apartments in the infill areas (existing suburbs). Even though I believe housing prices will eventually plateau, it will take many years for wages to catch up to house prices. So, the building industry is going to have to come up with more innovative ways to build houses that are smaller, such as single-bedroom and two-bedroom housing, either as units, townhouses or apartments, or develop more micro lots.

This is a worry, given that amenities are compromised with this type of housing form, as discussed previously, with houses on small lots having no courtyards, trees, etc. If small lots are to continue, then we are going to need to see smaller houses that allow for only two bedrooms and a backyard, so balance and amenities are preserved. Different housing forms also need to be considered, and perhaps we can consider what the government has been doing in Western Australia to try to deliver more affordable housing that doesn't compromise amenities.

Demonstration Housing: The Influence of the Government

When we start to think about what the next incarnation could be for the Australian Dream, we need to turn our attention to a subject matter often referred to as the 'missing middle'. You may be thinking, "what does 'the middle' mean?" Well, it succinctly refers to medium-density housing – housing that is not single-residential housing characterised as a three-bedroom single- or two-storey house on a single block, but is also not defined as housing in a large apartment development. The former is often referred to as lower-density or traditional housing, and the latter is often referred to as high-density housing. Both are well established in the industry.

As we have discussed previously, a variety of single-residential housing has popped up in the industry, particularly in our new growth areas, over the last twenty years, with lots ranging from 100sqm to 350sqm. This has brought with it a whole new built form, which I think most would agree is less than desirable, and, while it's relatively affordable, it tends to be fraught with negative amenity and environmental side effects. With apartments, it immediately conjures up an image of a three or four-storey apartment block, usually located around transport hubs and activity centres.

So, what is the middle?

The middle, as we know it from the past thirty years, is unit development in the form of battle-axe lots. This has been discussed, and we are aware of some of the pitfalls of this type of development, so the industry needs something else that achieves a medium level of residential density, housing affordability and maintains some level of amenity. You may not remember, but Australian cities did have something that fit this description, and it was referred to as the maisonette built-form typology, which existed in the 1960s in low numbers, but fell out of favour when city forms and housing became structured around the single-residential suburban home, highway and car.

A maisonette is simply a two-storey apartment development that looks like a two-storey dwelling. They used to come in sizes of four to eight apartments and varied in size from single-bedroom apartments to three-bedroom apartments – although it was more common to have single- and two-bedroom apartments. While not prolific in Australian cities during the 1960s, the maisonette offered the industry an affordable entry into the property market and allowed some variety to cater for different lifestyles and demographics. This building typology, however, was lost and hasn't been seen in Australian cities for over forty years… until recently.

The modern maisonette is something that a colleague of mine and I have had a direct influence in reincarnating within the industry, at least from a Western Australian perspective. The first modern version of the maisonette was created in the Mandurah Junction Project, which I led from 2008 to 2014. It showcased maisonette housing as an affordable housing option in transit-oriented development locations. This demonstration, which was a government initiative, set the standard for the industry and is a classic example of how, when the government leads and works with the private sector, the market can change and new built-form typologies can be achieved, effectively creating a new market.

Case Study: Maisonette (Mandurah Junction Project)

The Mandurah Junction Project developed by LandCorp (now DevelopmentWA) is a transit-oriented development located at the very end of the Perth southern suburbs railway line, and it was completed in 2007. The project consists of approximately fifteen hectares of land adjacent to the Mandurah Train Station and was earmarked for a transit-oriented development utilising the close proximity of the Mandurah Train Station. The project consists of 9,500sqm of retail and commercial floor space and approximately 950 dwellings catering for a population of between 2,000 and 2,500 people. The development is distinct, as it promotes a variety of built forms – including mixed-use development next to the train station, three- and four-storey apartment developments and a variety of single-residential housing options of various lot sizes. The development is also distinct because it was the first demonstration in the modern era of the maisonette apartment development – or in other words, the first demonstration of a two-storey apartment development.

During the planning phase of the Mandurah Junction Project, eager to do a demonstration of maisonette built form, I approached the urban designer, Malcom Mackay, who was big advocate for maisonette development, to create five lots within the Mandurah Junction Stage 1 area that could be set aside to demonstrate a new built-form typology. This was a first for the industry at the time, and was initially met with barriers within LandCorp, who felt the industry would not be ready for such a built form, since there were no standards or guidelines at the time that would promote such a built-form typology. The key to the project was to ensure we could create a new built-form typology that was not only successful from an affordability perspective, but could also be enhanced in future iterations and replicated across the industry.

Sitting down with Malcom Mackay, we created a lot that was approximately 500sqm in area, with dimensions that would enable two apartments to be located on the ground floor in a side-by-side configuration and two apartments at the second level, with one dwelling located towards the front of the lot and the second located towards the rear of the property. The lot would be serviced by a rear laneway, allowing the property to present as a two-storey development to the street front without a garage. Once the lots were created, we embarked upon a process of engagement with the building industry to solicit interest for the project and also set design guidelines that would support such a built form.

The process, while encouraging during the informal stage of engagement, was met with a lukewarm industry response during the formal tender stage, with builders asked to submit designs to partner with LandCorp in a house and land package arrangement. Upon conclusion of the tender process, only one submission and design was received from the building industry, and it came from BGC Construction. After finalising the design, a deal was supposed to have been struck between LandCorp and BGC on a partnership to deliver the new built form, but BGC got cold feet at the last minute, and instead we approached the Department for Housing (the state government social housing provider) to step in, which they did. The deal was that LandCorp would sell the land to the Department for Housing and BGC would build the dwellings. The first three lots consisted of four apartments and were completed in 2013; they were an immediate commercial success. The dwellings, which had two bedrooms and one bathroom, sold for between $210,000 and $230,000 within three months of construction.

For BGC, it was a steep learning curve, as there were standards associated with noise and fire ratings that needed to be navigated, and this added an additional construction cost. What resulted from the demonstration was a new and improved design by BGC and an immediate contract signed between BGC and the Department for Housing to construct a total of 140 such developments in the Perth metropolitan area. Just like that, the maisonette was reborn, and its new and improved versions resulted in hundreds of maisonettes being constructed both for the state and privately across the Perth metropolitan area from 2014 onwards.

In 2015, the Residential Design Codes were updated to include uniform provisions for Multiple Residential Housing, which essentially created the modern maisonette. This built form has been in full swing in Perth and provides a number of key benefits to the missing middle debate. Firstly, it creates much-needed housing diversity. In existing suburbs that are undergoing renewal, the previous building typologies were limited to either large two-storey houses on smaller lots, with three or four bedrooms, or smaller single-storey dwellings that included three bedrooms. With the advent of the maisonette, or two-storey multiple residential dwelling, you now have a mix of single and two-bedroom apartments. This is important for providing lifestyle diversity, allowing people to downsize from their initial home into smaller and more appropriate accommodation in the same suburb.

Figure 7.12: Maisonette in Mandurah Junction coupled with quality public open space creates a successful development[419]

The second key benefit of this form of development is that it is affordable. Previously, to enter a suburb in transition you would have a choice to purchase an existing house on a large block, which is expensive and prices most people out, or you could purchase a two-storey or single-storey townhouse, which is also expensive. If we use the middle suburb of Joondanna in Perth's northern suburbs, an original block with an existing house will set you back between $900,000 and $1,100,000, depending on the size of the block. A two-storey townhouse will set you back between $800,000 and $900,000. A single-storey townhouse will set you back between $600,000 and $700,000. Not very affordable, right? Well, with the introduction of maisonette development, a single-bedroom apartment will set you back approximately $380,000 and a two-bedroom between $400,000 and $450,000. All of a sudden, options open and you have affordability and diversity in your suburb.

The final benefit is that it is more sustainable. How? Because you can fit, for example, eight apartments on a block where, previously, you could only fit three townhouses. This means greater density and less housing that needs to be built on the city's fringes. The density is also seen as more acceptable because it's not four or five storeys in height, and therefore not imposing on a suburban area that traditionally accommodates single- and two-storey housing. So it achieves density without the stigma that comes with having large apartment developments in a suburban environment. It's no wonder this built form has been so popular.

---

[419] *'Pictures of Mandurah Junction Project, Perth'*, courtesy DevelopmentWA website, www.developmentwa.gov.au.

Maisonettes aren't perfect though. They also suffer from limited vegetation on site so can contribute to the 'heat island effect', similar to other infill development. Changes to the Residential Design Codes, however, in 2019 have ensured new maisonette developments provide tree protection areas and greater outdoor courtyards, which ensures improved amenities and more tree canopy. This is positive, as it shows that, as a planning community, we are learning, and what started as a humble development in Mandurah in 2013 is now morphing into a popular and sustainable built form option for our inner-suburban locations.

Old single-storey house on large block – $1,000,000

Modern two-storey townhouse on small block – $900,000

Modern single-storey townhouse on small block – $600,000-$700,000

Modern maisonette – $380,000-$450,000

Figure 7.13: Maisonettes – creating diverse housing in the suburbs[420]

While the reintroduction of the modern maisonette has helped to diversify the housing industry, there are other innovations in the pipeline that will help build the missing middle. One such example in Perth is LandCorp's (Now DevelopmentWA) White Gum Valley Project. The White Gum Valley Project isn't just innovative from a market and affordability perspective, but also exhibits environmental benefits that could be replicated.

---

[420] Photographs of Joondanna, Perth, from Sergio Famiano's photographic album, 2022.

Case Study: White Gum Valley (WGV) Project – Generation Y Project

The White Gum Valley Project is a state government – LandCorp (now DevelopmentWA) – project located 3 kilometres from Fremantle in the nearby suburb of White Gum Valley. The site, which is approximately 4 hectares in area, was formerly home to the Kim Beazley Primary School, which closed in 2008 and was deemed surplus to the state. The project's vision was to deliver approximately 80 new dwellings accommodating an estimated 180 people through a range of housing options, including maisonettes and single-residential homes.[421] While only a small development, LandCorp identified the project as a possible demonstration of the maisonette built form and a demonstration of the missing middle. The project was titled the 'Generation Y Home'.

Figure 7.14: Generation Y Demonstration Project[422]

The Generation Y Demonstration Housing Project is a practical demonstration of affordable, flexible and sustainable dwellings to suit a different approach to housing via a small footprint and small apartment arrangement. The Generation Y Home's purpose was to recognise the challenge of housing affordability and develop a building typology whereby young people could enter the property market by purchasing a small but well-designed single-bedroom apartment as part of a three-apartment complex. In addition to making it easier for first-time homeowners to enter the market, it also demonstrated housing diversity in a suburban setting.

The development provides an excellent demonstration of a housing solution that bridges the gap between the single house and the large apartment block by providing a smart design that includes three apartments in medium-density areas that integrate well with the streetscape. The project followed a design competition that was conducted jointly between LandCorp and the City of Fremantle, the Institute of Architects,

---

[421] *'Generation Y Home'*, WGV, courtesy DevelopmentWA website, www.developmentwa.gov.au 2021.
[422] *'Generation Y Home'*, WGV, courtesy DevelopmentWA website, www.developmentwa.gov.au 2021.

and the Office of the Government Architects. David Barr's design was selected and consisted of the following:

- three separate one-bedroom, one-bathroom apartments with private outdoor living spaces,
- architectural design features that blend harmoniously with surrounding suburban context,
- sizes that were small enough to be located on standard-sized residential blocks, and
- costs that were affordable enough to enable young singles to purchase.

The project has a compact footprint, consisting of a 250sqm block, which compares to the average-sized single-residential housing block of 241sqm. The density achieved is not at the expense of the liveability for inhabitants or neighbours, as each apartment has private and communal external areas, well-designed storage, generous ceiling heights and a high thermal efficiency.

The project is also a demonstration of sustainability, incorporating a design that is climate responsive by utilising solar passive design principles to ensure natural light and cross ventilation. It also utilises sustainable materials, such as 'green concrete', low carbon furnace slag – which provides thermal mass – in addition to using an exterior building material that was made of Colourbond sheeting and fibre cement cladding.[423] The apartment complex has also been designed to include a 9-kilowatt photovoltaic system with battery storage and a 10,000-litre underground rainwater harvesting tank supported by performance monitoring devices.[424] Finally, the landscaping incorporates recycled materials and water-wise planting with shared recycled brick planters for herbs and edible plants.

The project has been the recipient of many awards and is a clever and affordable demonstration of medium-density housing that could fit within a suburban, infill or outer-suburban context. It is a classic example of a demonstration project that could be replicated across the metropolitan area and exported to other states and territories as a viable alternative to the duplex or triplex battle-axe lot and could easily be modified to provide a two-bedroom variant.

---

[423] *'Generation Y Home'*, WGV, courtesy DevelopmentWA website, www.developmentwa.gov.au 2021.
[424] *'Generation Y Home'*, WGV, courtesy DevelopmentWA website, www.developmentwa.gov.au 2021.

Figure 7.15: Generation Y Building [425]

The Future of the Australian Dream
Tackling Affordability
As I have mentioned previously in this book, the issue of housing affordability will be one of the driving factors for the housing market for the foreseeable future. You may think this is just about the price of housing, which is inextricably linked to location, but the ongoing cost and management of a home are just as important. The latter point is where sustainability comes into the fold as a key player, and the two issues come together to achieve housing affordability and more sustainability in the built form at the same time. These issues can be tackled first on a macro scale – or, to put it another way, on a scale that affects all properties – and second on a micro level, where we look at the design of housing itself and the industry that supports it.

Housing Diversity: Reshaping the Australian Dream
Housing affordability, or the cost of a house, has many variables that affect it. Firstly, there is the land component, with the logic based on Von Thunen's theory of land–rent: the closer you are to the centre of the city, the higher the value of the land is on average.[426] This applies in a general sense within Australian cities, particularly given that Australian cities are highly centralised, with a strong core comprising of the central business district followed by a land-use mix and then suburban housing. While this is true, it is also true that cities have changed, and it is possible to have secondary centres where the land–rent theorem equally applies.

This can typically occur around distinct destinations within a city or areas where there are decentralised business cores. For example, in Perth, there is a hierarchy of

---

[425] 4*'Generation Y Home'*, WGV, courtesy DevelopmentWA website, www.developmentwa.gov.au 2021.
[426] Fujita, M and Thisse, J, *'Economic of Agglomeration'*, Cambridge University press, August 2013.

key strategic centres, which are the secondary activity and employment areas outside of the CBD, so while, in a macro sense the land–rent theorem applies to the city core, it also applies to the strategic centres, which act as a secondary core, usually supported by significant transport infrastructure in road and passenger rail. In other cities, such as Melbourne, it would also be supported by mid-tier transport, such as light rail. The transit-oriented development then acts as a mini core, where Von Thunen's theorem applies. Accordingly, land values are highest in the core and immediately around it because it is well serviced by a variety of amenities, and then there are particular city-based circumstances that affect property values, which tend to be associated around water bodies, such as rivers and the ocean, in Australia. Generally speaking, if you are located in close proximity to rivers and oceans, your land values are usually higher than those of property that is further away.

So land is a significant factor in the value of housing, and subject to location, the larger the land parcel the greater the value of the land. Link this with land use (the development potential of your land), and you have a complete picture of what affects land values in a city. Aside from land use, many of the other factors are largely fixed; although this could be different in new growth areas where elements such as planned transport and proximity to planned activity centres would have an influence. The point of all this discussion is that as policymakers in the town planning, real estate industry, and as politicians, we generally only have the lever of land use to affect land values; that and taxation. I will focus on both as an answer to Australia's affordability crisis.

To me, it is not fair that property values are so high that many of the next generation won't be able to afford to buy a house. If you are a young person living in Sydney, for example, unless you are a beneficiary of a major endowment, there is no way that it would be possible to afford the average house price of $1.5 million. Even the lower end of this scale, say $800,000, is unaffordable. It would be fair to say that even if you combine the incomes of two people, it would still be nearly impossible to afford a property, with median incomes hovering around $90,000. It's just not possible, and this is the sad reality that now confronts the younger generation in this so-called lucky country of ours. This isn't right when you consider shelter as a given human right (remember Maslow's hierarchy of needs?).

So, if land is a significant factor in the cost of housing, the logic would follow that the smaller the land parcel, the more affordable the house will be. We have seen the industry trying to do this by reducing lots to 100sqm in area, but the problem is they put a single-storey house on it that covers 80-90% of the lot, which creates all sorts of issues around amenity and tree-canopy loss. So, the alternative is not to reduce lot areas and covering it with a house, the solution is twofold: we need to go two storey, and we need to look at smaller housing units that actually reflect the market we are selling to. The problem with the first option is that two-storey housing is more expensive than single-storey housing. This may be true, but a smaller dwelling that is only one or two bedrooms in a two-storey configuration could offset the cost of a three-bedroom single-storey house that almost covers the entire lot.

New House Design for the Australian Dream in New Growth and Infill Areas

When creating affordable housing in new suburban locations, we need to tackle the issue from two fronts. Firstly, through lot size and secondly, through house size. If we get away from the notion that you need to have a three- or four-bedroom home and a double garage, all of a sudden affordable housing designs become a possibility.

I have prepared a number of housing designs that have been costed and provide options for new suburban and infill areas. This includes 'front-loaded' housing options that are compared with more contemporary designs in the industry, from the perspectives of affordability, amenity and sustainability. With more creative design, the contemporary options – while smaller dwellings on smaller lots – generally provide a much-needed balance in amenity and environment and are more affordable. Yes, you get less house for your dollar, but you get a better design and improved amenities, as well as a built form that caters for market needs. I am not sure why singles want to purchase a three-bedroom house for one or two people. If they decide to have a family, they can always sell their home and purchase a three-bedroom home – there is certainly plenty of choice, as there is no shortage of three- and four-bedroom homes in our cities. This requires a change in consumer sentiment and attitude, and also requires demonstration, which is where the government and the private sector can come in.

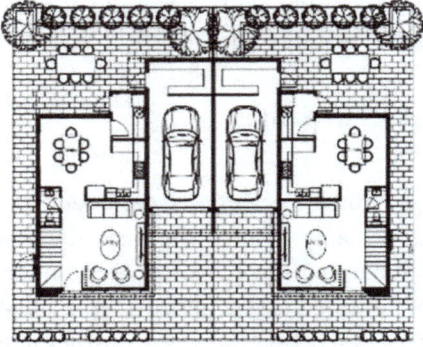
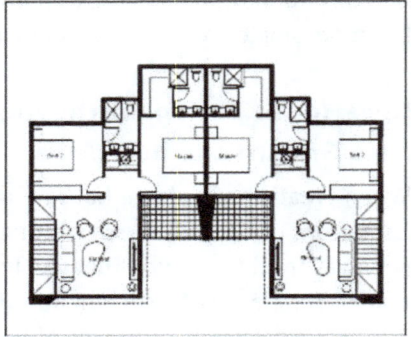

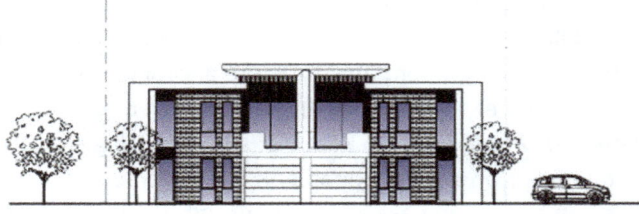

Block dimension: 10m wide x 17m deep
Block size: 170sqm
Dwelling size: 160sqm
Dwelling makeup: 2 bed, 2 bath, 1 garage

Perth Market	Sydney Market	Melbourne Market	Brisbane Market
Inner City Location (North Perth) Total Cost - **$600,000** Land value - $1,600/sqm Construction cost - $2,000/sqm	Inner City Location (Bardwell Park) Total Cost - **$865,000** Land value - $3,200/sqm Construction cost - $2,000/sqm	Inner City Location (Blackburn) Total Cost - **$630,000** Land value - $1,800/sqm Construction cost - $2,000/sqm	Inner City Location (Stafford Heights) Total Cost - **$580,000** Land value - $1,500/sqm Construction cost - $2,000/sqm
Outer Suburb (Baldivis) Total Cost - **$400,000** Land value - $460/sqm Construction cost - $2,000/sqm	Outer Suburb (Blacktown) Total Cost - **$595,000** Land value - $1,600/sqm Construction cost - $2,000/sqm	Outer Suburb (Craigieburn) Total Cost - **$530,000** Land value - $1,200/sqm Construction cost - $2,000/sqm	Outer Suburb (Caboolture) Total Cost - **$410-415,000** Land value - $520/sqm Construction cost - $2,000/sqm

Figure 7.16: Compact two-storey, two-bedroom home [427]

---

[427] 471 *'New House Design's'*, Copyright, Sergio Famiano 2022.

Micro-Planning the Australian Dream   291

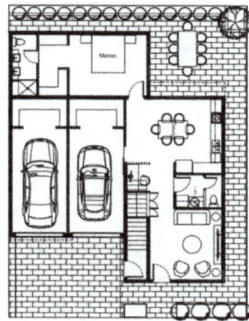

Block dimension: 12.6m wide x 17m deep
Block size: 214sqm
Dwelling size/makeup:
Ground – 1 bed, 2 bath, 1 garage 98sqm
Upper – 2 bed, 2 bath, 1 garage 109sqm

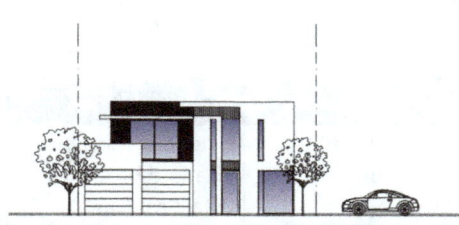

Perth Market	Sydney Market	Melbourne Market	Brisbane Market
Inner City Location (North Perth) Total Cost (Unit 1) - **$375,000** Total Cost (Unit 2) - **$395,000** Land value - $1,600/sqm Construction cost - $2,000/sqm	Inner City Location (Bardwell Park) Total Cost (Unit 1) - **$555,000** Total Cost (Unit 2) - **$565,000** Land value - $3,200/sqm Construction cost - $2,000/sqm	Inner City Location (Blackburn) Total Cost (Unit 1) - **$395,000** Total Cost (Unit 2) - **$415,000** Land value - $1,800/sqm Construction cost - $2,000/sqm	Inner City Location (Stafford Heights) Total Cost (Unit 1) - **$360,000** Total Cost (Unit 2) - **$385,000** Land value - $1,500/sqm Construction cost - $2,000/sqm
Outer Suburb (Baldivis) Total Cost (Unit 1) - **$250,000** Total Cost (Unit 2) - **$270,000** Land value - $460/sqm Construction cost - $2,000/sqm	Outer Suburb (Blacktown) Total Cost (Unit 1) - **$375,000** Total Cost (Unit 2) - **$395,000** Land value - $1,600/sqm Construction cost - $2,000/sqm	Outer Suburb (Craigieburn) Total Cost (Unit 1) - **$330,000** Total Cost (Unit 2) - **$350,000** Land value - $1,200/sqm Construction cost - $2,000/sqm	Outer Suburb (Caboolture) Total Cost (Unit 1) - **$255,000** Total Cost (Unit 2) - **$275,000** Land value - $520/sqm Construction cost - $2,000/sqm

Figure 7.17: Compact Multiple Residential development – Missing Middle[428]

---

[428] *'New House Designs'*, Copyright, Sergio Famiano 2022.

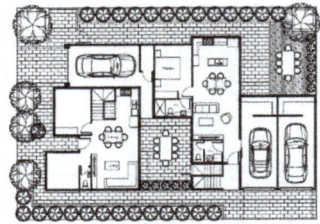
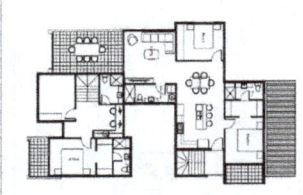

Block dimension: 24.2m wide x 17m deep
Block size: 411sqm
Dwelling size/makeup:
Ground – 1 bed, 2 bath, 1 garage 91sqm
Ground/upper – 3 bed, 2 bath, 1 garage 120sqm
Upper – 2 bed, 2 bath, 1 garage 116sqm

Perth Market	Sydney Market	Melbourne Market	Brisbane Market
Inner City Location (North Perth) Total Cost (Unit 1) - **$405,000** Total Cost (Unit 2) - **$465,000** Total Cost (Unit 3) - **$455,000** Land value - $1,600/sqm Construction cost - $2,000/sqm	Inner City Location (Bardwell Park) Total Cost (Unit 1) - **$625,000** Total Cost (Unit 2) - **$680,000** Total Cost (Unit 3) - **$675,000** Land value - $3,200/sqm Construction cost - $2,000/sqm	Inner City Location (Blackburn) Total Cost (Unit 1) - **$435,000** Total Cost (Unit 2) - **$495,000** Total Cost (Unit 3) - **$485,000** Land value - $1,800/sqm Construction cost - $2,000/sqm	Inner City Location (Stafford Heights) Total Cost (Unit 1) - **$390,000** Total Cost (Unit 2) - **$450,000** Total Cost (Unit 3) - **$455,000** Land value - $1,500/sqm Construction cost - $2,000/sqm
Outer Suburb (Baldivis) Total Cost (Unit 1) - **$250,000** Total Cost (Unit 2) - **$305,000** Total Cost (Unit 3) - **$300,000** Land value - $460/sqm Construction cost - $2,000/sqm	Outer Suburb (Blacktown) Total Cost (Unit 1) - **$405,000** Total Cost (Unit 2) – **$465,000** Total Cost (Unit 3) - **$455,000** Land value - $1,600/sqm Construction cost - $2,000/sqm	Outer Suburb (Craigieburn) Total Cost (Unit 1) - **$350,000** Total Cost (Unit 2) - **$410,000** Total Cost (Unit 3) - **$400,000** Land value - $1,200/sqm Construction cost - $2,000/sqm	Outer Suburb (Caboolture) Total Cost (Unit 1) - **$260,000** Total Cost (Unit 2) - **$315,000** Total Cost (Unit 3) - **$310,000** Land value - $520/sqm Construction cost - $2,000/sqm

Figure 7.18: Micro Multiple Residential development – Missing Middle[429]

---

[429] 473 *'New House Designs'*, Copyright, Sergio Famiano 2022.

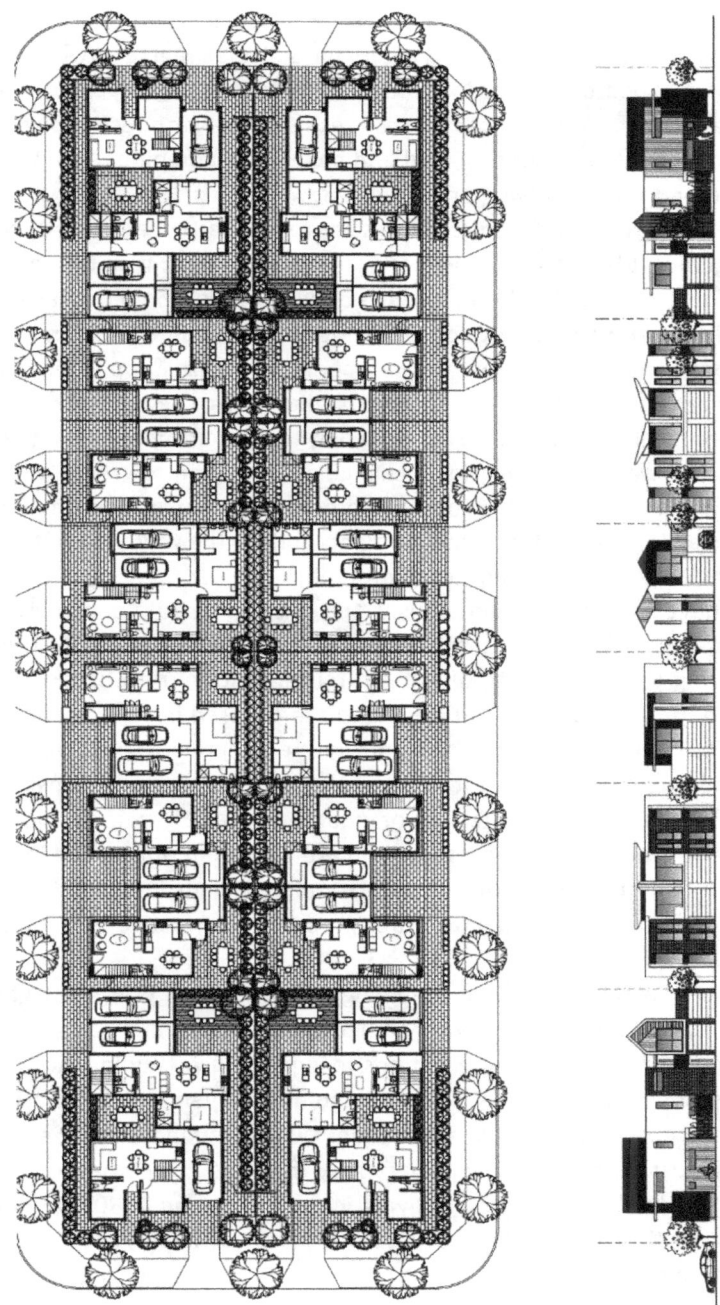

Figure 7.19: Micro multiple residential development – missing middle block design[430]

---

[430] *'New House Designs'*, Copyright, Sergio Famiano 2022.

Just by looking at the examples above, you can see how you can have creative and efficient design that is affordable and caters for a diverse market. Two-storey designs that focus on two bedrooms, and in some cases reducing the garage to one garage that still allows a second uncovered car bay, can result in smaller house designs, as well as smaller blocks that are better designed and have more amenities than their contemporary three-bedroom and two-garage designs.

There are enormous efficiencies in this approach, particularly if you scale up; you can save significant land area and achieve diversity and density in the same instance. Now, I am not saying we should create rows of just two-bedroom houses – no. We can mix it up with three-bedroom options for larger households, or we can have a row of two-bedroom houses with a row of three-bedroom houses opposite. You can chop and change at your will, and this improves land efficiency, diversity and affordability. This is the approach that should be mandated by the government in our new suburban areas to ensure we are catering for a changing population to create affordable and more social dynamic and flexible suburbs, rather than the oversized and monotonous suburbs that are being created at the moment. And, by the way, we can fit trees in the lot, which improves amenity and the environment.

As we have reflected on previously, the missing middle is a key issue in our cities and is a subject matter that needs to be tackled head on. At the moment, we are carving up our large traditional suburban blocks into battle-axe lots that are devoid of outdoor spaces and trees and are covered in concrete and rooftops. This needs to change, not only from a design perspective to achieve an improved amenity and environment, but it needs to change to improve housing diversity. Practically 99% of all duplex, triplex or quadraplex battle-axe developments are either three- or four-bedrooms homes and are crammed onto small lots. We need to mix it up and start introducing single- and two-bedroom housing typologies to improve the use of limited space, design and housing diversity for a changing population.

This also calls for mixing and matching options so we don't just get monotonous single-storey and two-storey three-bedroom houses, but perhaps a combination of apartment and townhouse options to support diversity in places. The above examples demonstrate that there could be significant diversity in housing that can be affordable and sustainable at the same time. What we need is for the building and real estate industries to stop telling everybody they need three or four bedrooms in a home for resale value. We are not living in the 1960s and 1980s anymore, where everybody is getting married and having three kids. Nowadays, people are deferring marriage or not getting married at all. When they are getting married, they are having one to two children and, in some cases, none at all. So why would we need so many three- and four-bedroom homes? As mentioned previously, it is because we are told we need them.

People need to start thinking about what they really need rather than what marketing companies and real estate agents are telling them. It is normal to live in a single-bedroom or two-bedroom home for ten years and then upsize for twenty or thirty years to cater for a family, and then downsize again when the children have moved out. This makes sense, so don't get caught in the trap that you need to have a family home ten years before you decide to have a family. It's a tremendous burden to maintain a large house, and this is completely unnecessary for one or two people.

A Carrot or Stick Approach?

One method of ensuring greater affordable housing could be to encourage or mandate it through policy or else to leave it up to the market to respond. It's the carrot or stick approach. In my experience, we need a bit of both. Humans are creatures of habit, and it's difficult to break a habit and try something new. This has certainly been what I have witnessed in my twenty-five-plus years in the industry. You need to mandate something to get it in the system and change the habit, and then you can relax and take your foot off the accelerator for a bit.

Remember photovoltaic cells? Remember when they first came out in the 2000s in Australia? The government provided an incentive by subsidising producers, and this resulted in a steady uptake of the system in households and also resulted in the expansion of the industry, bringing more competitors to the market. I remember when I was leading the Mandurah Junction Project back in 2010; we included in our house and land packages a 1.5-kilowatt photovoltaic system with every house sold. At the time, the system was worth $6,000. As uptake of the system began to increase in the 2010s, there were more competitors, and therefore prices dropped, allowing the government to step out and reduce its rebate. Now, in 2022, you can get a 6.6-kilowatt system for less than $3,000, and they are everywhere. Amazing, isn't it? But it takes a bit of commitment, time and pressure to change the market.

In housing, we need to start seeing a twofold approach for bringing housing diversity to the industry. We have seen in previous examples that we can build affordable, well designed, single- and two-bedroom apartments, such as the Generation Y Project, rather than building monotonous, environmentally damaging lots covered by a house. What we need to see is the government mandating through the State Government Planning Policy a minimum number of single- and two-bedroom housing to be provided in new urban areas. We already see this in government policy where apartment development is proposed, usually in infill or existing suburban locations where there is a planning policy requiring a minimum number of single and two-bedroom dwellings in any given apartment development. We need to now see this transpire in new suburban development.

In Western Australia, for example, this would require the Liveable Neighbourhoods Policy being updated to require a minimum number of single- and two-bedroom dwellings in new estates. This may appear as an overreach by the government, but if we allow the market to continue with driving this agenda, all we will see is three- and four-bedroom housing on small blocks in our new suburban locations. We need to get more sophisticated in our approach and start planning for a holistic or diversified community – and an affordable one. If this requirement is mandated, the industry will whinge for a while, but eventually they will get used to it and start producing housing that meets the single- and two-bedroom brief. If we couple these changes with design guidelines modelled around demonstration housing, such as the Generation Y Project, we can then provide a pathway for developers to deliver quality and affordable housing. I have faith in the industry, in that they will eventually design and build quality housing, if shown how to do so. This 'stick approach' will also help to change the narrative around housing in our city, as the industry will be forced to start 'talking up' the benefits of transitional housing, since their bottom line will depend on it.

The above initiative is going to be important, since, for a more sustainable city, we are going to need to start to curb the expansive changes in our city's 'growth boundaries'. As mentioned previously, in most cities the majority of new housing is occurring on the urban fringes, in the form of new urban development. Well, this needs to change, with the majority of new development needing to occur in existing suburban locations, where existing infrastructure, such as telecommunications, sewer, roads, etc., can be utilised. The industry will argue, however, that if we reduce the level of new housing on the fringes, assuming demand is maintained, it will drive up prices of land in existing urban/suburban areas. I agree with this notion, since new urban developments are controlled by developers who respond to market demand, while most infill developments are controlled by thousands of different land owners who may be motivated by priorities other than developing their land to respond to market needs. It is here where the government needs to step in, and I know what I am about to say will be construed as controversial, but unfortunately it will be necessary to shift the balance from new development on the fringes to infill areas in our existing suburbs. The government needs to incentivise infill development, and it needs to do this via a number of methods, which I will explain below.

Government Grants

Firstly, many state governments in Australia offer a First Homeowners' Grant to anyone buying or building a home for the first time. Currently, the grant is skewed towards people building a new home for the first time. This is good, because it encourages the construction industry, but falls short in another way, because more often than not they are constructing housing in new urban areas on the fringes of our cities, which is what we need to reduce or discourage.

The state governments, therefore, need to refocus and provide larger grants to home buyers who purchase or construct housing in existing areas, rather than new growth areas. The incentive needs to be increased as well, so it is not $10,000 but more in the region of $50,000 to $80,000 for new or existing housing in existing areas. This is necessary, since housing in more traditional neighbourhoods closer to the city core is generally more expensive (due to the land). You may think, "how can this be paid for?" Well, simply reduce the incentive given to new construction in new growth areas and increase taxation on investment properties. The former is fairly simple, but the latter is more involved.

As an example, in Western Australia, if you have an investment property, you pay a land tax. This is in addition to the Metropolitan Region Improvement Tax, which provides money to the Metropolitan Improvement Fund – a fund currently held by the State Government Planning Institution. This money is then used to purchase land to affect the Metropolitan Region Scheme's objectives. This includes paying for land for major roads, public open space and reserves, to mention a few. My suggestion to fund an increase in the First Homeowners' Grants is to increase the land tax on investment properties and funnel the additional money to the First Homeowners' Grant fund. Because land tax is an expense that applies to investment properties, it is a legitimate tax deduction, so if we increase land tax by, say, 50%, then half of that would be returned to the investor through the tax process. The balance comes out of the investor's pocket.

That's fair, right? I mean, if we are honest with ourselves, the wealthier people in society are the ones snapping up investment properties making themselves richer, and in the process they are driving up housing prices and pricing out young people from the market. It is only fair that they then give a small piece of the pie back to first home buyers, who are being squeezed out of the market. The property investment industry is huge, and every one property that is purchased by property investors helps drive up the price of housing, especially those who have more than two or three properties – and trust me, there are many who fit into this category.

Property investment and the negative gearing tax system that supports it, helps to maintain a middle class and helps the rich get richer, so it is only fair that, together, they help the unfortunate youth to get a leg up on the property ladder. As a property investor myself, I wouldn't have a problem paying an extra $500 a year in land tax if it means young people have a better chance of entering the housing market and if it also encourages more sustainable built forms by promoting development in infill areas.

In case you have your doubts about the impact of investors on the property market, especially in driving up prices, then let me give you some sobering statistics. According to CoreLogic, in 2021 there were a little over 10.5 million dwellings in Australia worth a staggering $7.1 trillion.[431] Of a population that is now 26 million and growing, there are 2.2 million people who own investment properties in Australia, which is just under

---

[431] Forbes, K *'How Many Australian's Own and Investment Property'*, propertyupdate.com, 2021.

10% of the population.[432] Most of the investors are in the higher age bracket, showing that baby boomers and Generation X are by far the biggest investors in the country, with people below the age of thirty barely getting a mention. This is not surprising, since many people under thirty can barely afford a home, let alone the luxury of an investment property.

Investor age	Percentage
60 or more	27.83%
Between 50 and 59	31.67%
Between 40 and 49	24.65%
Between 30 and 39	14.22%
Younger than 30	1.63%

Figure 7.20: Investment properties as a break down by age[433]

When you break down the statistics even further, it gets more interesting. CoreLogic has noticed that there is a growing trend of investors acquiring more property, with nearly 30% of investors owning more than one investment property. This trend is increasing, which is adding to the price pressure on housing and further blocking young people from owning their first homes. This means the property gap is getting wider, with more and more properties being purchased by investors, making it harder and harder for first home buyers to enter the property market.

Number of investment properties	Percentage	Percentage increase since 2021
1	71% (1.57 million)	2.3%
2	19% (418,000)	2.7%
3	6% (129,784)	3%
4	2% (47,469)	2.2%
5	1% (19,861)	1.8%
6 or more	1% (20,756)	2%

Figure 7.21: Number of investment properties per investors[434]

---

[432] Forbes, K *'How Many Australian's Own and Investment Property'*, propertyupdate.com, 2021.
[433] Forbes, K *'How Many Australian's Own and Investment Property'*, propertyupdate.com, 2021.
[434] Forbes, K *'How Many Australian's own and Investment Property'*, propertyupdate.com, 2021.

I believe in the free market and the right for people to invest their hard-earned money into property, which provides rentals for those who are unable to afford a home and also allows for a middle class in Australia, but I believe this needs to be balanced, and, right now in Australia, it is not. Property prices have risen so high and so fast that it has made the few people who own investment properties, in particular the baby boomers and Generation X, very wealthy, leaving other generations behind. Remember our property boom has occurred over a relatively short period of time. In 1980, the average house price in Sydney was $18,700. By 1990, it rose to $184,000.[435] By 2000, it was $312,000.[436] In 2010, it was $575,000.[437] Now, it is just over $1.5 million.[438] The average annual wage in 1990 was $28,000.[439] Now it is $90,000.[440] So, in 1990 in Sydney, the average house price was equivalent to two years of gross wages. It has now grown to a staggering 15 years during COVID-19.

The average house price across Australia is now $980,000, and the average income around $90,000. The average house price is equivalent to ten years of gross wages.[441] This is a massive gap between house prices and income, and it has largely occurred over the last twenty years. It is easy to see who has benefited the most from this boom. It has been the baby boomers and Generation X. The former cohort were in their 40s during the 1980s, so from the 1980s to 2000 they would have been snapping up properties for a fraction of the price they are going for today. Generation X were in their 30s and 40s during the 1990s and would have done the same. Poor Generation Y and Generation Z won't be so lucky, with house prices now too expensive to even contemplate purchasing a first home.

The argument in favour of taxing wealthy landowners, particularly those who have more than one investment property, is strong and justified. While the tax on a per property basis could be modest, possibly $500 extra a year (indexed to inflation), the benefits for first home buyers would be significant. Who wants to see young people struggling to have a home? Babies born from 2010 onwards are shaping up to be the first generation not be able to afford a house. Accordingly, assistance is required, and there is a precedent to justify the type of support being suggested. Remember the returning World War Two veterans? The returning veterans were beneficiaries of government subsidies not only as a thank you for their contribution towards the war effort, but also because many left the labour market to fight a war and needed assistance to get back on their feet when they returned.

---

[435] 'Australian House Prices Over the Last 50 Years', Datamentary, 2021.
[436] 'Australian House Prices Over the Last 50 Years', Datamentary, 2021.
[437] 'Australian House Prices Over the Last 50 Years', Datamentary, 2021.
[438] 'Australian House Prices Over the Last 50 Years', Datamentary, 2021.
[439] 'Australian average Weekly Wages', Trading Economics, 2021.
[440] 'Australian average Weekly Wages', Trading Economics, 2021.
[441] 'Australian average Weekly Wages', Trading Economics, 2021.

A government-led approach, therefore, has a precedent, and indeed there is the First Homeowners' Grant today, which provides first home buyers with some modest relief. What occurred immediately after the Second World War with government support for homeowners is needed now to assist the younger generations of this 'lucky country' to get a place they can call their own. As suggested, I believe this could be achieved through expanding the scope of the First Homeowners' Grant, and the grant can be skewed to facilitate the delivery of more compact affordable housing in existing built-up areas, where there is less drain on state government budgets to provide services and transport infrastructure. This would slow down the growth of new suburban areas, which also means reducing government expenditure on services and transport infrastructure for these areas. The money saved could be repurposed to support diversified and affordable housing in existing areas. Think about it. Governments spend huge amounts of money in new suburban areas – new roads, services, regional parks, wastewater treatment and schools. Reducing new suburban areas means reducing the burden of delivering these services.

Reducing Transportation Costs

As I've mentioned, tackling housing affordability is a twofold approach. One is the cost of the house and land itself, the second is the ongoing running cost of a home. In the new suburban estates on the city's fringes, the cost of purchasing a new house and land is less than purchasing a house and land in existing areas closer to the city core (Von Thunene's theory). However, as discussed earlier, it is significantly more costly to live in a new suburban home than in a house closer to the city core. This is because properties located closer to the city core have greater access to services and live closer to amenities and employment areas and have more reliable public transport. The latter is a significant cost in running a house. People living in existing built-up areas close to the city and close to amenities can get away with being less dependent on private vehicle transportation.

It is, therefore, possible that a family of four in an existing suburban location close to public transport can live with one less vehicle. Families living on the fringes, however, are dependent on two vehicles, since areas of employment, amenities, shops and special interest areas are located a long distance away. The impact of having one less car is enormous, as can be seen in the table below, which is based on vehicles that cost approximately $30,000.

	Vehicle cost: outer-suburban areas (2022)*	Vehicle cost: inner-suburban areas (2022)**
Vehicle licensing	$2,500	$1,250
Vehicle insurance	$2,000	$1,000
Maintenance costs	$3,000	$1,000
Running costs (fuel/oil)	$10,500	$3,250
Vehicle depreciation	$4,800***	$2,400***
Public transport costs	$200	$1,500
Total (1 year)	**$23,000**	**$10,400**
Total (10 years)	**$230,000**	**$104,000**

Figure 7.22: Vehicle cost comparison – inner versus outer suburbs[442]

*Vehicle costs based on two vehicles (at 2022 prices).

**Vehicle costs based on one vehicle (at 2022 prices).

***Depreciation based on 15% annually – amount is averaged over 10 years.

Note: The example provided is from Perth, Western Australia.

As you can see by the simple example above, there is a significant difference in transport costs alone. The difference could represent a significant deduction from a mortgage, especially if you take into consideration travel costs equivalent over thirty years, which is the average life of a mortgage. We, therefore, need to stop building new suburbs in the middle of nowhere and start consolidating our cities. I know this is unrealistic, but at the very least we need to slow it down and push for a more significant amount of housing to be provided in existing urban areas. Then, combined with good public transport, people will have the choice to have just one car per family, which will reduce environmental impacts and mortgage stress.

Reducing the Running Costs of a Home: The Role of Sustainability

Sustainability plays a key role in reducing household costs. Why? Because it's about us reducing our dependence on fossil fuels and using free energy generated by the sun, wind and rain. It's that simple. We will look at water and electricity, which represent the biggest household bills in a modern home.

Water Costs

Saving money on water usage can only be done by reducing the household's water consumption. How do you do that though? Australia's climate is hot, and, in most

---

[442] *'Investigative work undertaken by Sergio Famiano'*, 2021.

areas (with the exception of Queensland) rainfall is irregular. The notion of putting in rainwater tanks is somewhat helpful, because you are guaranteed water in winter to supply some of the summer consumption, but once it runs out you are left relying on scheme water. The best way of reducing water usage is by reducing the need to use it in the first place. This can be done through various means. Firstly, by reducing water usage inside the house. This could be achieved by:

- implementing water saving practices i.e., limiting time in showers,
- harvesting water from rain i.e., installing rainwater tanks,
- recycling grey water by using wastewater from the laundry and toilet to irrigate the garden, reducing reliance on scheme water, and
- employing water saving appliances i.e., dish washers.

All of the above contribute towards reduced water consumption inside a house. At the moment, the requirement for water saving devices is optional within housing, but I think it needs to become mandatory. In Australia, for example, the Water Efficiency Labelling and Standards (WELS) rating system is used to determine the level of sustainability in water usage and is reflected in star ratings, with the higher number of stars meaning a more sustainable water system. The industry needs to start mandating a minimum WELS rating in new developments. This occurs in some developments but only if sought by the developer. It needs to be mandated across the board.

The second method of reducing water usage is by reducing water consumption outside the home. This means less water usage in our gardens. This can be achieved through smart design, where garden areas are consolidated, rather than spread over large areas, and by using drought-resistant planting. By selecting Australian native vegetation over imported species, you could cut down on water consumption on your garden by half.

The Australian Government 'Your Home' website (https://www.yourhome.gov.au/) suggests that, if you follow the above measures, you could reduce overall water consumption in a house by up to 40%.[443] That is a big saving. Let's put it in perspective by using some real numbers. According to the Australian Bureau of Statistics, the average Australian uses 340 litres of water per day.[444] If we multiply this by 365 days and again by 2.53 (average household size), the average house consumes roughly 313,973 litres (or 313 kilolitres) of water a year. This equates to roughly a cost of $750 per annum (using Sydney's price of $2.35 per kilolitre), not including service costs and charges.

If we reduce water consumption by 40%, the savings could be up to $15,000 per household over a forty year period. Doesn't seem like much, but think of our

---

[443] 'Australia Guide to Sustainability Homes', Australian Government, https://www.yourhome.gov.au/.
[444] 'Australia Guide to Sustainability Homes', Australian Government, https://www.yourhome.gov.au/.

environment. The water savings equates to approximately 5,000,000 litres, or 5,000 kilolitres, of water per household every forty years . That's a lot of water. Multiply that by the number of households in Australia, and you get a ridiculous number.

Electricity Costs

As with water, the electricity costs associated with a house can be reduced by reducing your reliance on electricity to power your home. The first method of doing this is consuming less electricity. For example, instead of having three TVs and two fridges, just have one of each. Instead of having a standard project home builder, cookie-cutter-design of a home, spend a little extra on the design to ensure improved passive solar orientation, which will result in less reliance on lighting and air conditioning. If all these measures are not possible, and you have to have your modern comforts, then I would suggest investing in photovoltaic solar panels and a battery. The savings are quite remarkable, and you would be reducing your ecological footprint by drawing power from the sun. According to a study by the Auscan Electrical Group, the average Australian household consumption of electricity can vary depending upon the size and scale of the home. The following examples are provided below:

Household type	Electricity consumption per day (kilowatts)	Electricity consumption per year (kilowatts)	Annual cost of electricity	Cost over fifteen years
Household A: Suburban home with two parents and two kids	41	15,000	$3,999	$59,985
Household B: Suburban home with a couple	23	8,300	$2,212	$33,180
Household C: Apartment with two parents and a child	13.7	5,000	$1,333	$19,995
Household D: Apartment with a single retiree	7	2,500	$666	$9,990

*Cost based on 26.66 cents per kilowatt (2022 prices)

Figure 7.23: Different household electricity consumption[445]

---

[445] Auscan Services, electrical, air-conditioning and data https://auscanservices.com.au/how-much-power-is-needed-to-run-an-average-home/ 2022.

The household that consumes the greatest electricity is the suburban home with a family. Apartments naturally consume significantly less electricity, even when taking consumption into consideration a per capita basis. If we were to look at the same scenario and install a photovoltaic system for each dwelling type, applying a 6.6 kilowatt system for the suburban home and a 1.5 kilowatt system for the apartments, we can see the savings over an annual basis and over a fifteen year period, which is the expected life of the photovoltaic cells.

Household type	Electricity consumption per day (kilowatts)	Electricity consumption per year (kilowatts)	Annual cost of electricity	Cost over fifteen years	PV cell cost	Annual savings**	Fifteen year savings**	Net savings
Household A: Suburban home with two parents and two kids	41	15,000	$3,999	$59,985	$4,000	$1,800	$27,000	**$23,000**
Household B: Suburban home with a couple	23	8,300	$2,212	$33,180	$4,000	$1,800	$27,000	**$23,000**
Household C: Apartment with two parents and a child	13.7	5,000	$1,333	$19,995	$2,500	$600	$9,000	**$8,400**
Household D: Apartment with a single retiree	7	2,500	$666	$9,990	$2,500	$600	$9,000	**$8,400**

*Cost based on 26.66 cents per kilowatt (2022 prices)
**Government purchase price based on 7 cents per kilowatt (2022) + electricity savings based on optimisation of peak consumption

Figure 7.24: Electricity savings per household type[446]

---

[446] Auscan Services, electrical, air-conditioning and data https://auscanservices.com.au/how-much-power-is-needed-to-run-an-average-home/ 2022.

Parting Words on the Australian Dream
Reflecting on the Past and the Present

As we have seen throughout history, the Australian Dream has been omnipresent in the Australian conscious. There may have been different trends, different housing cycles and different influences – social, economic and political – but the outcome throughout Australia's short history has always been the same: Australians aspire to purchase a home of their own. If you ask any Australian, they will tell you that home ownership is part of the "Australian way of life". In a poll undertaken by the Australian National University in 2017, which included over 2,500 Australians, the question was posed: is owning a home part of the Australian way of life? The answer was an emphatic "yes". Just over 92% of survey participants indicated home ownership was very much part of the Australian way of life, with a paltry 8% thinking otherwise.[447]

As we have seen throughout this book, the great Australian Dream can mean several things – freedom to do what you want, egalitarianism – but for the most part it is the dream of home ownership. This notion is interesting when you compare it to other countries. In America, the great American Dream is synonymous with the freedom to be who you want, but Americans agree it also includes home ownership. Other countries, even wealthy countries such as Germany, see home ownership differently. In Germany, home ownership is lower than Australia and the United States, with renting featuring more predominately. Other countries, such as Singapore, have a greater percentages of state ownership of housing, again with most people renting.

It is interesting that home ownership is still so prominent in Australia in 2022. With so many Australians now facing mortgage stress and a whole generation effectively priced out of home ownership in Australia, it shows the power of the Australian Dream and its luring effect on the population, even when it is now out of reach for many.

So now we have some of the highest property values in the world. The prospect of owning a home comes with a massive mortgage, and unfortunately, for the first time perhaps, we have a generation of Australians thinking home ownership is beyond their grasp. As we have seen, the dream of home ownership in Australia is still alive – in spirit at least.

We know Australians are concerned with obtaining home ownership, so it will become a political issue. From the same Australian National University study, over 70% of Australians are very concerned home ownership is becoming unattainable for younger generations.[448] Only 14% do not think this is the case.[449] It appears, at least for the short-term, and especially because of COVID-19, that housing prices are going to continue to rise. The Australian National University's polling shows that approximately

---

[447] Belot, H, *'Six charts that tell you about housing affordability in Australia'*, ABC News, Federal Budget, May 2017.
[448] Belot, H, *'Six charts that tell you about housing affordability in Australia'*, ABC News, Federal Budget, May 2017.
[449] Belot, H, *'Six charts that tell you about housing affordability in Australia'*, ABC News, Federal Budget, May 2017.

84% of people think prices will continue to increase over the next five years, with only 10% thinking prices will stay the same.[450] If this turns out to be true, I hate to think what the median house price in Sydney will be in another five years.

The Future

As discussed in this book, I am concerned that the egalitarian principles that seem to go hand in hand with the Australian Dream, staring from the beginning of British settlement through to the 1970s, are today slipping away. When we look at history, you can define the rise and fall of housing affordability in this country. Migrants coming to Australia en masse post the Second World War and the advent of socialism and communism cemented the notion of home ownership as a public policy priority via government intervention and management to ensure Australia had a middle class who could afford a home and car; this kept the population happy and content so they would not stray towards communism. The advent of communism, in particular, kept the notion of extreme market-based capitalism at bay and meant a hybrid of capitalism – democracy and egalitarianism – would define Australia, the place we have come to love.

The fall of communism in the 1980s was a double-edge sword. Since then, Australia has been influenced by prevailing market-based economic theory emanating from the Thatcher and Reagan era, and it seems the 'bull of capitalism' has been let loose, with deregulation and financial incentives for the wealthy and upper middle class of the 1980s and 1990s being the instruments driving property investment and prices through the roof. Benefiting from the boom in investment properties and the financial rewards that come with this are the wealthy and middle class. This is at the expense of future generations.

This theory is sound. It has not only happened to the property market but also to education, with university degrees largely being free until the late 1980s. Australia is moving in the same direction as the United States, where a basic degree will now set you back $50,000; the cost is increasing at a rate faster than wages or inflation. Couple this debt with a mortgage on a Sydney home, and very quickly you can begin to appreciate that young Australians get very depressed about their financial predicaments.

Apart from the general circumstances – such as the fall of communism, rise of neo-liberalism economics and or Reagan economics, which has infected the Western world – if we start breaking apart the structural influences that have conspired to create an affordable housing crisis, we notice one of the major culprits is the provision of tax benefits for the wealthy through negative gearing.

Negative gearing, as discussed previously, clearly encourages property investment, resulting in creating competition in the market between home buyers and investors. This is obvious. But, as mentioned previously, there are too many people

---

[450] Belot, H, *'Six charts that tell you about housing affordability in Australia'*, ABC News, Federal Budget, May 2017.

invested in the cycle of property investment now for governments to break this link. The Labor opposition led by Bill Shorten tried to do this in the federal election of 2019, hoping to mobilise the young in Australia to support his policy shift, but apparently there aren't enough young people in our ageing population, because Shorten and his Labor party lost the unlosable election. It is interesting, because polls at the time showed Australians would be supportive of removing negative gearing from the arsenal of property investment.

In the same Australian National University poll in 2017 leading up to the election, only 25% of people opposed or strongly opposed removing negative gearing.[451] Just over 50% agreed to remove it, and 25% were neither here nor there on the issue.[452] You might excuse Bill Shorten for being confident that his major election platform would be supported by the populace. For the immediate future, I don't see negative gearing being reversed. It is clear now there are too many Australians invested in property and using negative gearing for it to be removed altogether.

I do suggest, however, that it should gradually be reduced. Apart from it taking a brave politician to get rid of negative gearing altogether, I think there would be some support for it to be limited. As mentioned previously, we could see negative gearing limited to just one property, in addition to your place of residence. This would mean people with more than one investment property wouldn't reap the benefits of negative gearing, and, accordingly, this would limit the exploits of greed by discouraging people to have five investment properties and reap the tax benefits from them. This could be phased out firstly by limiting negative gearing to two properties, and then bringing it down to one. By taking this structured approach over ten or so years, you will minimise radical disruption to the property market.

The First Homeowners' Grant is the other obvious lever to pull to encourage younger people to get into the property market, but this has to be done carefully to encourage new development in existing areas over new fringe suburban locations. Governments and policymakers hate the First Homeowners' Grant and love it at the same time. They love it, because, politically, they are giving money to people who tend to vote for you when they are handed money, and the development industry loves it because it stimulates development. They hate it because developers can get greedy and pump up prices to capture a slice of the grant, or sometimes all of it. This means the government is virtually giving money to developers. But what do you do? If you can't get rid of negative gearing, which is competing with first home buyers, you have to give something to first home buyers to give them a chance.

As we have discussed, wages have been supressed, as they are aligned with inflation, which has been kept low to prevent wage-led inflation in the economy. So the

---

[451] Belot, H, *'Six charts that tell you about housing affordability in Australia'*, ABC News, Federal Budget, May 2017.
[452] Belot, H, *'Six charts that tell you about housing affordability in Australia'*, ABC News, Federal Budget, May 2017.

only recourse is to give first home buyers a grant. As mentioned previously, the grant needs to mean something, and, frankly, $10,000 doesn't cut it. For existing areas, it needs to be between $50,000 and $80,000 and kept at just $20,000 for new development on the fringes.

The Australian population supports adjusting the First Homeowners' Grant. A total of 83% of survey participants in the Australian National University Poll strongly support the First Homeowners' Grant and it increasing.[453] This is a resounding vote of confidence from the Australian population. Like I have said, it can be paid for by taxing property investors more through the land tax process. This is equitable and also represents a tax deduction for the property investor.

Another opportunity for helping fund a more significant First Homeowners' Grant could be by taxing vacant land holdings. Nothing is more of a blight than a vacant block on the street doing nothing. A vacant property does not contribute towards society, as it doesn't provide a home for an owner–occupier or a renter. By taxing such landholdings, it forces land owners to develop the land for either a home or rental, which assists the property market by adding greater supply to the property market. The tax can then be used to support the expanded First Homeowners' Grant.

Of course, the above incentive- and taxed-based approaches can't be done in isolation, and I see town planning and the property market playing a significant role in changing the form of the Australian Dream in a way that makes it more affordable. The need to change planning policy to require diversity of housing and greater quantities of it, supported by quality design, needs to be instituted as part of the framework and no longer seen as a 'nice to have'. Yes, it may result in some cost increases in the short-term as developers come to terms with not being able to roll out the Model T home anymore, but eventually they will change their tunes and work with the system.

Right now, in Western Australia, the state government's release of the *Residential Design Codes Volume 2: Apartment Design* is a living example. Prior to 2019, to build an apartment you just had to have the right zoning and meet setback, building height, plot ratio and car parking requirements. There was no emphasis on design quality. Now, through the latest iteration of the Residential Design Codes, you have to pay significant attention to site planning, vegetation retention or planting, amenity creation and overall design to create hospitable and well-designed apartments. This approach is backed up by the design review process, as mentioned earlier. This has resulted in vast improvements in apartment design in Western Australia and is an approach that other Australian states have adopted previously with great success. This design-led approach now needs to be imbedded into smaller housing.

I see the town planning framework across Australia changing from a ridged framework to a performance-based approach with a focus on design and sustainability. This means training in town planning needs to change to have a focus on design and a

---

[453] *'ANU Finds the Great Australian Dream is Fading'*, Australian National University, May 2017.

more flexible assessment framework that encourages and supports good design outcomes. I have provided examples of different housing forms that are design focused and would support changing demographics in Australia. We now need to change the planning framework to ensure this type of housing – diverse and well designed – is provided in Australian cities.

The improvements in the town planning industry will result in a slow end to the days where you could create a lot covered by 75% house. Suburban blocks and infill blocks will have to pay more attention to the environment and design in general. I also see a shift in housing type away from the typical three- and four-bedroom home in inner and suburban locations to greater diversity in single and two-bedroom homes and apartments being constructed. This will need to be induced by planning policy but will eventually be taken up by the development industry when affordability becomes an issue and developers begin responding to performance-based planning, which requires such housing through the provision of amenity in housing design. Again, there will be a greater emphasis on providing for the environment and creating better links between indoor and outdoor amenities than just focusing on designing the biggest house possible. This will force the industry to design smaller houses, as you will have to build a second storey if you want to maintain the same housing size on the current sizing of blocks.

Perhaps optimistically, I see a shift in the way our cities are designed in a broad sense. They will be more place-based and diverse in housing, with a greater link between housing, mixed-use and place, which will transform new suburban locations that are largely monotonous in nature. I see a greater role of public transport in our cities, especially in cities like Perth, Sydney, Brisbane and Melbourne. We are going to see a greater level of investment in mid-tier public transport, such as light rail and trackless trams. This will be needed as our cities become too congested with the automobile, and these options will be demanded by the development industry, to support the redevelopment of our existing locations. We are already starting to see this across Australia in cities such as Brisbane, the Gold Coast and Sydney, where billions of dollars are being invested in light rail. Perth is starting to look at it, and I think we will see light rail or trackless trams coming into circulation by 2035.

I think investment in public transport is critical, as I don't believe autonomous vehicles will be the panacea to our transport system. I think they are still ten to twenty years away in being operationalised en masse, and even then, they are talking about the autonomous vehicle being in private ownership. This won't solve the congestion problems faced by our growing cities, so it comes back to the issue that is the elephant in the room. We need to get people out of cars and into public transport, and walking and cycling, which is not only more efficient, but is also more environmentally friendly.

Over the next twenty years, I see a vision of the Australian Dream coming back to its egalitarian roots, where the government and industry work together to ensure home ownership is accessible to all and not just the wealthy few. I see a mass transfer of equity and wealth from the baby boomers to Generation X and Y, as baby boomers will be passing on, and many have properties and wealth to give up. This, of course, is not widespread, but it does represent the death of the first generation to have investment properties, so if they don't spend all their money and provide an inheritance, they would also be the first generation to hand over assets that constitute more than one property to their children. This may provide some relief for Generation X and Y, but doesn't do much for Generation Z, who are in their teenage years and early twenties now and have Generation X parents, who have another thirty to forty years of life left in them. It's the Generation Z also who are faced with the $1.5 million price tag for housing in Sydney, as Generation X and Y bought into the property market when prices were lower.

I also see policymakers diverting more tax dollars towards first home buyers to encourage them into the industry. This will be funded by property investors, as it should be, and will be a foil for not removing negative gearing altogether. This will come out of necessity, since, over the next twenty years, it will be the Generation Z dominating the workforce, and they will be demanding a fair shake at the prop-erty tree, or else they will vote accordingly. I also see property prices slowing, given the increasing affordability issue that will reduce the number of people who can buy a property; however, this may stabilise if more assistance comes in the form of an expanded First Homeowners' Grant, as mentioned above.

For Generation Z, however, it will be a dream just to own a home, and they can forget about purchasing investment property. Therefore, investment into property by Generation Z will mostly be out of reach for the next twenty to forty years. This will also be the trend as population growth begins to slow. That's not to say population growth in Australia won't continue, it will, but we won't see the same level of popula-tion growth as we've seen over the last seventy years. It will slow as we have fewer babies and immigration becomes more restricted.

There is much to be hopeful about for the future of the Australian Dream if we adopt the above vision for the next twenty years. Generation Z will have a chance at the property ladder, our cities will be better planned, the housing stock will be more reflective of our society's needs, and it will be more environmentally friendly, with the heat island effect reduced and less of our urban fringe destroyed to make way for new housing. More sustainable and reliable public transport will reduce travel-ling costs and environmental impacts and will make our cities more resilient and flexible in times of supply shock related to fossil fuels.

Above all, I am hopeful for the next generation. Everybody deserves a chance at owning a home. It is a fundamental human right, so, if we are going to see the Australian Dream alive and well in the future, things need to change, and I believe they will.

ABOUT THE AUTHOR

Sergio Famiano has spent over a quarter of a century working in the town planning and development industry in Perth, Western Australia, spending thirteen years working for the State Developer (LandCorp, now DevelopmentWA), leading key transformational projects, such as the Cockburn Coast (Shoreline), Mandurah Junction, the China Green Development in Subiaco and the Perth City Link Project. In recent years, Sergio has turned his attention towards the sustainable development of town centres in brownfield and new urban growth areas, applying Jan Gehl's principles of people-first planning and design.

Sergio has spent much of his career at the forefront of implementing change in the planning and development of Perth, applying New Urbanist and transit-oriented development principles and focusing away from car-dominated planning and design. He is an expert in urban rejuvenation, urban design, town centre development and housing affordability.

www.ingramcontent.com/pod-product-compliance
Lightning Source LLC
Chambersburg PA
CBHW082109230426
43671CB00015B/2642